CHILDREN OF THE WHALES

Story and Art by Abi Umeda

Volume

14

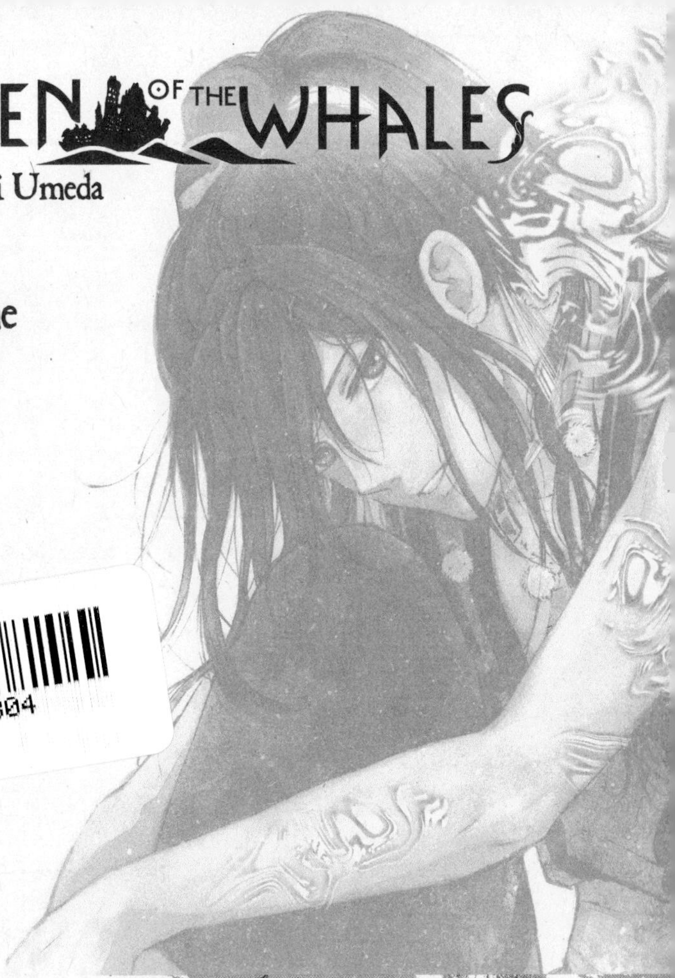

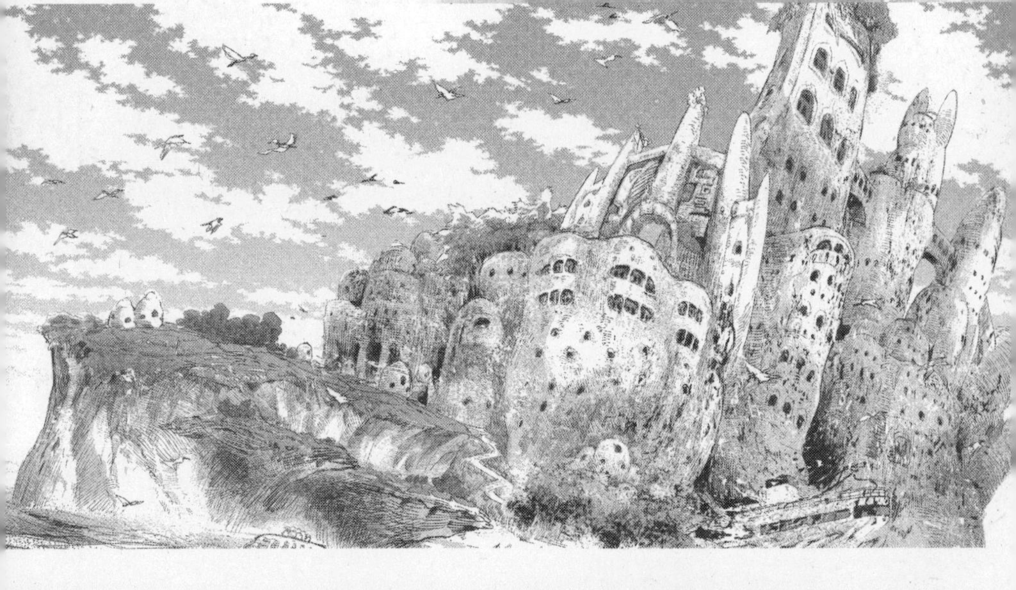

On the Mud Whale

Ouni
(Marked, 16 years old)
A very powerful thymia user who possesses the strength of a daimona. He is being held on Karcharías after being defeated by Orca.

Lykos
(Marked, 14 years old)
A girl from the Allied Empire who comes aboard the Mud Whale. She is being held on Karcharías by Orca.

Chakuro
(Marked, 14 years old)
The young archivist of the Mud Whale. His desire to save Lykos and Ouni from Orca's clutches leads him to clash with Suou.

Former Allied Empire

Orca
(Marked)
A powerful thymia user and Lykos's brother. He has seized the battleship Karcharías and declared his independence from the empire.

Shuan
(Marked, 26 years old)
Former commander of the Vigilante Corps. He took on Orca in Amonlogia in an attempt to save Ouni, but was no match for the imperial commander.

Suou
(Unmarked, 17 years old)
Mayor of the Mud Whale. He declares that the people of the Mud Whale will seek a new home immediately and not stop to rescue Lykos and Ouni.

Allied Empire

The Emperor
The most powerful man in the empire bears an uncanny resemblance to Chakuro. He seeks Faláina and plans to crush Orca's insurrection.

Former Allied Empire

Itía
The archivist on the battleship Skyros before it sank. Orca saved her from execution, and she later agreed to marry him.

Former Allied Empire

Liontari
(Marked)
He joined the invasion of Amonlogia as Orca's jester and stays on Karcharías after the revolt.

Glossary of the Sea of Sand

The Mud Whale	A huge, drifting island-ship. Those in the empire who resisted giving up their emotions were exiled here, along with all their descendants.
Thymia	Telekinetic power derived from emotions.
The Marked	The 90 percent of the Mud Whale population who are thymia users. They are all short-lived.
The Unmarked	The members of the Mud Whale population who cannot use thymia. Unlike the Marked, they are long-lived.
Nous	A unique organism that obtains energy from peoples' emotions and gives people the power of thymia in return.
Nous Fálaina	A Nous that dwells deep within the Belly of the Mud Whale. Unlike other Nouses, it consumes the life force of humans rather than their emotions.
The Allied Empire	A large nation on the Sea of Sand that controls its citizenry through the Nouses and their absorption of emotions.
Daímonas	A legend from the empire. A being said to be able to destroy a Nous.

A Record of the Mud Whale and the Sea of Sand

Year 93 of the Sand Exile.

The Mud Whale drifts endlessly through the Sea of Sand, home to about 500 people who know nothing of the outside world.

The dream of a new home in Amonlogia is dead. While most of the people of the Mud Whale managed to escape the violence, Lykos and Ouni were captured by their longtime nemesis, Orca. Chakuro and the others are wracked with despair, especially once Suou declares that they will seek a new home immediately and not make any attempt to rescue the captives.

"The Mud Whale was our entire world."

Table of Contents

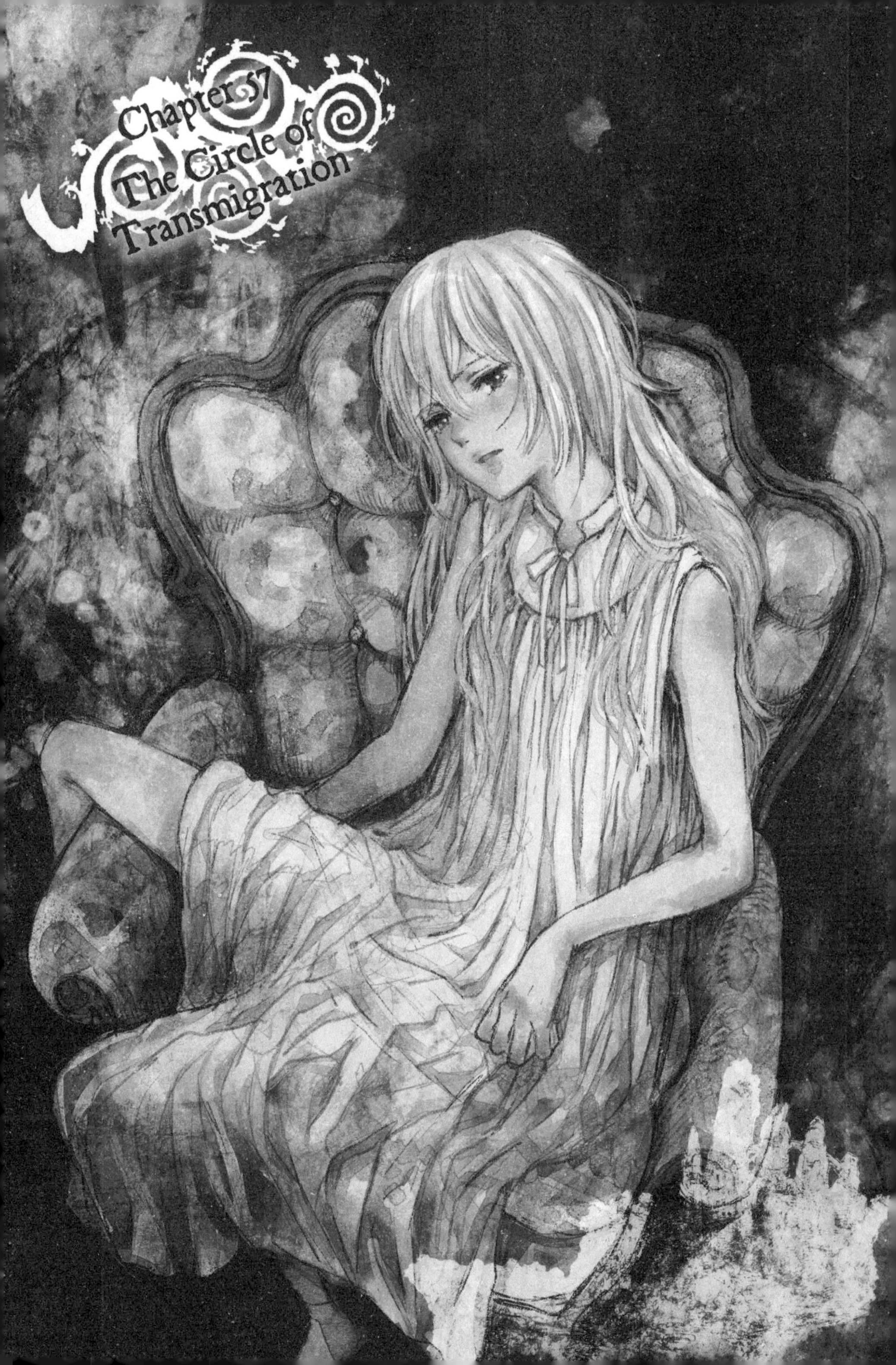
Chapter 57
The Circle of Transmigration

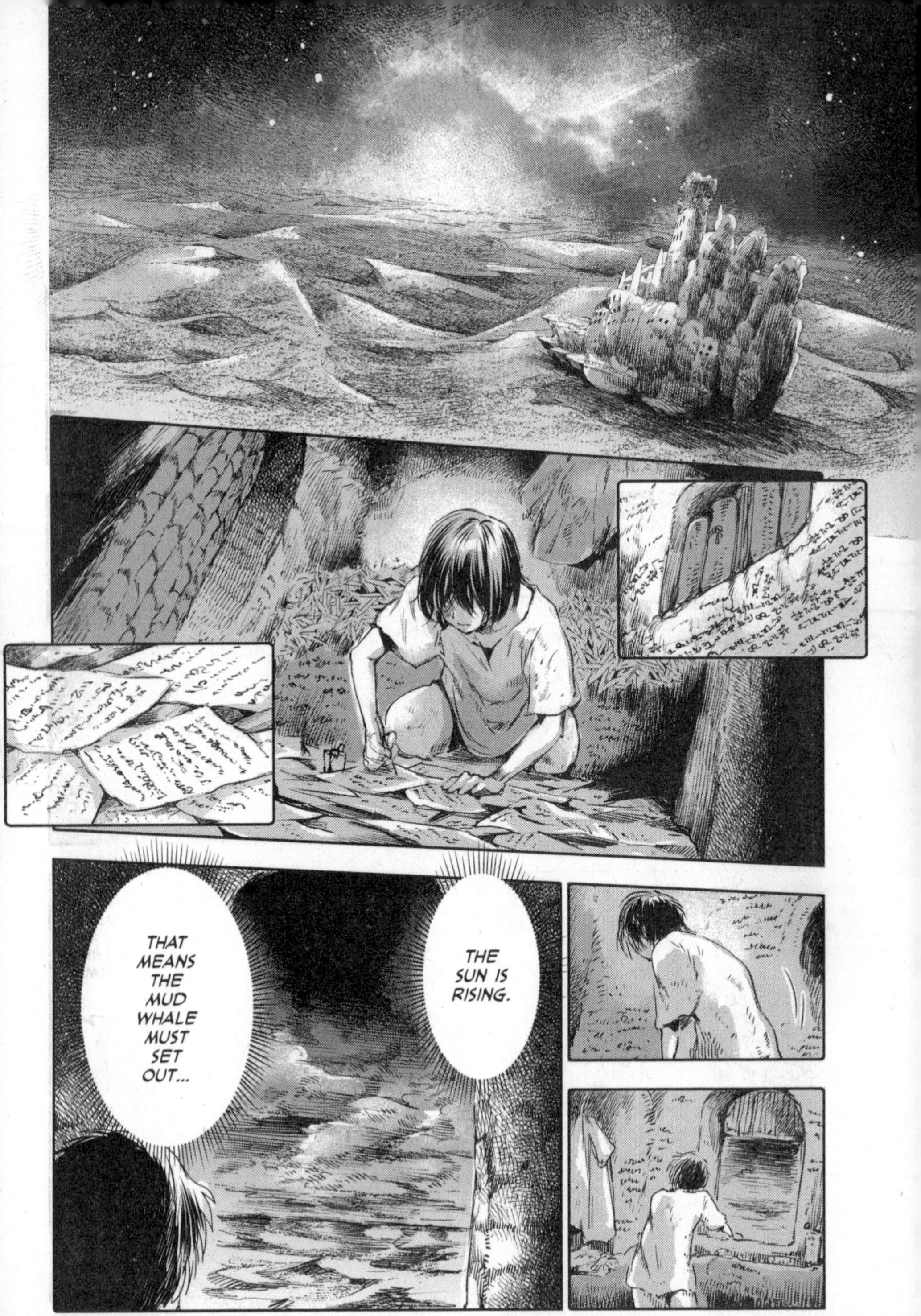
THE SUN IS RISING.
THAT MEANS THE MUD WHALE MUST SET OUT...

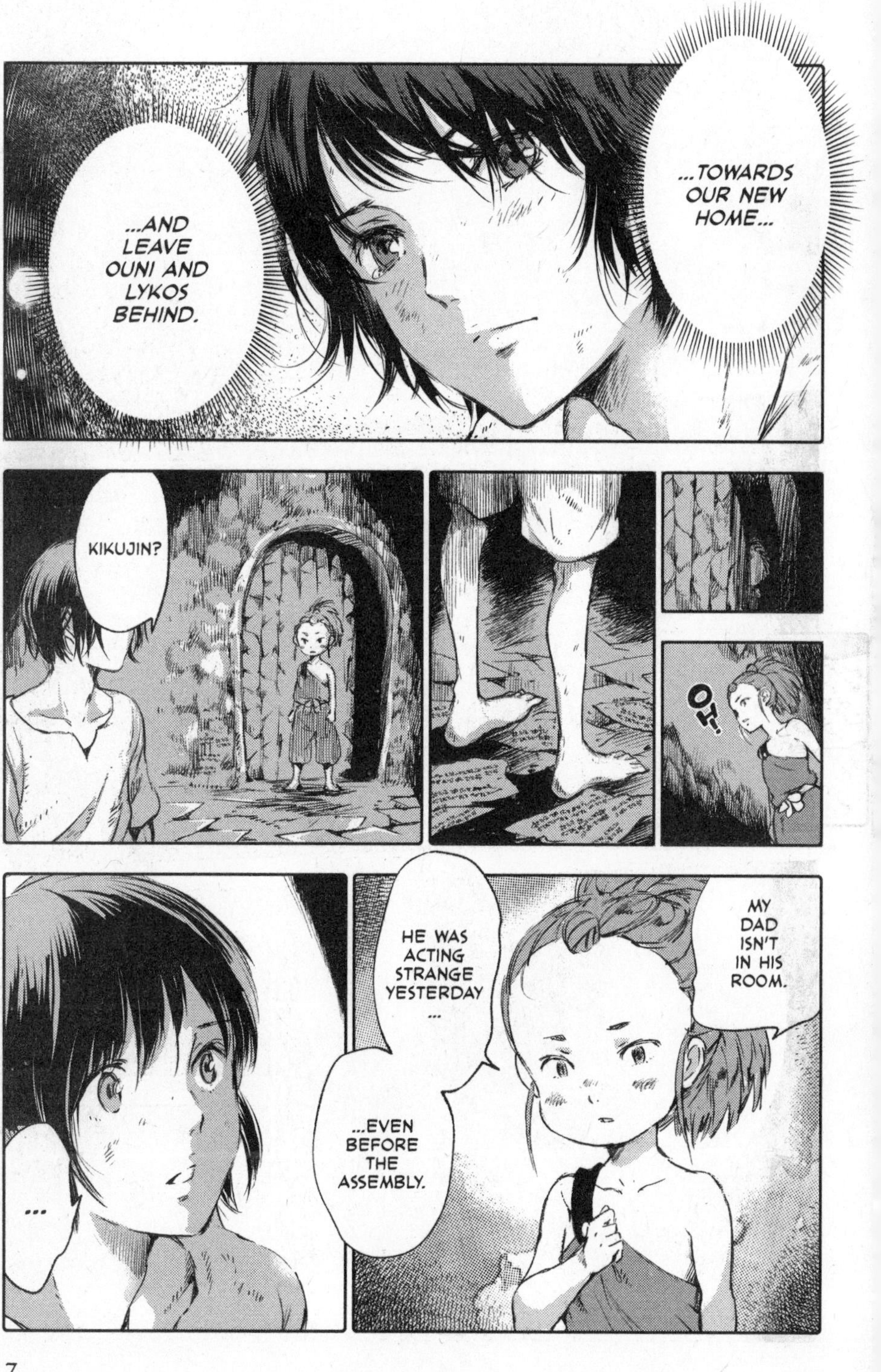
...TOWARDS OUR NEW HOME...
...AND LEAVE OUNI AND LYKOS BEHIND.
OH!
KIKUJIN?
MY DAD ISN'T IN HIS ROOM.
HE WAS ACTING STRANGE YESTERDAY ...
...EVEN BEFORE THE ASSEMBLY.
...

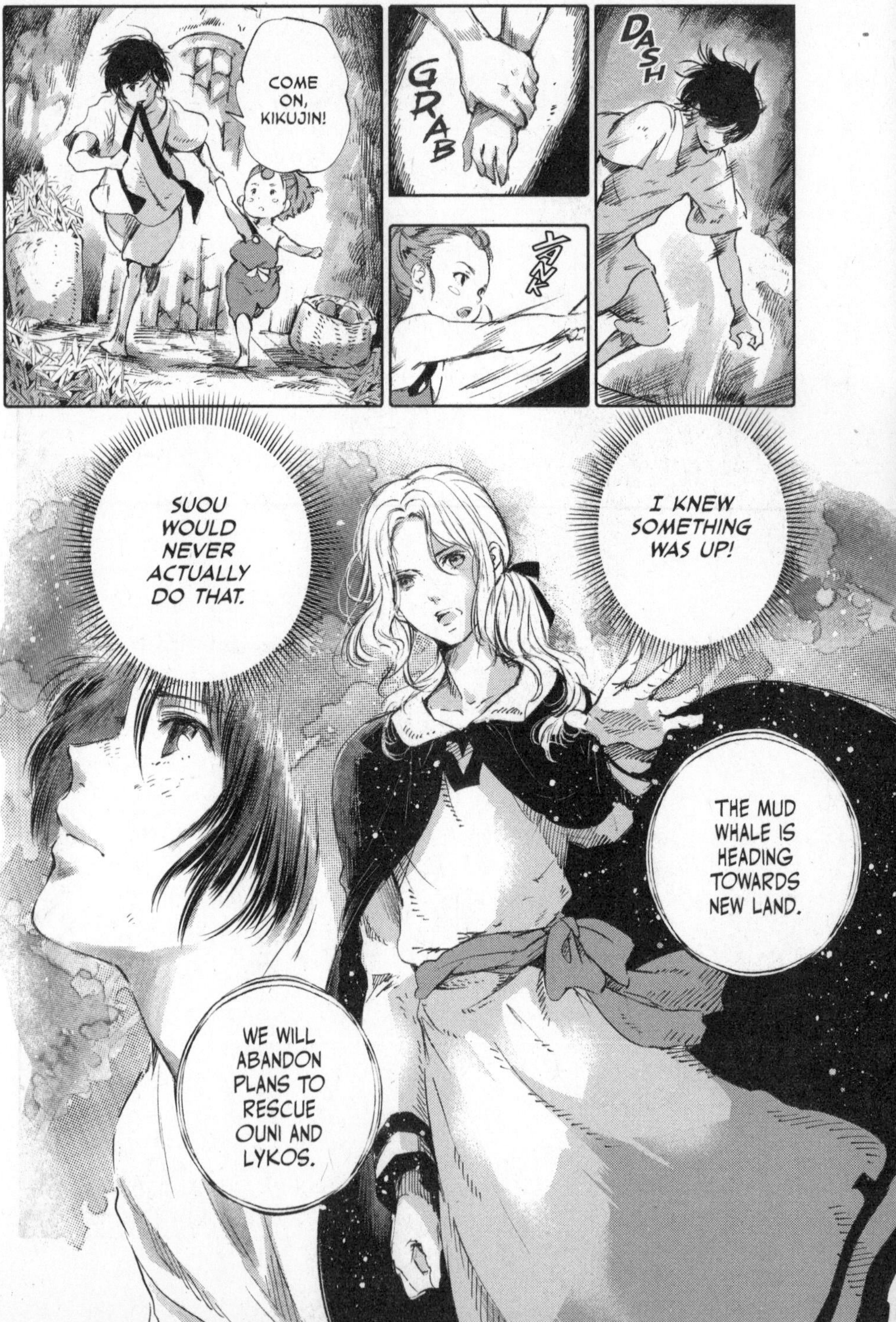
DASH
GRAB
YANK
COME ON, KIKUJIN!
I KNEW SOMETHING WAS UP!
SUOU WOULD NEVER ACTUALLY DO THAT.
THE MUD WHALE IS HEADING TOWARDS NEW LAND.
WE WILL ABANDON PLANS TO RESCUE OUNI AND LYKOS.

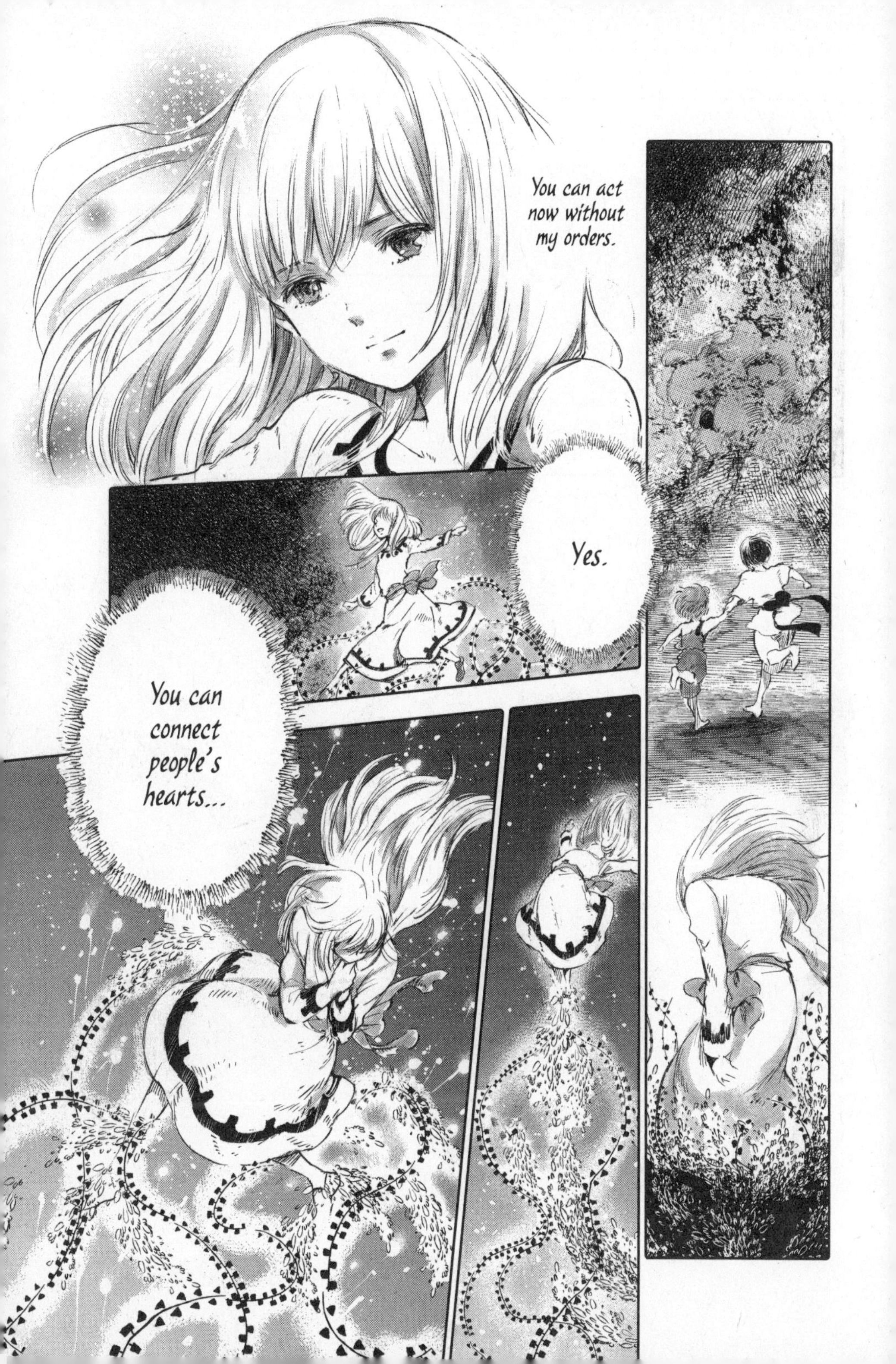
You can act now without my orders.
Yes.
You can connect people's hearts...

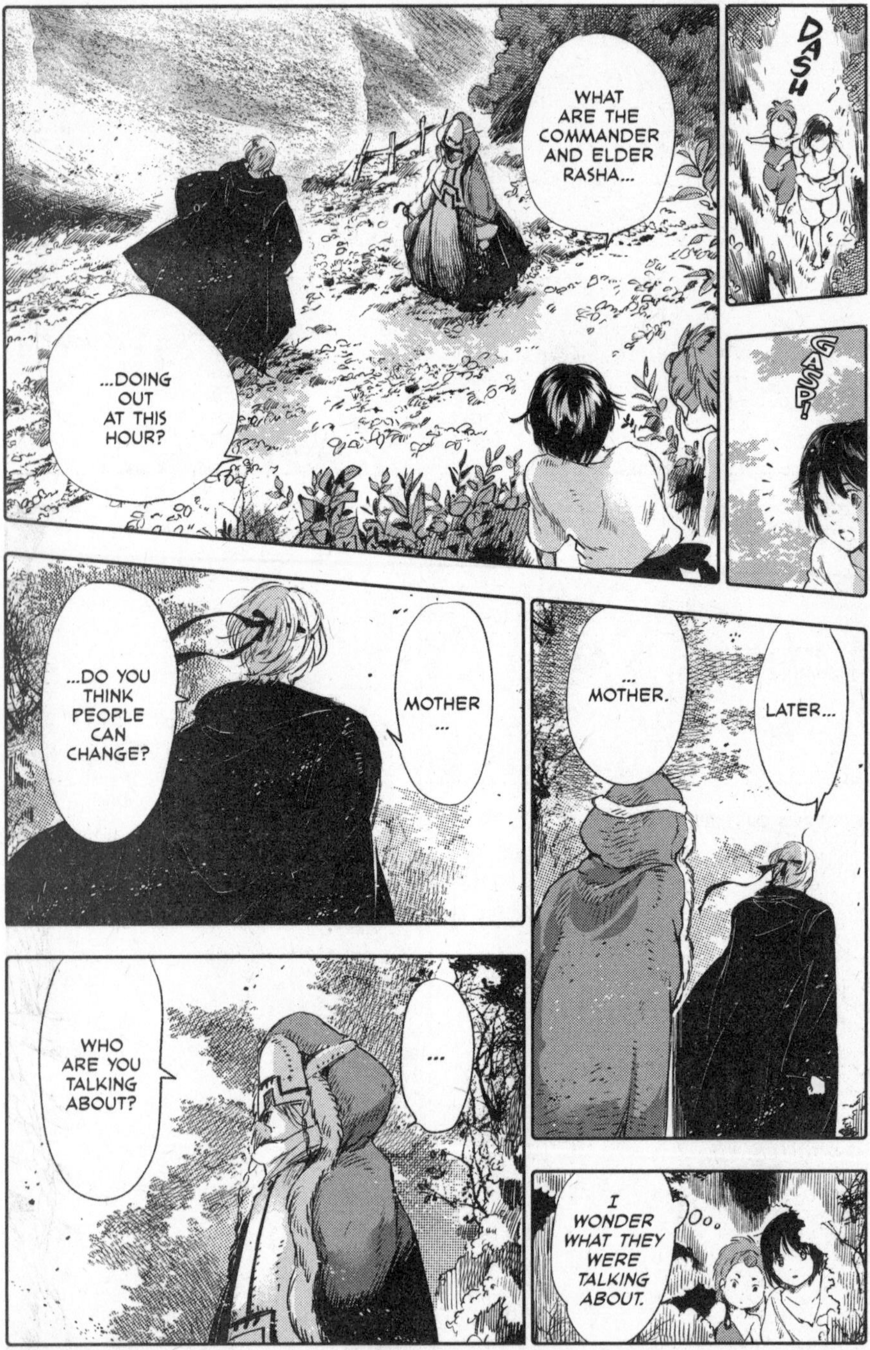
DASH
GASP!
WHAT ARE THE COMMANDER AND ELDER RASHA...
...DOING OUT AT THIS HOUR?
MOTHER ...
...DO YOU THINK PEOPLE CAN CHANGE?
WHO ARE YOU TALKING ABOUT?
...
LATER...
... MOTHER.
I WONDER WHAT THEY WERE TALKING ABOUT.

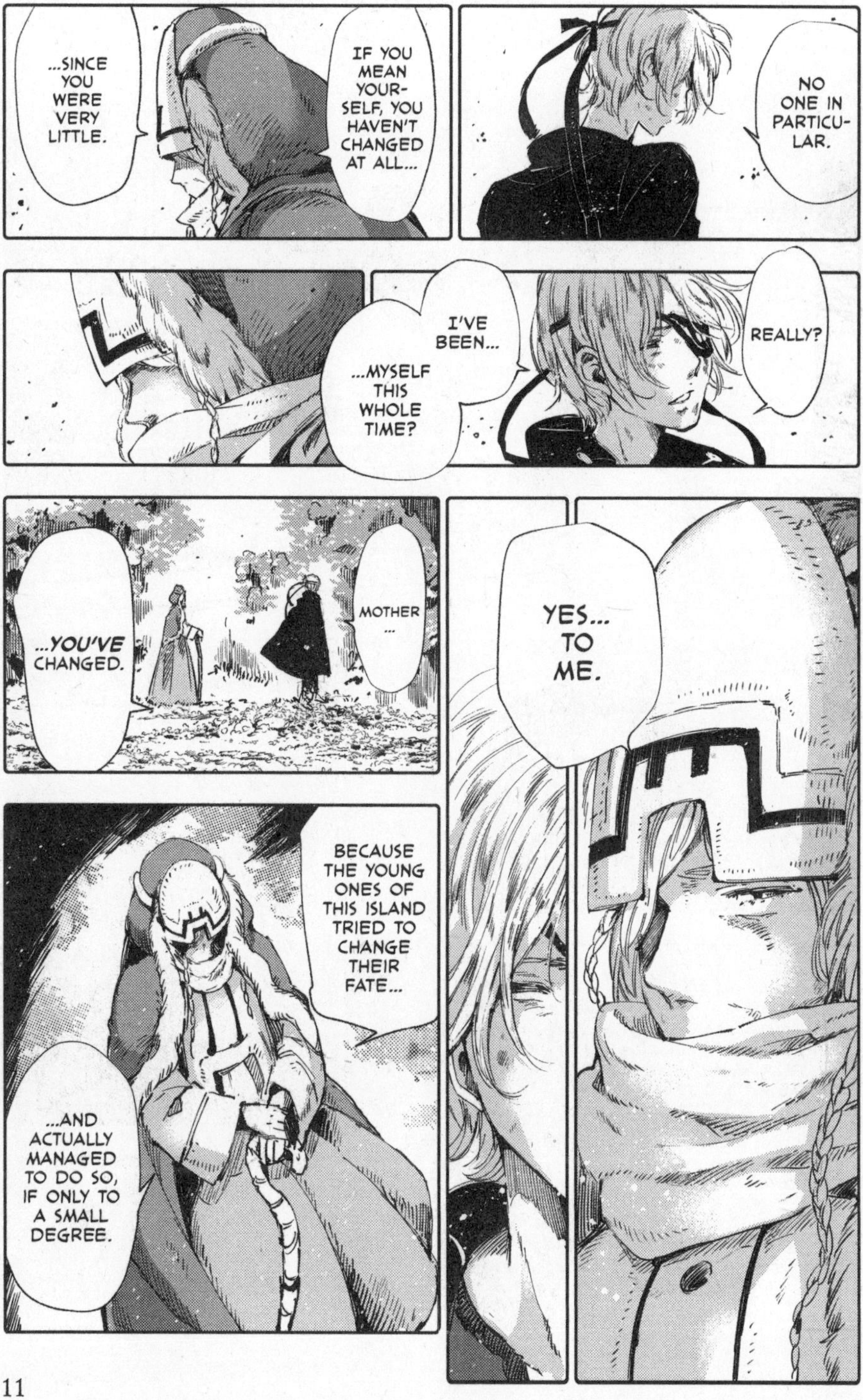
NO ONE IN PARTICULAR.
IF YOU MEAN YOURSELF, YOU HAVEN'T CHANGED AT ALL...
...SINCE YOU WERE VERY LITTLE.
REALLY?
I'VE BEEN...
...MYSELF THIS WHOLE TIME?
YES... TO ME.
MOTHER...
...YOU'VE CHANGED.
BECAUSE THE YOUNG ONES OF THIS ISLAND TRIED TO CHANGE THEIR FATE...
...AND ACTUALLY MANAGED TO DO SO, IF ONLY TO A SMALL DEGREE.

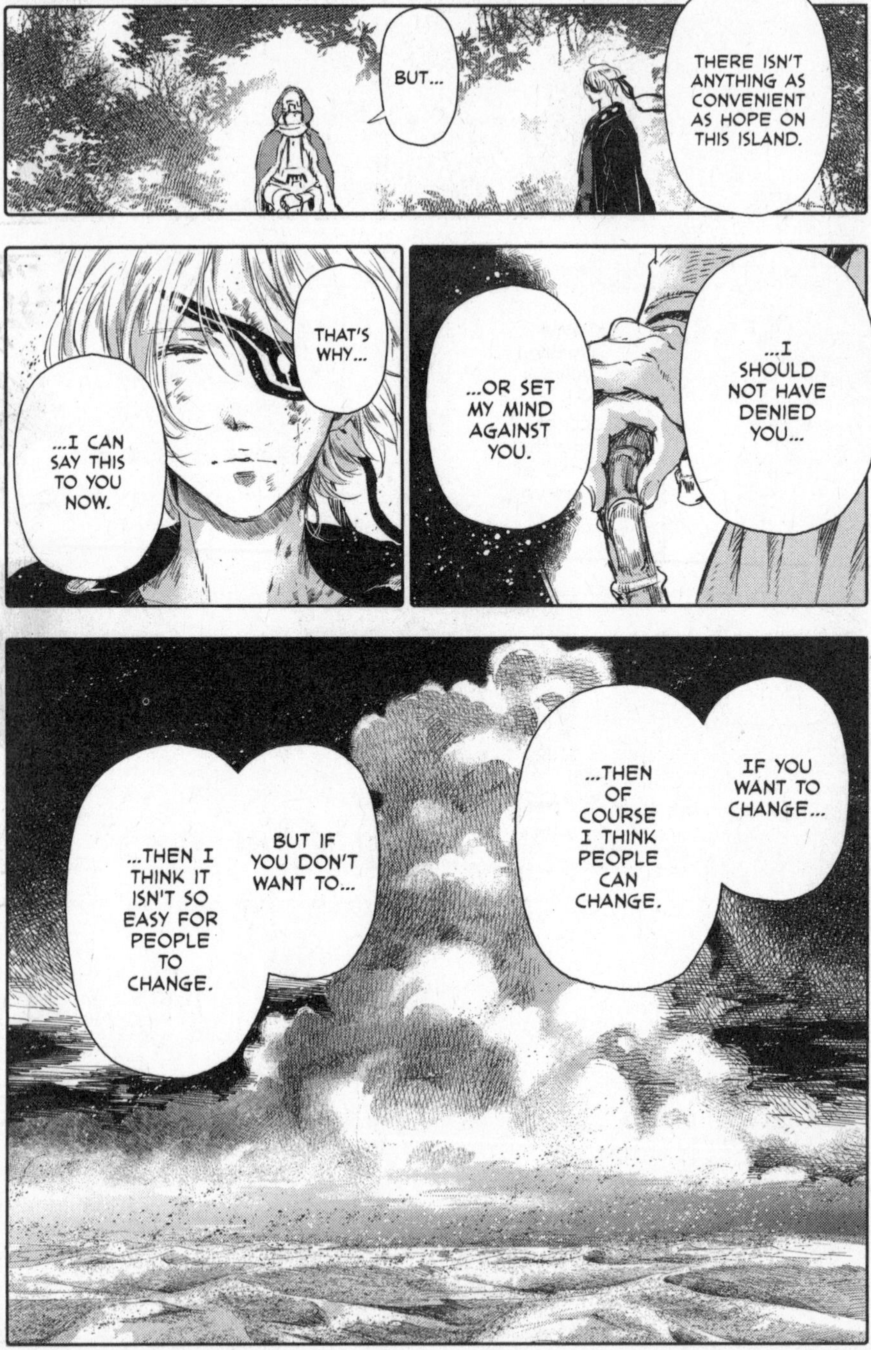
THERE ISN'T ANYTHING AS CONVENIENT AS HOPE ON THIS ISLAND.
BUT...
...I SHOULD NOT HAVE DENIED YOU...
...OR SET MY MIND AGAINST YOU.
THAT'S WHY...
...I CAN SAY THIS TO YOU NOW.
IF YOU WANT TO CHANGE...
...THEN OF COURSE I THINK PEOPLE CAN CHANGE.
BUT IF YOU DON'T WANT TO...
...THEN I THINK IT ISN'T SO EASY FOR PEOPLE TO CHANGE.

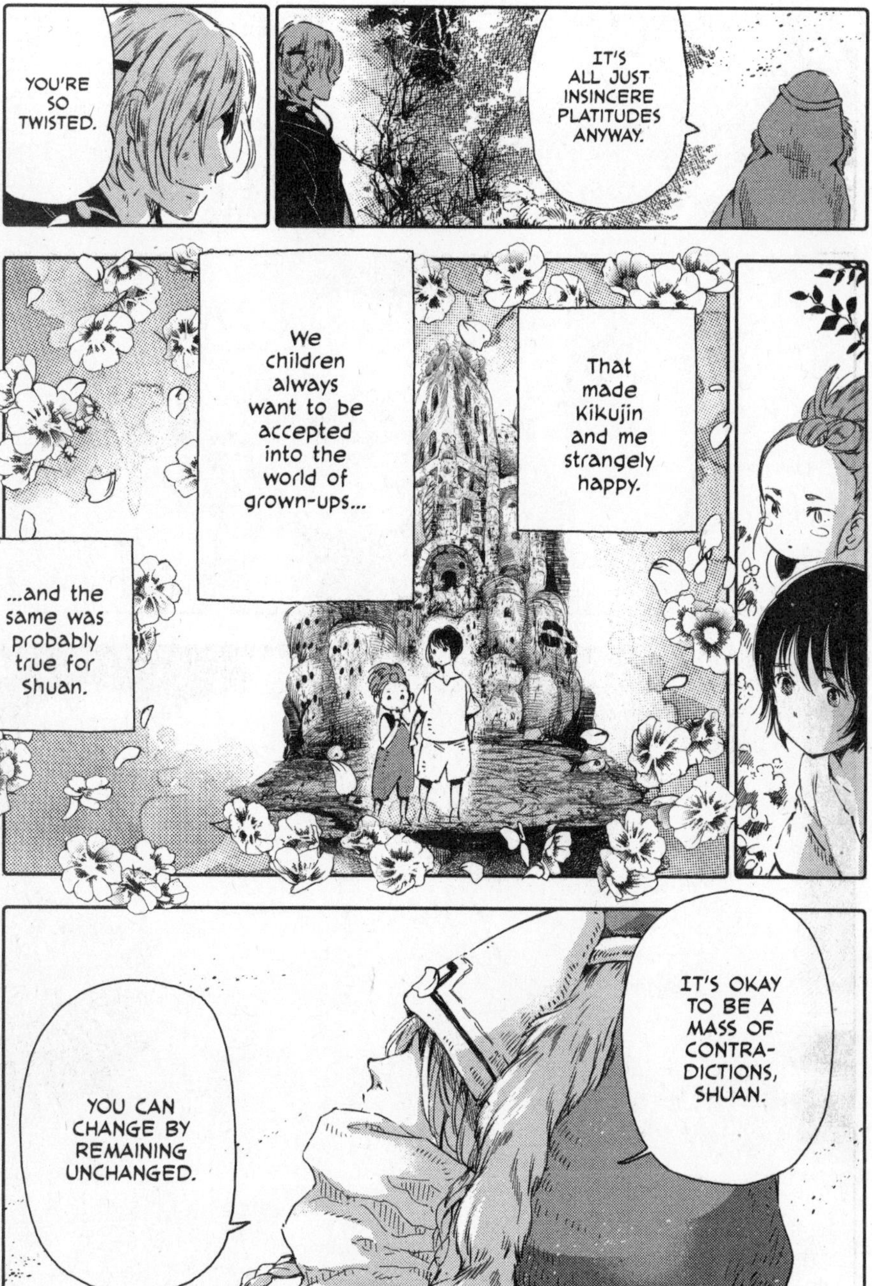
IT'S ALL JUST INSINCERE PLATITUDES ANYWAY.
YOU'RE SO TWISTED.
That made Kikujin and me strangely happy.
We children always want to be accepted into the world of grown-ups...
...and the same was probably true for Shuan.
IT'S OKAY TO BE A MASS OF CONTRA-DICTIONS, SHUAN.
YOU CAN CHANGE BY REMAINING UNCHANGED.

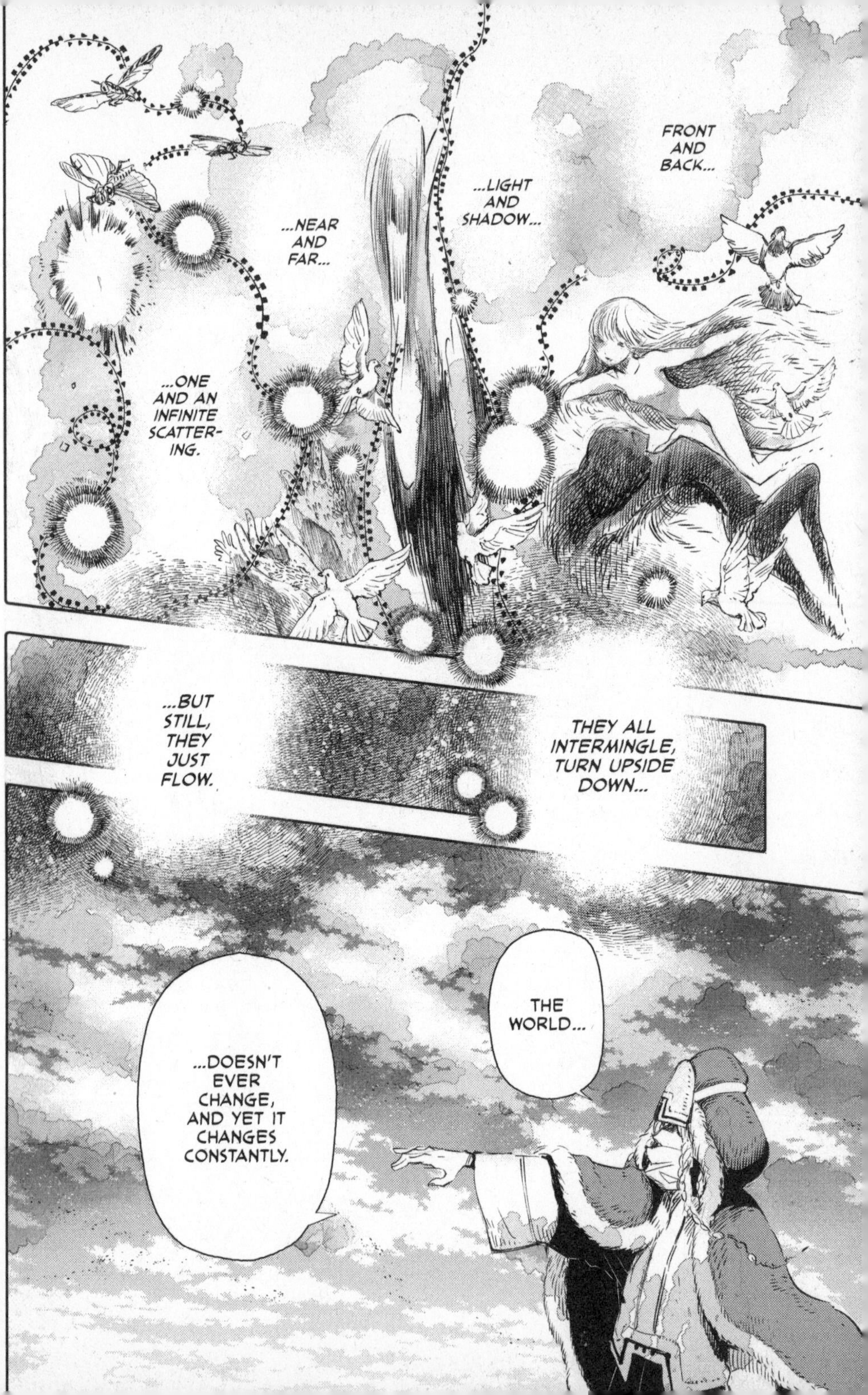
FRONT AND BACK...
...LIGHT AND SHADOW...
...NEAR AND FAR...
...ONE AND AN INFINITE SCATTERING.
THEY ALL INTERMINGLE, TURN UPSIDE DOWN...
...BUT STILL, THEY JUST FLOW.
THE WORLD...
...DOESN'T EVER CHANGE, AND YET IT CHANGES CONSTANTLY.

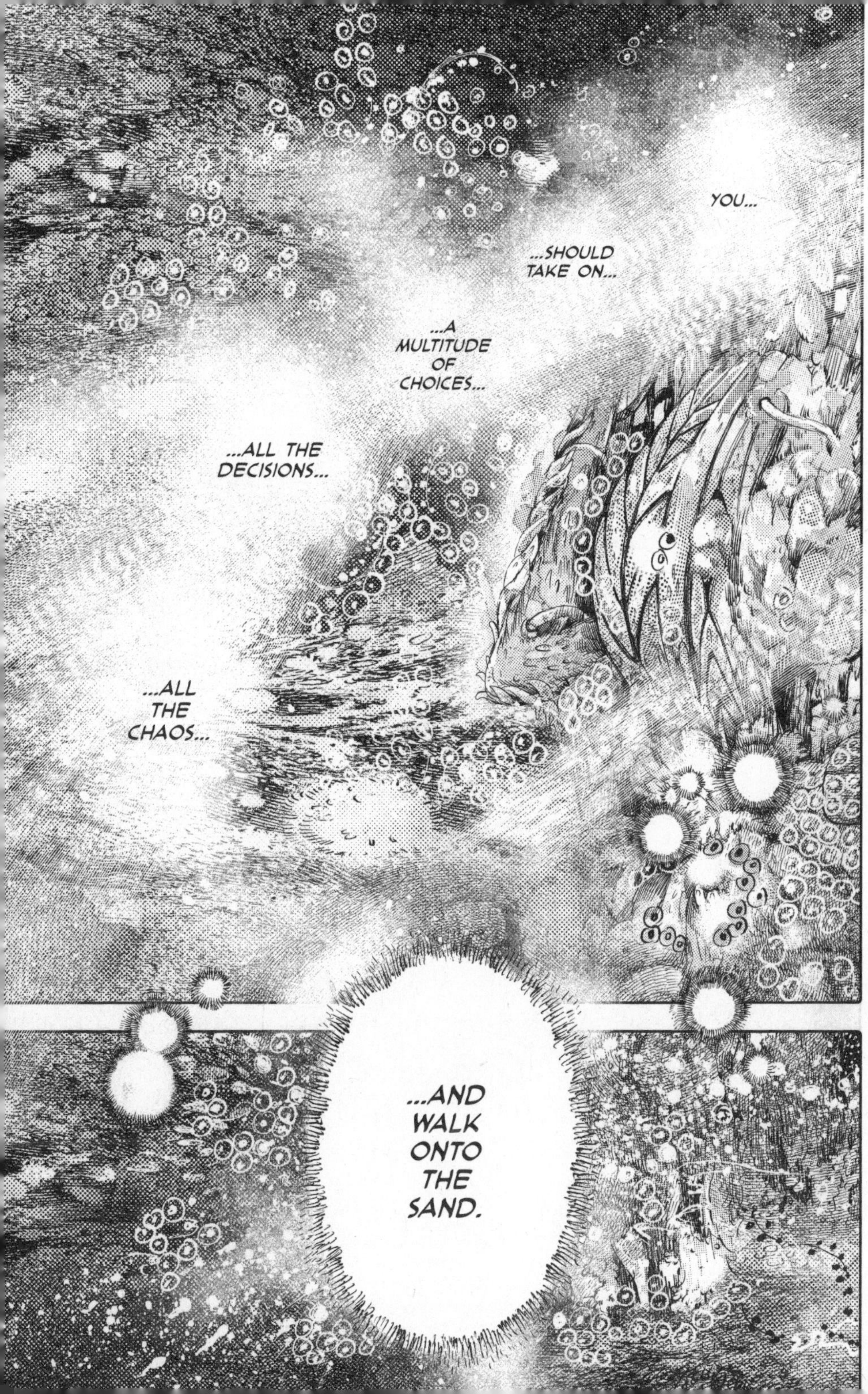
YOU...
...SHOULD TAKE ON...
...A MULTITUDE OF CHOICES...
...ALL THE DECISIONS...
...ALL THE CHAOS...
...AND WALK ONTO THE SAND.

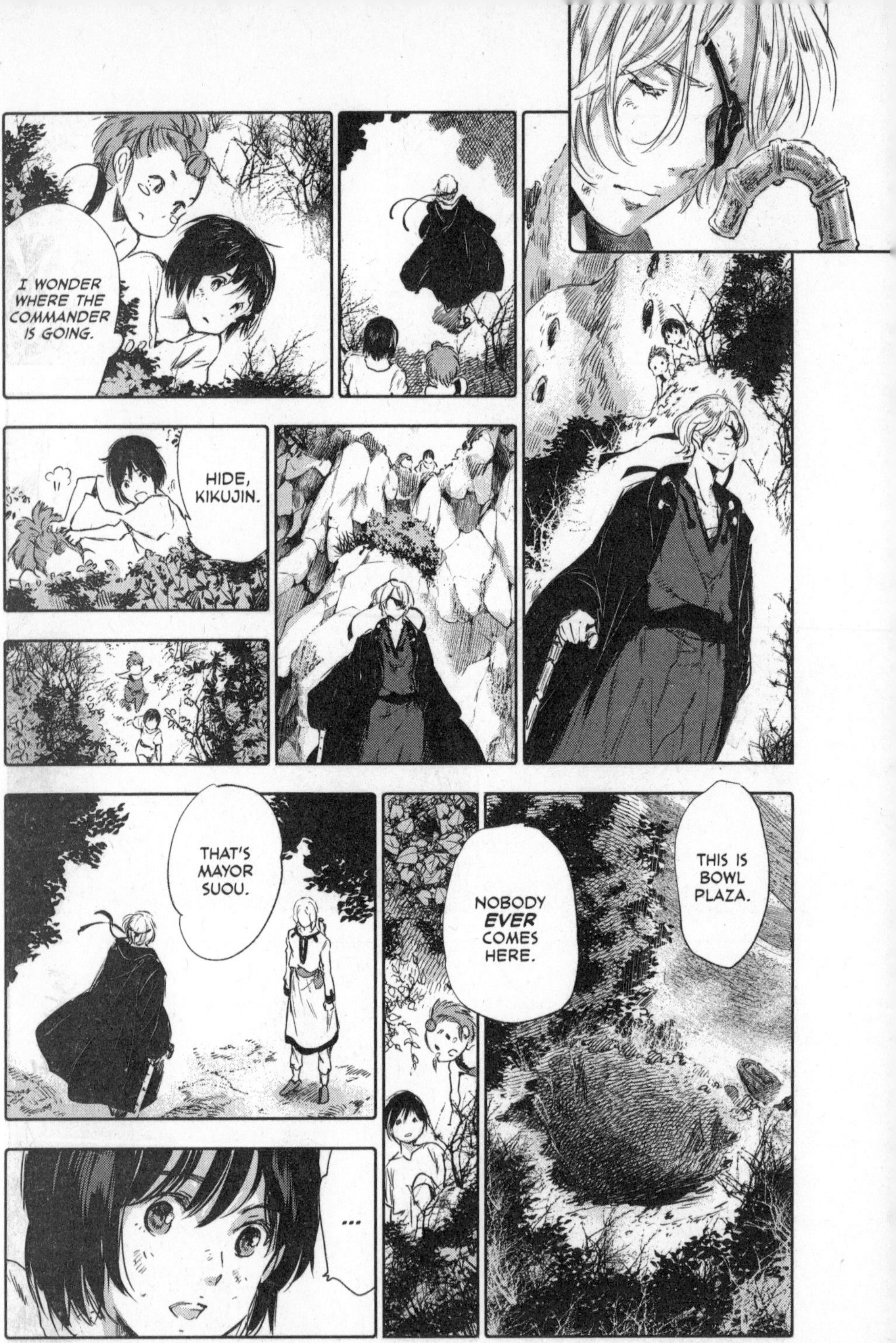
I WONDER WHERE THE COMMANDER IS GOING.
HIDE, KIKUJIN.
THIS IS BOWL PLAZA.
NOBODY *EVER* COMES HERE.
THAT'S MAYOR SUOU.
...

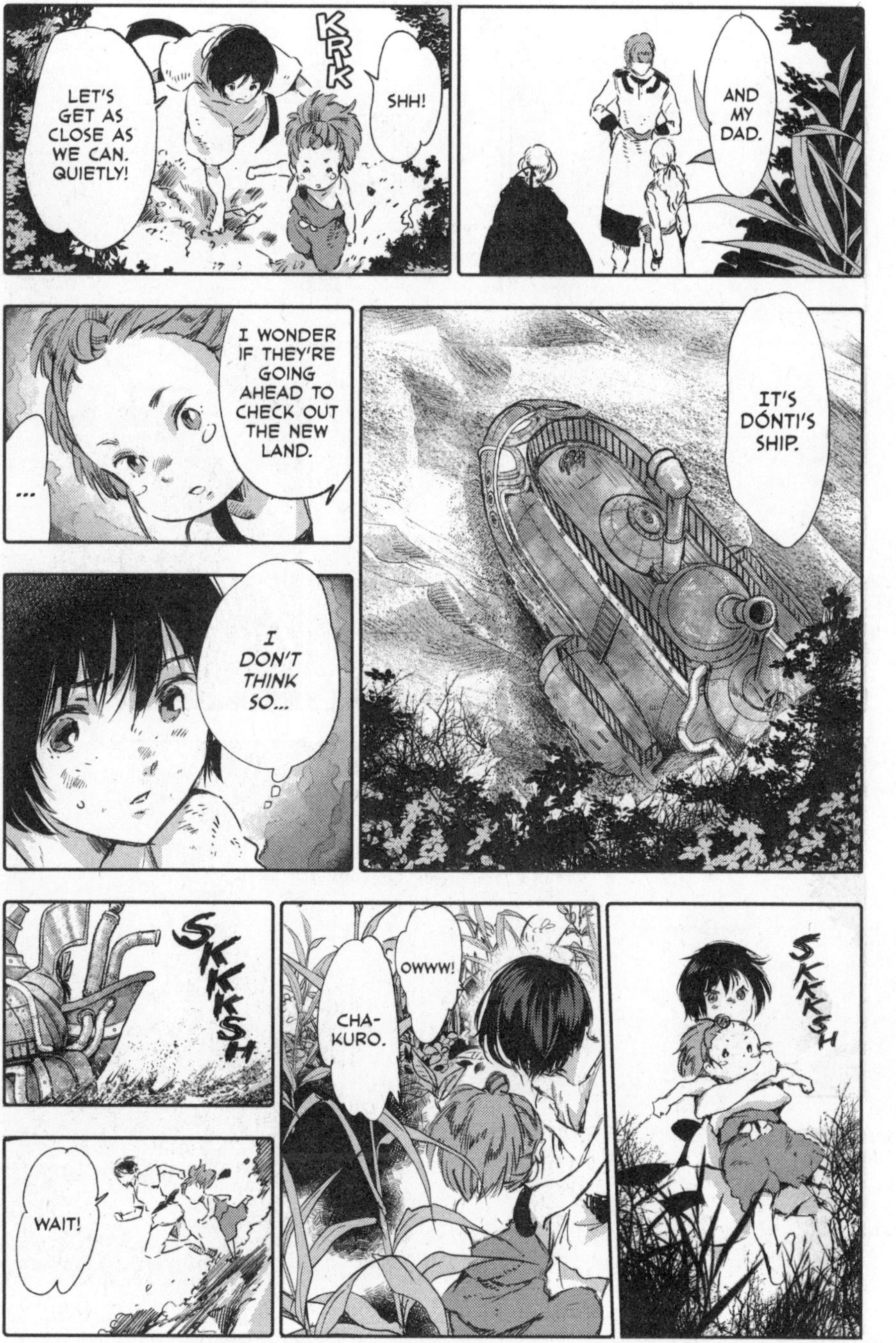
AND MY DAD.
KRIK
SHH!
LET'S GET AS CLOSE AS WE CAN. QUIETLY!
IT'S DÓNTI'S SHIP.
I WONDER IF THEY'RE GOING AHEAD TO CHECK OUT THE NEW LAND.
...
I DON'T THINK SO...
SKKKSH
OWWW!
CHA-KURO.
SKKKSH
WAIT!

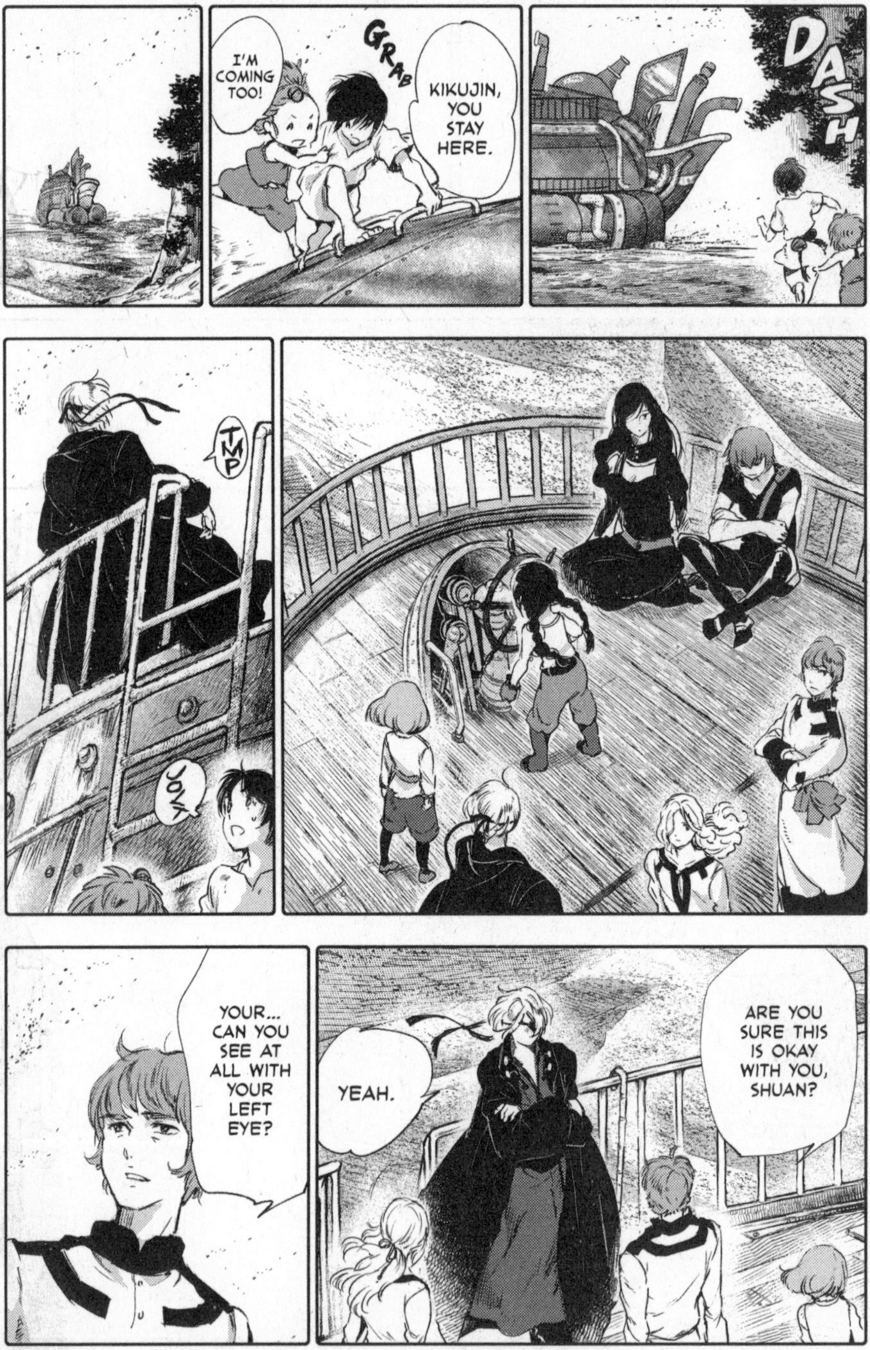
DASH
KIKUJIN, YOU STAY HERE.
GRAB
I'M COMING TOO!
TMP
JOLT
ARE YOU SURE THIS IS OKAY WITH YOU, SHUAN?
YEAH.
YOUR... CAN YOU SEE AT ALL WITH YOUR LEFT EYE?

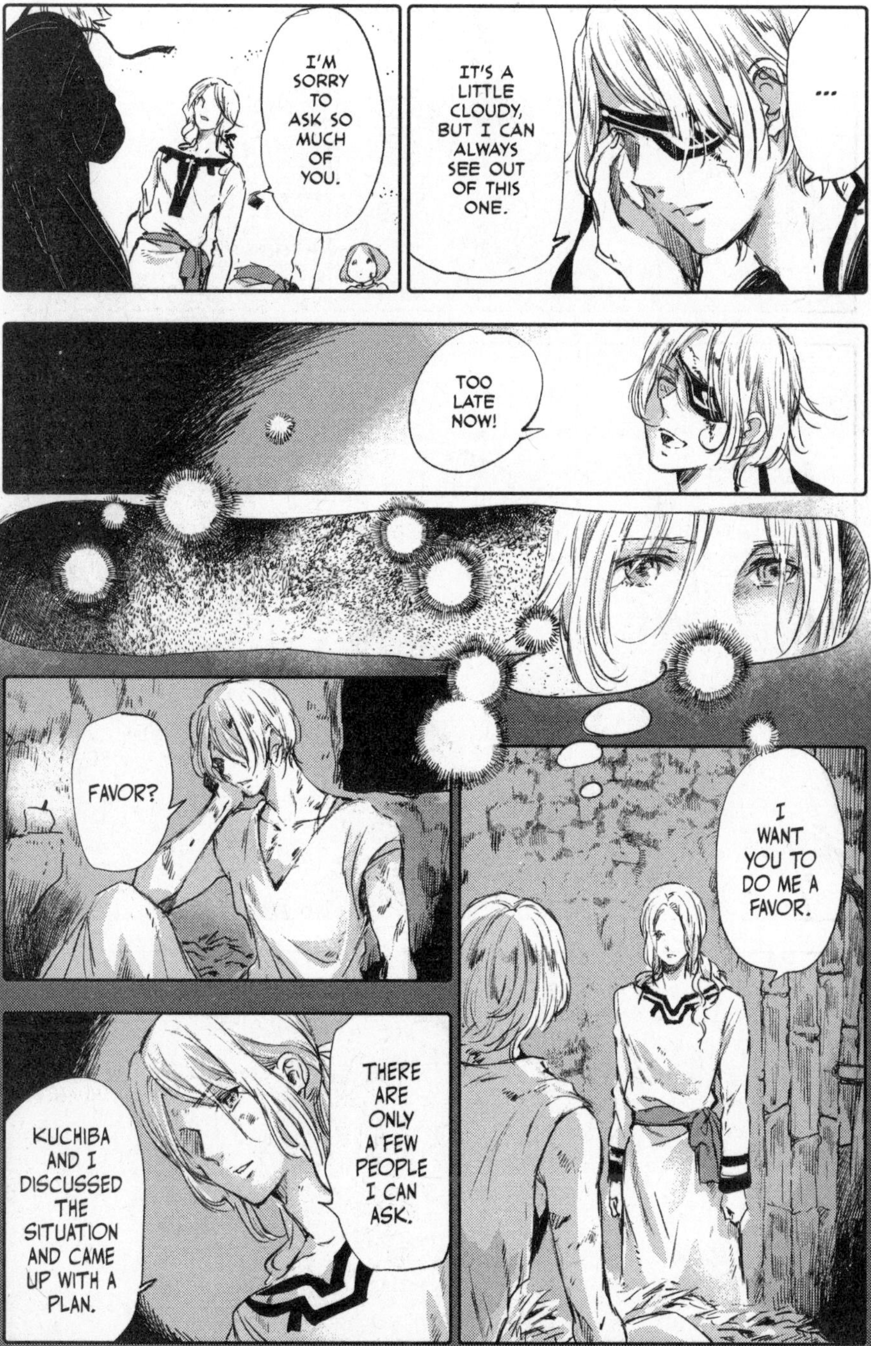
...
IT'S A LITTLE CLOUDY, BUT I CAN ALWAYS SEE OUT OF THIS ONE.
I'M SORRY TO ASK SO MUCH OF YOU.
TOO LATE NOW!
I WANT YOU TO DO ME A FAVOR.
FAVOR?
THERE ARE ONLY A FEW PEOPLE I CAN ASK.
KUCHIBA AND I DISCUSSED THE SITUATION AND CAME UP WITH A PLAN.

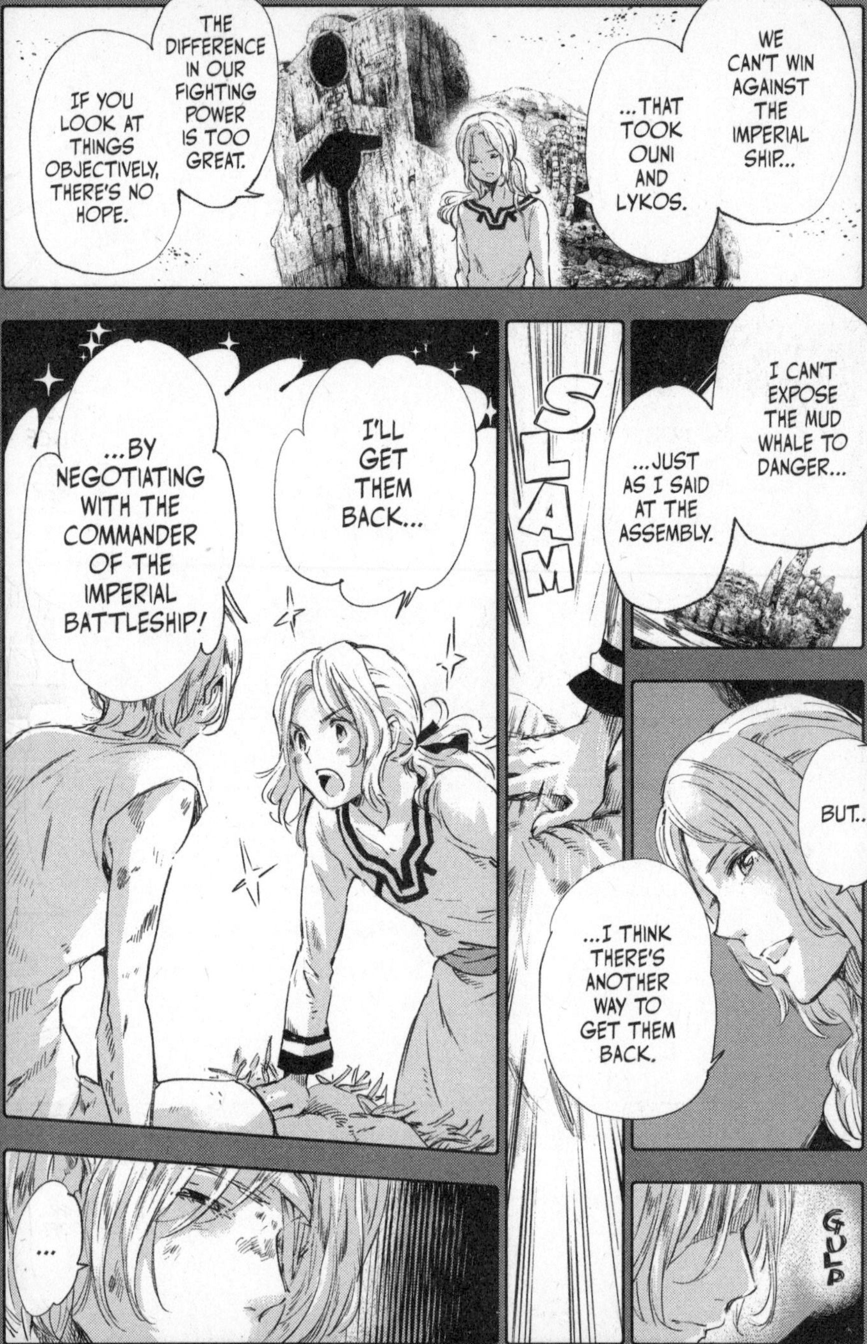
WE CAN'T WIN AGAINST THE IMPERIAL SHIP...
...THAT TOOK OUNI AND LYKOS.
THE DIFFERENCE IN OUR FIGHTING POWER IS TOO GREAT.
IF YOU LOOK AT THINGS OBJECTIVELY, THERE'S NO HOPE.
I CAN'T EXPOSE THE MUD WHALE TO DANGER...
...JUST AS I SAID AT THE ASSEMBLY.
BUT...
...I THINK THERE'S ANOTHER WAY TO GET THEM BACK.
GULP
SLAM
I'LL GET THEM BACK...
...BY NEGOTIATING WITH THE COMMANDER OF THE IMPERIAL BATTLESHIP!
...

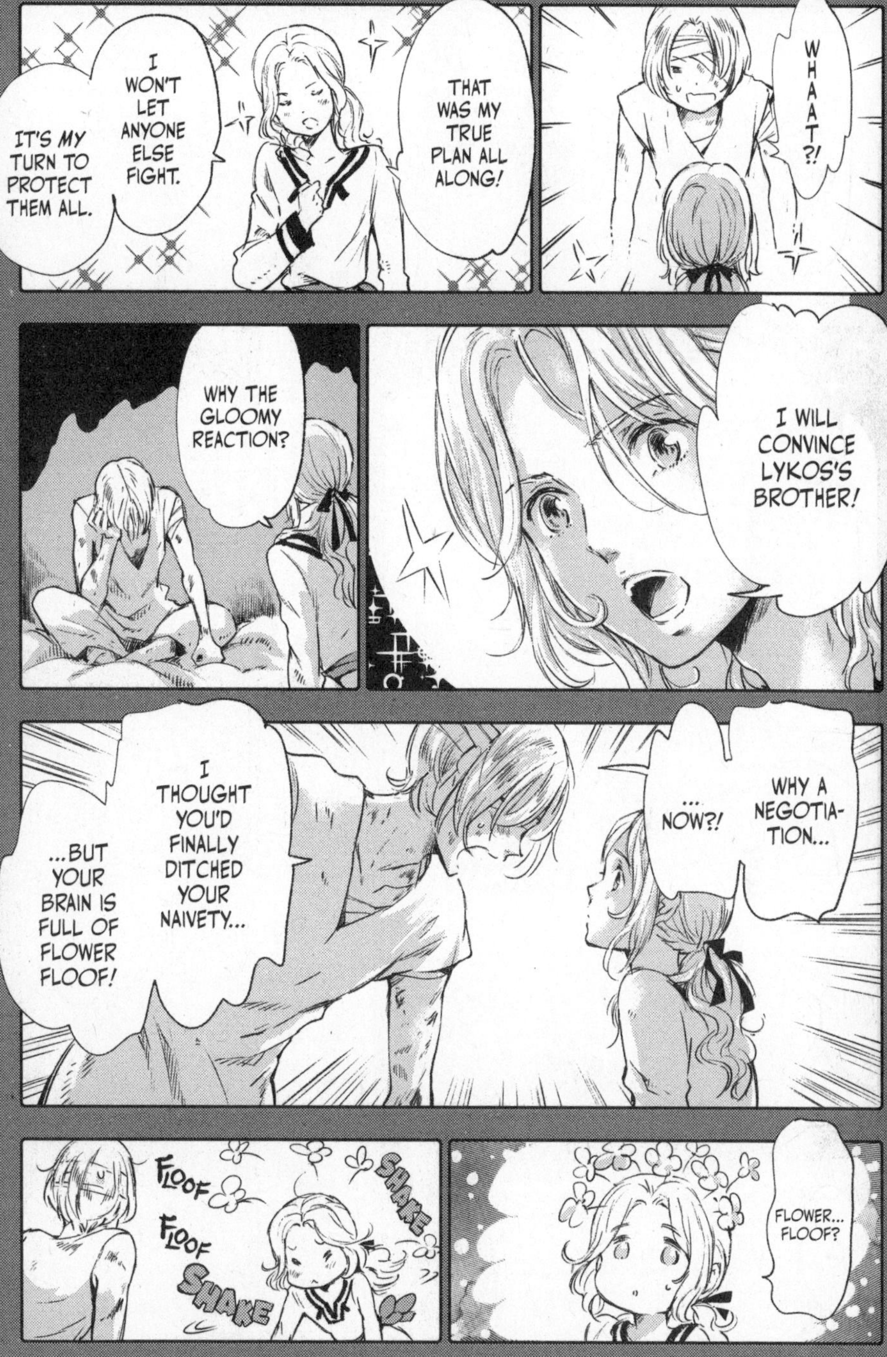
WHAAT?!
THAT WAS MY TRUE PLAN ALL ALONG!
I WON'T LET ANYONE ELSE FIGHT.
IT'S MY TURN TO PROTECT THEM ALL.
I WILL CONVINCE LYKOS'S BROTHER!
WHY THE GLOOMY REACTION?
WHY A NEGOTIA-TION...
...NOW?!
I THOUGHT YOU'D FINALLY DITCHED YOUR NAIVETY...
...BUT YOUR BRAIN IS FULL OF FLOWER FLOOF!
FLOWER... FLOOF?
SHAKE
FLOOF
FLOOF
SHAKE

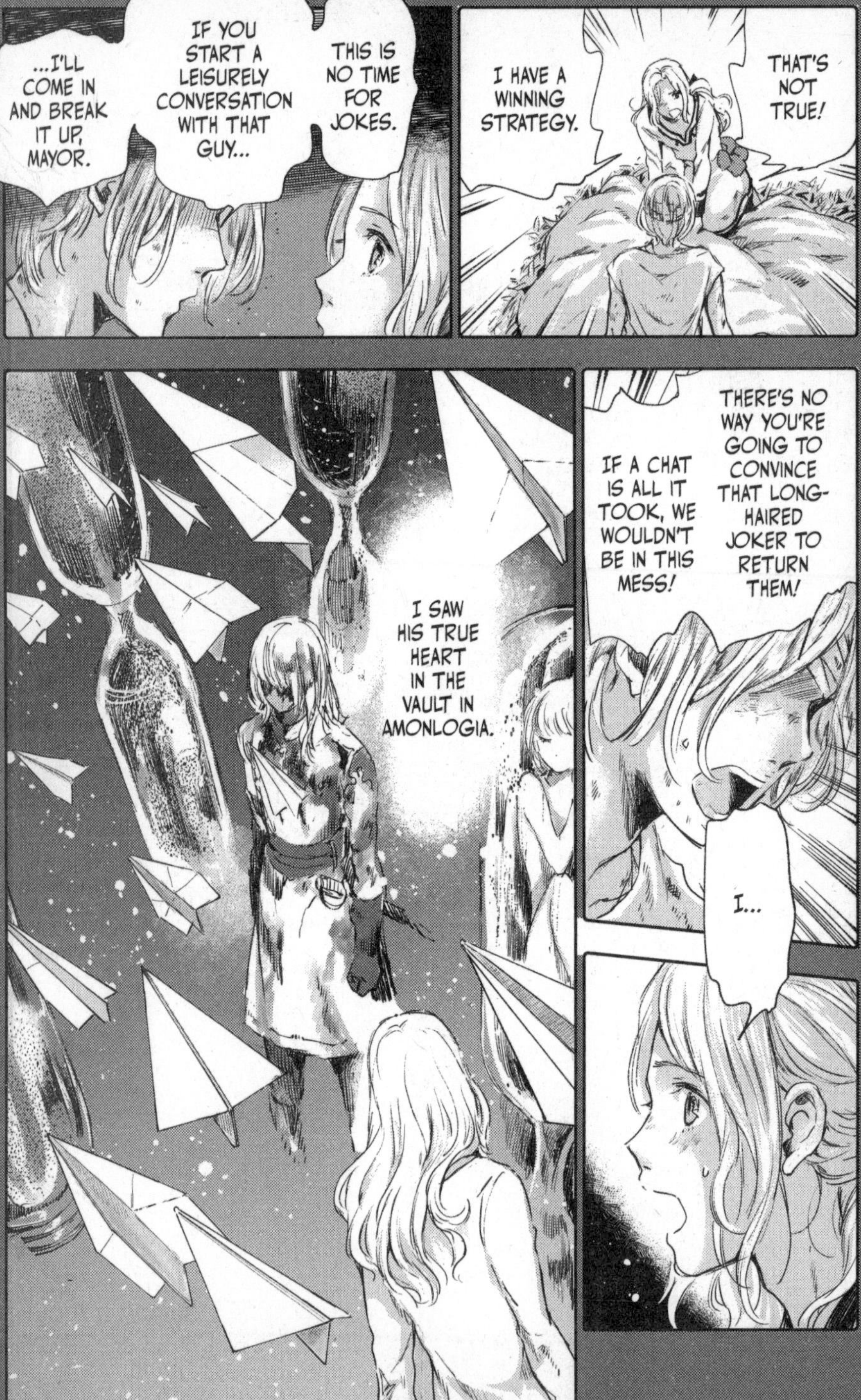
THAT'S NOT TRUE!
I HAVE A WINNING STRATEGY.
THIS IS NO TIME FOR JOKES.
IF YOU START A LEISURELY CONVERSATION WITH THAT GUY...
...I'LL COME IN AND BREAK IT UP, MAYOR.
THERE'S NO WAY YOU'RE GOING TO CONVINCE THAT LONG-HAIRED JOKER TO RETURN THEM!
IF A CHAT IS ALL IT TOOK, WE WOULDN'T BE IN THIS MESS!
I...
I SAW HIS TRUE HEART IN THE VAULT IN AMONLOGIA.

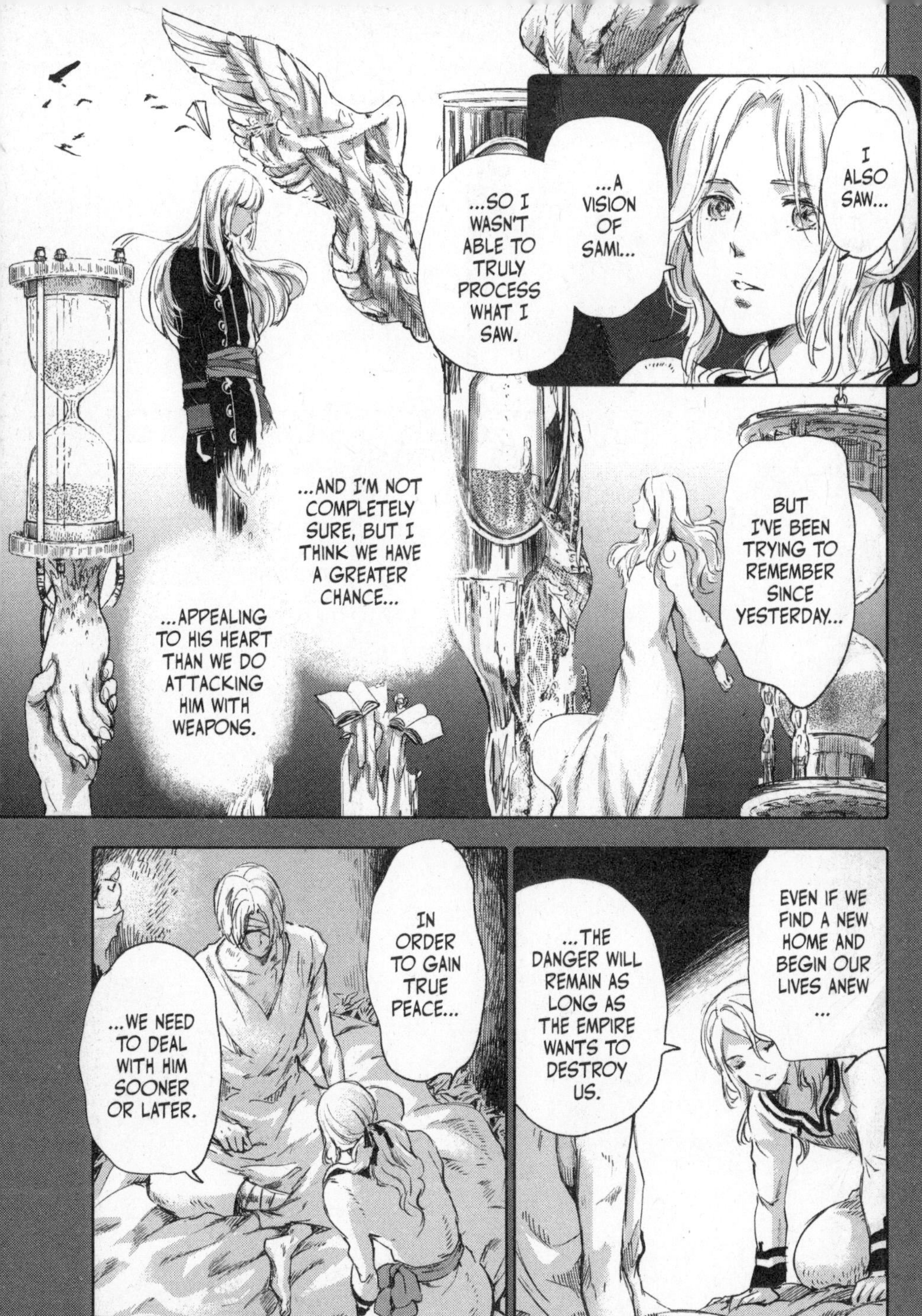
I ALSO SAW...
...A VISION OF SAMI...
...SO I WASN'T ABLE TO TRULY PROCESS WHAT I SAW.
BUT I'VE BEEN TRYING TO REMEMBER SINCE YESTERDAY...
...AND I'M NOT COMPLETELY SURE, BUT I THINK WE HAVE A GREATER CHANCE...
...APPEALING TO HIS HEART THAN WE DO ATTACKING HIM WITH WEAPONS.
EVEN IF WE FIND A NEW HOME AND BEGIN OUR LIVES ANEW ...
...THE DANGER WILL REMAIN AS LONG AS THE EMPIRE WANTS TO DESTROY US.
IN ORDER TO GAIN TRUE PEACE...
...WE NEED TO DEAL WITH HIM SOONER OR LATER.

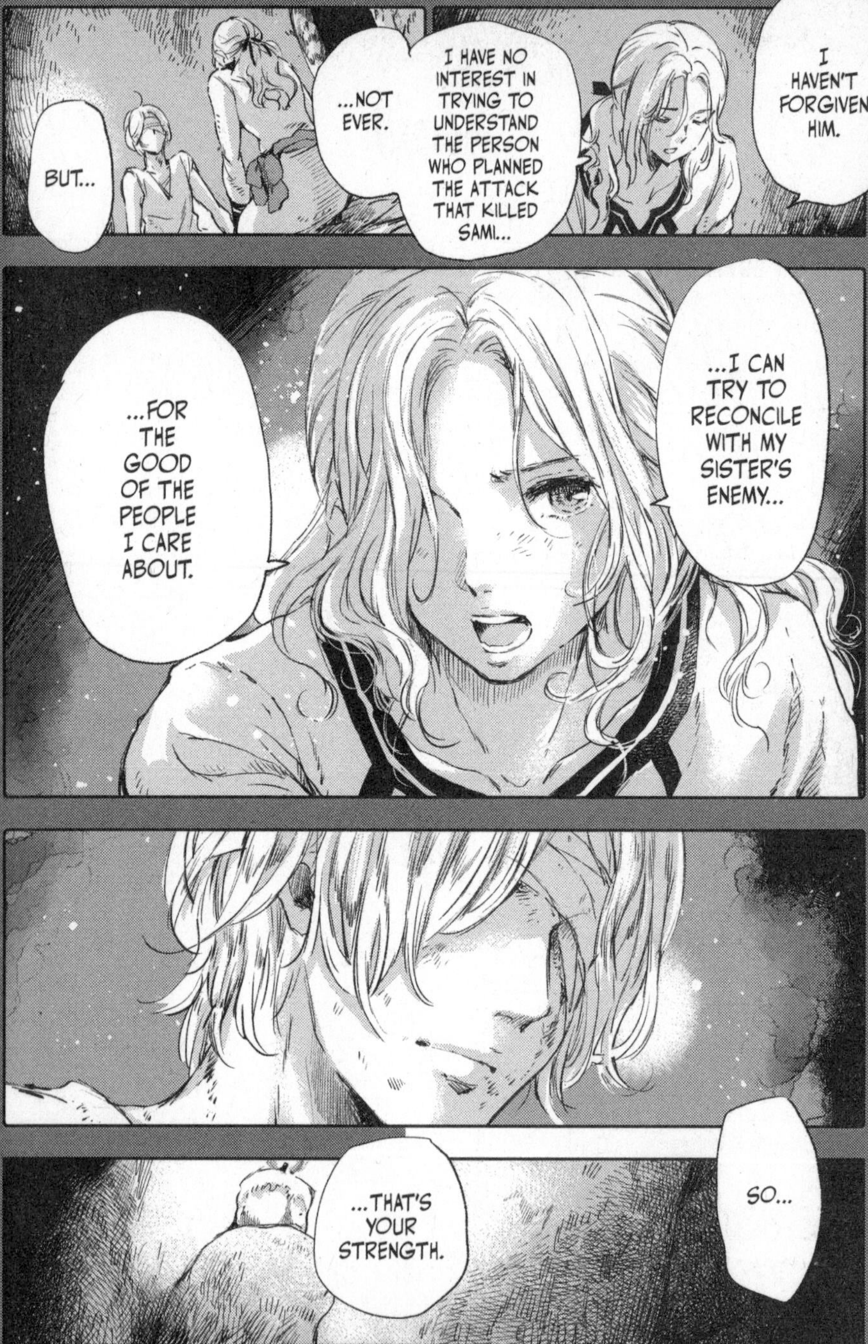
I HAVEN'T FORGIVEN HIM.
I HAVE NO INTEREST IN TRYING TO UNDERSTAND THE PERSON WHO PLANNED THE ATTACK THAT KILLED SAMI...
...NOT EVER.
BUT...
...I CAN TRY TO RECONCILE WITH MY SISTER'S ENEMY...
...FOR THE GOOD OF THE PEOPLE I CARE ABOUT.
SO...
...THAT'S YOUR STRENGTH.

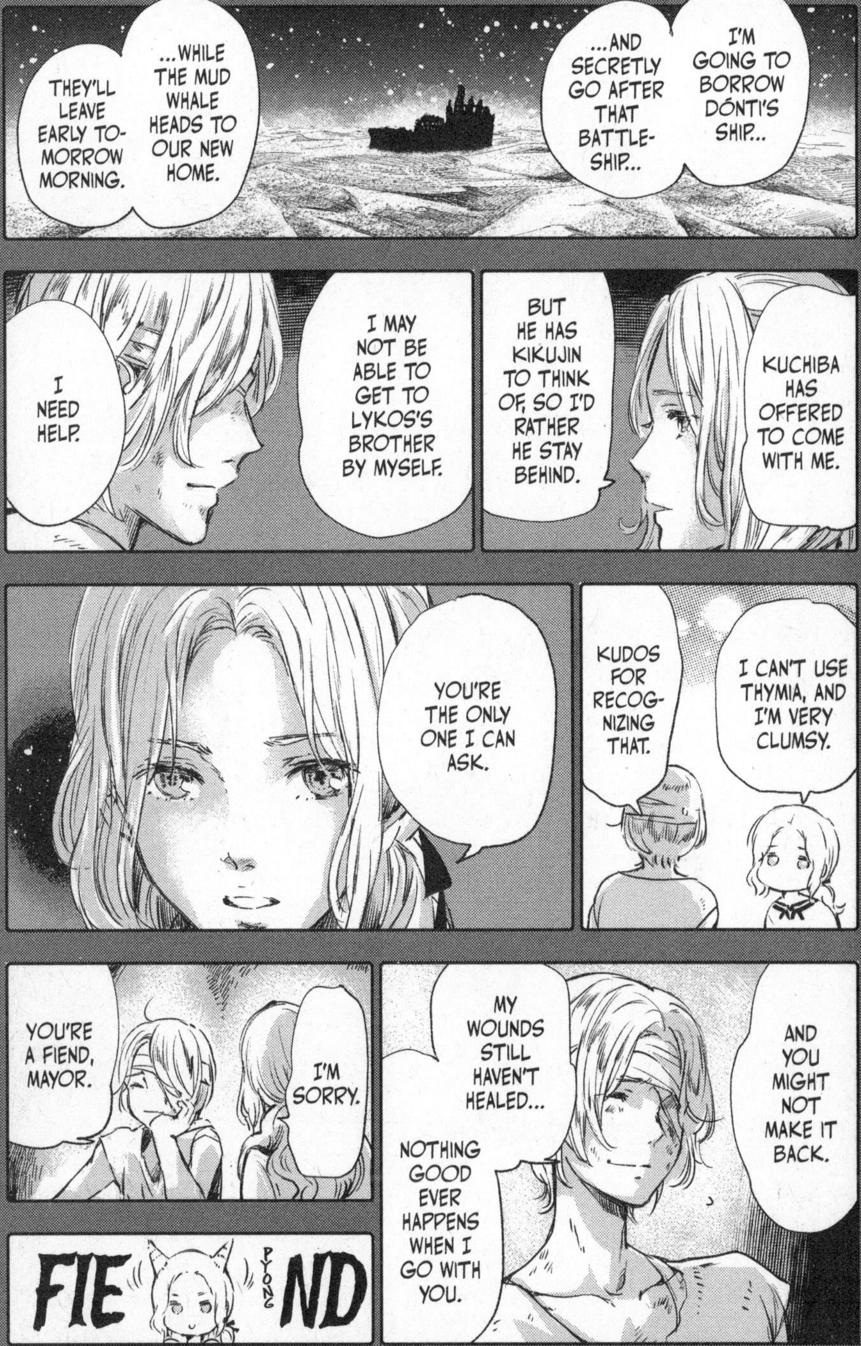
I'M GOING TO BORROW DÓNTI'S SHIP...
...AND SECRETLY GO AFTER THAT BATTLE-SHIP...
...WHILE THE MUD WHALE HEADS TO OUR NEW HOME.
THEY'LL LEAVE EARLY TO-MORROW MORNING.
KUCHIBA HAS OFFERED TO COME WITH ME.
BUT HE HAS KIKUJIN TO THINK OF, SO I'D RATHER HE STAY BEHIND.
I MAY NOT BE ABLE TO GET TO LYKOS'S BROTHER BY MYSELF.
I NEED HELP.
I CAN'T USE THYMIA, AND I'M VERY CLUMSY.
KUDOS FOR RECOG-NIZING THAT.
YOU'RE THE ONLY ONE I CAN ASK.
AND YOU MIGHT NOT MAKE IT BACK.
MY WOUNDS STILL HAVEN'T HEALED...
NOTHING GOOD EVER HAPPENS WHEN I GO WITH YOU.
I'M SORRY.
YOU'RE A FIEND, MAYOR.
FIE
PYONG
ND

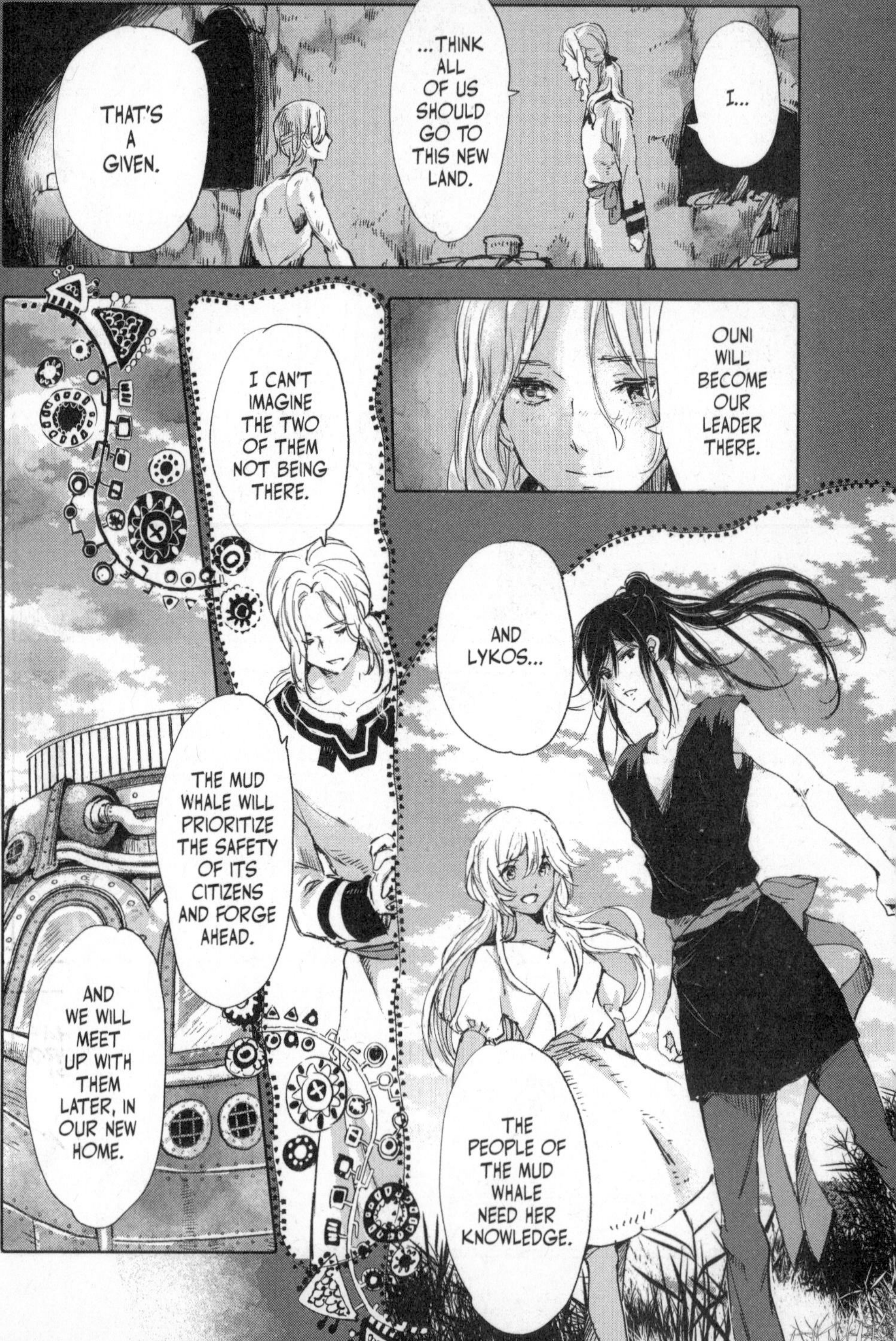
I...
...THINK ALL OF US SHOULD GO TO THIS NEW LAND.
THAT'S A GIVEN.
OUNI WILL BECOME OUR LEADER THERE.
AND LYKOS...
THE PEOPLE OF THE MUD WHALE NEED HER KNOWLEDGE.
I CAN'T IMAGINE THE TWO OF THEM NOT BEING THERE.
THE MUD WHALE WILL PRIORITIZE THE SAFETY OF ITS CITIZENS AND FORGE AHEAD.
AND WE WILL MEET UP WITH THEM LATER, IN OUR NEW HOME.

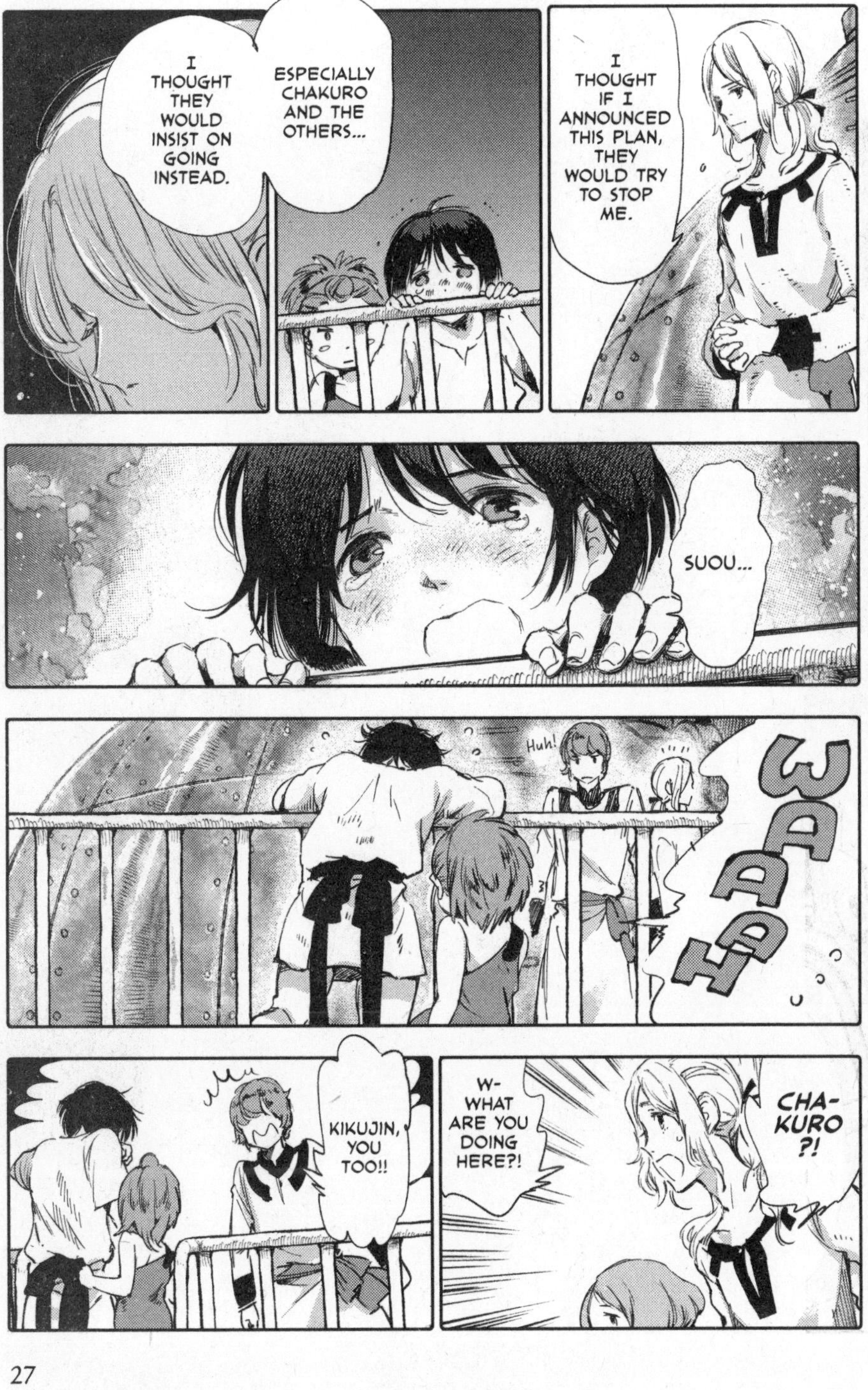
I THOUGHT IF I ANNOUNCED THIS PLAN, THEY WOULD TRY TO STOP ME.
ESPECIALLY CHAKURO AND THE OTHERS...
I THOUGHT THEY WOULD INSIST ON GOING INSTEAD.
SUOU...
WAAAH
Huh!
CHA-KURO?!
W-WHAT ARE YOU DOING HERE?!
KIKUJIN, YOU TOO!!

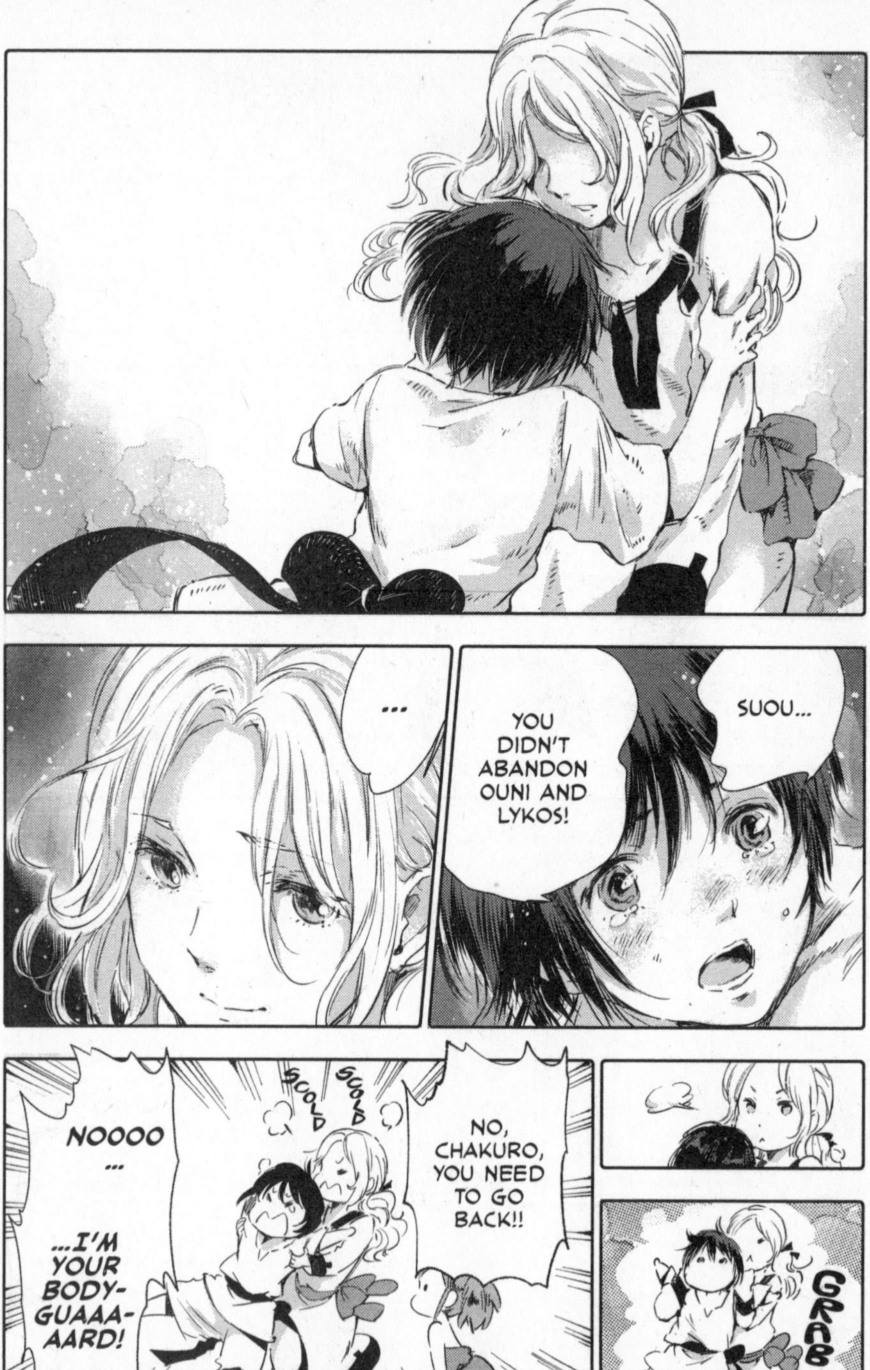
SUOU...
YOU DIDN'T ABANDON OUNI AND LYKOS!
...
GRAB
NO, CHAKURO, YOU NEED TO GO BACK!!
SCOLD SCOLD
NOOOO ...
...I'M YOUR BODY-GUAAA-AARD!

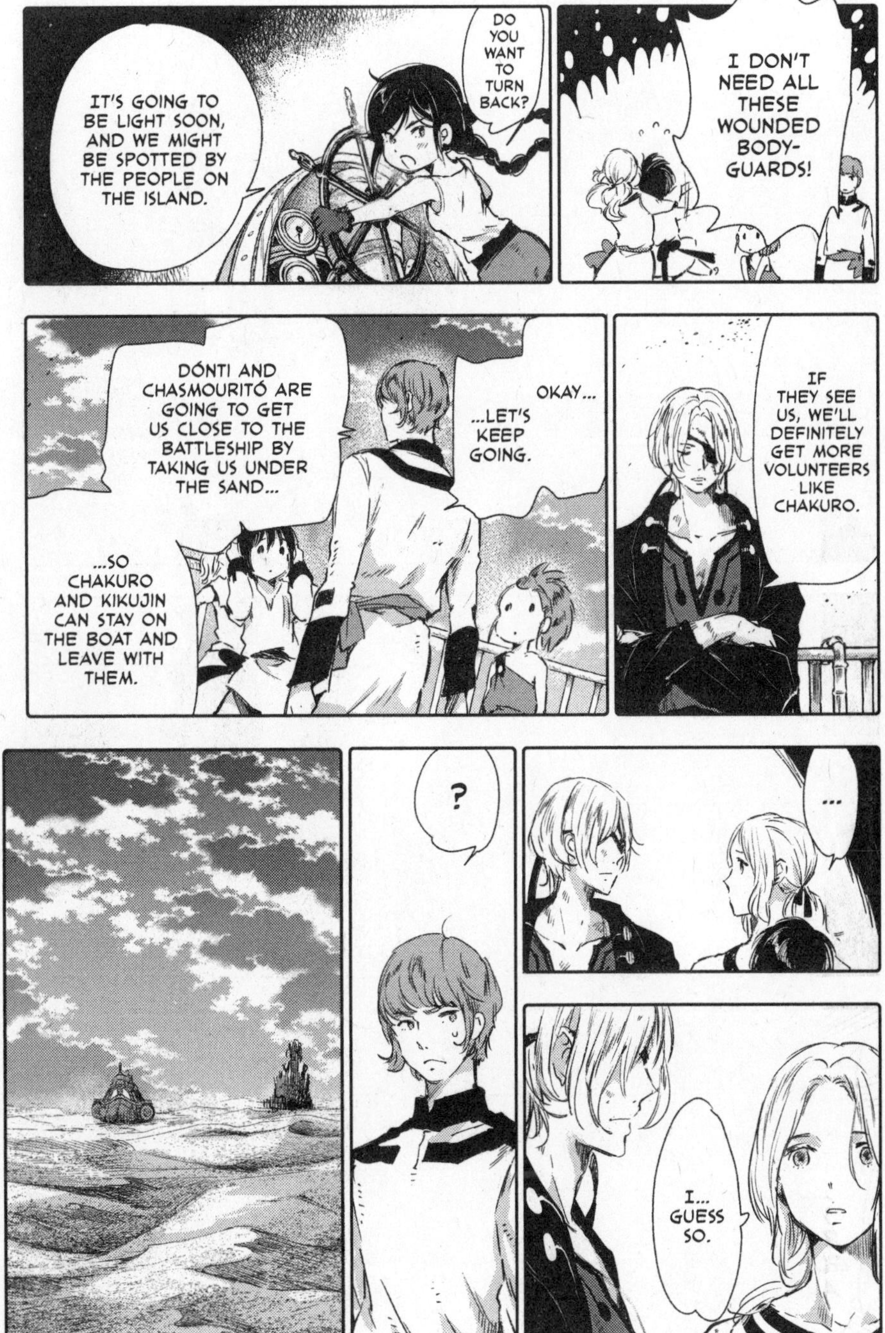
I DON'T NEED ALL THESE WOUNDED BODY-GUARDS!
DO YOU WANT TO TURN BACK?
IT'S GOING TO BE LIGHT SOON, AND WE MIGHT BE SPOTTED BY THE PEOPLE ON THE ISLAND.
IF THEY SEE US, WE'LL DEFINITELY GET MORE VOLUNTEERS LIKE CHAKURO.
OKAY...
...LET'S KEEP GOING.
DÓNTI AND CHASMOURITÓ ARE GOING TO GET US CLOSE TO THE BATTLESHIP BY TAKING US UNDER THE SAND...
...SO CHAKURO AND KIKUJIN CAN STAY ON THE BOAT AND LEAVE WITH THEM.
...
I... GUESS SO.
?

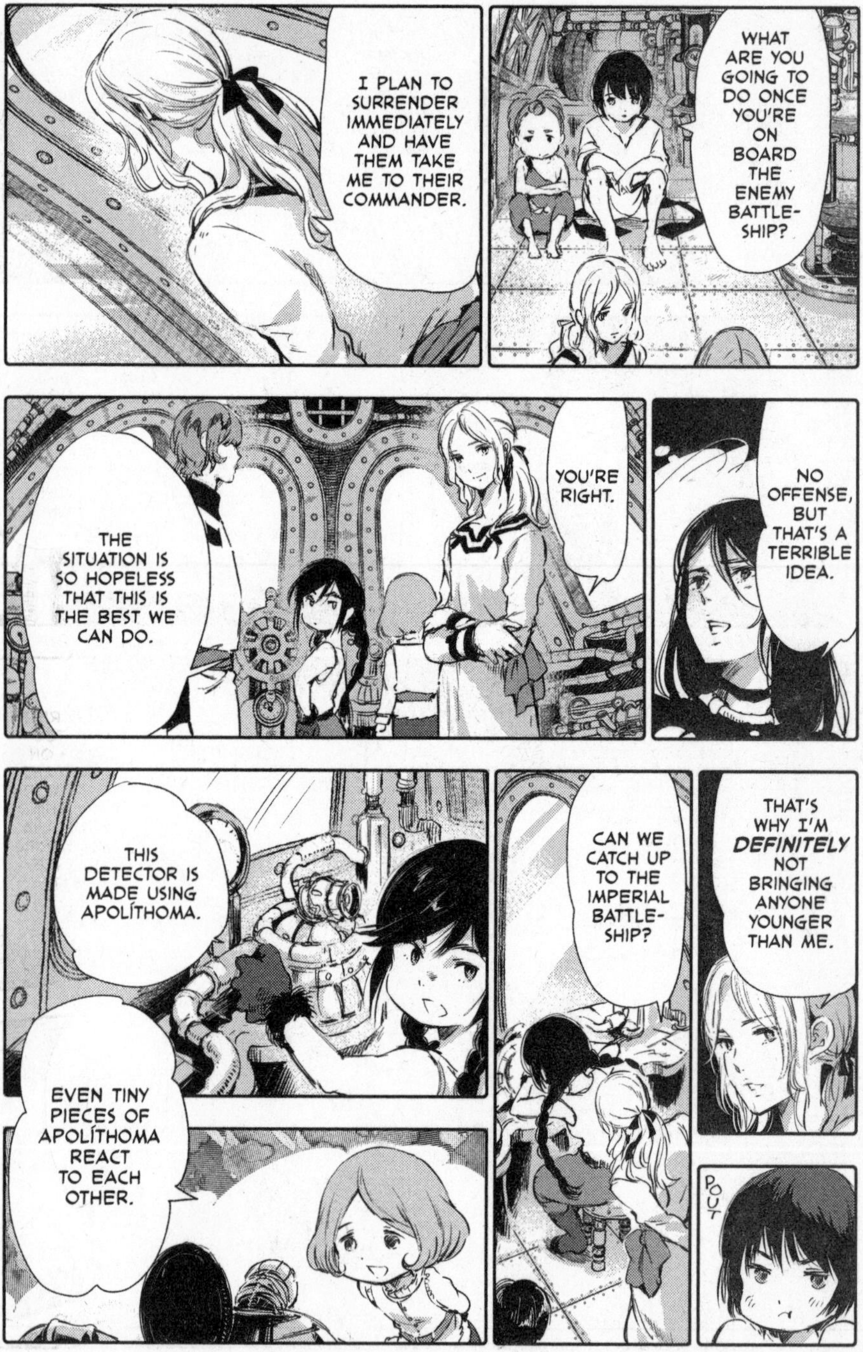
WHAT ARE YOU GOING TO DO ONCE YOU'RE ON BOARD THE ENEMY BATTLE-SHIP?
I PLAN TO SURRENDER IMMEDIATELY AND HAVE THEM TAKE ME TO THEIR COMMANDER.
NO OFFENSE, BUT THAT'S A TERRIBLE IDEA.
YOU'RE RIGHT.
THE SITUATION IS SO HOPELESS THAT THIS IS THE BEST WE CAN DO.
THAT'S WHY I'M *DEFINITELY* NOT BRINGING ANYONE YOUNGER THAN ME.
POUT
CAN WE CATCH UP TO THE IMPERIAL BATTLE-SHIP?
THIS DETECTOR IS MADE USING APOLÍTHOMA.
EVEN TINY PIECES OF APOLÍTHOMA REACT TO EACH OTHER.

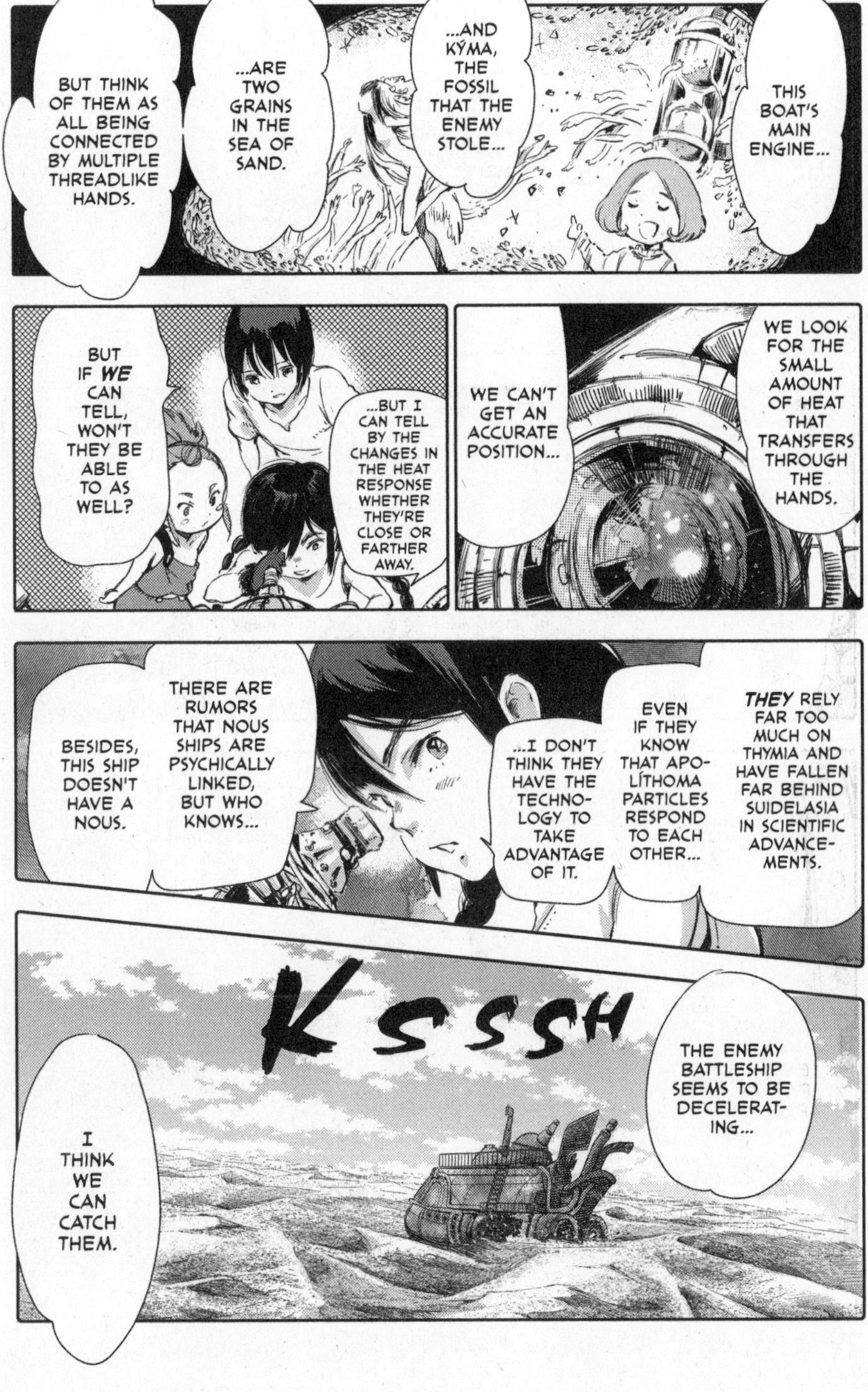
THIS BOAT'S MAIN ENGINE...
...AND KÝMA, THE FOSSIL THAT THE ENEMY STOLE...
...ARE TWO GRAINS IN THE SEA OF SAND.
BUT THINK OF THEM AS ALL BEING CONNECTED BY MULTIPLE THREADLIKE HANDS.
WE LOOK FOR THE SMALL AMOUNT OF HEAT THAT TRANSFERS THROUGH THE HANDS.
WE CAN'T GET AN ACCURATE POSITION...
...BUT I CAN TELL BY THE CHANGES IN THE HEAT RESPONSE WHETHER THEY'RE CLOSE OR FARTHER AWAY.
BUT IF *WE* CAN TELL, WON'T THEY BE ABLE TO AS WELL?
THEY RELY FAR TOO MUCH ON THYMIA AND HAVE FALLEN FAR BEHIND SUIDELASIA IN SCIENTIFIC ADVANCEMENTS.
EVEN IF THEY KNOW THAT APOLÍTHOMA PARTICLES RESPOND TO EACH OTHER...
...I DON'T THINK THEY HAVE THE TECHNOLOGY TO TAKE ADVANTAGE OF IT.
THERE ARE RUMORS THAT NOUS SHIPS ARE PSYCHICALLY LINKED, BUT WHO KNOWS...
BESIDES, THIS SHIP DOESN'T HAVE A NOUS.
KSSSH
THE ENEMY BATTLESHIP SEEMS TO BE DECELERATING...
I THINK WE CAN CATCH THEM.

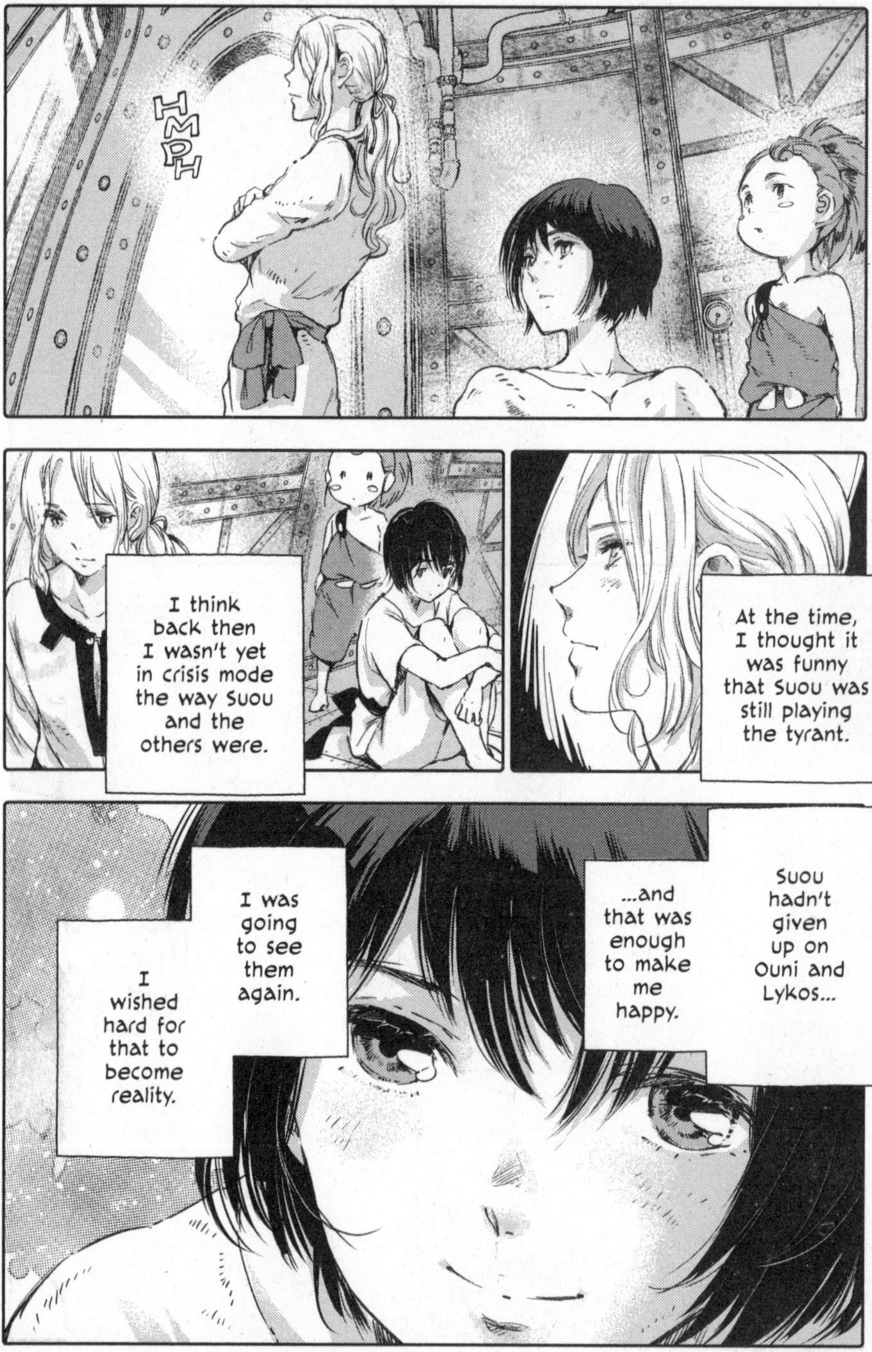
HMPH
At the time, I thought it was funny that Suou was still playing the tyrant.
I think back then I wasn't yet in crisis mode the way Suou and the others were.
Suou hadn't given up on Ouni and Lykos...
...and that was enough to make me happy.
I was going to see them again.
I wished hard for that to become reality.

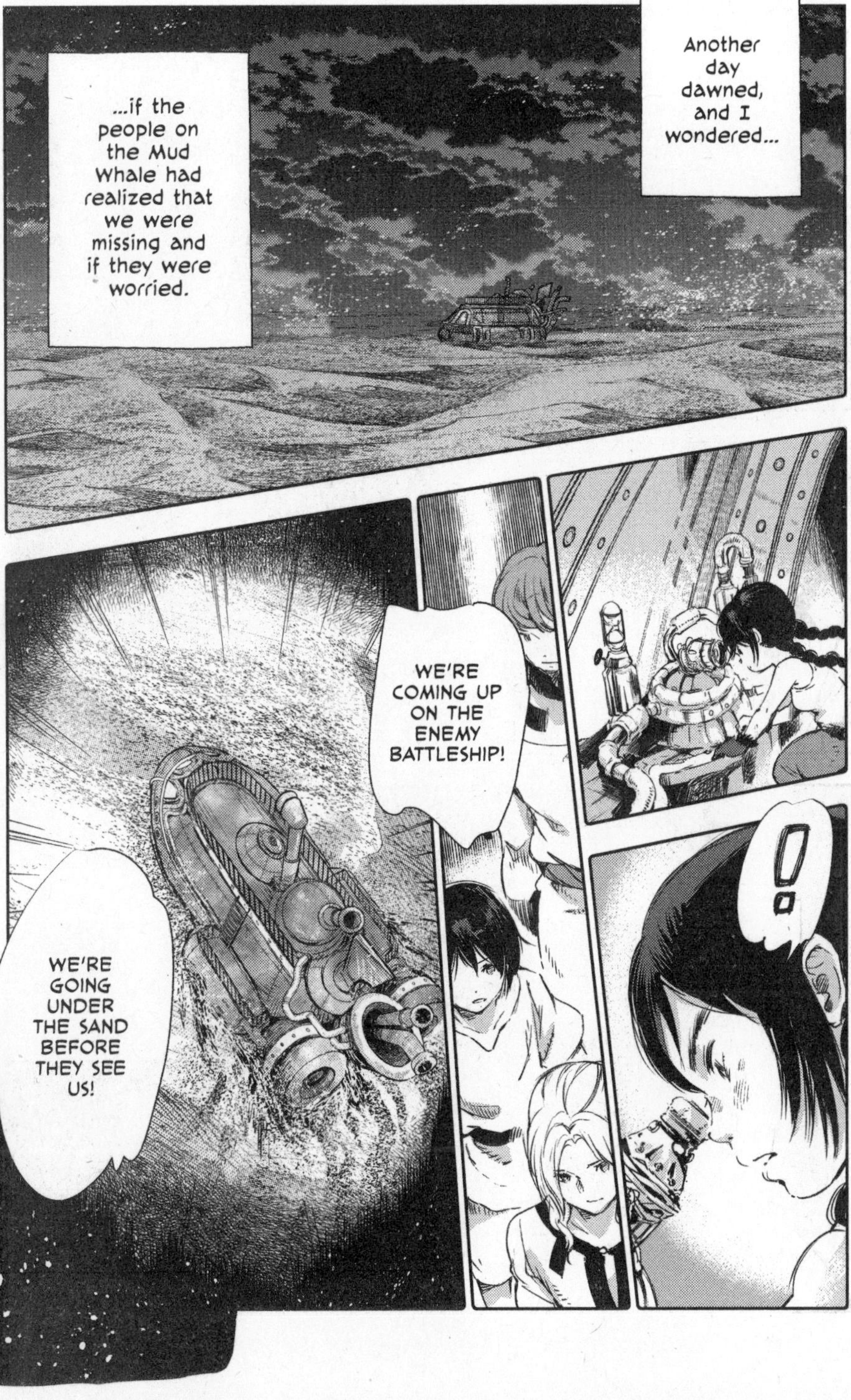

Another day dawned, and I wondered...
...if the people on the Mud Whale had realized that we were missing and if they were worried.
!
WE'RE COMING UP ON THE ENEMY BATTLESHIP!
WE'RE GOING UNDER THE SAND BEFORE THEY SEE US!

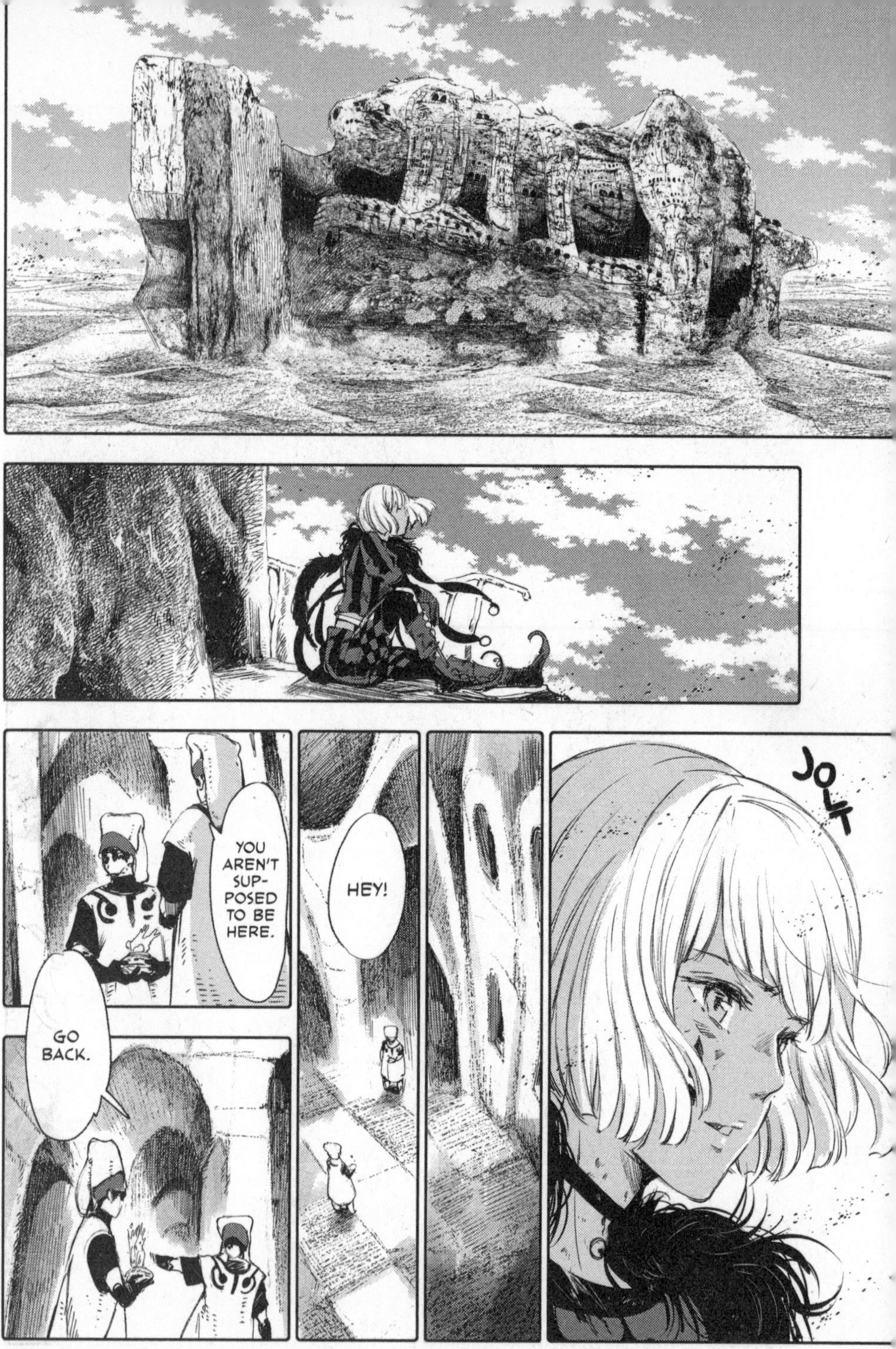
JOLT
HEY!
YOU AREN'T SUPPOSED TO BE HERE.
GO BACK.

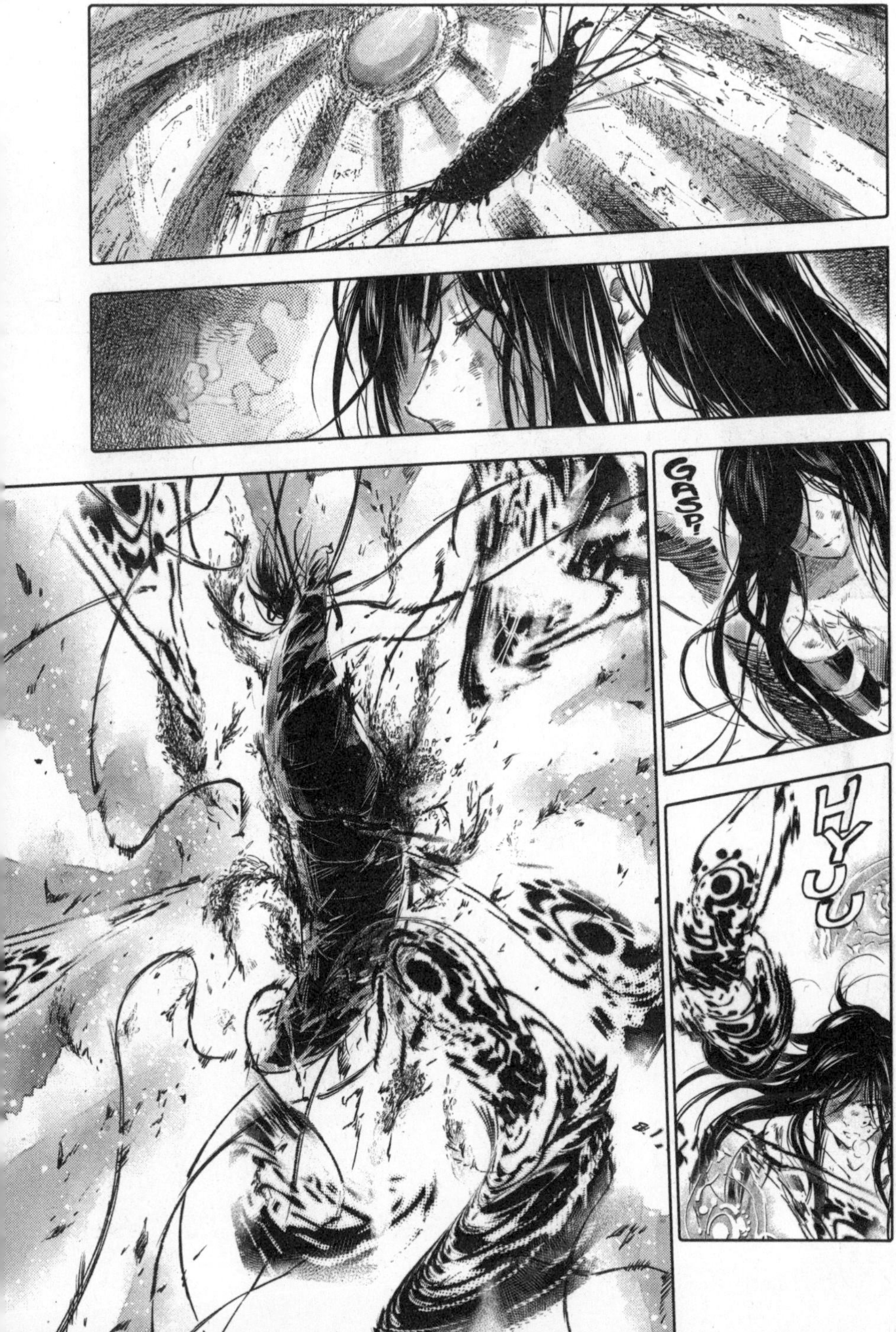
GASP!
HYJU

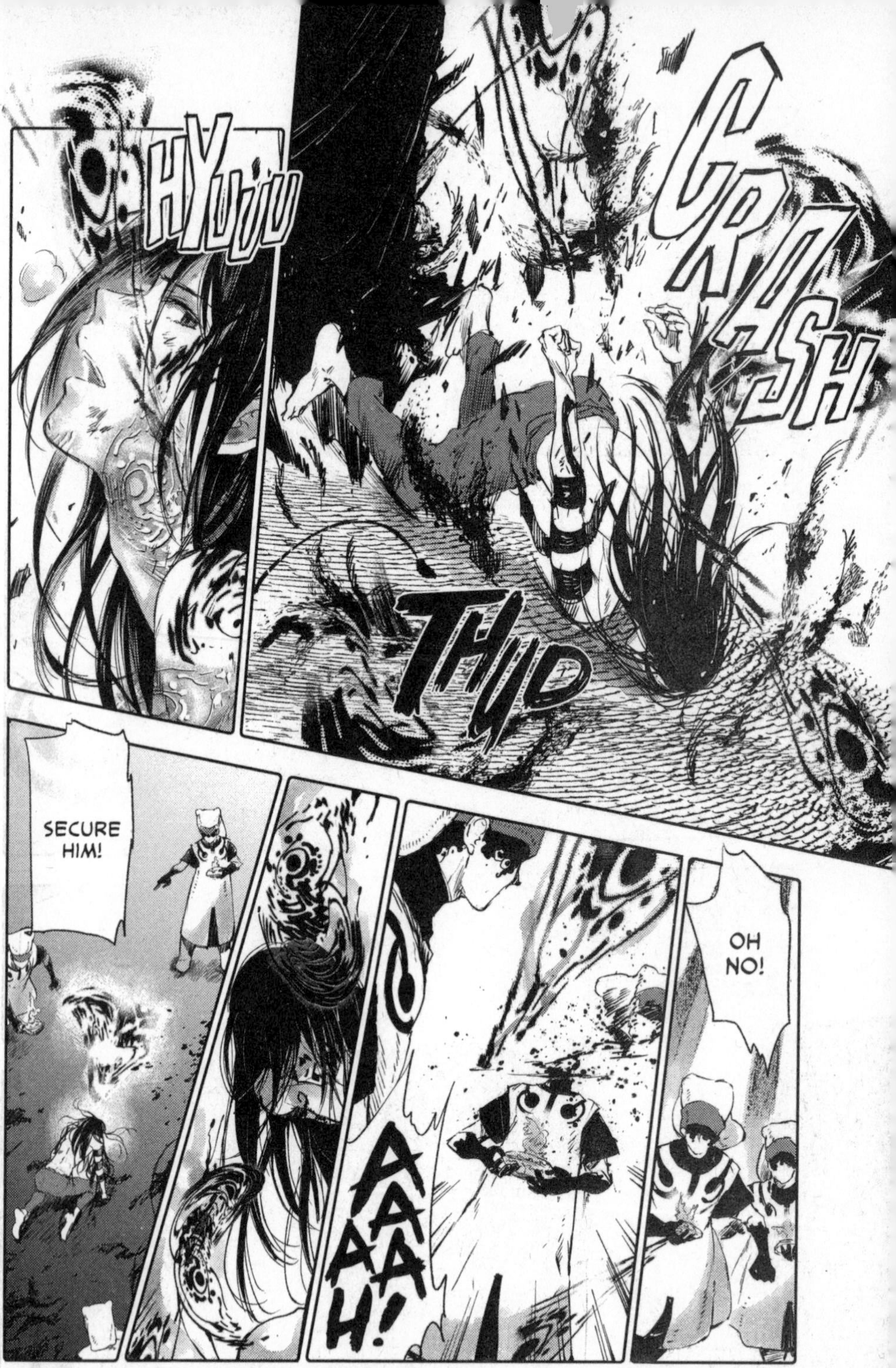
CRASH
THUD
HYUUUU
OH NO!
AAAAH!
SECURE HIM!

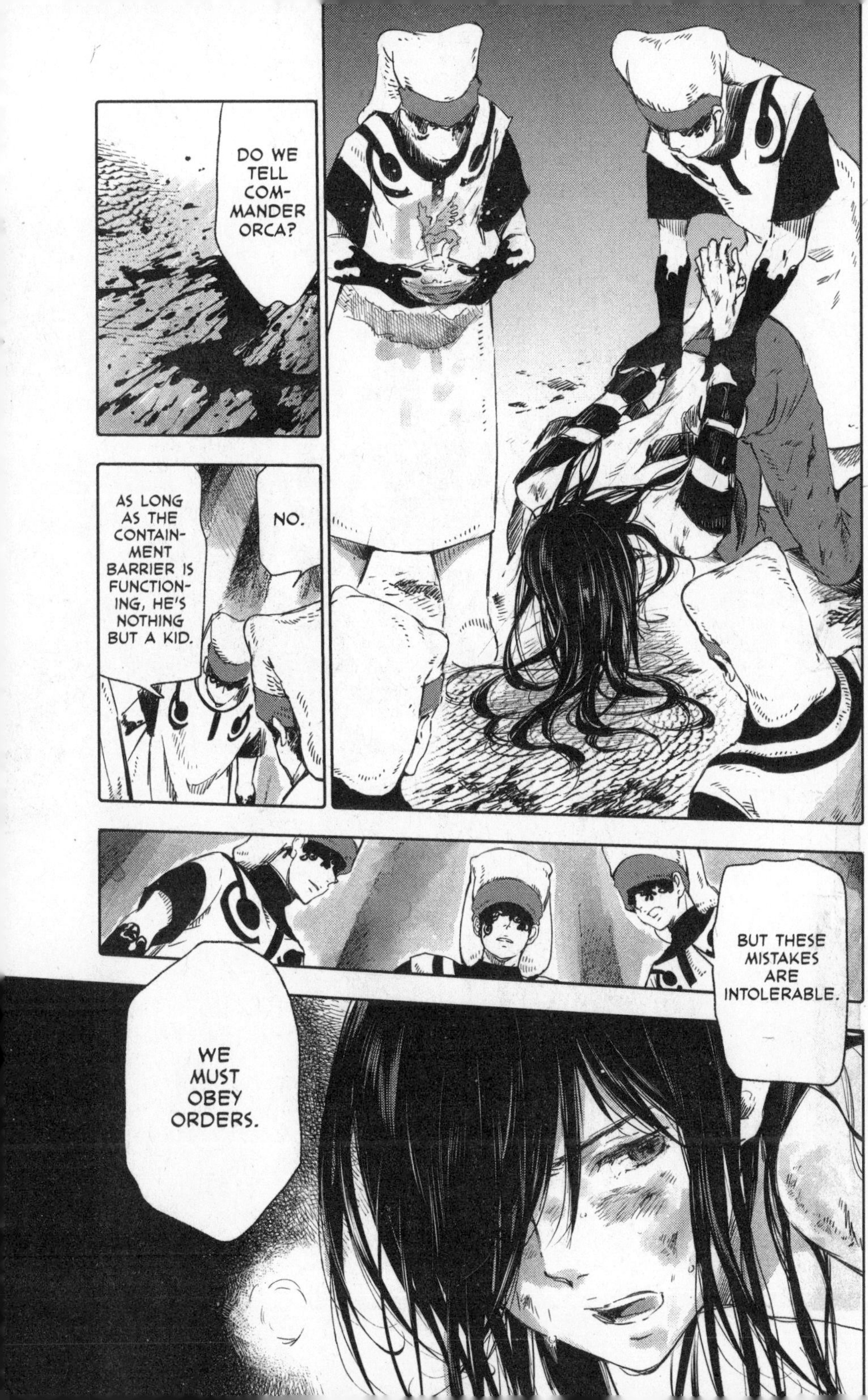
DO WE TELL COMMANDER ORCA?
NO.
AS LONG AS THE CONTAINMENT BARRIER IS FUNCTIONING, HE'S NOTHING BUT A KID.
BUT THESE MISTAKES ARE INTOLERABLE.
WE MUST OBEY ORDERS.

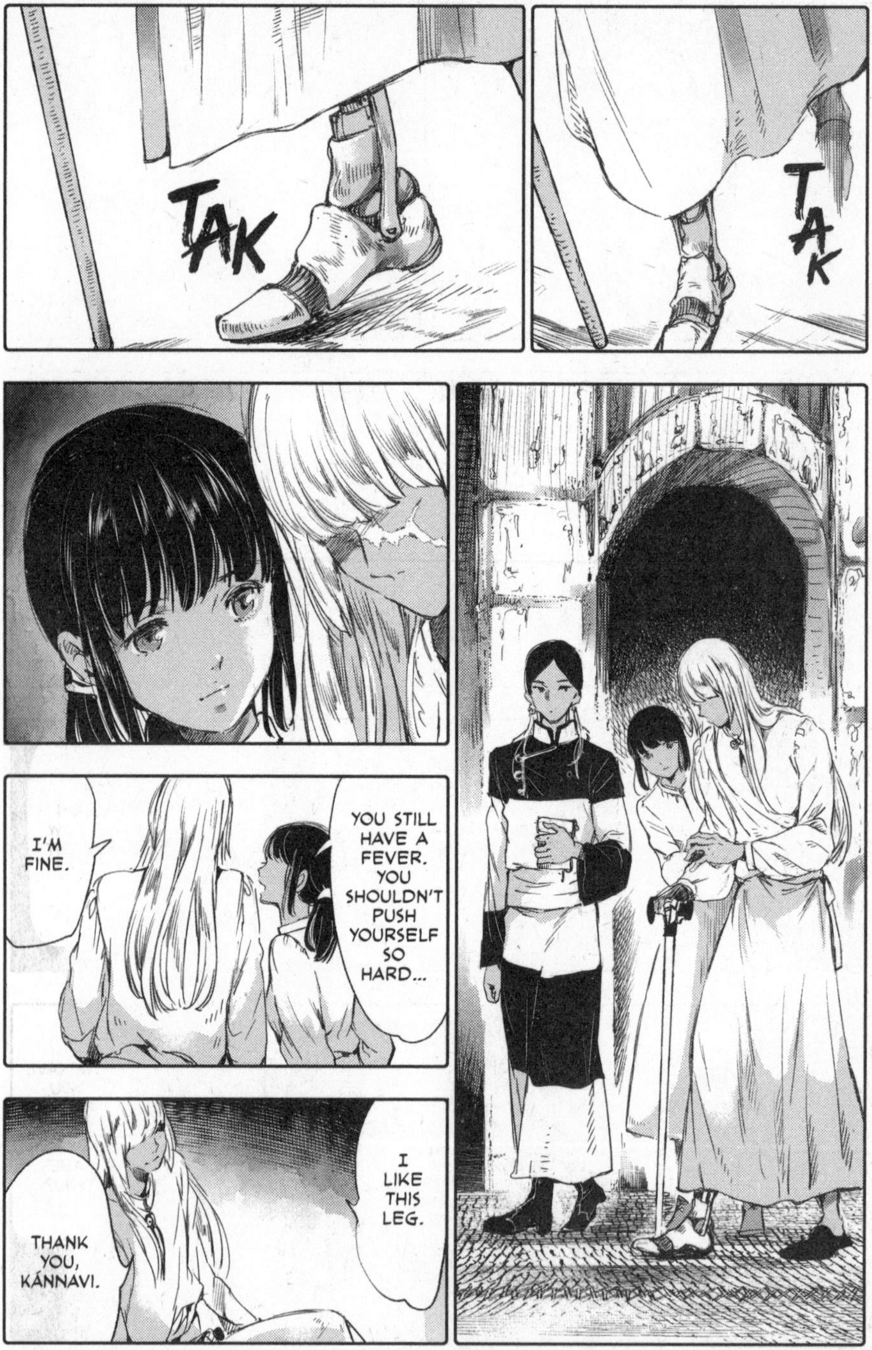
TAK
TAK
YOU STILL HAVE A FEVER. YOU SHOULDN'T PUSH YOURSELF SO HARD...
I'M FINE.
I LIKE THIS LEG.
THANK YOU, KÁNNAVI.

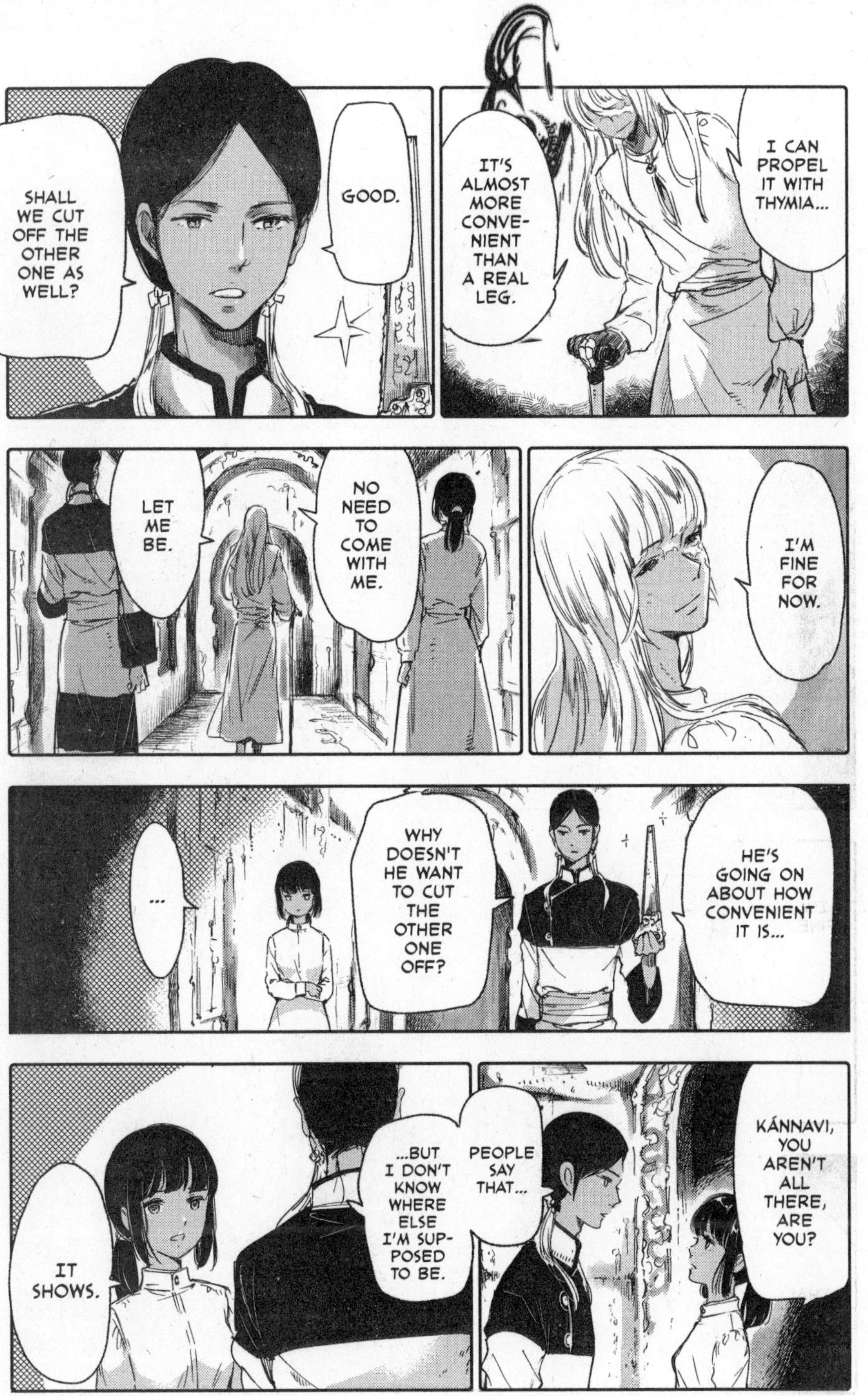
I CAN PROPEL IT WITH THYMIA...
IT'S ALMOST MORE CONVENIENT THAN A REAL LEG.
GOOD.
SHALL WE CUT OFF THE OTHER ONE AS WELL?
I'M FINE FOR NOW.
NO NEED TO COME WITH ME.
LET ME BE.
HE'S GOING ON ABOUT HOW CONVENIENT IT IS...
WHY DOESN'T HE WANT TO CUT THE OTHER ONE OFF?
...
KÁNNAVI, YOU AREN'T ALL THERE, ARE YOU?
PEOPLE SAY THAT...
...BUT I DON'T KNOW WHERE ELSE I'M SUPPOSED TO BE.
IT SHOWS.

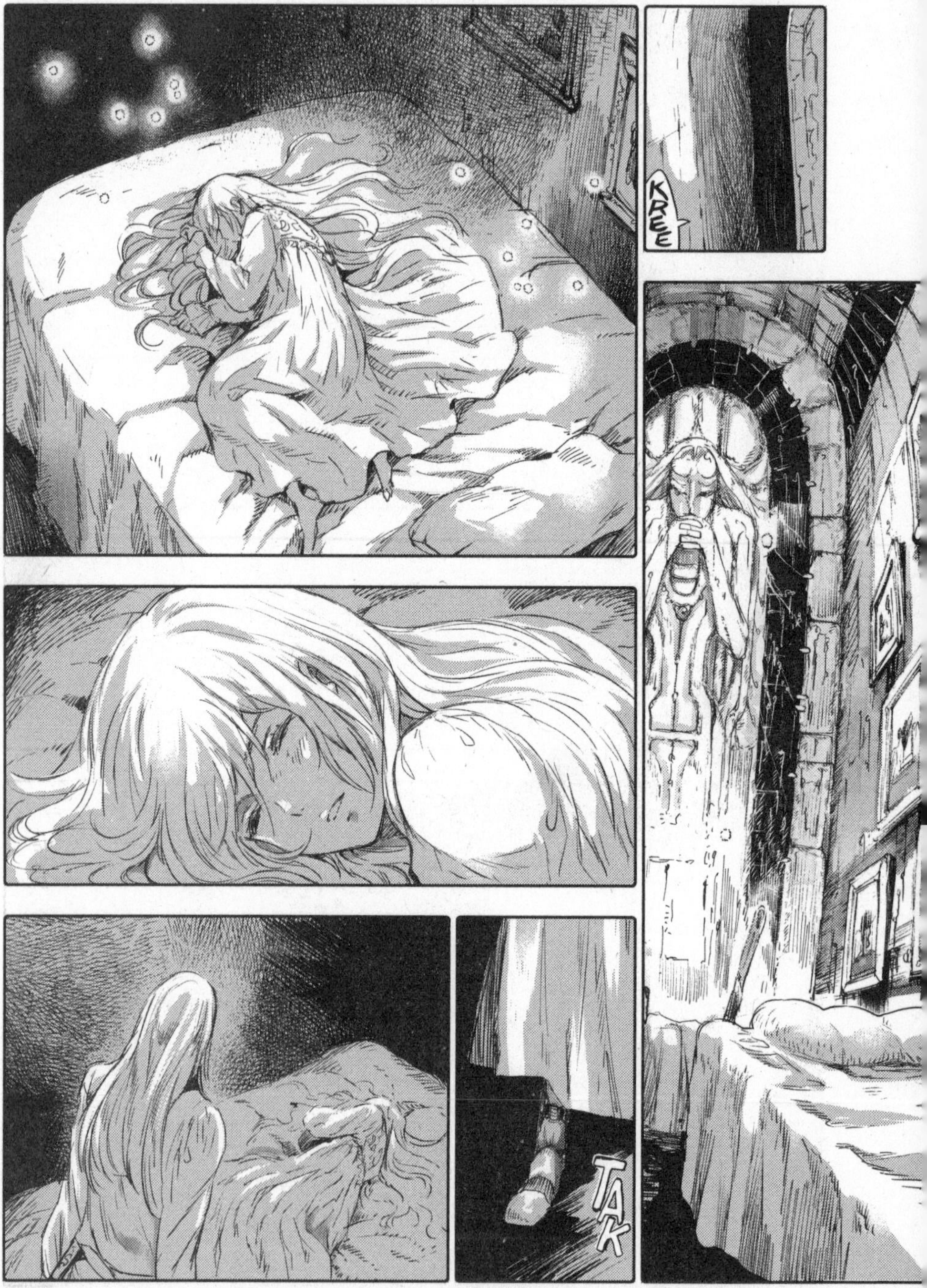
KREE
TAK

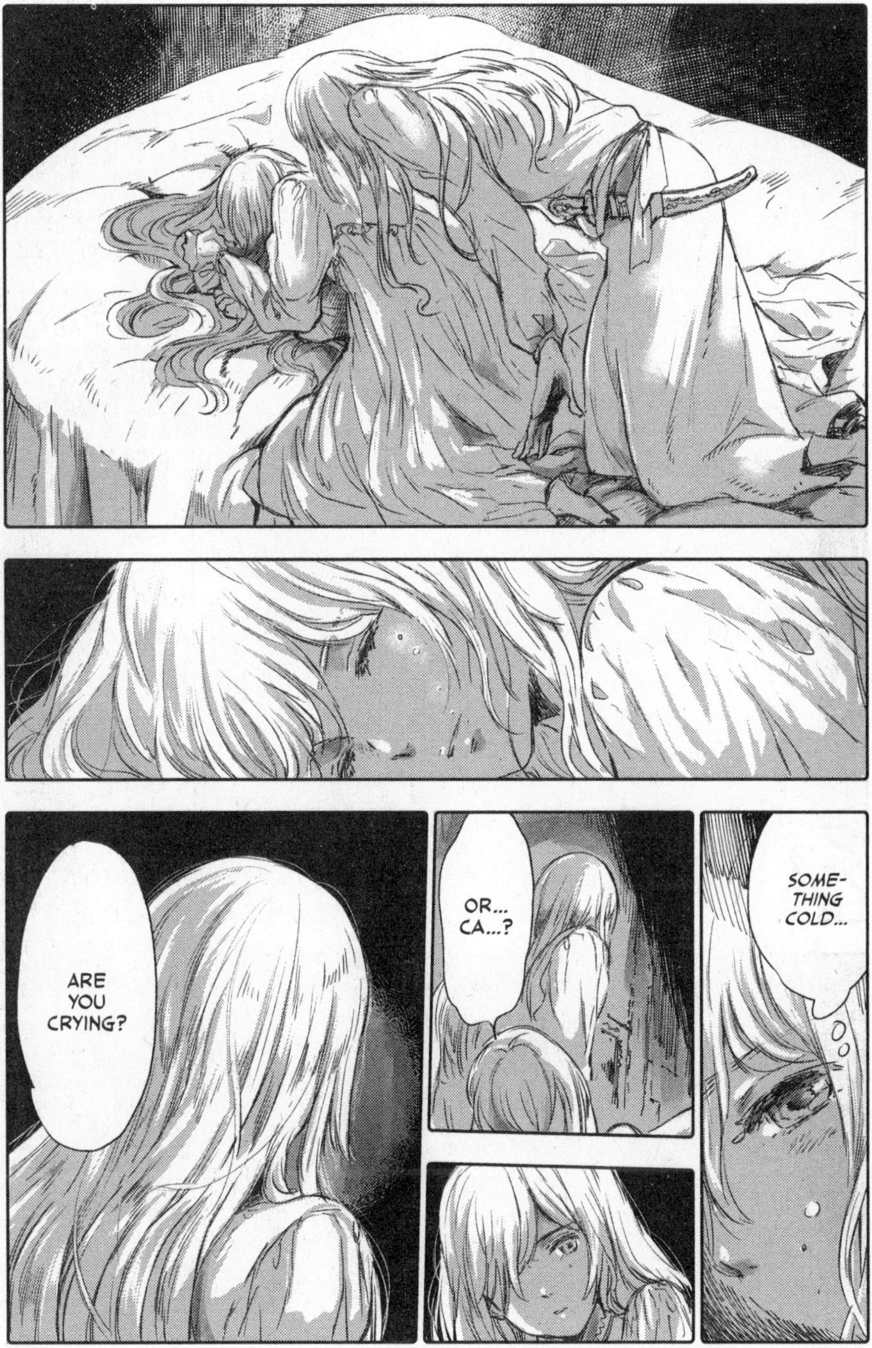
SOME-THING COLD...
OR... CA...?
ARE YOU CRYING?

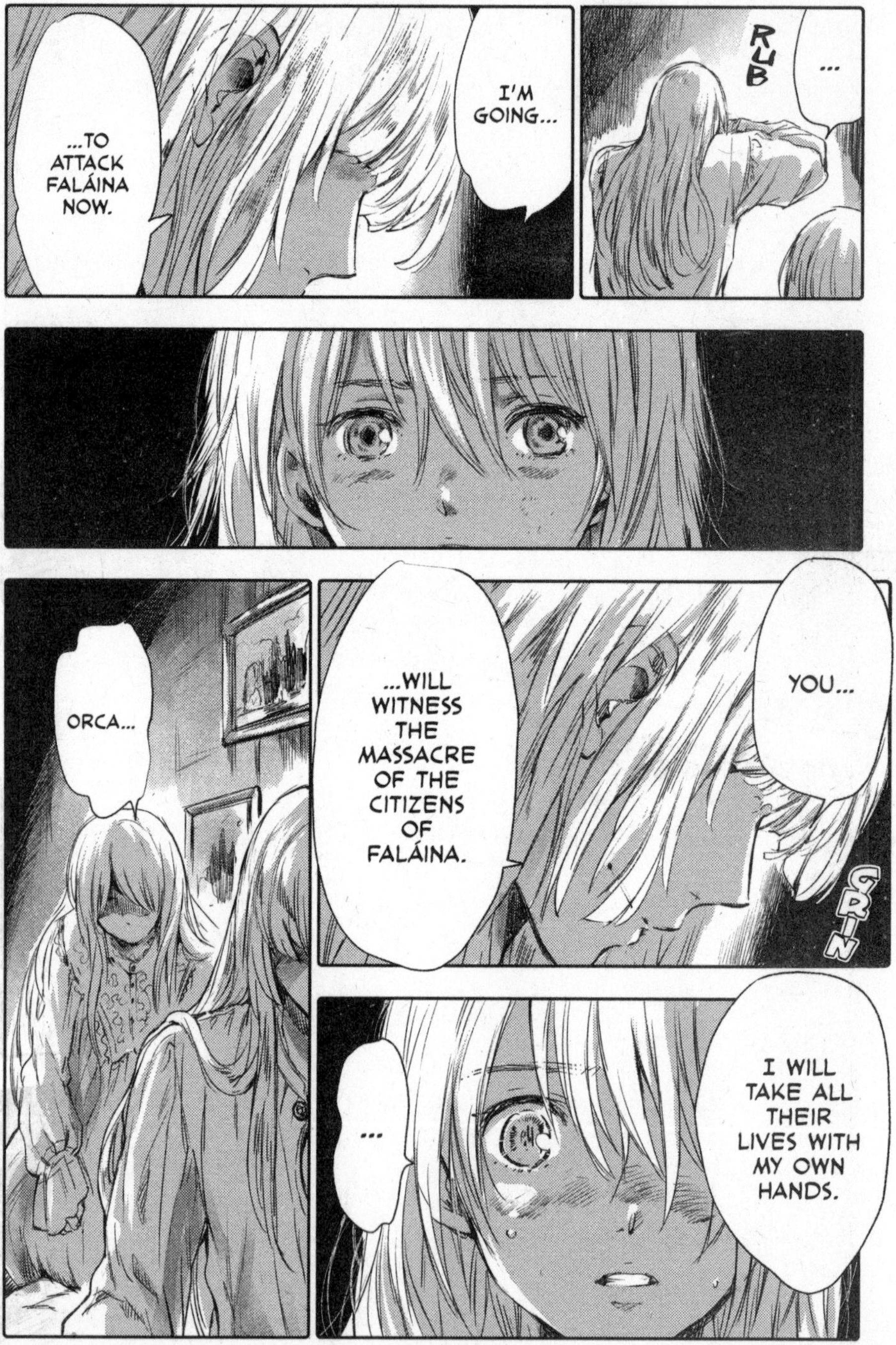
...
RUB
I'M GOING...
...TO ATTACK FALÁINA NOW.
YOU...
GRIN
...WILL WITNESS THE MASSACRE OF THE CITIZENS OF FALÁINA.
I WILL TAKE ALL THEIR LIVES WITH MY OWN HANDS.
...
ORCA...

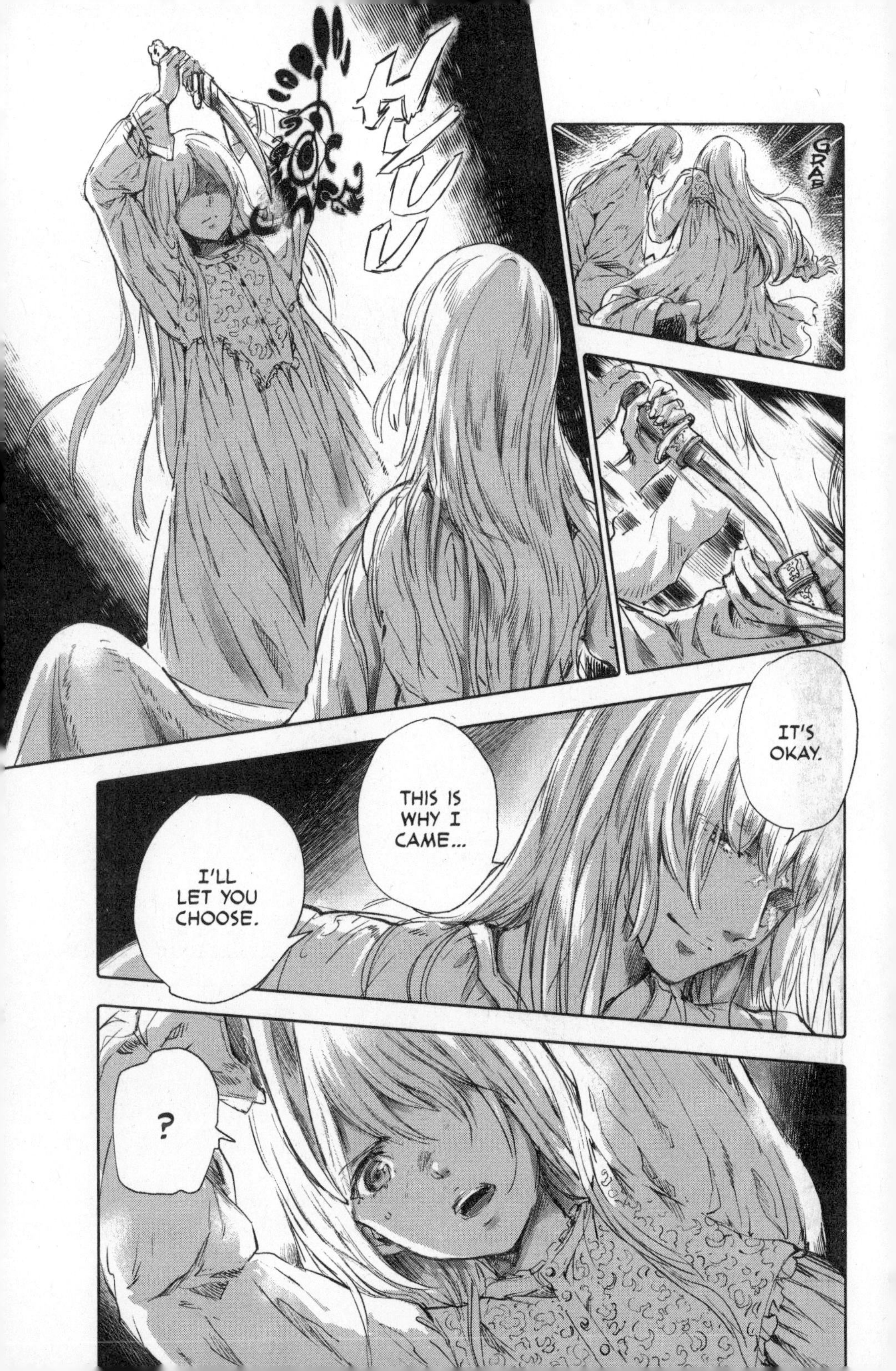
GRAB
IT'S OKAY.
THIS IS WHY I CAME...
I'LL LET YOU CHOOSE.
?

The Circle of Transmigration -The End-

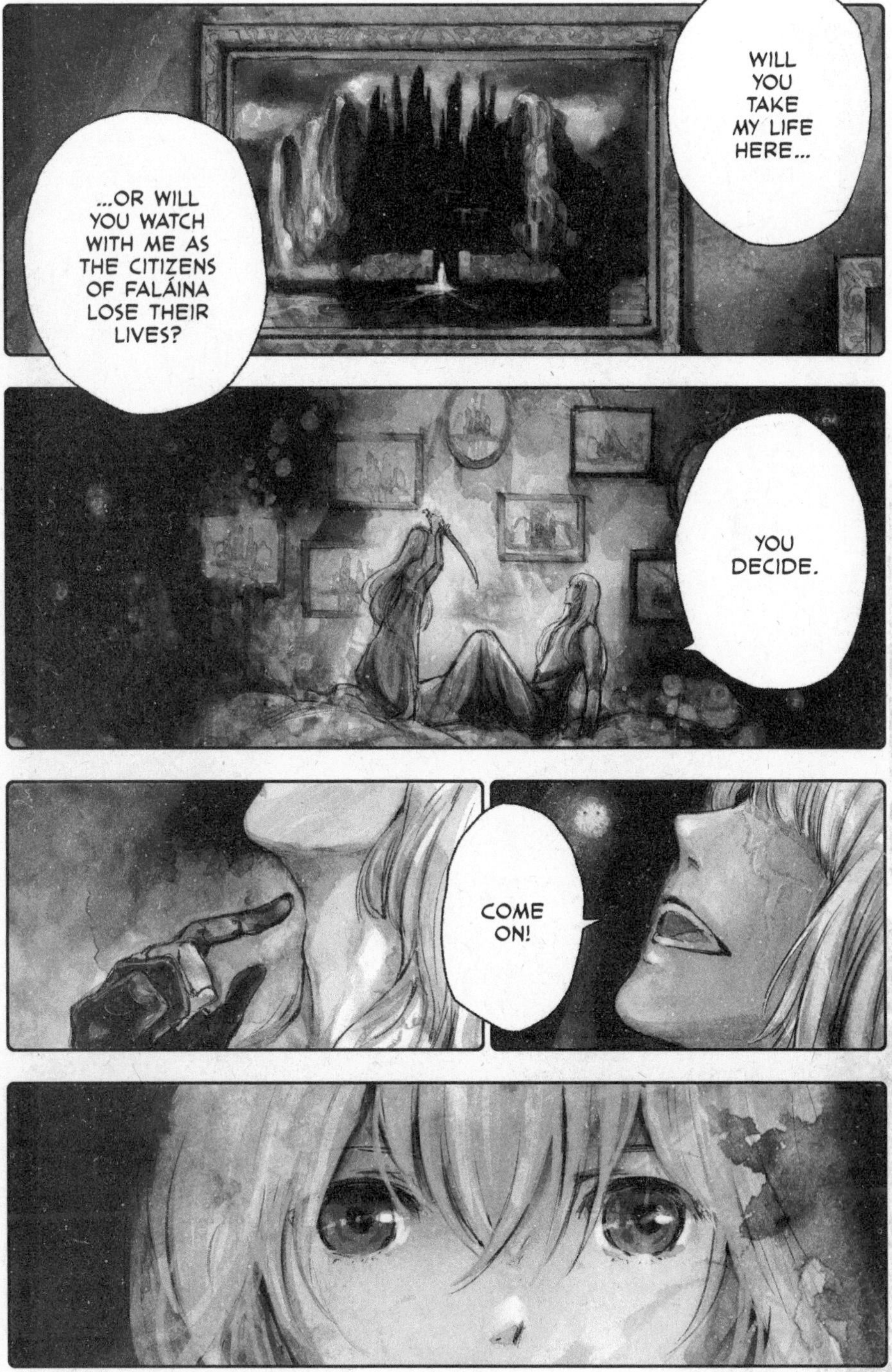
WILL YOU TAKE MY LIFE HERE...
...OR WILL YOU WATCH WITH ME AS THE CITIZENS OF FALÁINA LOSE THEIR LIVES?
YOU DECIDE.
COME ON!

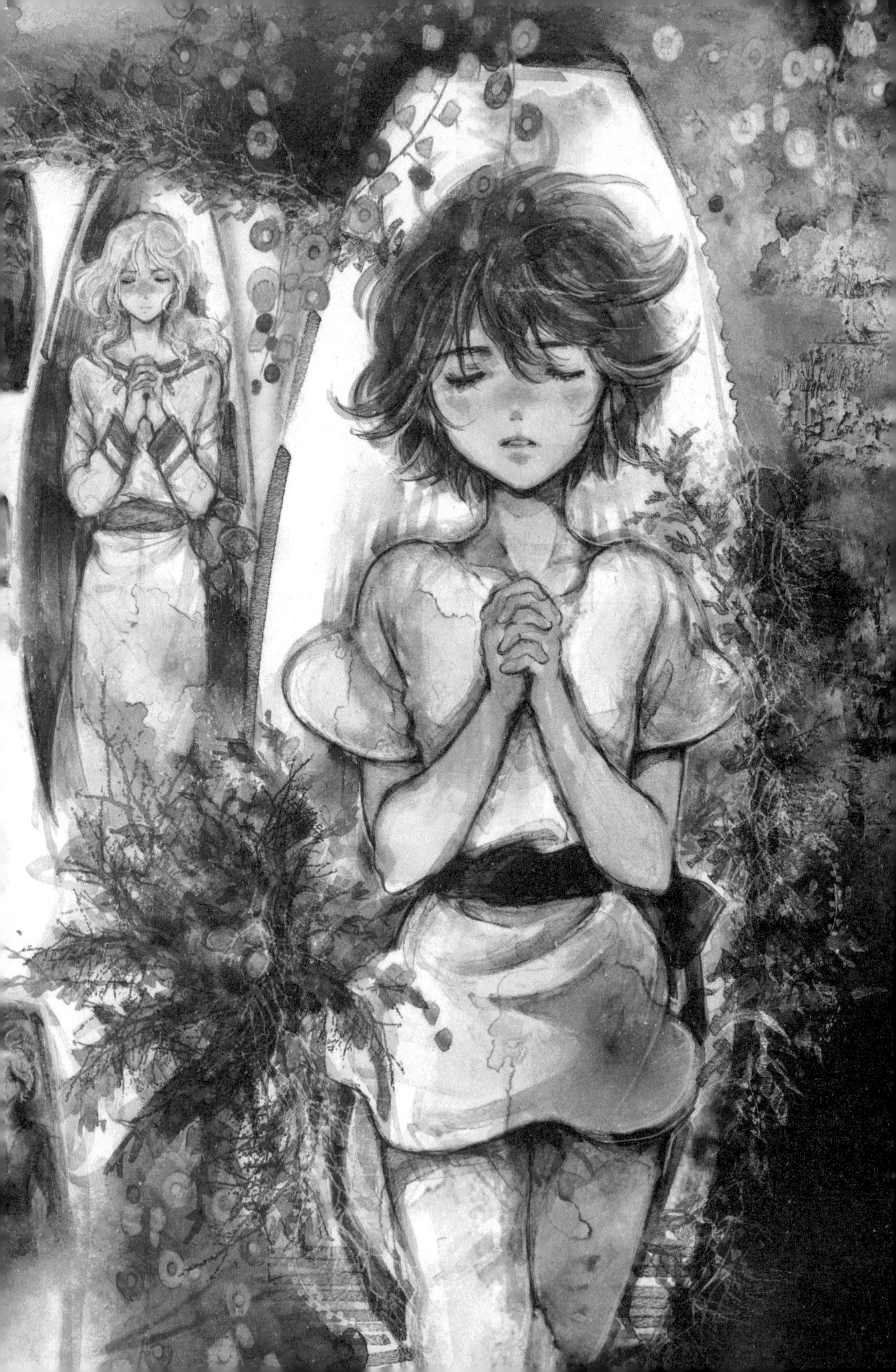

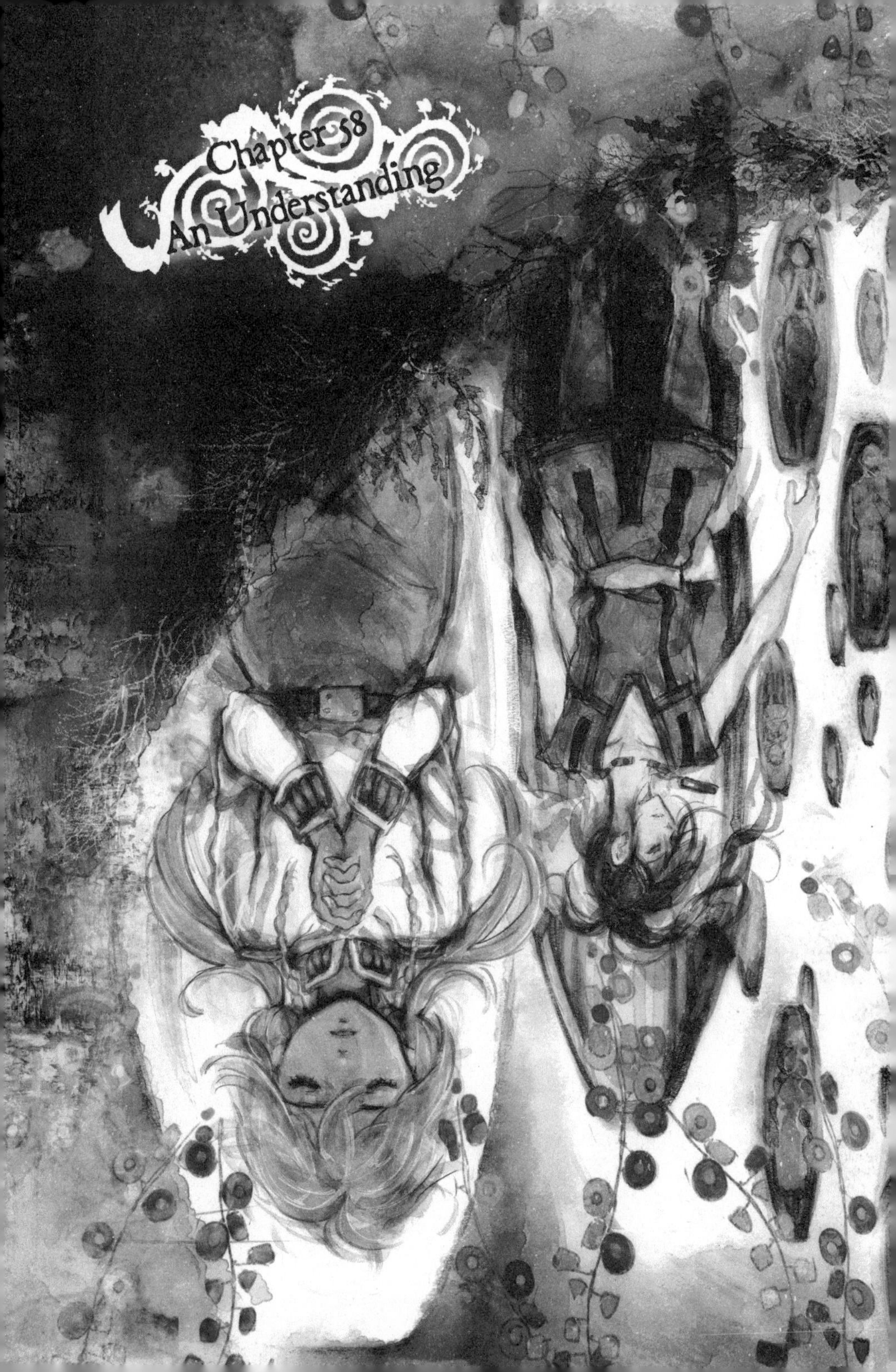
Chapter 58
An Understanding

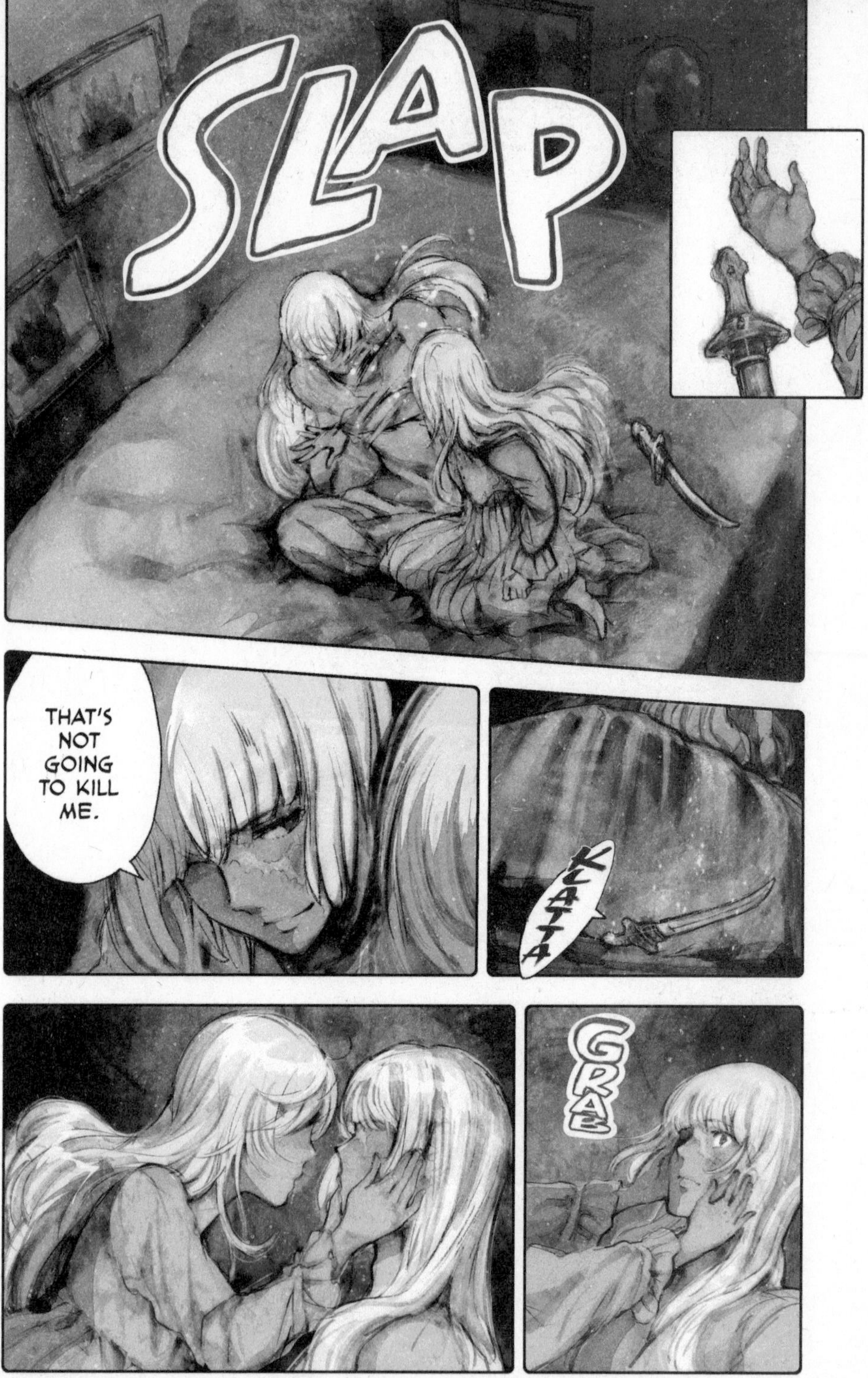
SLAP
KLATTA
THAT'S NOT GOING TO KILL ME.
GRAB

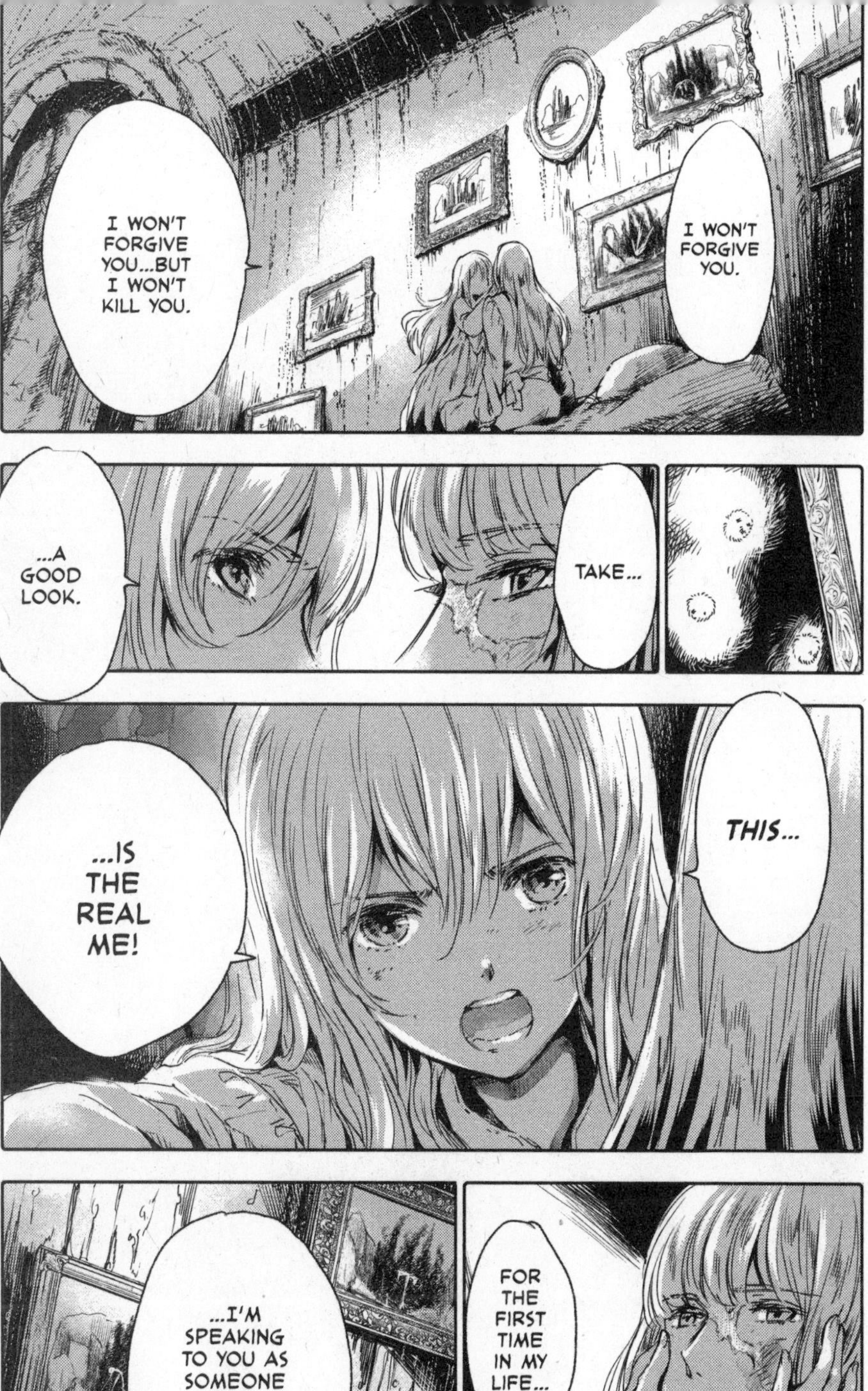
I WON'T FORGIVE YOU.
I WON'T FORGIVE YOU...BUT I WON'T KILL YOU.
TAKE...
...A GOOD LOOK.
THIS...
...IS THE REAL ME!
FOR THE FIRST TIME IN MY LIFE...
...I'M SPEAKING TO YOU AS SOMEONE WITH A HEART.

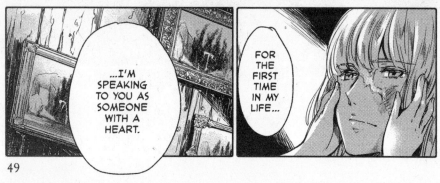

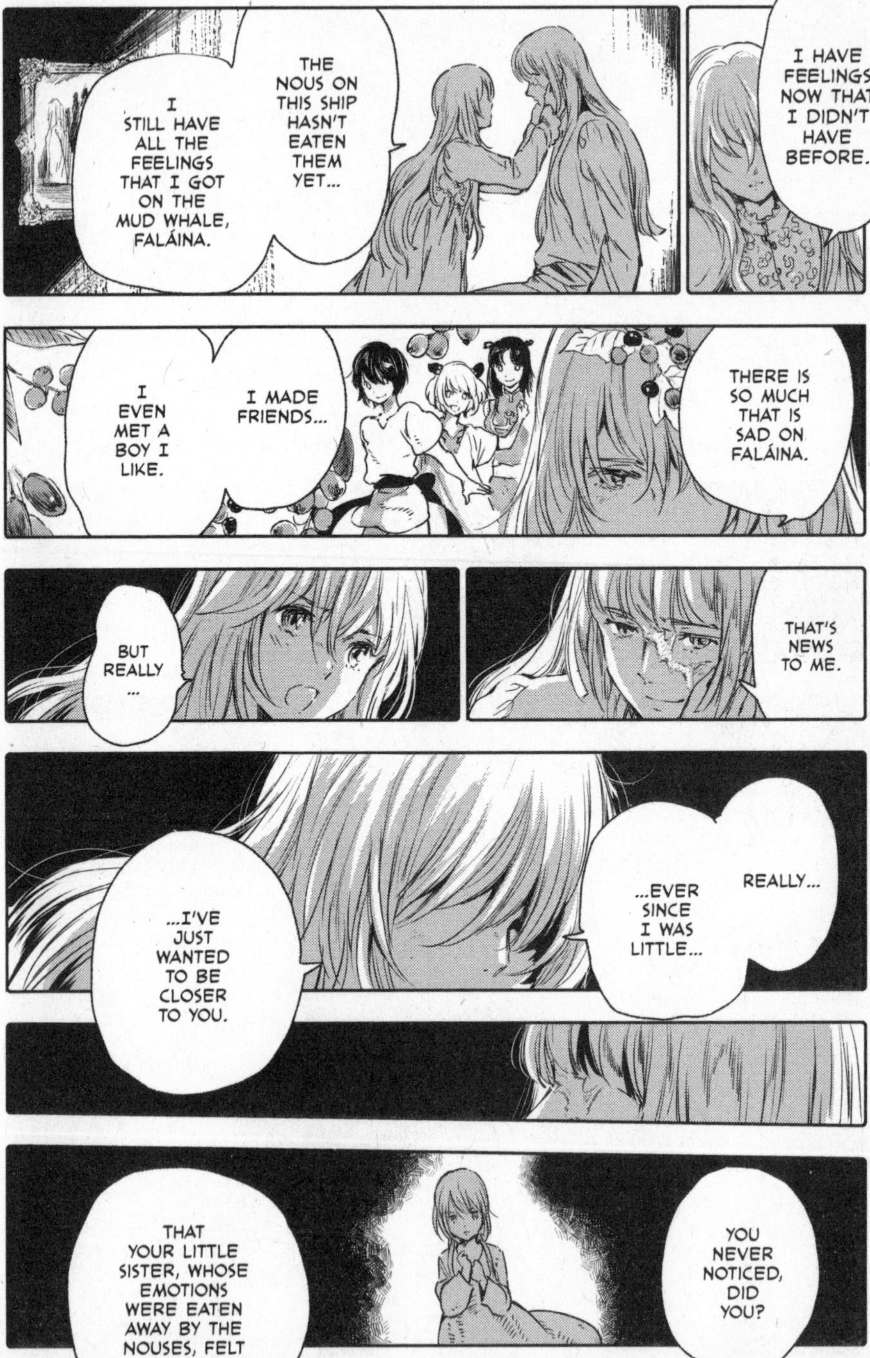
I HAVE FEELINGS NOW THAT I DIDN'T HAVE BEFORE.
THE NOUS ON THIS SHIP HASN'T EATEN THEM YET...
I STILL HAVE ALL THE FEELINGS THAT I GOT ON THE MUD WHALE, FALÁINA.
THERE IS SO MUCH THAT IS SAD ON FALÁINA.
I MADE FRIENDS...
I EVEN MET A BOY I LIKE.
THAT'S NEWS TO ME.
BUT REALLY ...
REALLY...
...EVER SINCE I WAS LITTLE...
...I'VE JUST WANTED TO BE CLOSER TO YOU.
YOU NEVER NOTICED, DID YOU?
THAT YOUR LITTLE SISTER, WHOSE EMOTIONS WERE EATEN AWAY BY THE NOUSES, FELT THAT WAY.

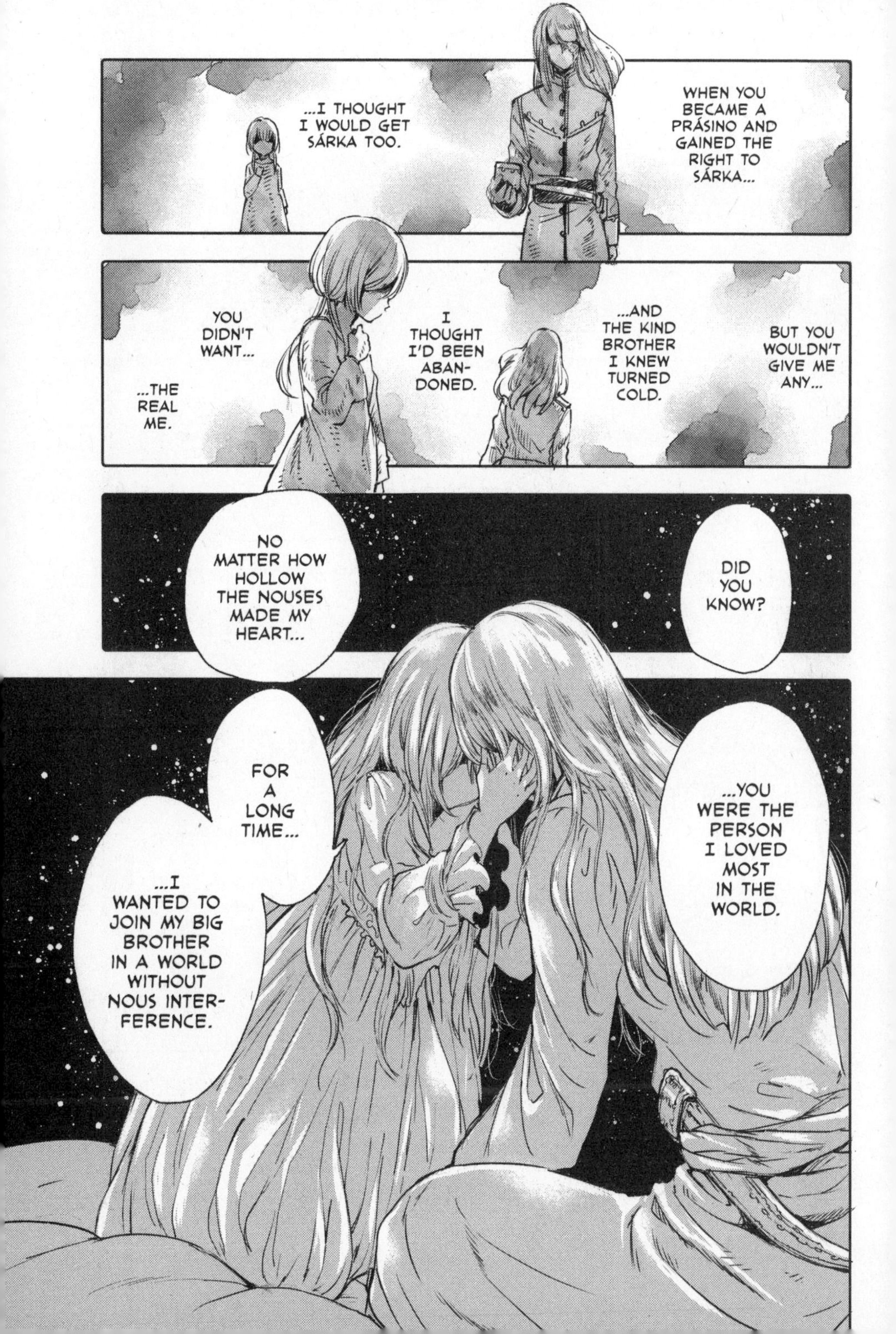
WHEN YOU BECAME A PRÁSINO AND GAINED THE RIGHT TO SÁRKA...
...I THOUGHT I WOULD GET SÁRKA TOO.
BUT YOU WOULDN'T GIVE ME ANY...
...AND THE KIND BROTHER I KNEW TURNED COLD.
I THOUGHT I'D BEEN ABANDONED.
YOU DIDN'T WANT...
...THE REAL ME.
DID YOU KNOW?
NO MATTER HOW HOLLOW THE NOUSES MADE MY HEART...
...YOU WERE THE PERSON I LOVED MOST IN THE WORLD.
FOR A LONG TIME...
...I WANTED TO JOIN MY BIG BROTHER IN A WORLD WITHOUT NOUS INTERFERENCE.

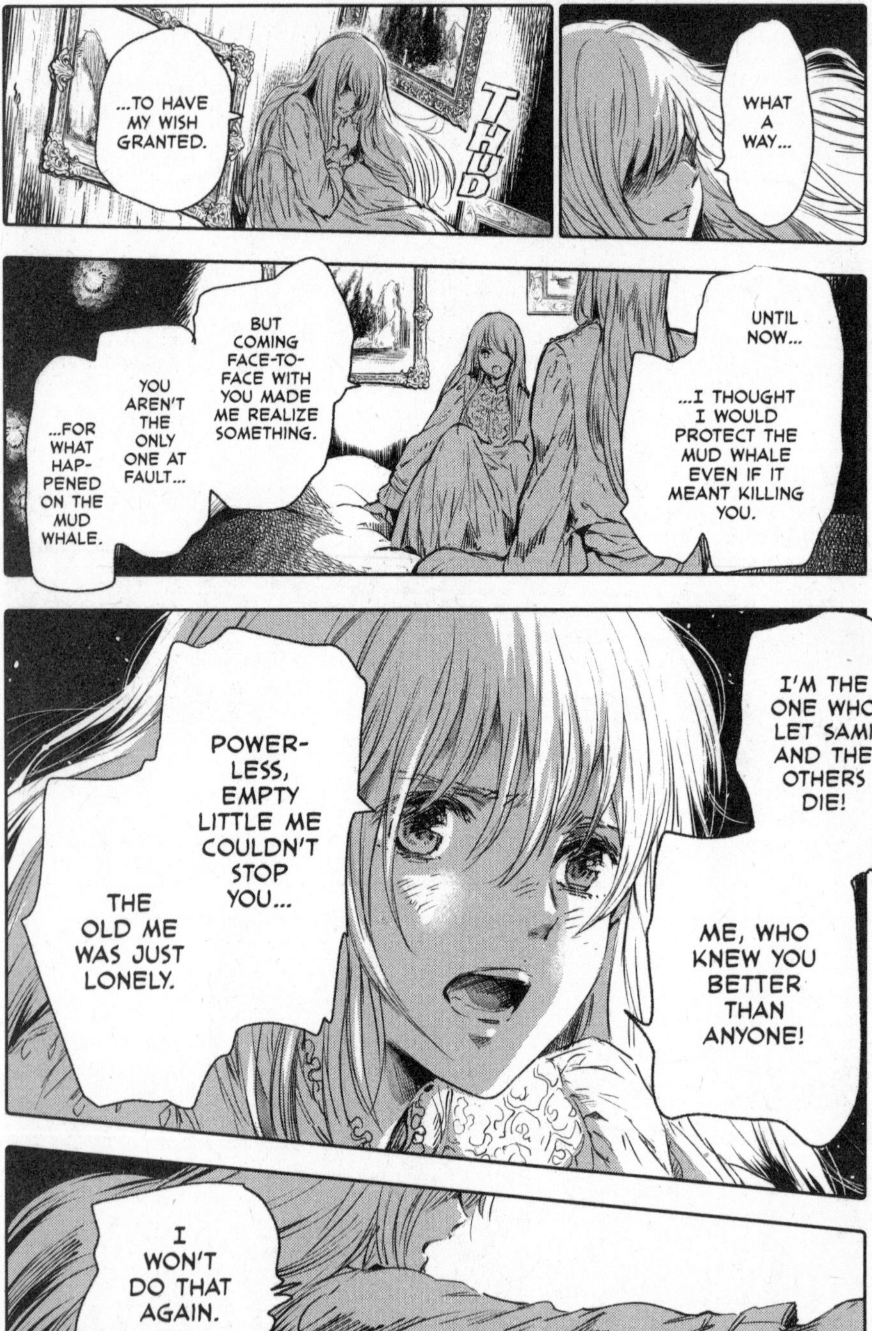
WHAT A WAY...
...TO HAVE MY WISH GRANTED.
THUD
UNTIL NOW...
...I THOUGHT I WOULD PROTECT THE MUD WHALE EVEN IF IT MEANT KILLING YOU.
BUT COMING FACE-TO-FACE WITH YOU MADE ME REALIZE SOMETHING.
YOU AREN'T THE ONLY ONE AT FAULT...
...FOR WHAT HAP-PENED ON THE MUD WHALE.
I'M THE ONE WHO LET SAMI AND THE OTHERS DIE!
ME, WHO KNEW YOU BETTER THAN ANYONE!
POWER-LESS, EMPTY LITTLE ME COULDN'T STOP YOU...
THE OLD ME WAS JUST LONELY.
I WON'T DO THAT AGAIN.

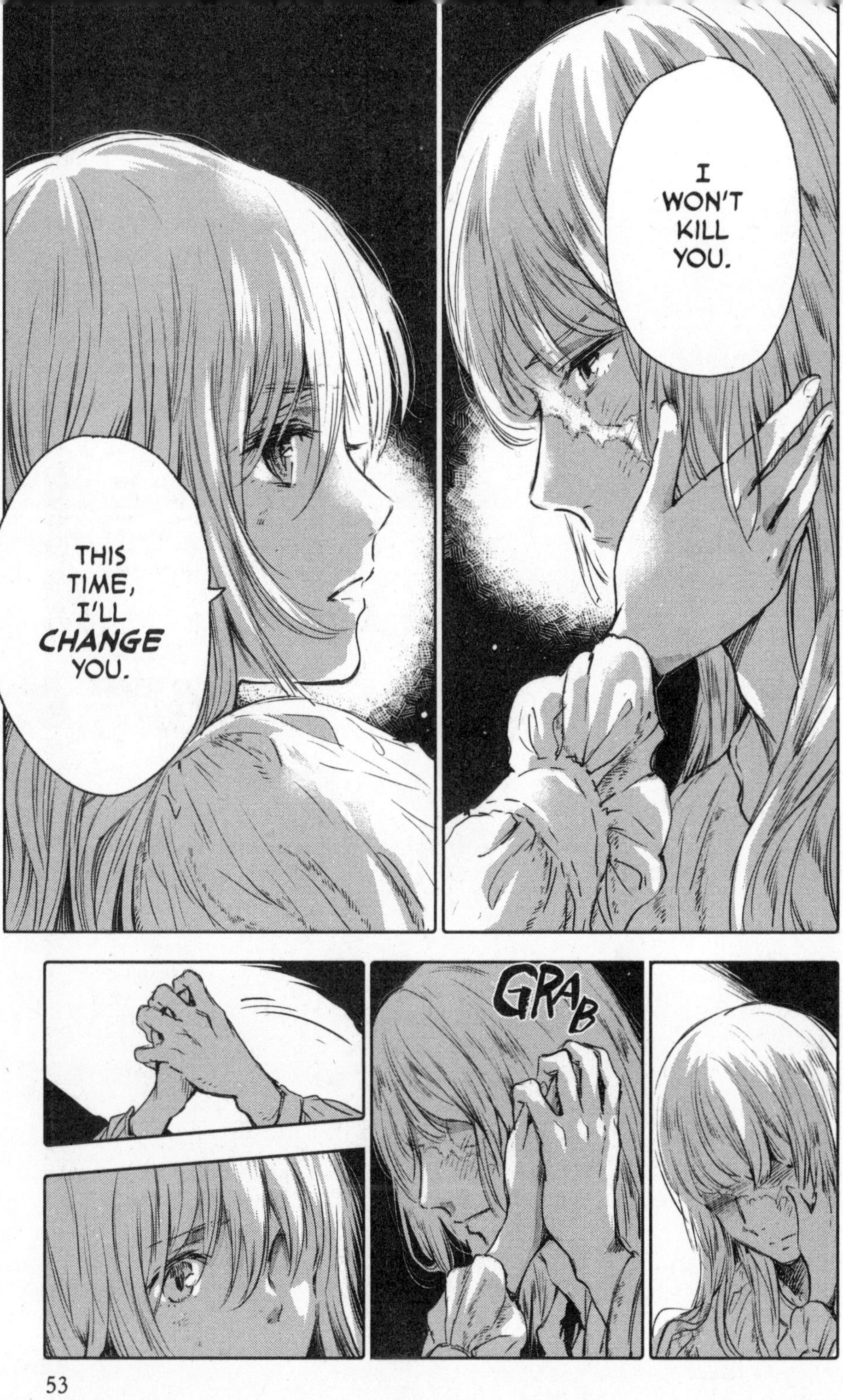
I WON'T KILL YOU.
THIS TIME, I'LL CHANGE YOU.
GRAB

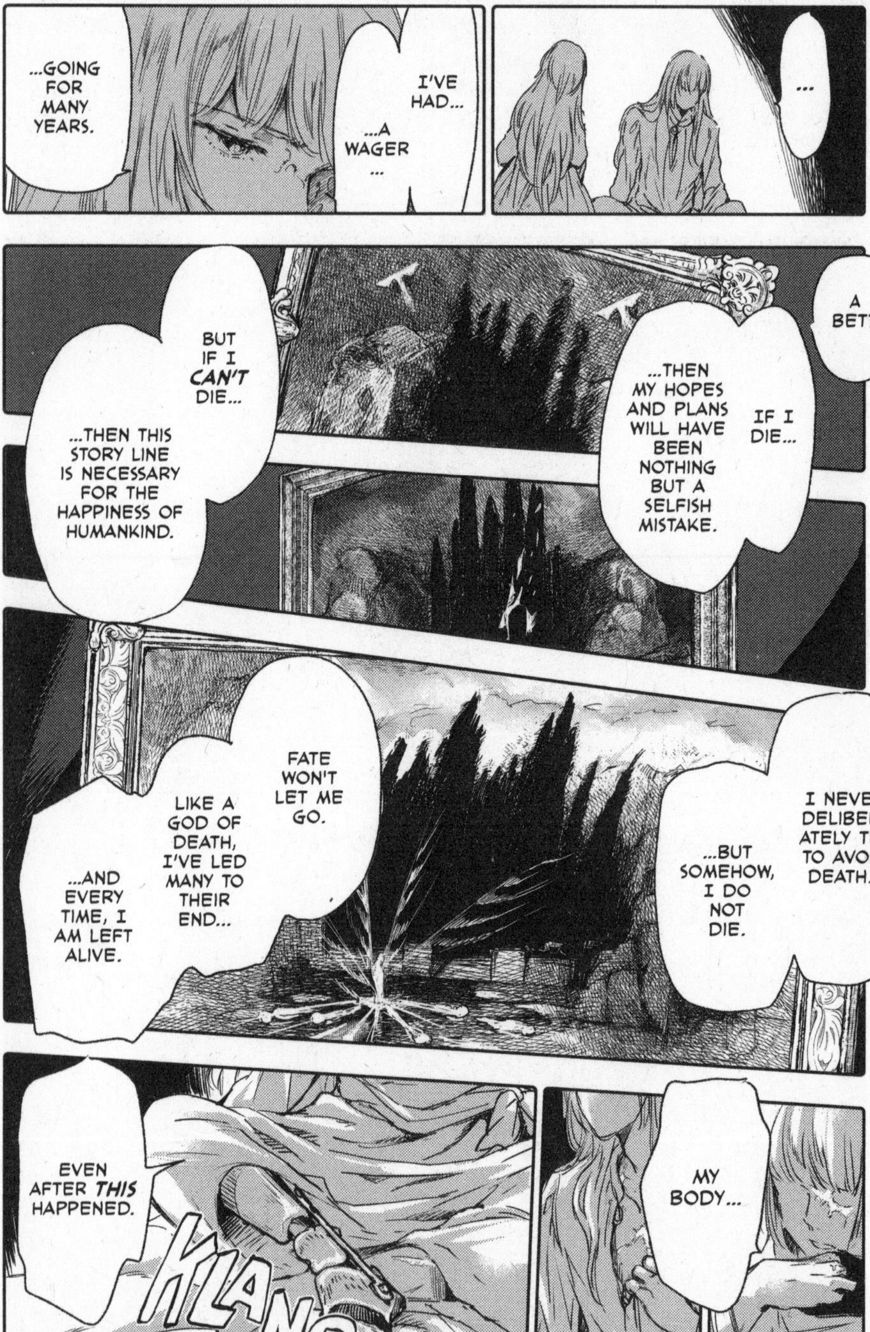
...
I'VE HAD...
...A WAGER...
...GOING FOR MANY YEARS.
A BET?
IF I DIE...
...THEN MY HOPES AND PLANS WILL HAVE BEEN NOTHING BUT A SELFISH MISTAKE.
BUT IF I *CAN'T* DIE...
...THEN THIS STORY LINE IS NECESSARY FOR THE HAPPINESS OF HUMANKIND.
I NEVER DELIBERATELY TRY TO AVOID DEATH...
...BUT SOMEHOW, I DO NOT DIE.
FATE WON'T LET ME GO.
LIKE A GOD OF DEATH, I'VE LED MANY TO THEIR END...
...AND EVERY TIME, I AM LEFT ALIVE.
MY BODY...
EVEN AFTER *THIS* HAPPENED.
KLANG

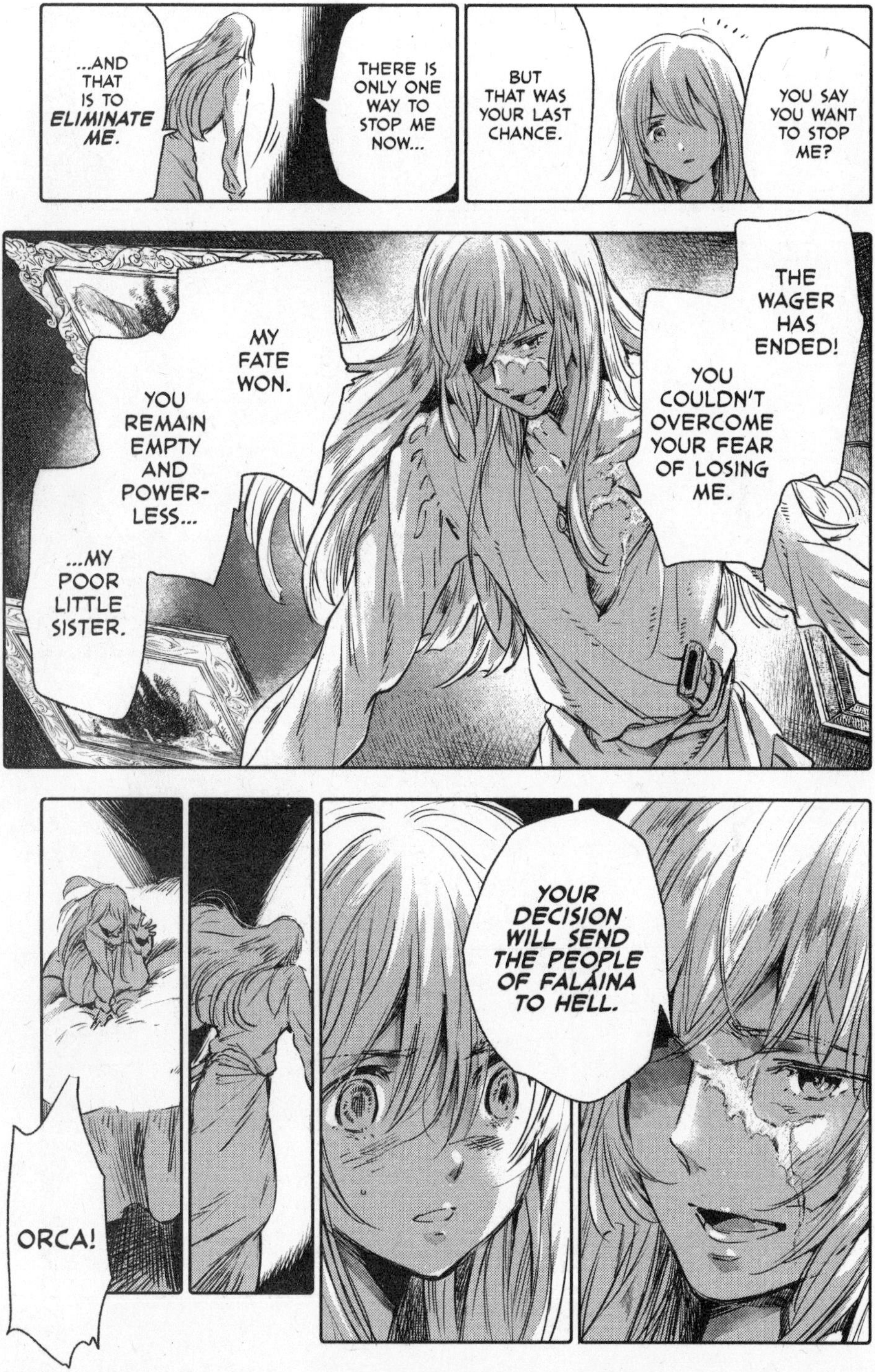
YOU SAY YOU WANT TO STOP ME?
BUT THAT WAS YOUR LAST CHANCE.
THERE IS ONLY ONE WAY TO STOP ME NOW...
...AND THAT IS TO *ELIMINATE ME*.
THE WAGER HAS ENDED!
YOU COULDN'T OVERCOME YOUR FEAR OF LOSING ME.
MY FATE WON.
YOU REMAIN EMPTY AND POWERLESS...
...MY POOR LITTLE SISTER.
YOUR DECISION WILL SEND THE PEOPLE OF FALAINA TO HELL.
ORCA!

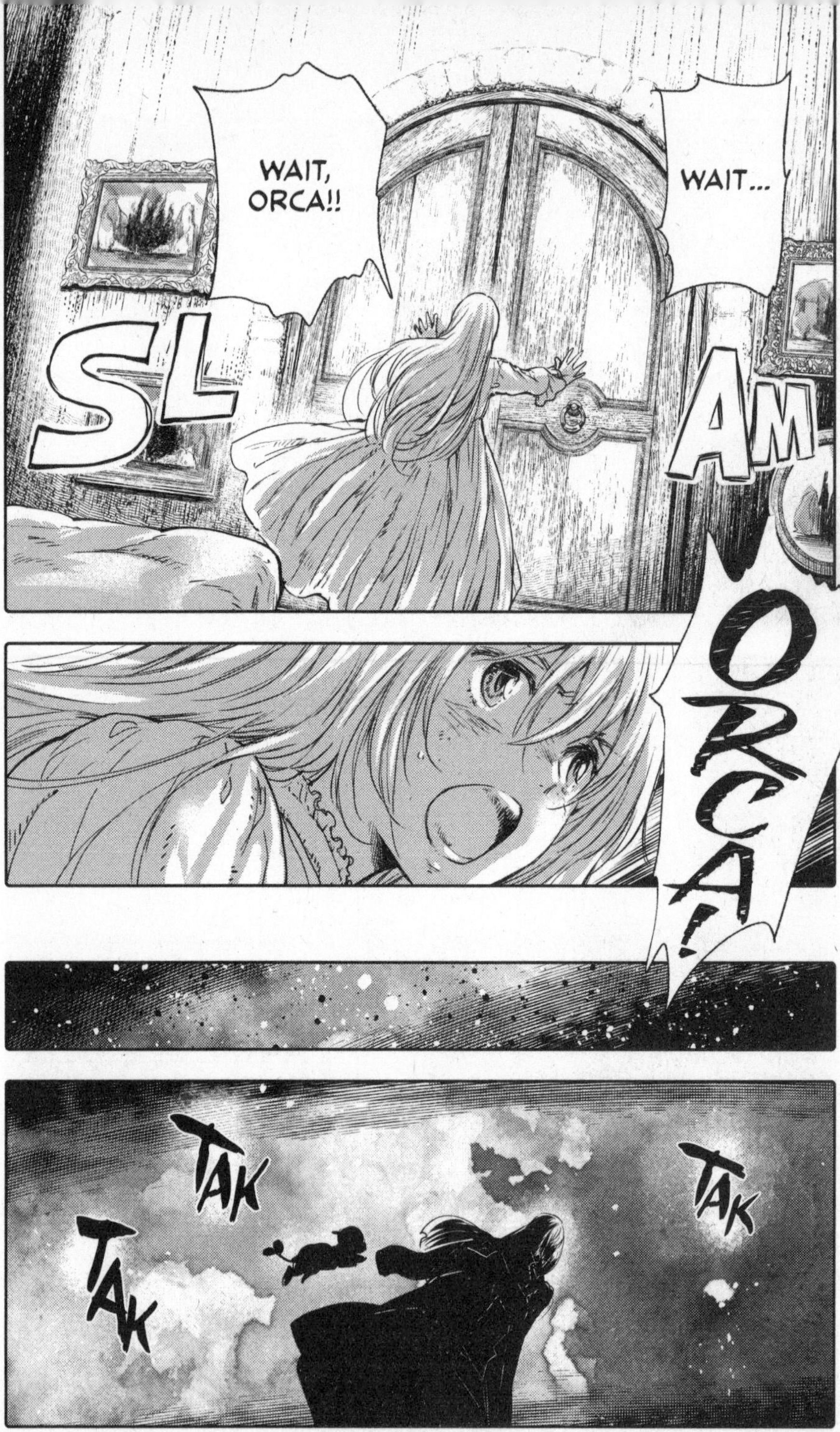
WAIT...
WAIT, ORCA!!
SL
AM
ORCA!
TAK
TAK
TAK

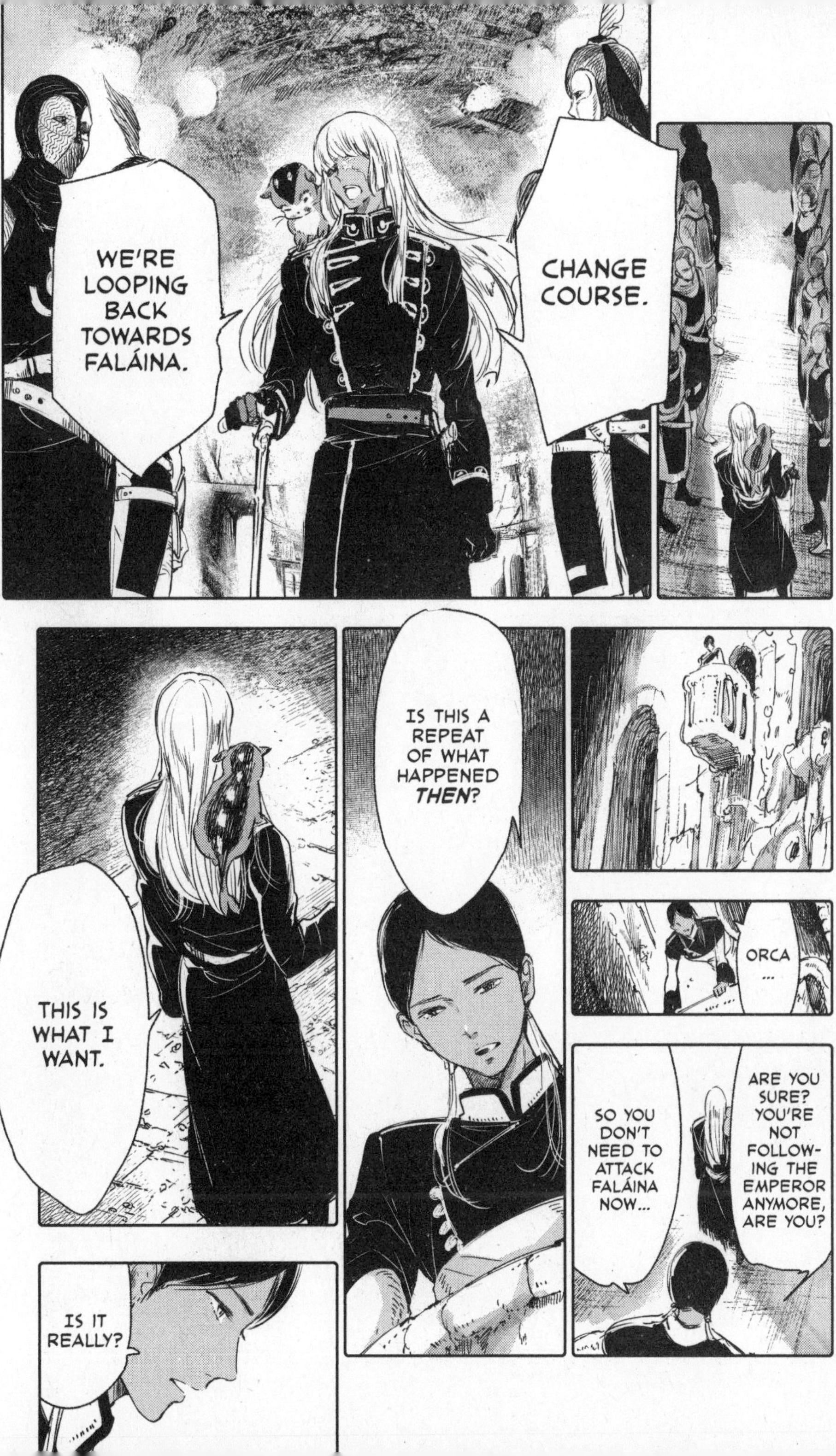
CHANGE COURSE.
WE'RE LOOPING BACK TOWARDS FALÁINA.
ORCA ...
ARE YOU SURE? YOU'RE NOT FOLLOW-ING THE EMPEROR ANYMORE, ARE YOU?
SO YOU DON'T NEED TO ATTACK FALÁINA NOW...
IS THIS A REPEAT OF WHAT HAPPENED *THEN*?
THIS IS WHAT I WANT.
IS IT REALLY?

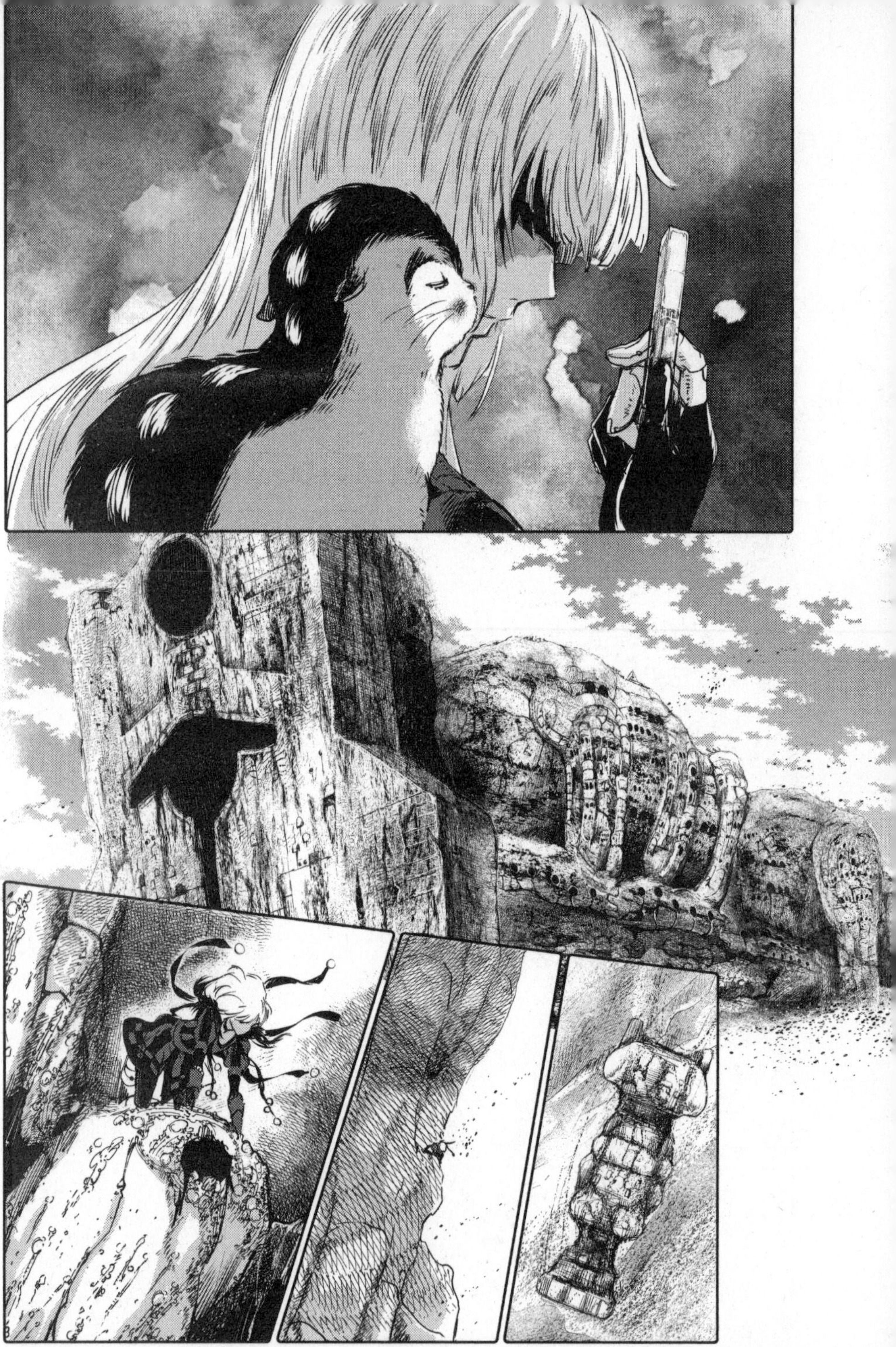

SHIING

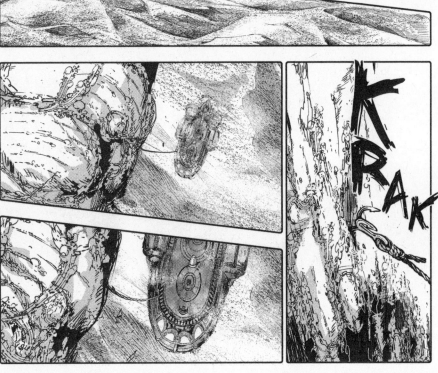

KRAK

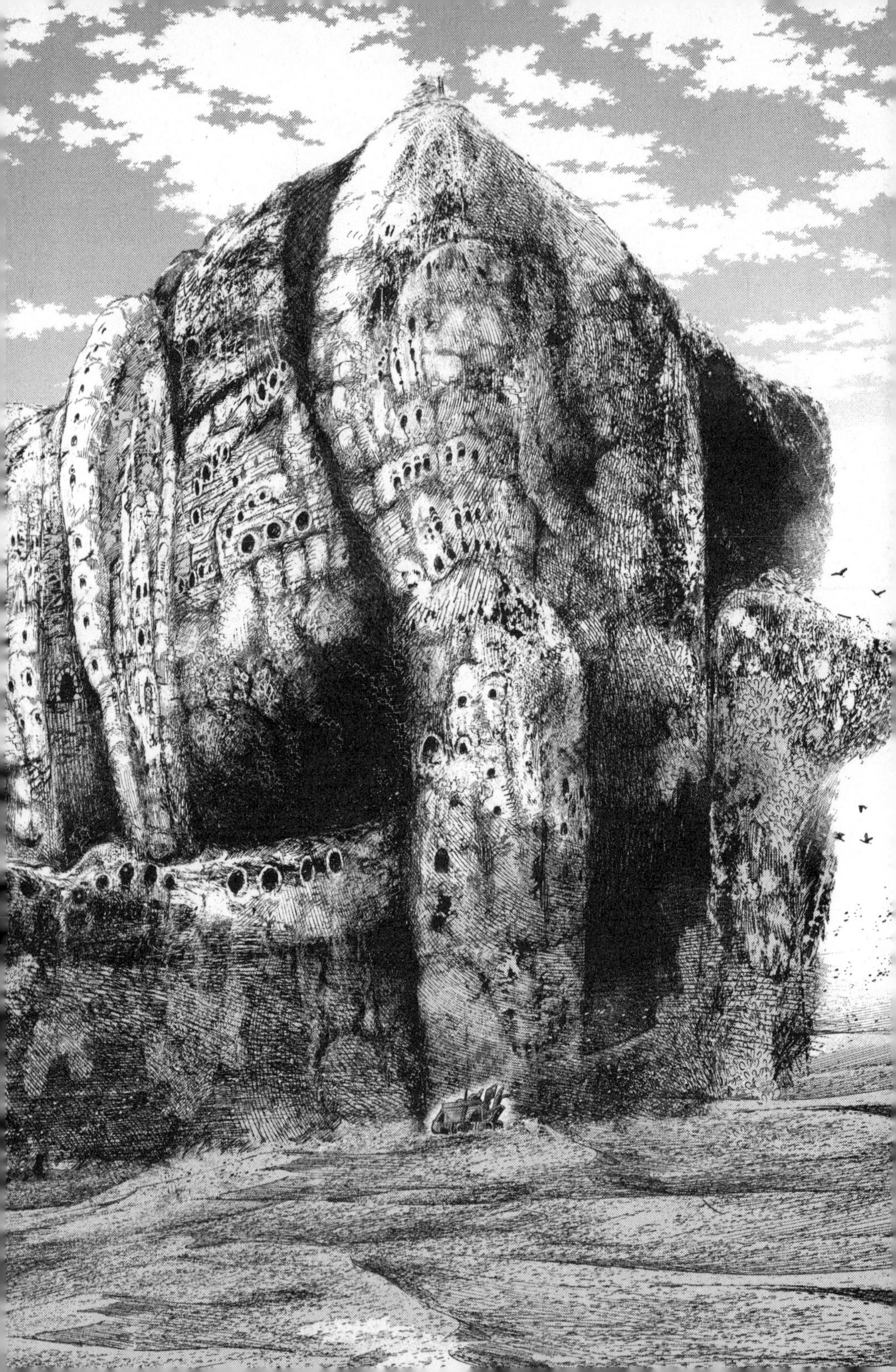

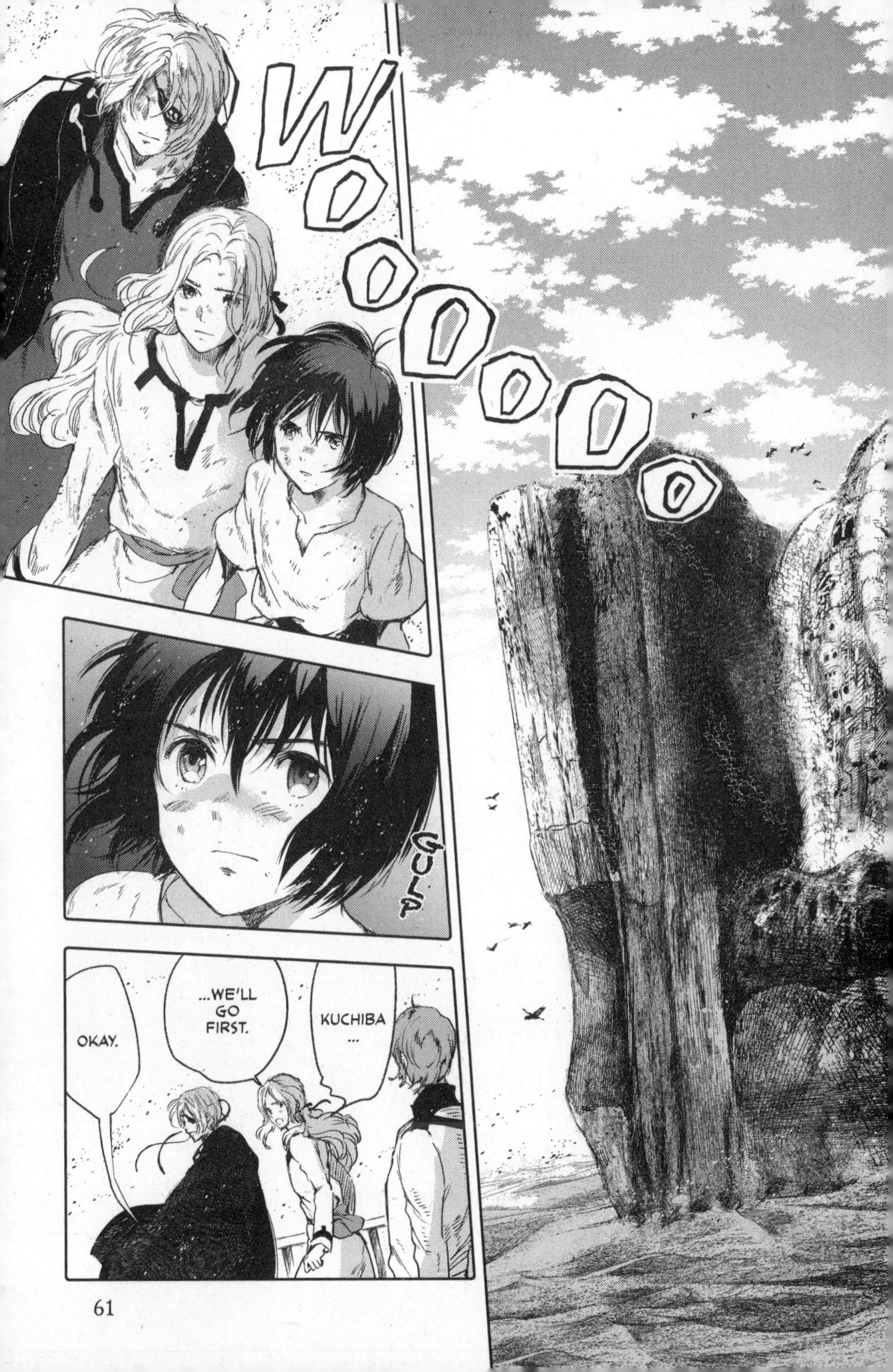
WOOOOOOO
GULP
KUCHIBA ...
...WE'LL GO FIRST.
OKAY.

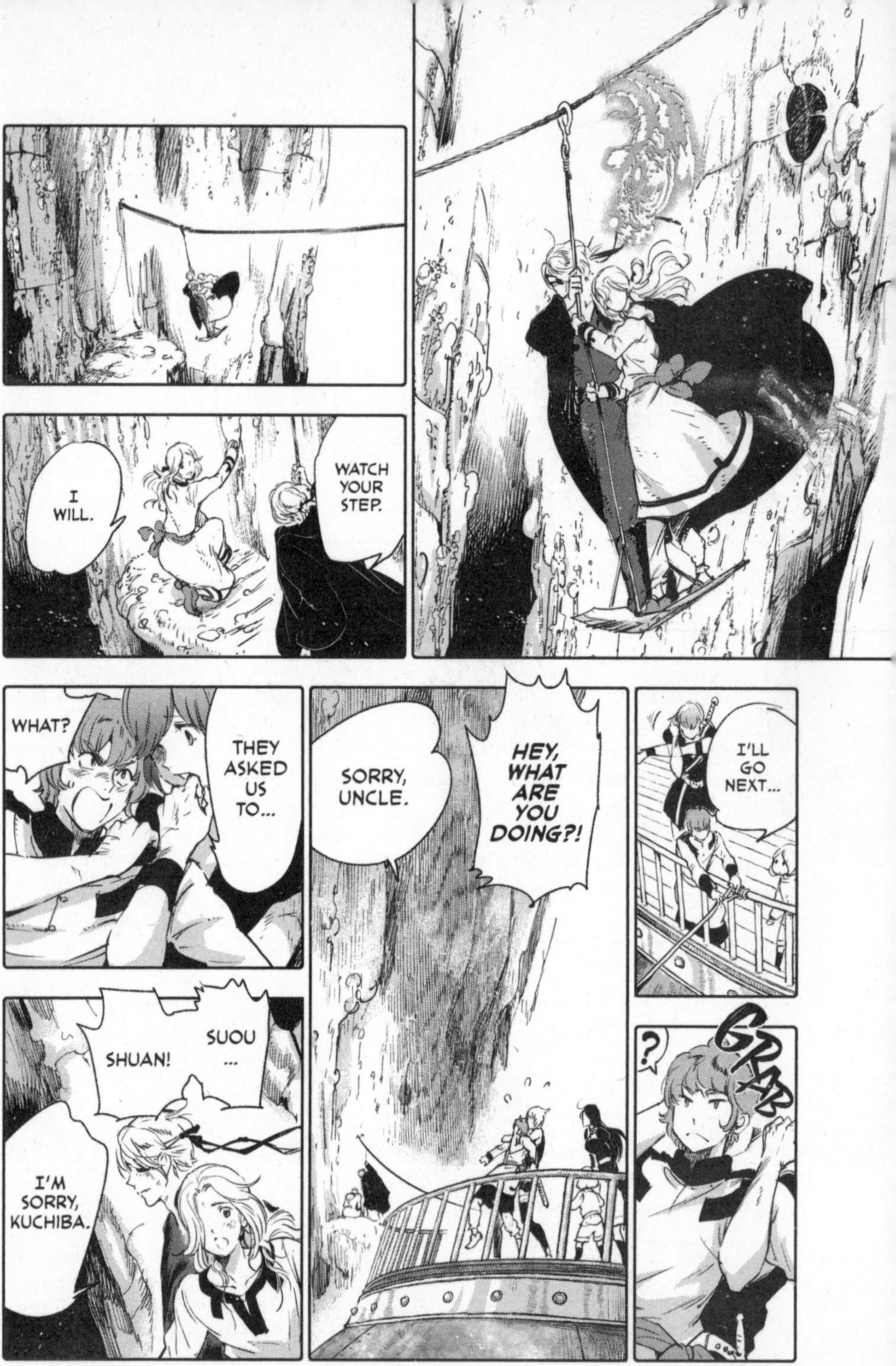
WATCH YOUR STEP.
I WILL.
I'LL GO NEXT...
?
GRAB
HEY, WHAT ARE YOU DOING?!
SORRY, UNCLE.
THEY ASKED US TO...
WHAT?
SUOU ...
SHUAN!
I'M SORRY, KUCHIBA.

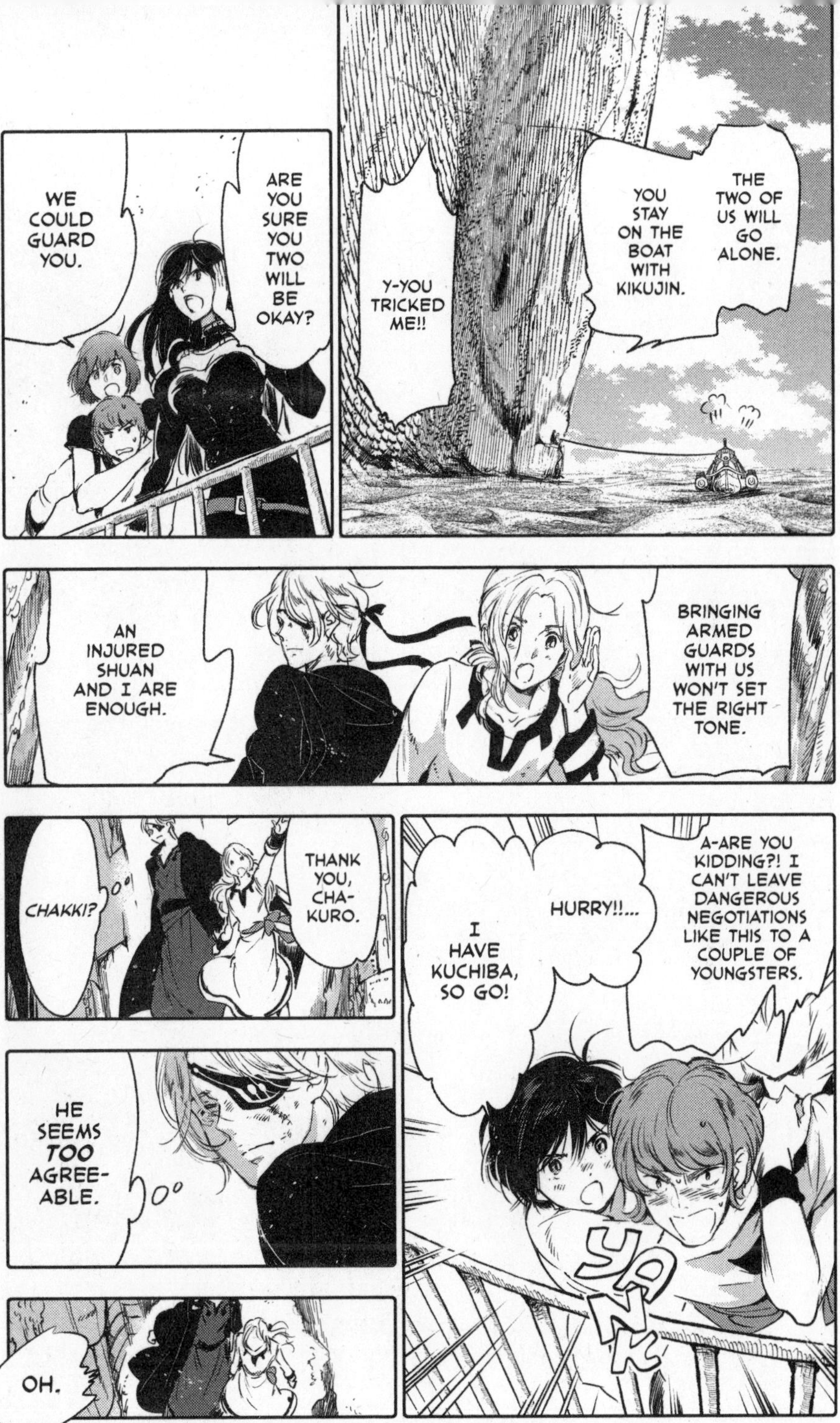
THE TWO OF US WILL GO ALONE.
YOU STAY ON THE BOAT WITH KIKUJIN.
Y-YOU TRICKED ME!!
ARE YOU SURE YOU TWO WILL BE OKAY?
WE COULD GUARD YOU.
BRINGING ARMED GUARDS WITH US WON'T SET THE RIGHT TONE.
AN INJURED SHUAN AND I ARE ENOUGH.
A-ARE YOU KIDDING?! I CAN'T LEAVE DANGEROUS NEGOTIATIONS LIKE THIS TO A COUPLE OF YOUNGSTERS.
HURRY!!...
I HAVE KUCHIBA, SO GO!
YANK
THANK YOU, CHA-KURO.
CHAKKI?
HE SEEMS *TOO* AGREE-ABLE.
OH.

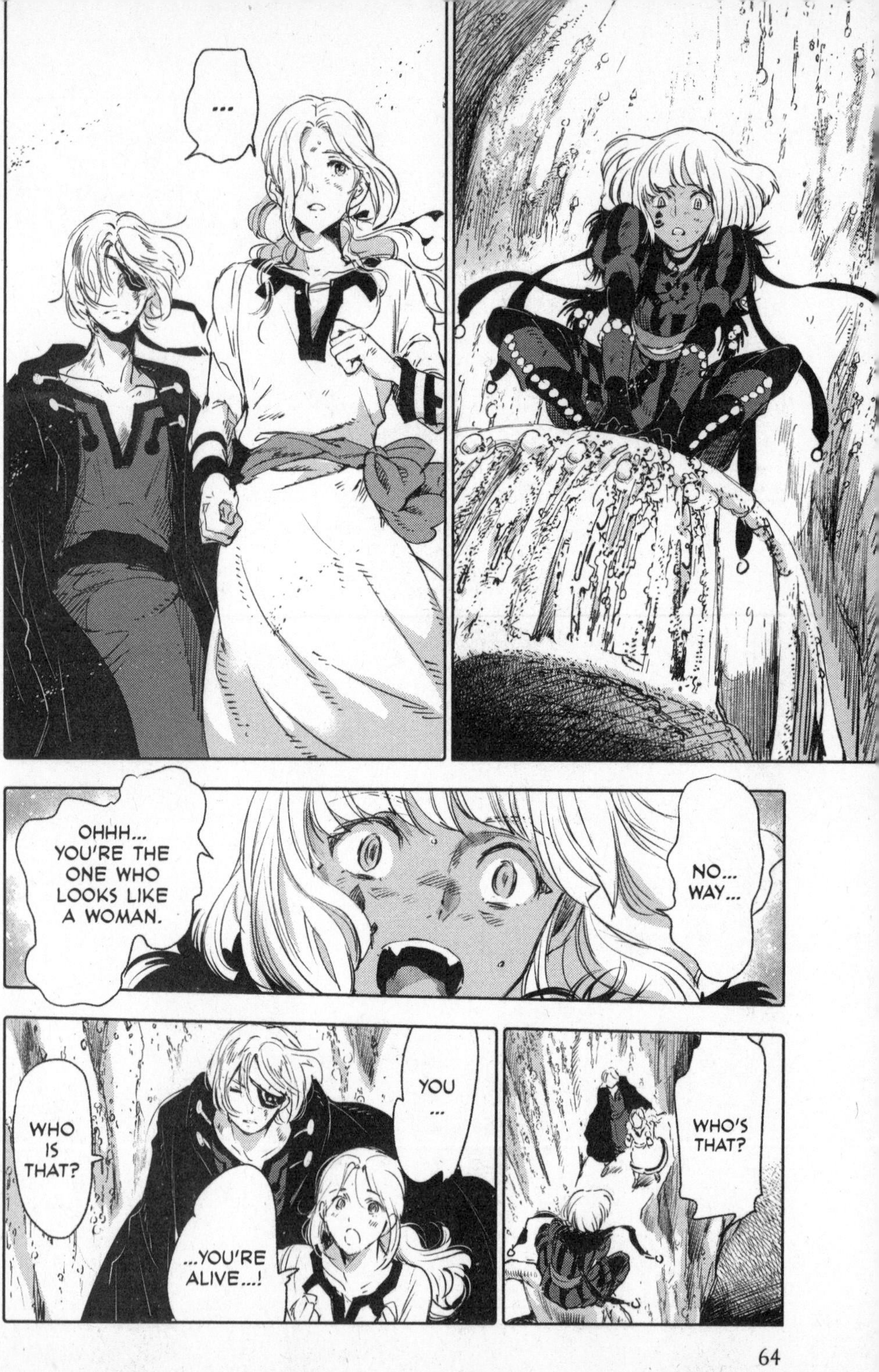
...
NO... WAY...
OHHH... YOU'RE THE ONE WHO LOOKS LIKE A WOMAN.
WHO'S THAT?
YOU ...
...YOU'RE ALIVE...!
WHO IS THAT?

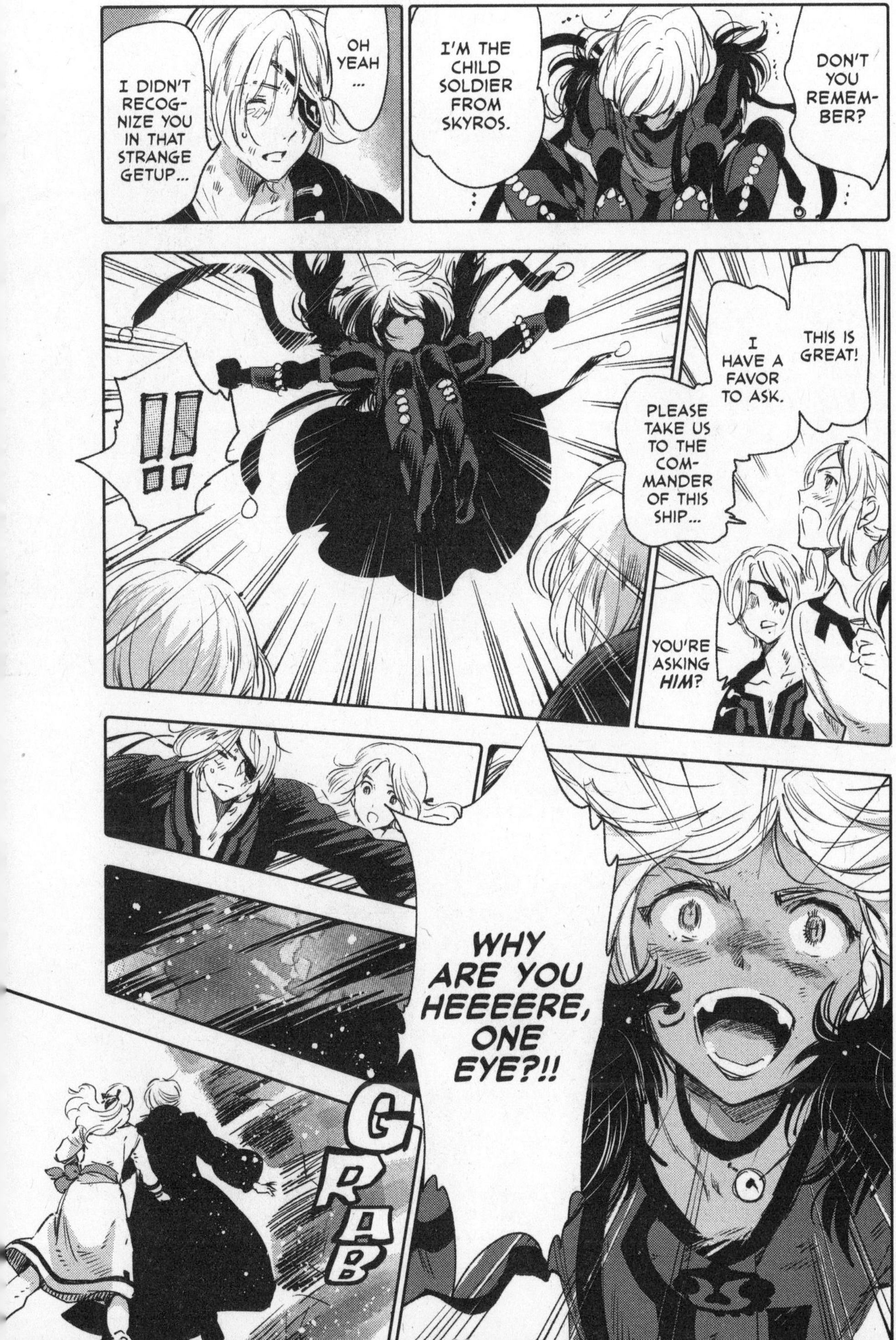
DON'T YOU REMEMBER?
I'M THE CHILD SOLDIER FROM SKYROS.
OH YEAH ...
I DIDN'T RECOGNIZE YOU IN THAT STRANGE GETUP...
THIS IS GREAT!
I HAVE A FAVOR TO ASK.
PLEASE TAKE US TO THE COMMANDER OF THIS SHIP...
YOU'RE ASKING *HIM*?
!!
WHY ARE YOU HEEEERE, ONE EYE?!!
GRAB

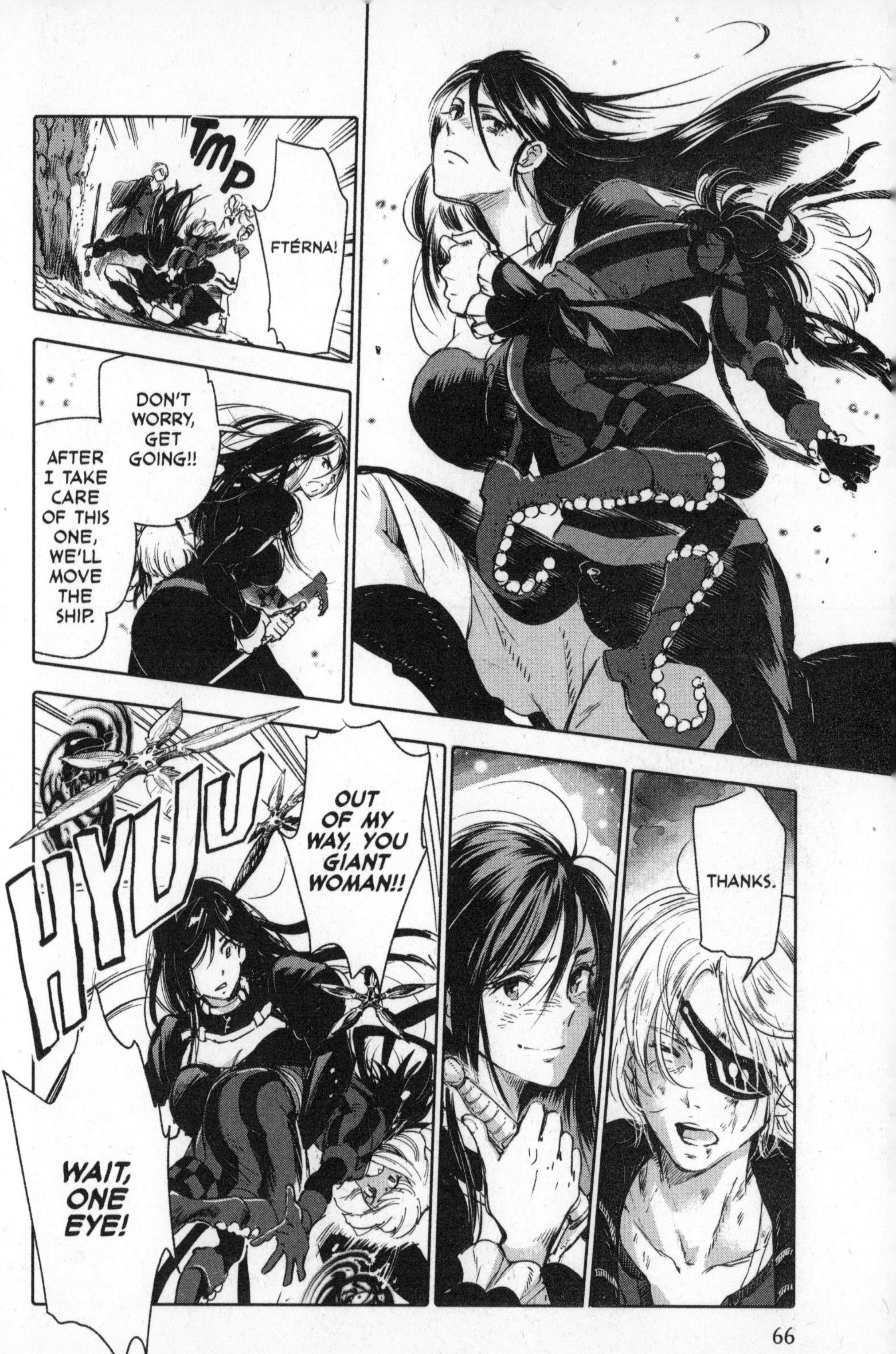
TMP
FTÉRNA!
DON'T WORRY, GET GOING!!
AFTER I TAKE CARE OF THIS ONE, WE'LL MOVE THE SHIP.
THANKS.
OUT OF MY WAY, YOU GIANT WOMAN!!
HYUU
WAIT, ONE EYE!

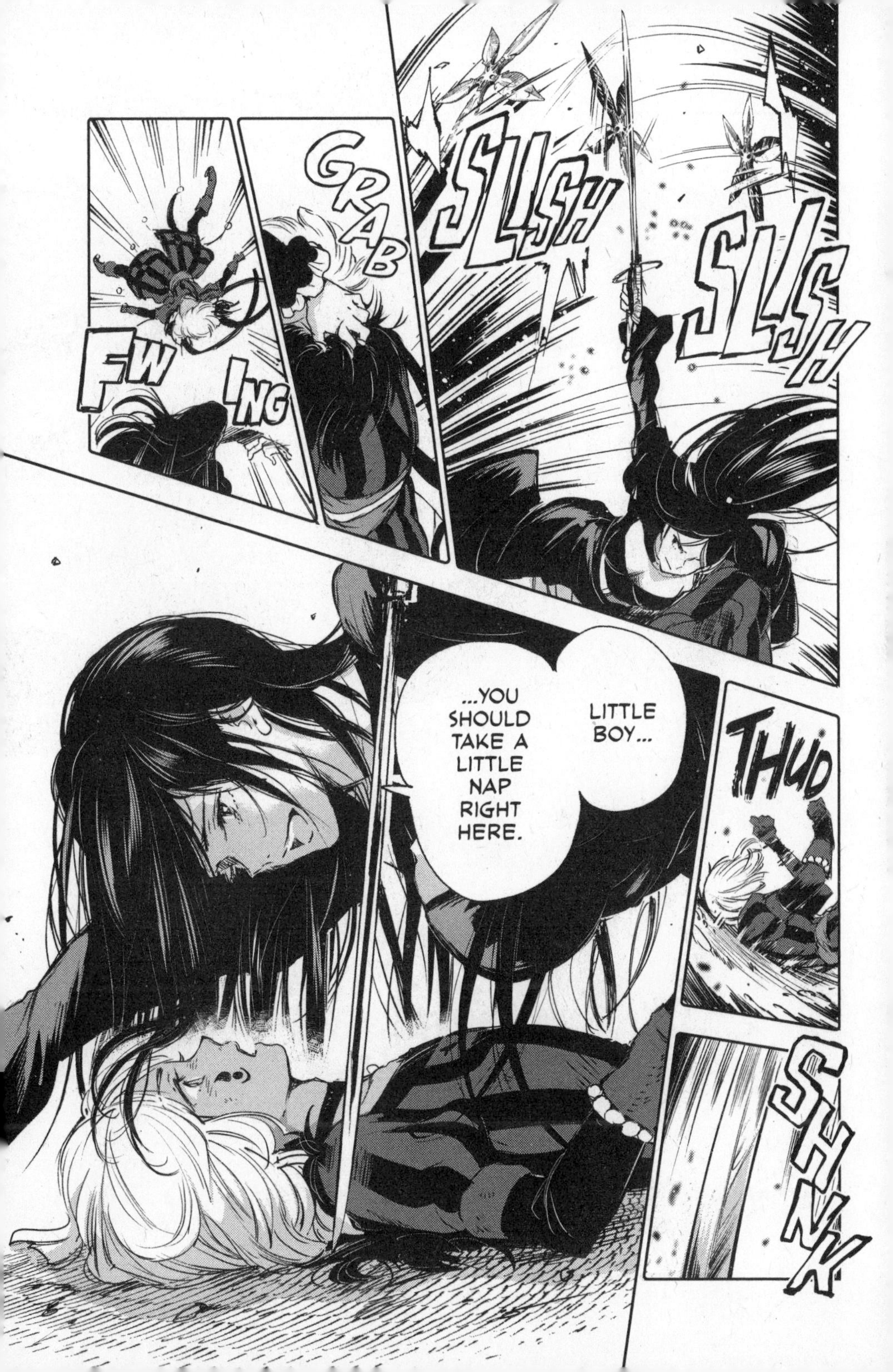
SLISH
SLISH
GRAB
FWING
THUD
SHNK
LITTLE BOY...
...YOU SHOULD TAKE A LITTLE NAP RIGHT HERE.

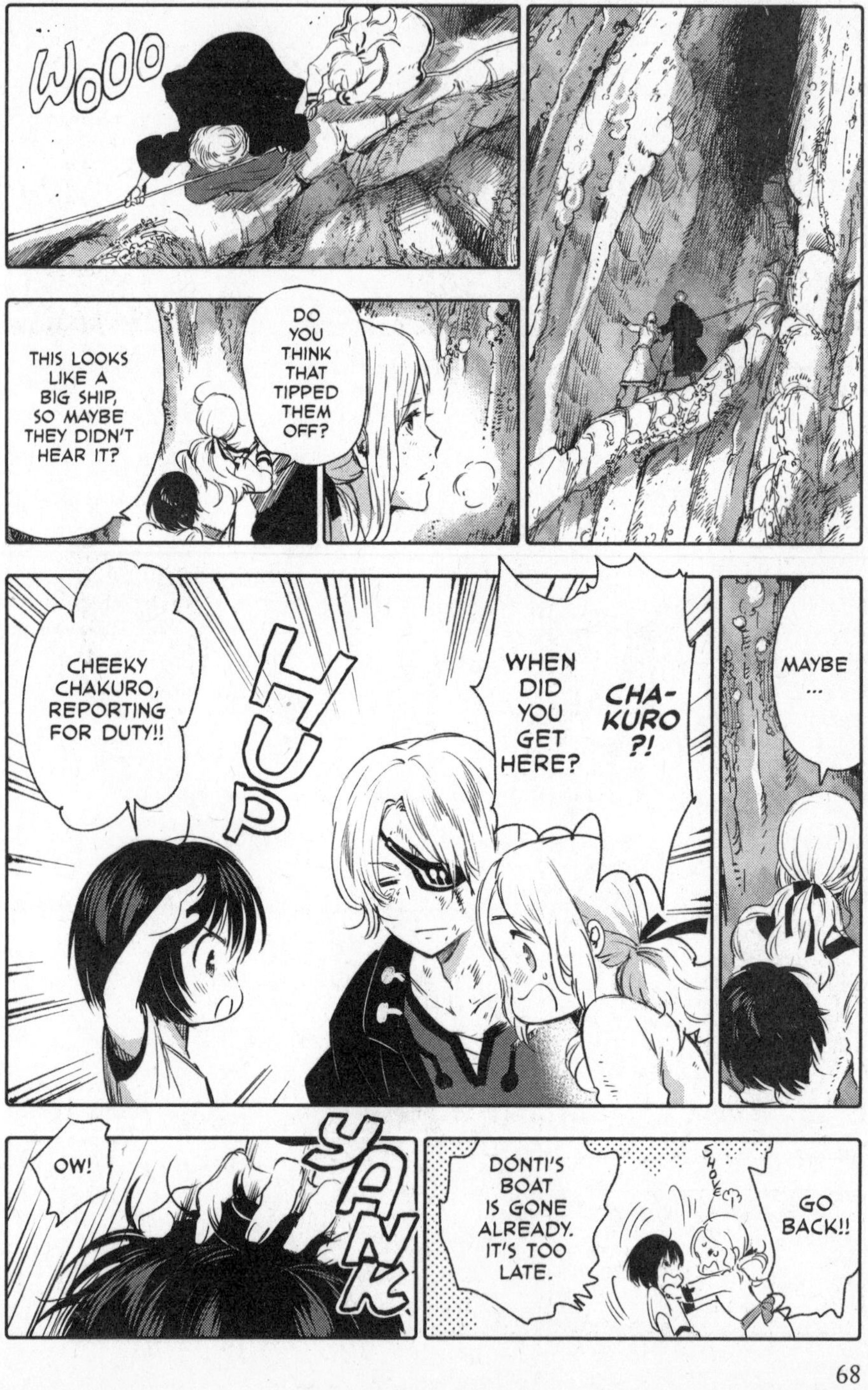

WoOO
DO YOU THINK THAT TIPPED THEM OFF?
THIS LOOKS LIKE A BIG SHIP, SO MAYBE THEY DIDN'T HEAR IT?
MAYBE ...
CHA-KURO?!
WHEN DID YOU GET HERE?
HUP
CHEEKY CHAKURO, REPORTING FOR DUTY!!
GO BACK!!
SHOVE
DÓNTI'S BOAT IS GONE ALREADY. IT'S TOO LATE.
YANK
OW!

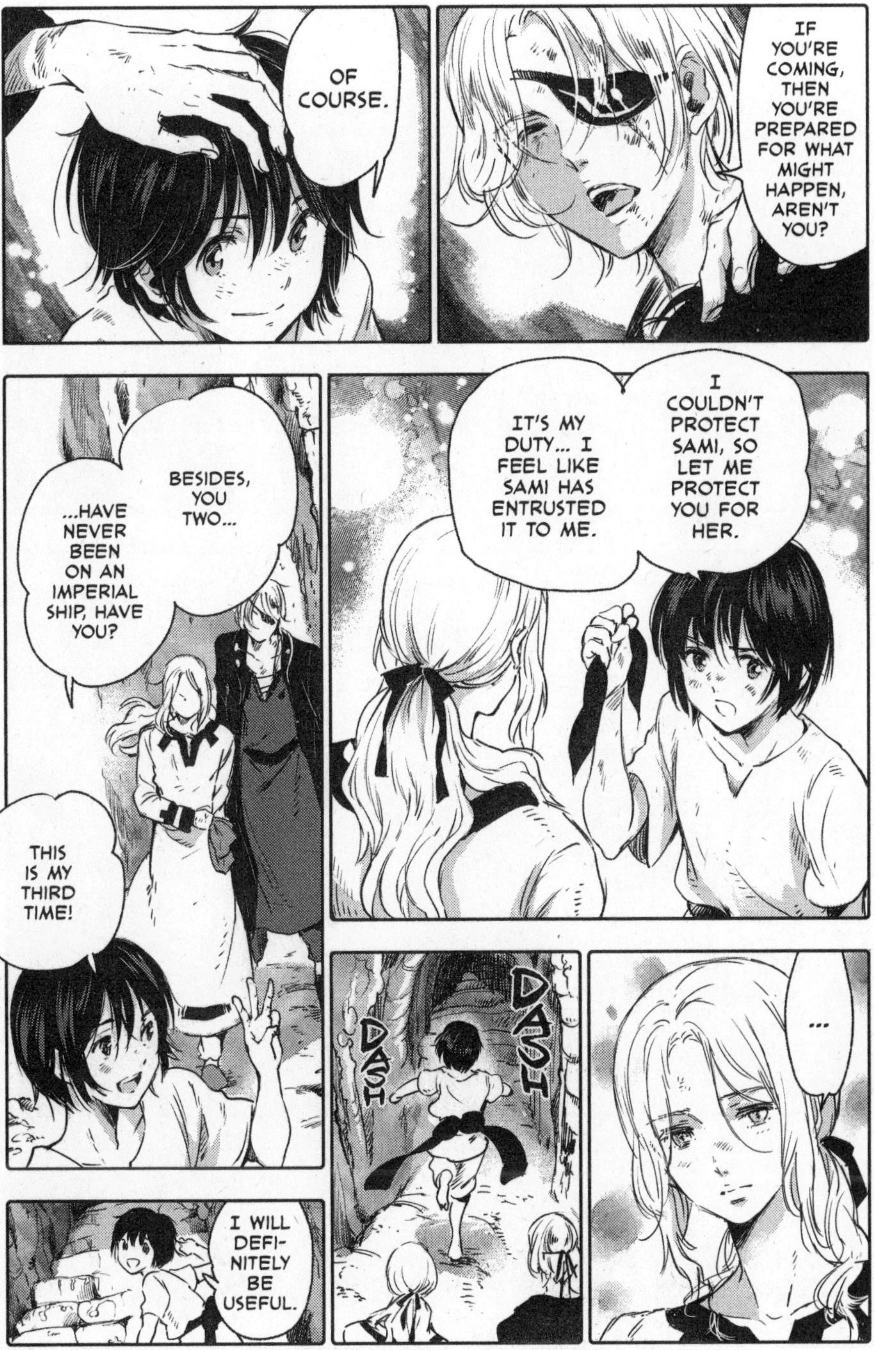
IF YOU'RE COMING, THEN YOU'RE PREPARED FOR WHAT MIGHT HAPPEN, AREN'T YOU?
OF COURSE.
I COULDN'T PROTECT SAMI, SO LET ME PROTECT YOU FOR HER.
IT'S MY DUTY... I FEEL LIKE SAMI HAS ENTRUSTED IT TO ME.
BESIDES, YOU TWO...
...HAVE NEVER BEEN ON AN IMPERIAL SHIP, HAVE YOU?
THIS IS MY THIRD TIME!
...
DASH
DASH
I WILL DEFI-NITELY BE USEFUL.

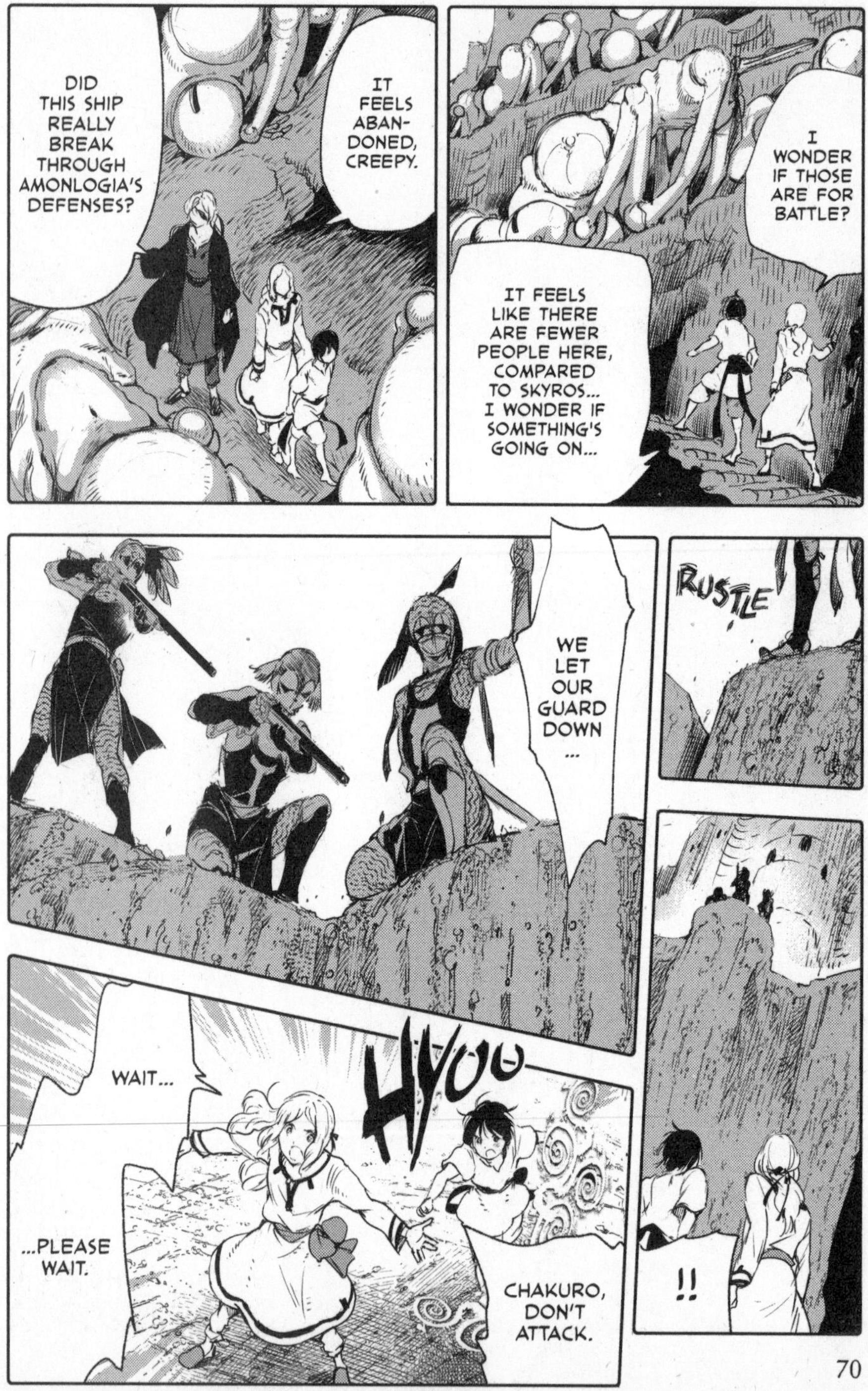
I WONDER IF THOSE ARE FOR BATTLE?
IT FEELS LIKE THERE ARE FEWER PEOPLE HERE, COMPARED TO SKYROS... I WONDER IF SOMETHING'S GOING ON...
IT FEELS ABAN-DONED, CREEPY.
DID THIS SHIP REALLY BREAK THROUGH AMONLOGIA'S DEFENSES?
RUSTLE
!!
WE LET OUR GUARD DOWN ...
HYUU
WAIT...
CHAKURO, DON'T ATTACK.
...PLEASE WAIT.

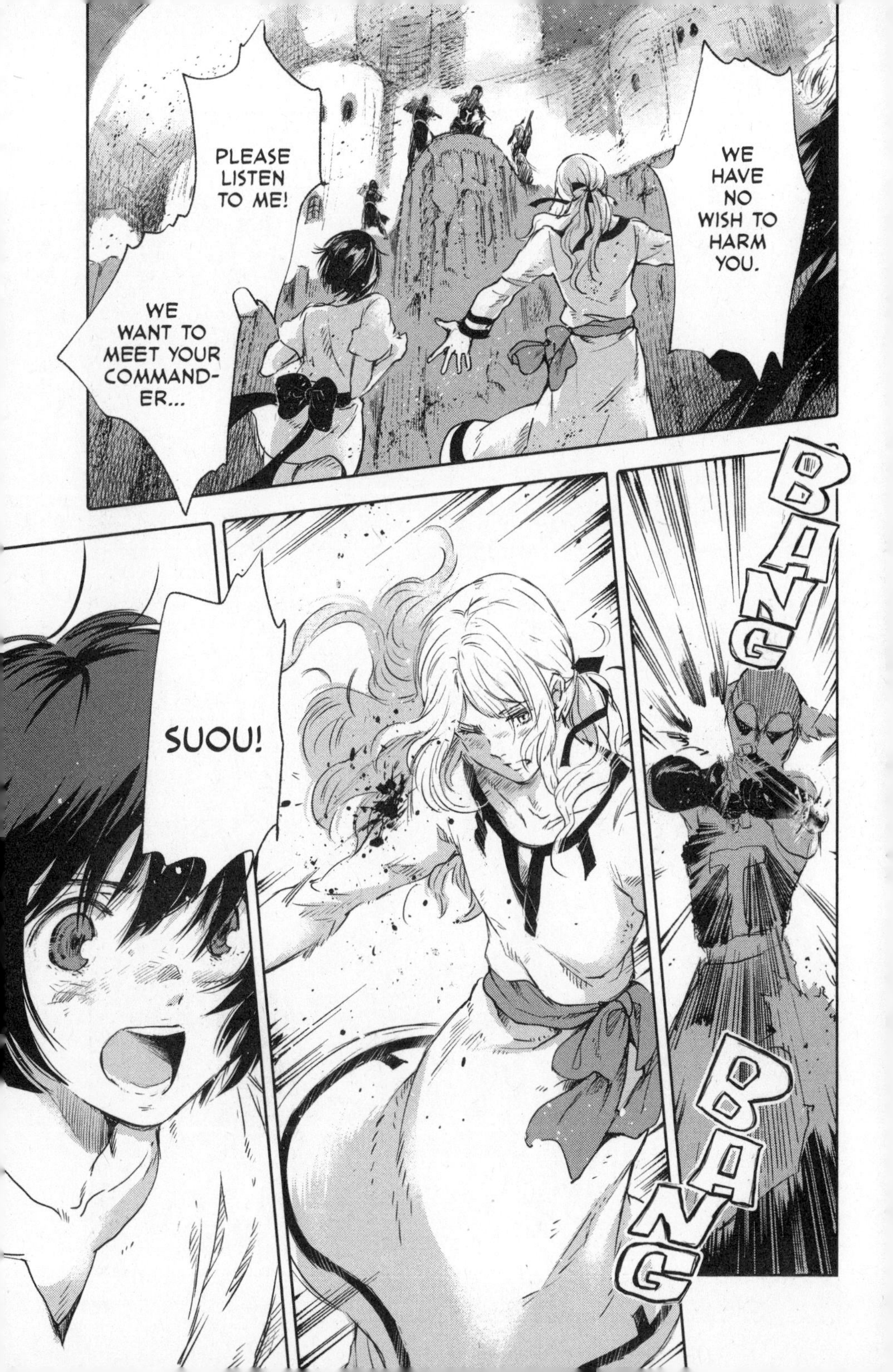
WE HAVE NO WISH TO HARM YOU.
PLEASE LISTEN TO ME!
WE WANT TO MEET YOUR COMMANDER-ER...
BANG
BANG
BANG
SUOU!

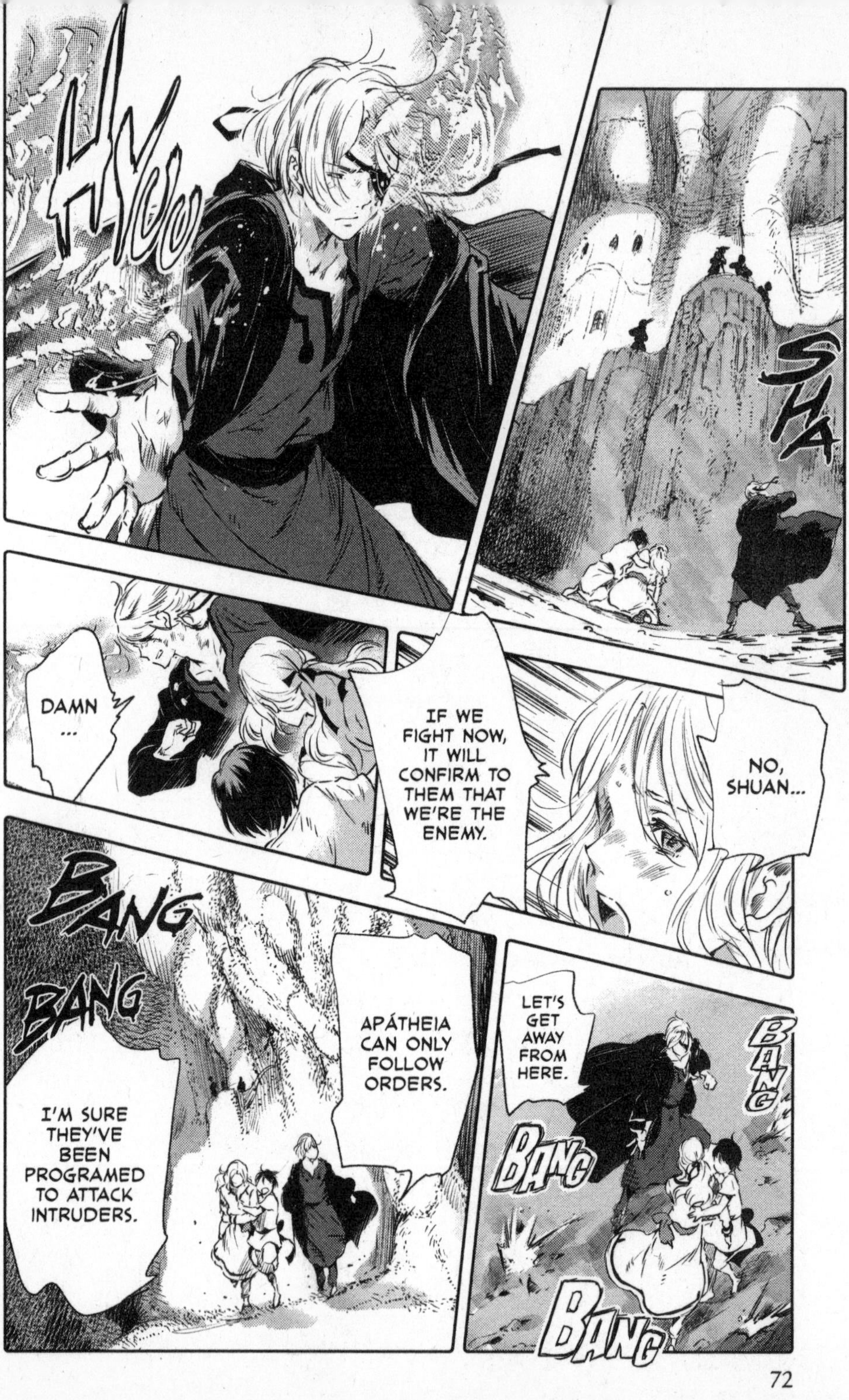
SHA
HYOO
NO, SHUAN...
IF WE FIGHT NOW, IT WILL CONFIRM TO THEM THAT WE'RE THE ENEMY.
DAMN ...
BANG
LET'S GET AWAY FROM HERE.
BANG
BANG
BANG
BANG
APÁTHEIA CAN ONLY FOLLOW ORDERS.
I'M SURE THEY'VE BEEN PROGRAMED TO ATTACK INTRUDERS.

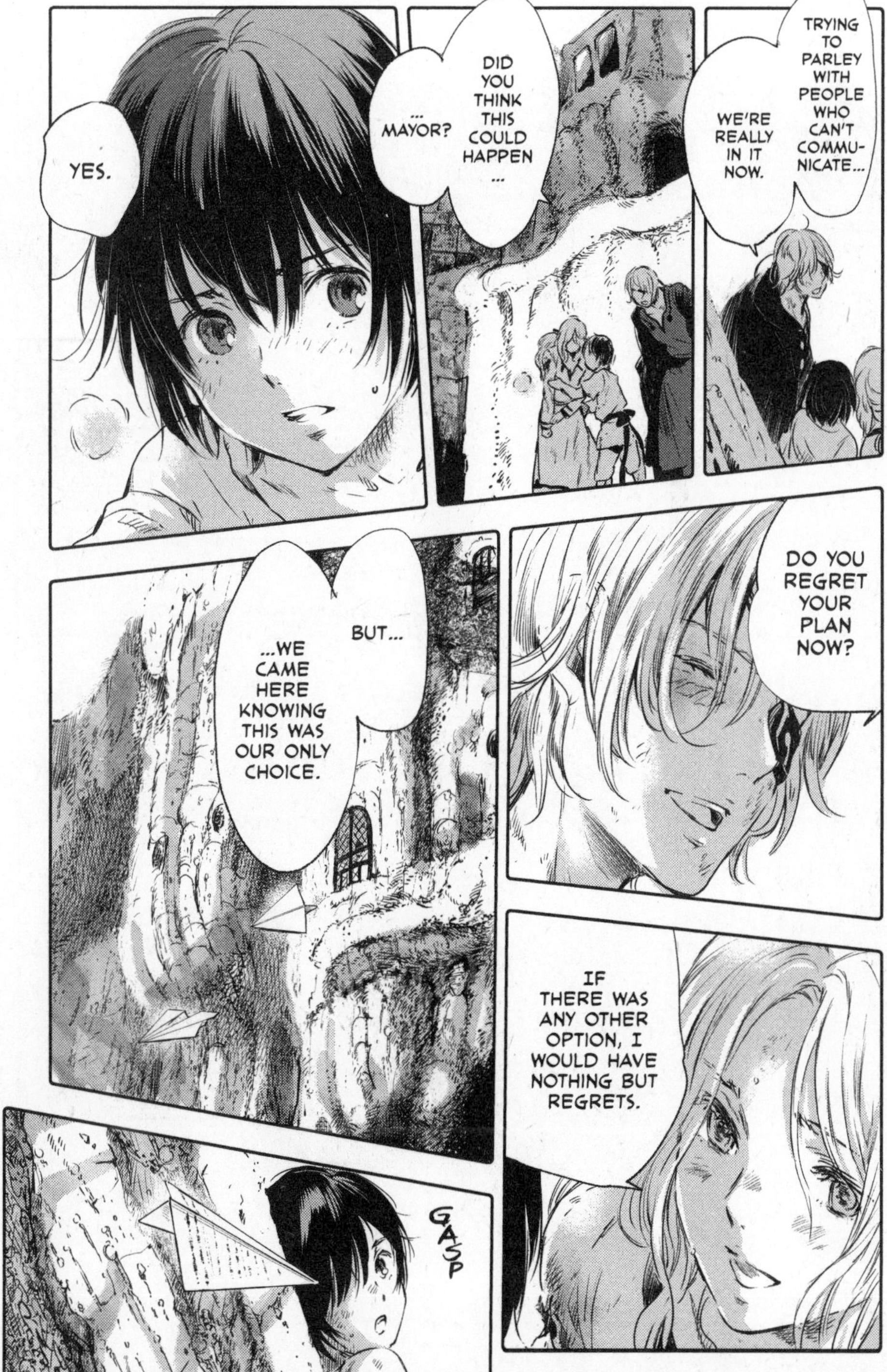

TRYING TO PARLEY WITH PEOPLE WHO CAN'T COMMUNICATE...
WE'RE REALLY IN IT NOW.
DID YOU THINK THIS COULD HAPPEN ...
... MAYOR?
YES.
DO YOU REGRET YOUR PLAN NOW?
IF THERE WAS ANY OTHER OPTION, I WOULD HAVE NOTHING BUT REGRETS.
BUT...
...WE CAME HERE KNOWING THIS WAS OUR ONLY CHOICE.
GASP

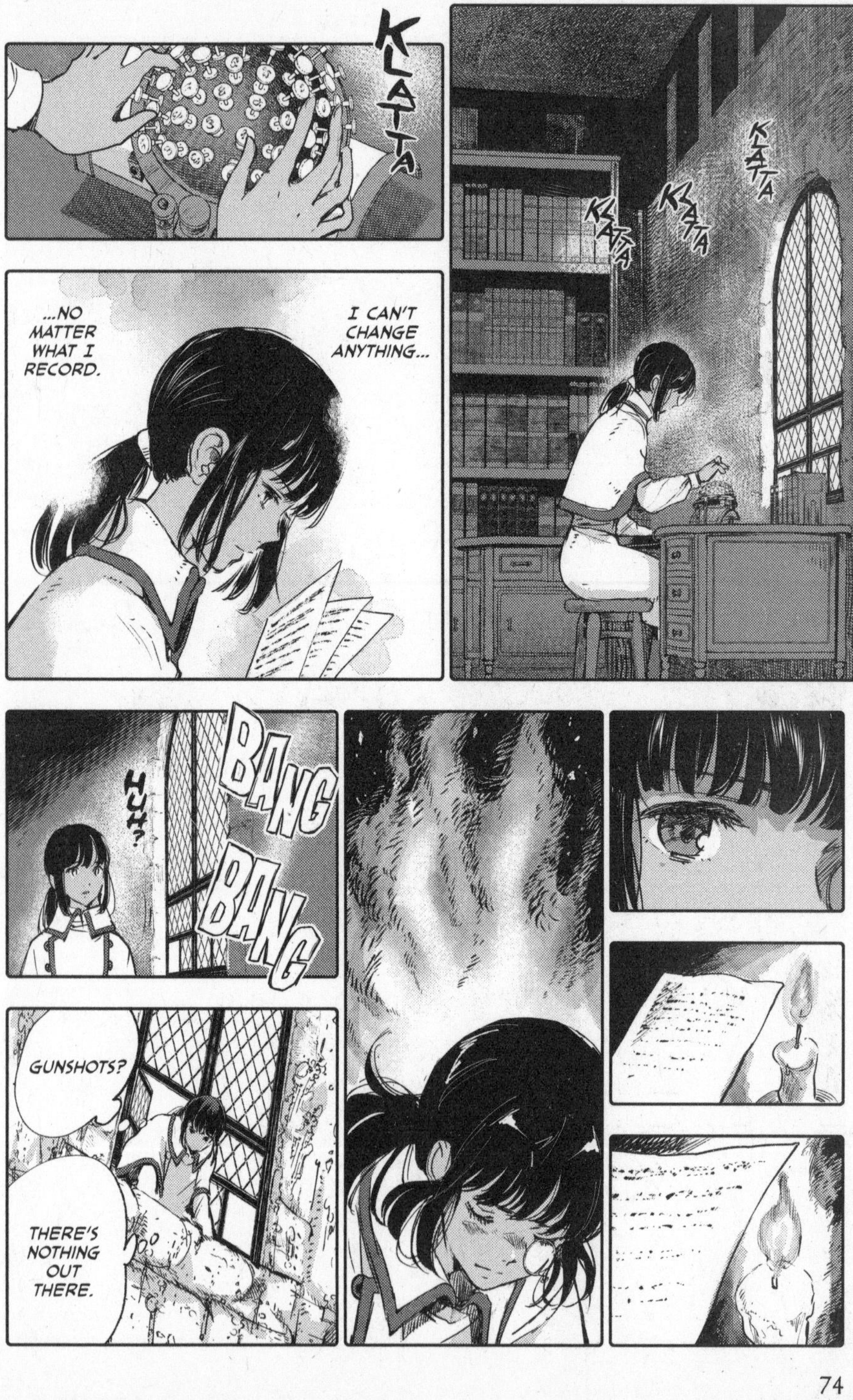
KLATTA
KLATTA
KLATTA
KLATTA
I CAN'T CHANGE ANYTHING...
...NO MATTER WHAT I RECORD.
BANG
BANG
HUH?
GUNSHOTS?
THERE'S NOTHING OUT THERE.

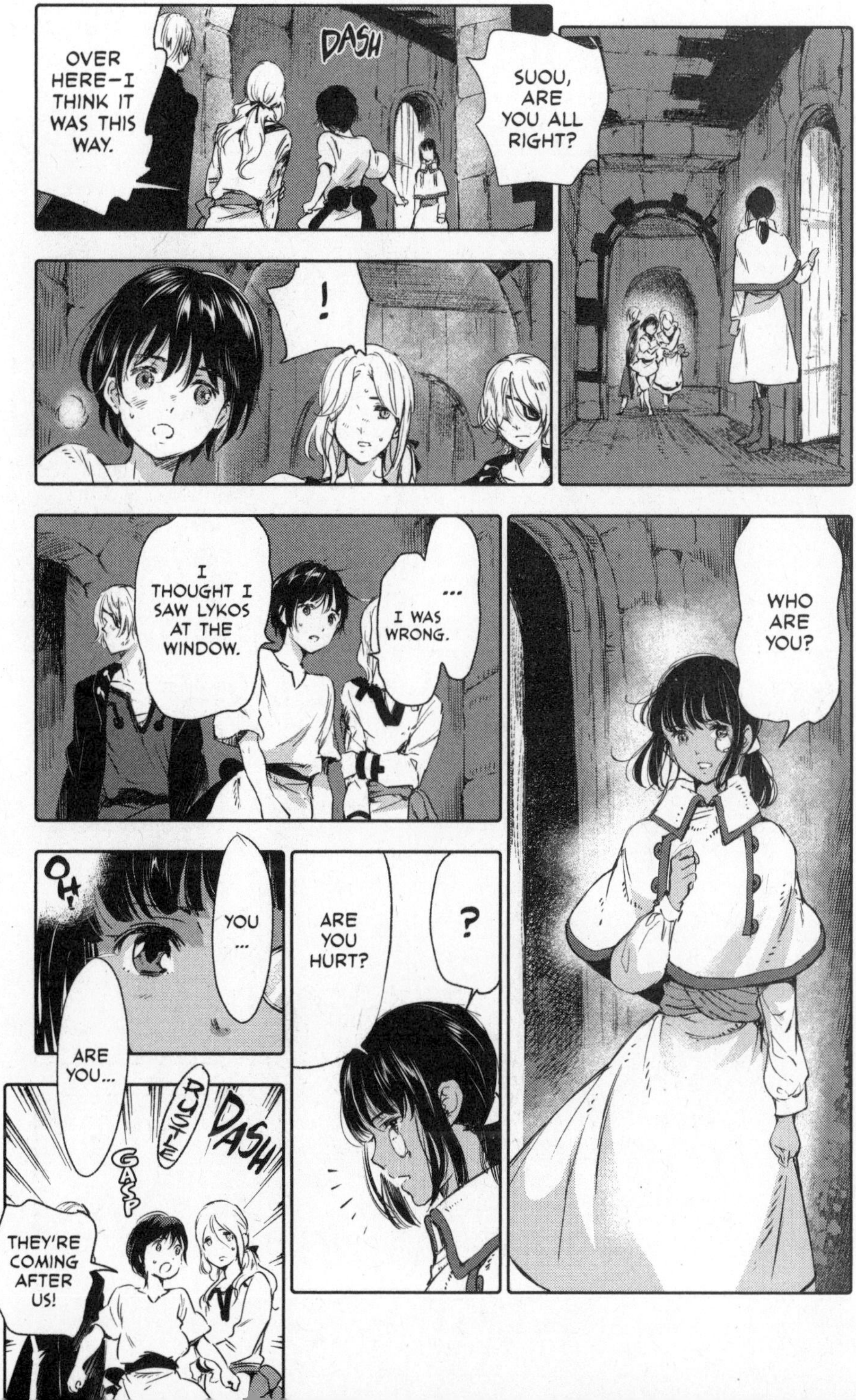
SUOU, ARE YOU ALL RIGHT?
OVER HERE—I THINK IT WAS THIS WAY.
DASH
!
WHO ARE YOU?
... I WAS WRONG.
I THOUGHT I SAW LYKOS AT THE WINDOW.
?
ARE YOU HURT?
OH!
YOU ...
ARE YOU...
DASH
RUSTLE
GASP
THEY'RE COMING AFTER US!

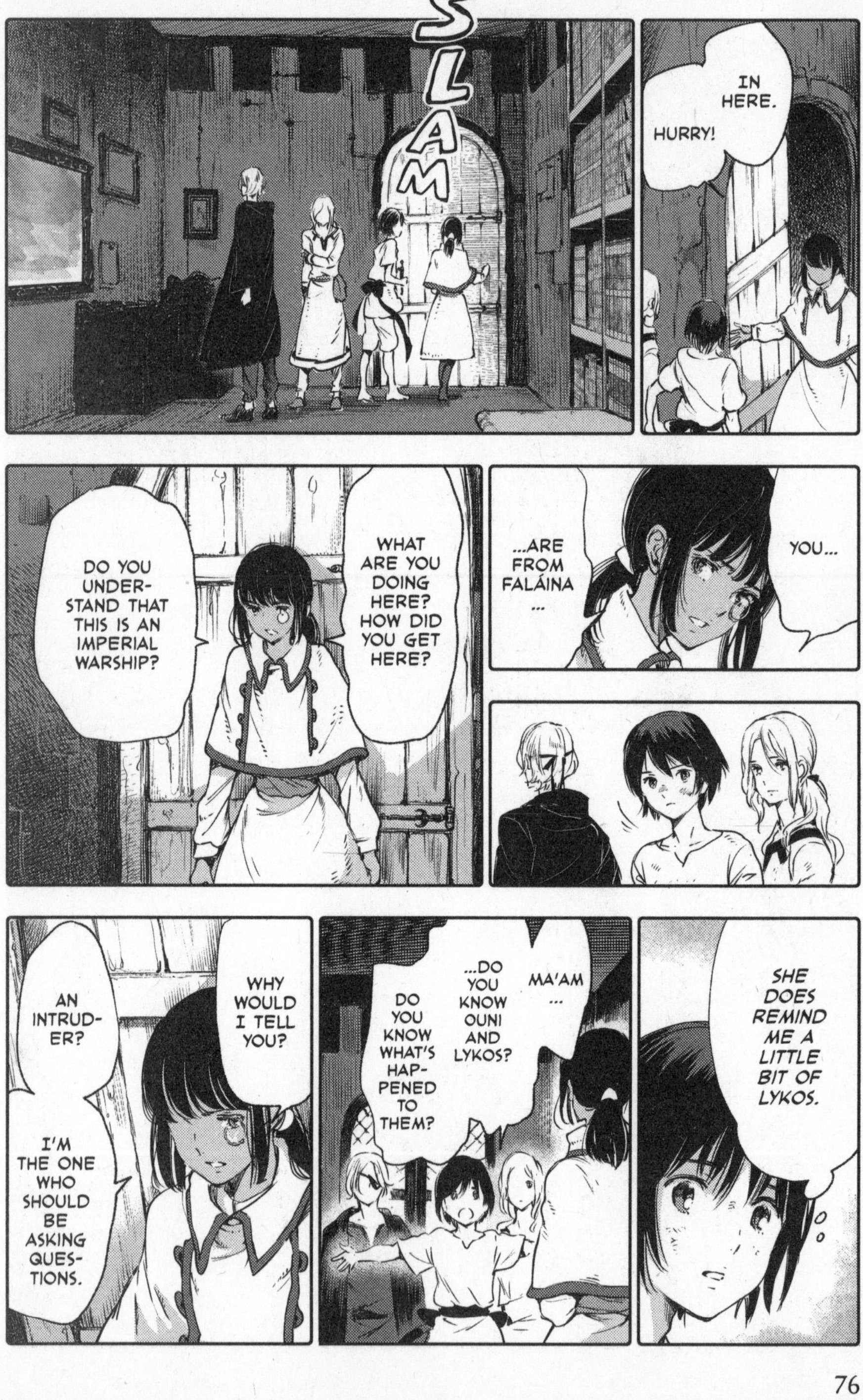
IN HERE.
HURRY!
SLAM
YOU...
...ARE FROM FALÁINA ...
WHAT ARE YOU DOING HERE? HOW DID YOU GET HERE?
DO YOU UNDER-STAND THAT THIS IS AN IMPERIAL WARSHIP?
SHE DOES REMIND ME A LITTLE BIT OF LYKOS.
MA'AM ...
...DO YOU KNOW OUNI AND LYKOS?
DO YOU KNOW WHAT'S HAP-PENED TO THEM?
WHY WOULD I TELL YOU?
AN INTRUD-ER?
I'M THE ONE WHO SHOULD BE ASKING QUES-TIONS.

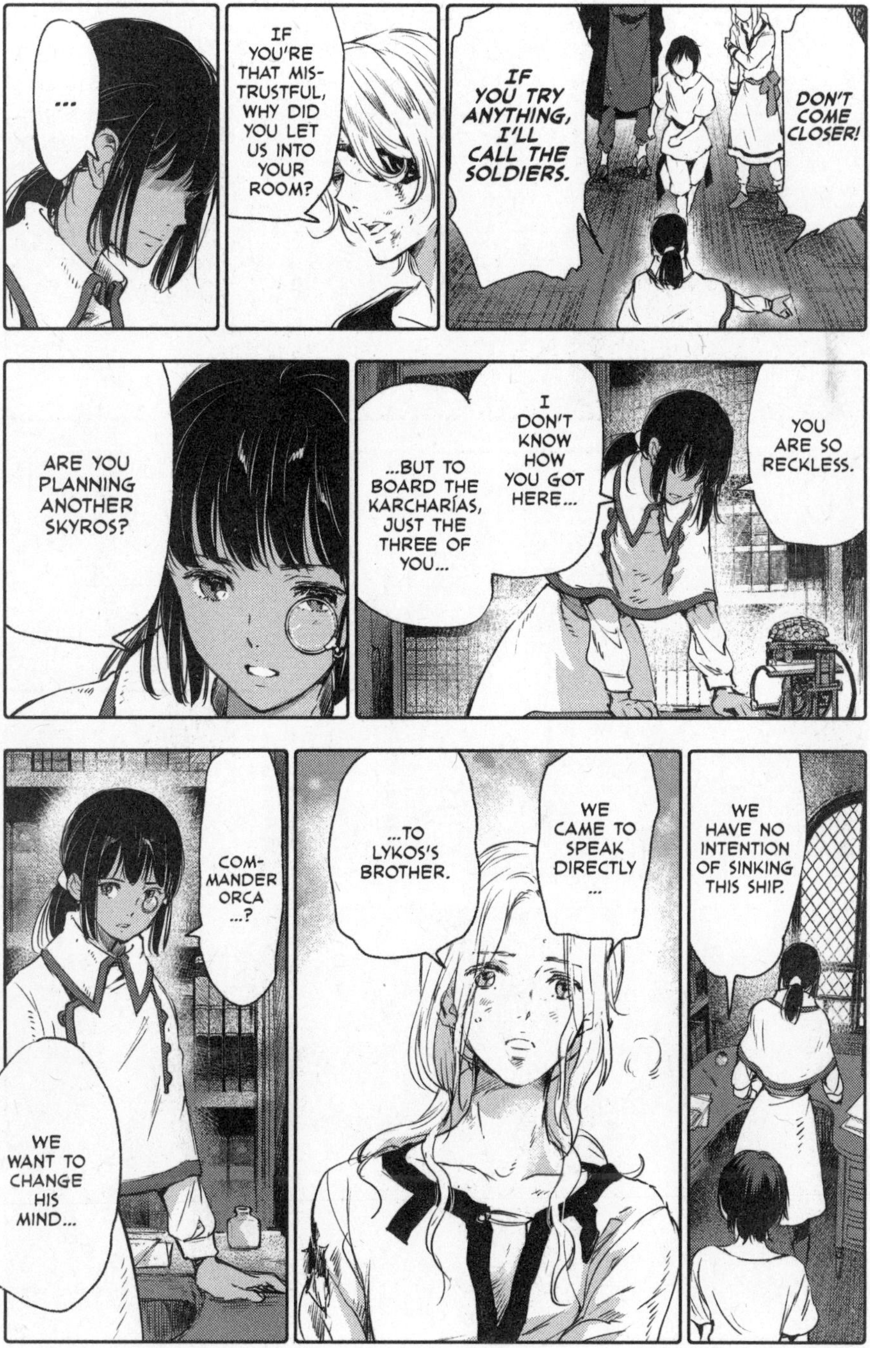
DON'T COME CLOSER!
IF YOU TRY ANYTHING, I'LL CALL THE SOLDIERS.
IF YOU'RE THAT MIS-TRUSTFUL, WHY DID YOU LET US INTO YOUR ROOM?
...
YOU ARE SO RECKLESS.
I DON'T KNOW HOW YOU GOT HERE...
...BUT TO BOARD THE KARCHARÍAS, JUST THE THREE OF YOU...
ARE YOU PLANNING ANOTHER SKYROS?
WE HAVE NO INTENTION OF SINKING THIS SHIP.
WE CAME TO SPEAK DIRECTLY ...
...TO LYKOS'S BROTHER.
COM-MANDER ORCA ...?
WE WANT TO CHANGE HIS MIND...

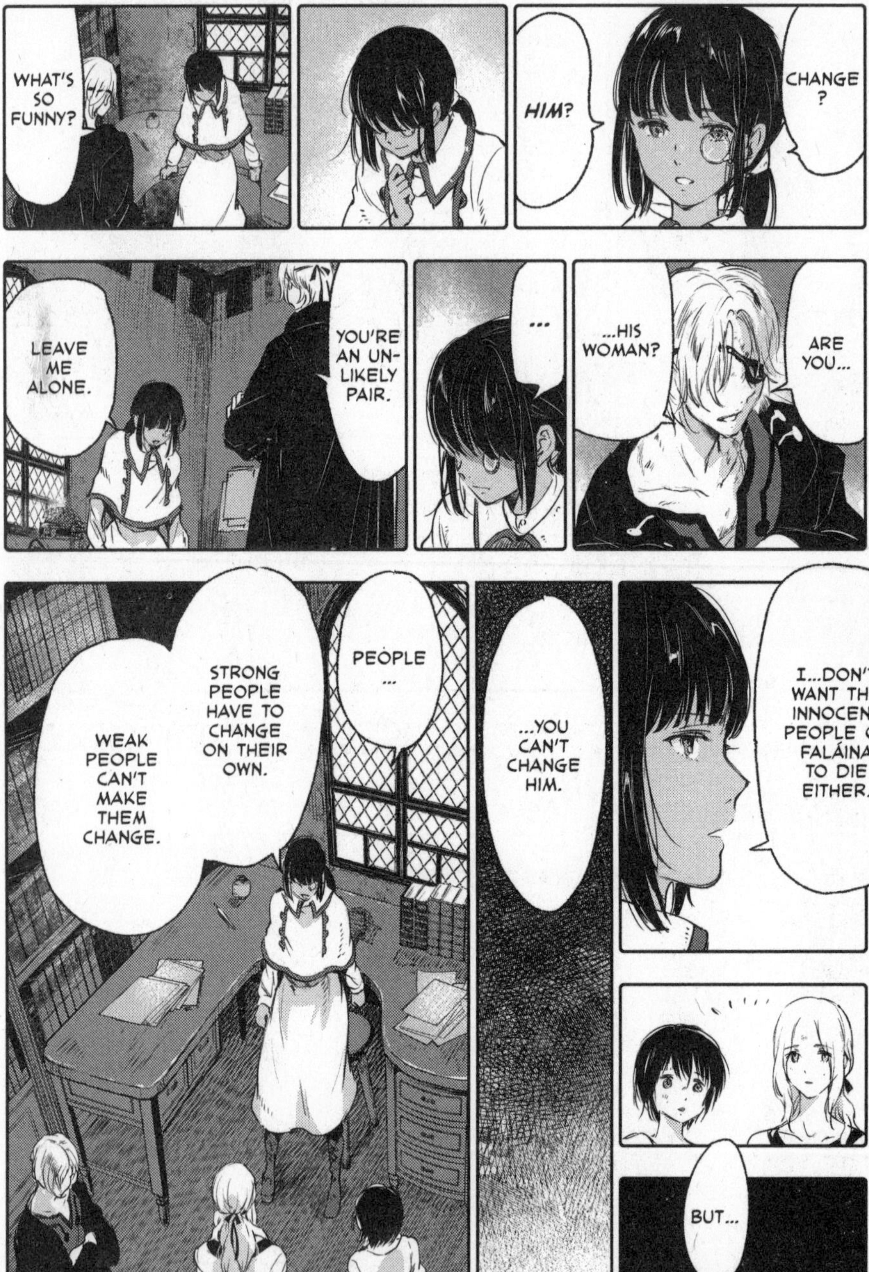
CHANGE ?
HIM?
WHAT'S SO FUNNY?
ARE YOU...
...HIS WOMAN?
...
YOU'RE AN UN-LIKELY PAIR.
LEAVE ME ALONE.
I...DON'T WANT THE INNOCENT PEOPLE OF FALÁINA TO DIE EITHER.
BUT...
...YOU CAN'T CHANGE HIM.
PEOPLE ...
STRONG PEOPLE HAVE TO CHANGE ON THEIR OWN.
WEAK PEOPLE CAN'T MAKE THEM CHANGE.

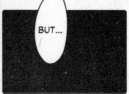

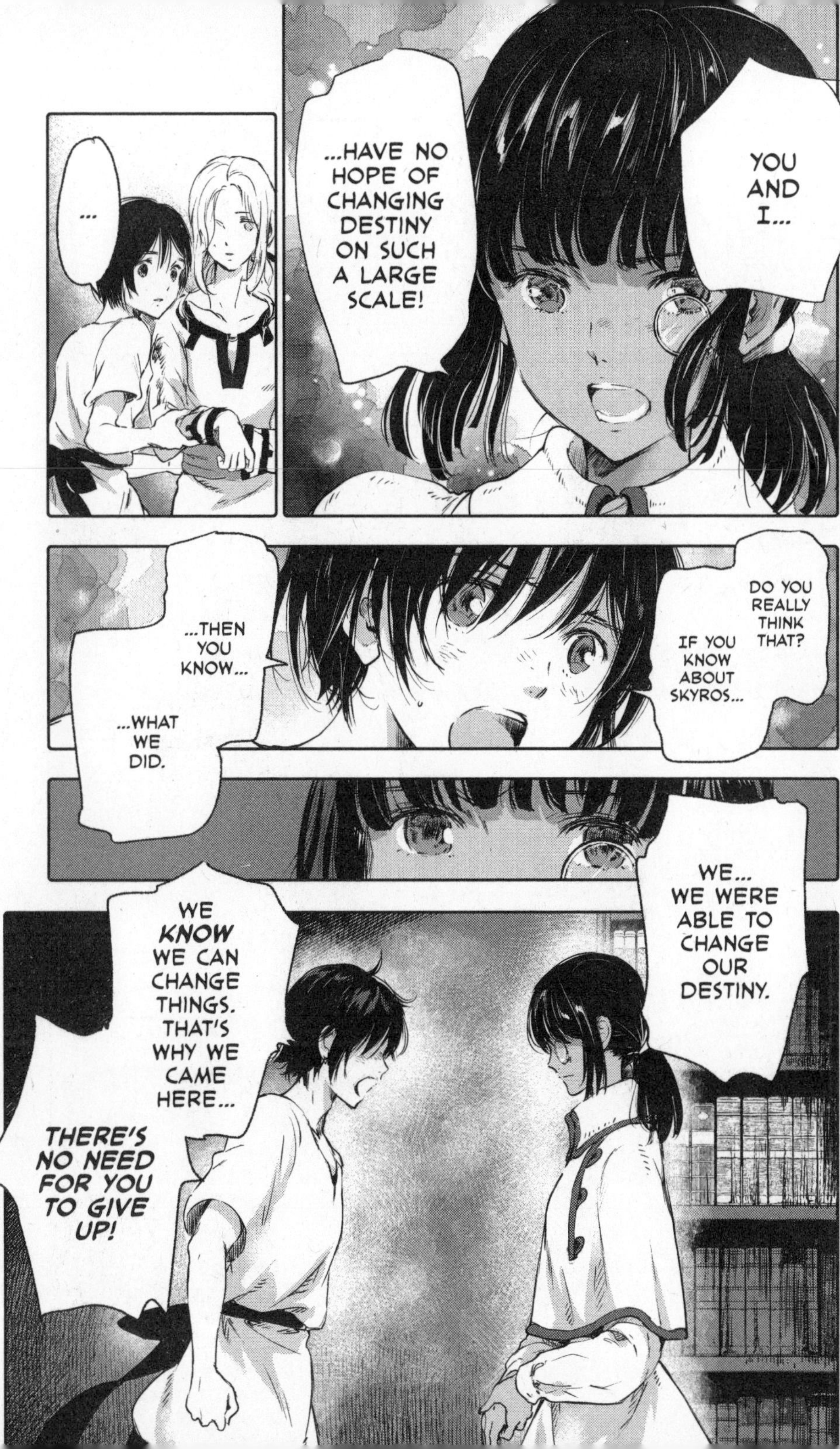
YOU AND I...
...HAVE NO HOPE OF CHANGING DESTINY ON SUCH A LARGE SCALE!
...
DO YOU REALLY THINK THAT?
IF YOU KNOW ABOUT SKYROS...
...THEN YOU KNOW...
...WHAT WE DID.
WE... WE WERE ABLE TO CHANGE OUR DESTINY.
WE *KNOW* WE CAN CHANGE THINGS. THAT'S WHY WE CAME HERE...
THERE'S NO NEED FOR YOU TO GIVE UP!

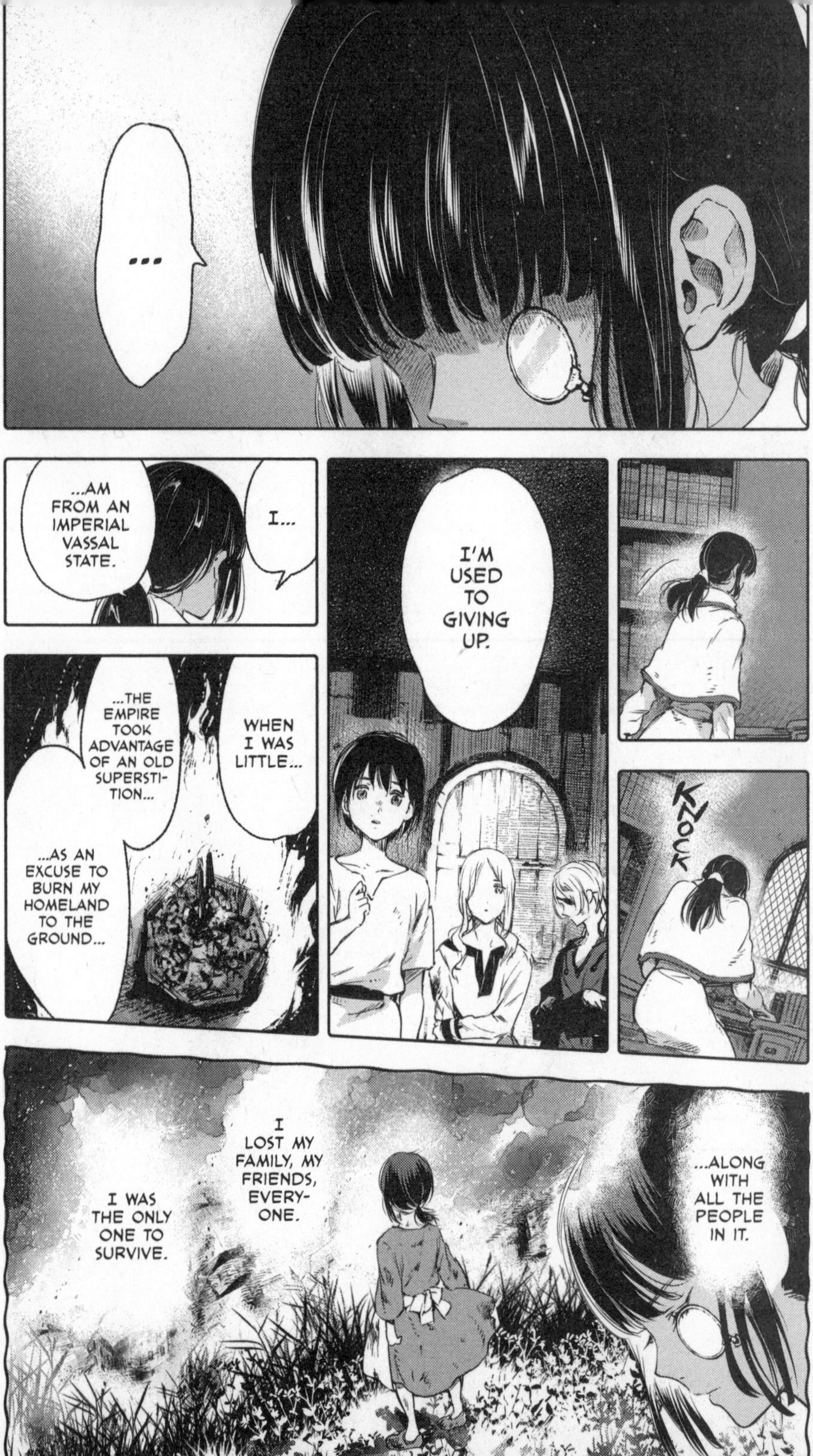
...
KNOCK
I'M USED TO GIVING UP.
I...
...AM FROM AN IMPERIAL VASSAL STATE.
WHEN I WAS LITTLE...
...THE EMPIRE TOOK ADVANTAGE OF AN OLD SUPERSTITION...
...AS AN EXCUSE TO BURN MY HOMELAND TO THE GROUND...
...ALONG WITH ALL THE PEOPLE IN IT.
I LOST MY FAMILY, MY FRIENDS, EVERYONE.
I WAS THE ONLY ONE TO SURVIVE.

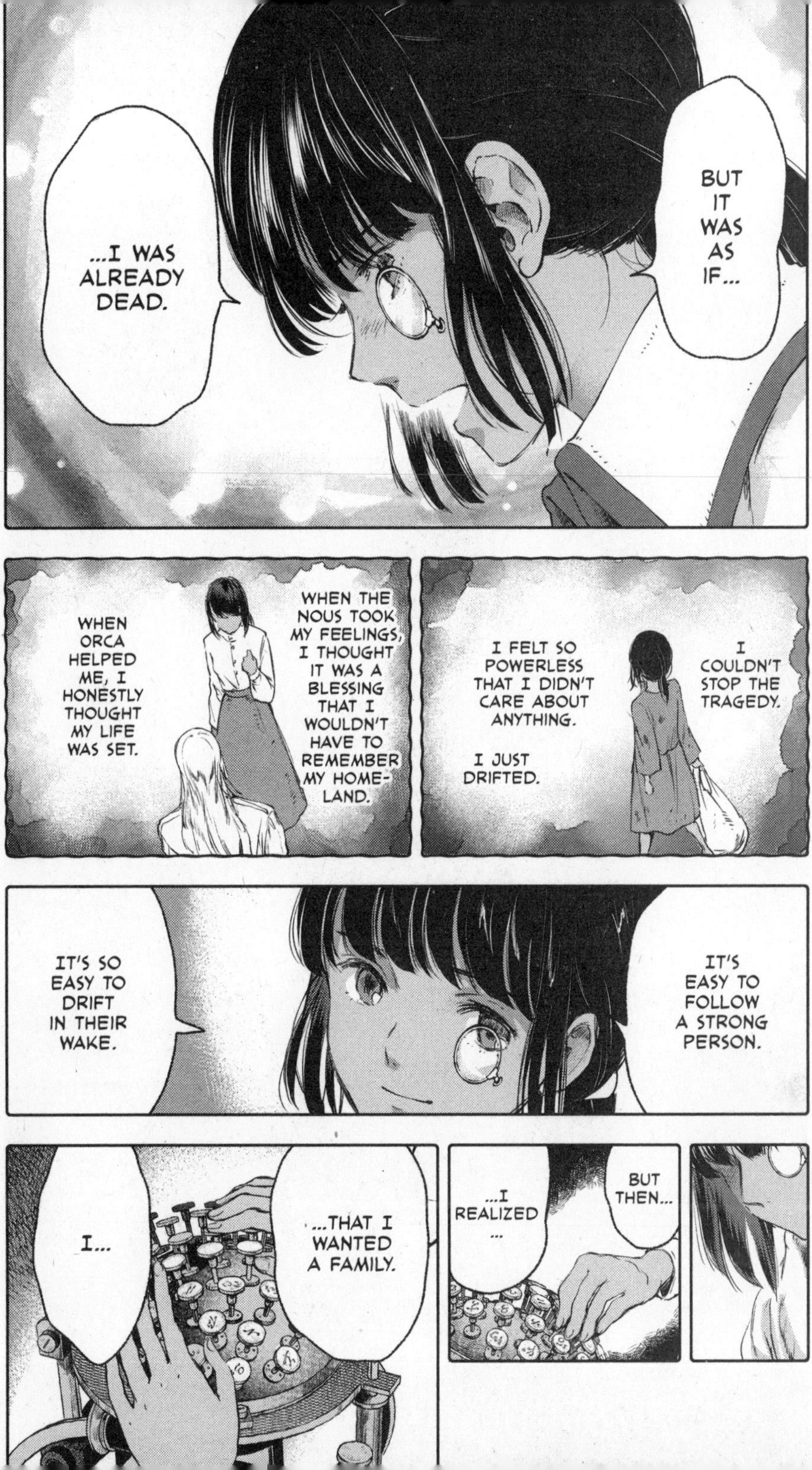
BUT IT WAS AS IF...
...I WAS ALREADY DEAD.
I COULDN'T STOP THE TRAGEDY.
I FELT SO POWERLESS THAT I DIDN'T CARE ABOUT ANYTHING.
I JUST DRIFTED.
WHEN THE NOUS TOOK MY FEELINGS, I THOUGHT IT WAS A BLESSING THAT I WOULDN'T HAVE TO REMEMBER MY HOME-LAND.
WHEN ORCA HELPED ME, I HONESTLY THOUGHT MY LIFE WAS SET.
IT'S EASY TO FOLLOW A STRONG PERSON.
IT'S SO EASY TO DRIFT IN THEIR WAKE.
BUT THEN...
...I REALIZED...
...THAT I WANTED A FAMILY.
I...

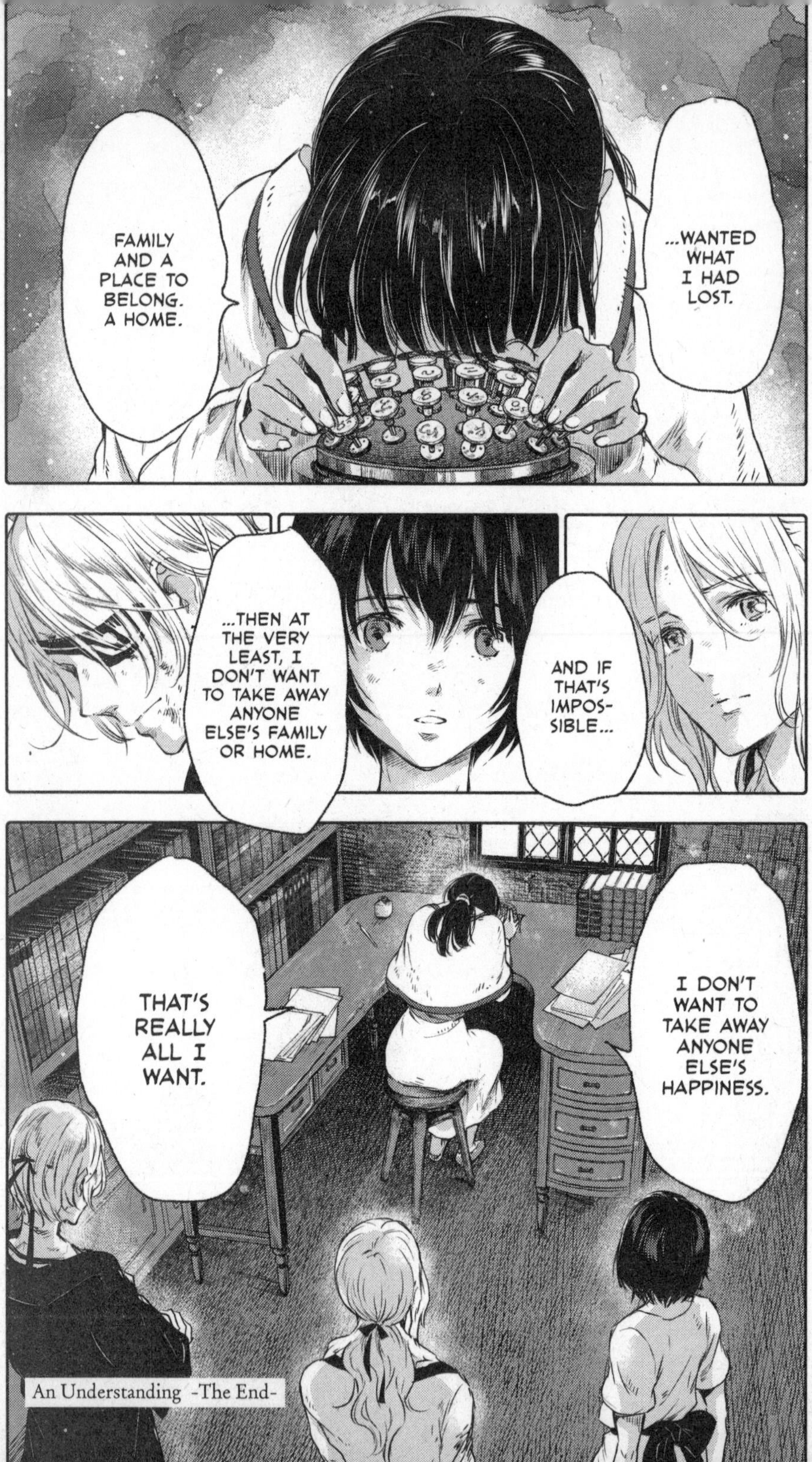
...WANTED WHAT I HAD LOST.
FAMILY AND A PLACE TO BELONG. A HOME.
AND IF THAT'S IMPOS-SIBLE...
...THEN AT THE VERY LEAST, I DON'T WANT TO TAKE AWAY ANYONE ELSE'S FAMILY OR HOME.
I DON'T WANT TO TAKE AWAY ANYONE ELSE'S HAPPINESS.
THAT'S REALLY ALL I WANT.
An Understanding -The End-

TIME: Mon Jun 06 2022 05:43PM
INSTITUTION: 9alam
NAME: CHI, STEVEN
RECORD #:   p24024673

TITLE: Children of the whales. Volume 14
 / story and art by Abi Umeda ; translat
ion, JN Productions ; touch-up art & let
tering, Annaliese Christman.
AUTHOR: Umeda, Abi, author, artist.
CALL #: TEEN MANGA Children Of v.14
BARCODE: 330291080002259sact
RECORD #:   i82584916@9sact
LOCATION: Martin Luther King Jr Teen Are
a

Return above item to 15 - Sacramento Pub
lic Library

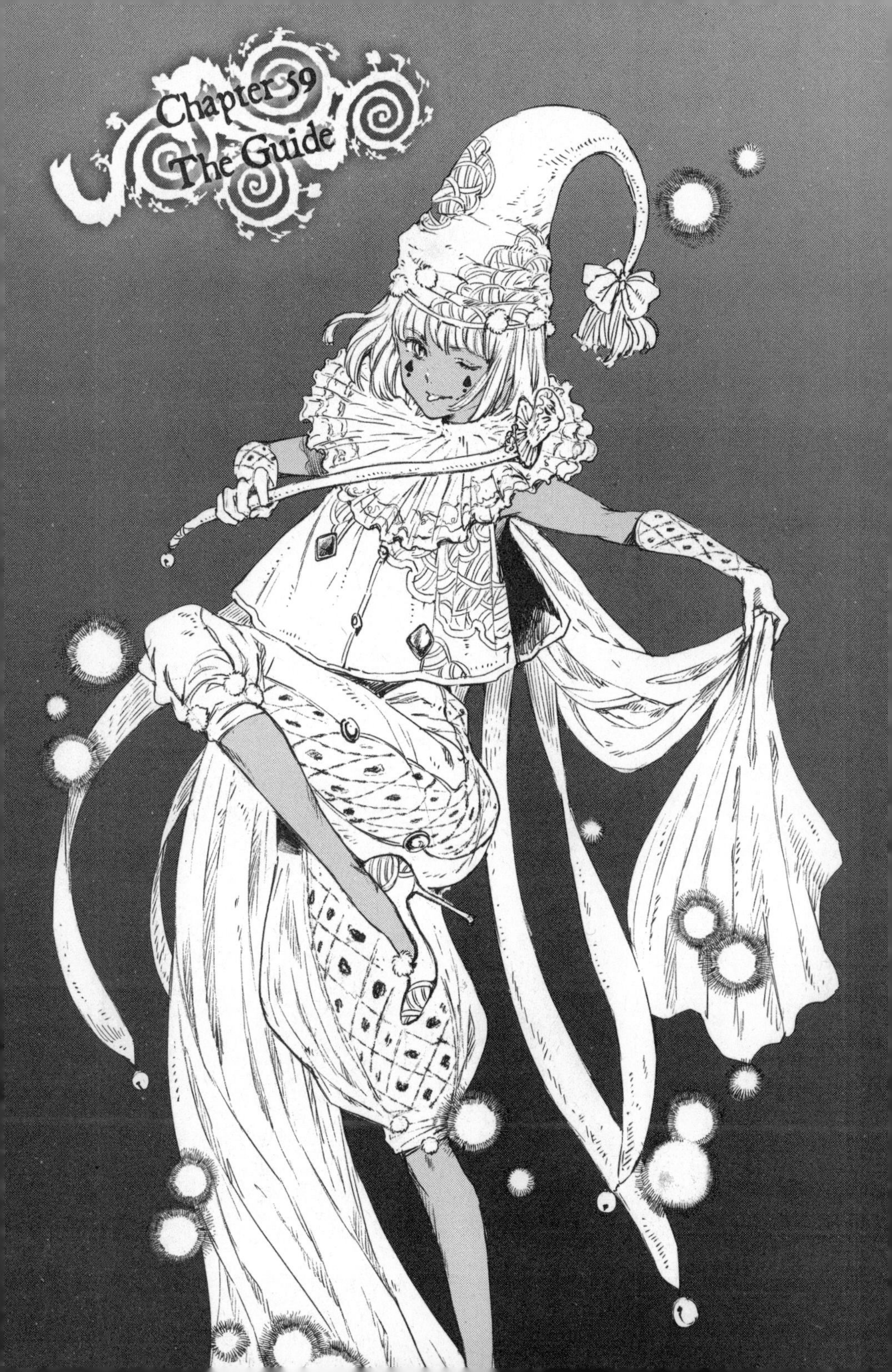
Chapter 59
The Guide

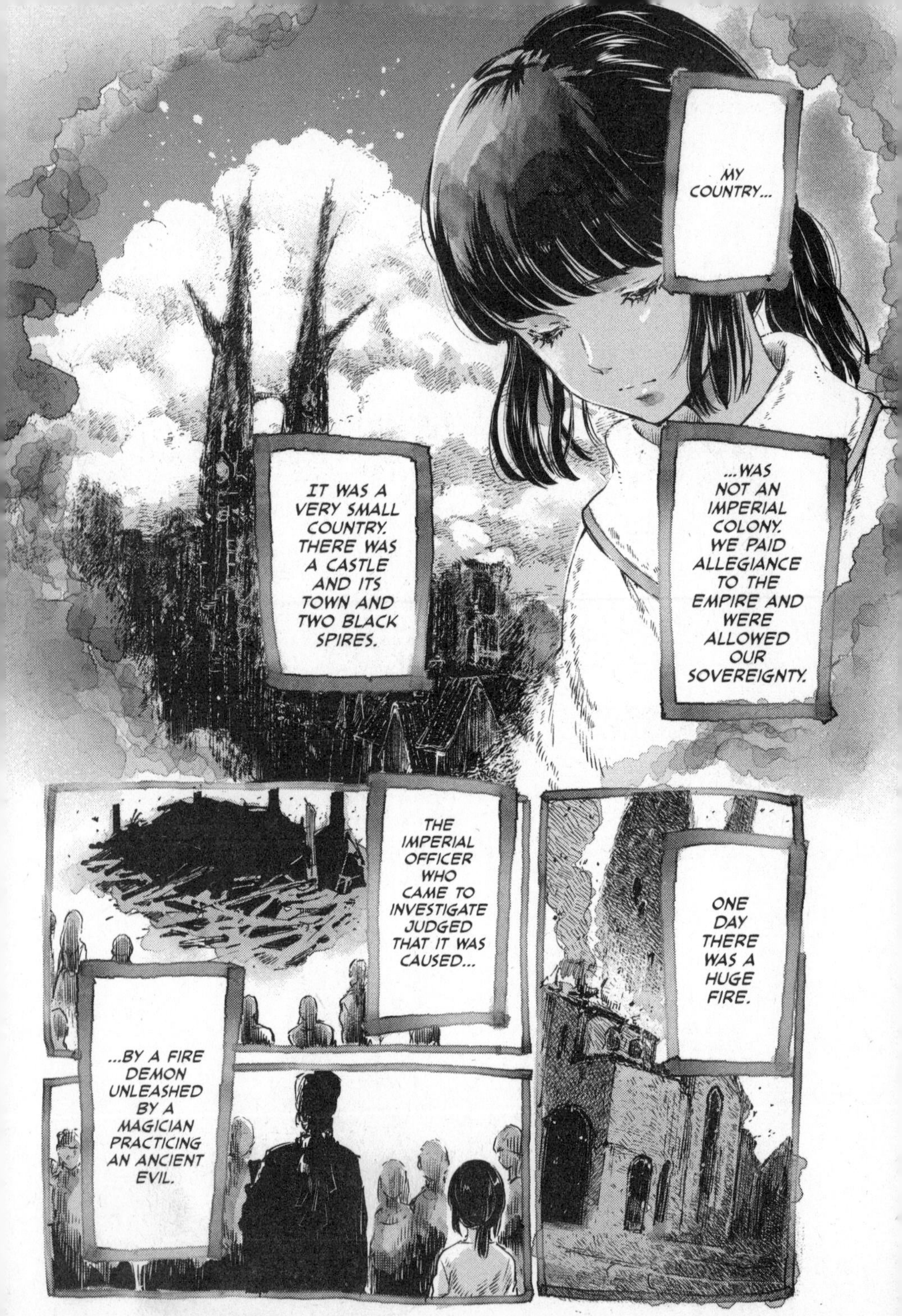
MY COUNTRY...
...WAS NOT AN IMPERIAL COLONY. WE PAID ALLEGIANCE TO THE EMPIRE AND WERE ALLOWED OUR SOVEREIGNTY.
IT WAS A VERY SMALL COUNTRY. THERE WAS A CASTLE AND ITS TOWN AND TWO BLACK SPIRES.
ONE DAY THERE WAS A HUGE FIRE.
THE IMPERIAL OFFICER WHO CAME TO INVESTIGATE JUDGED THAT IT WAS CAUSED...
...BY A FIRE DEMON UNLEASHED BY A MAGICIAN PRACTICING AN ANCIENT EVIL.

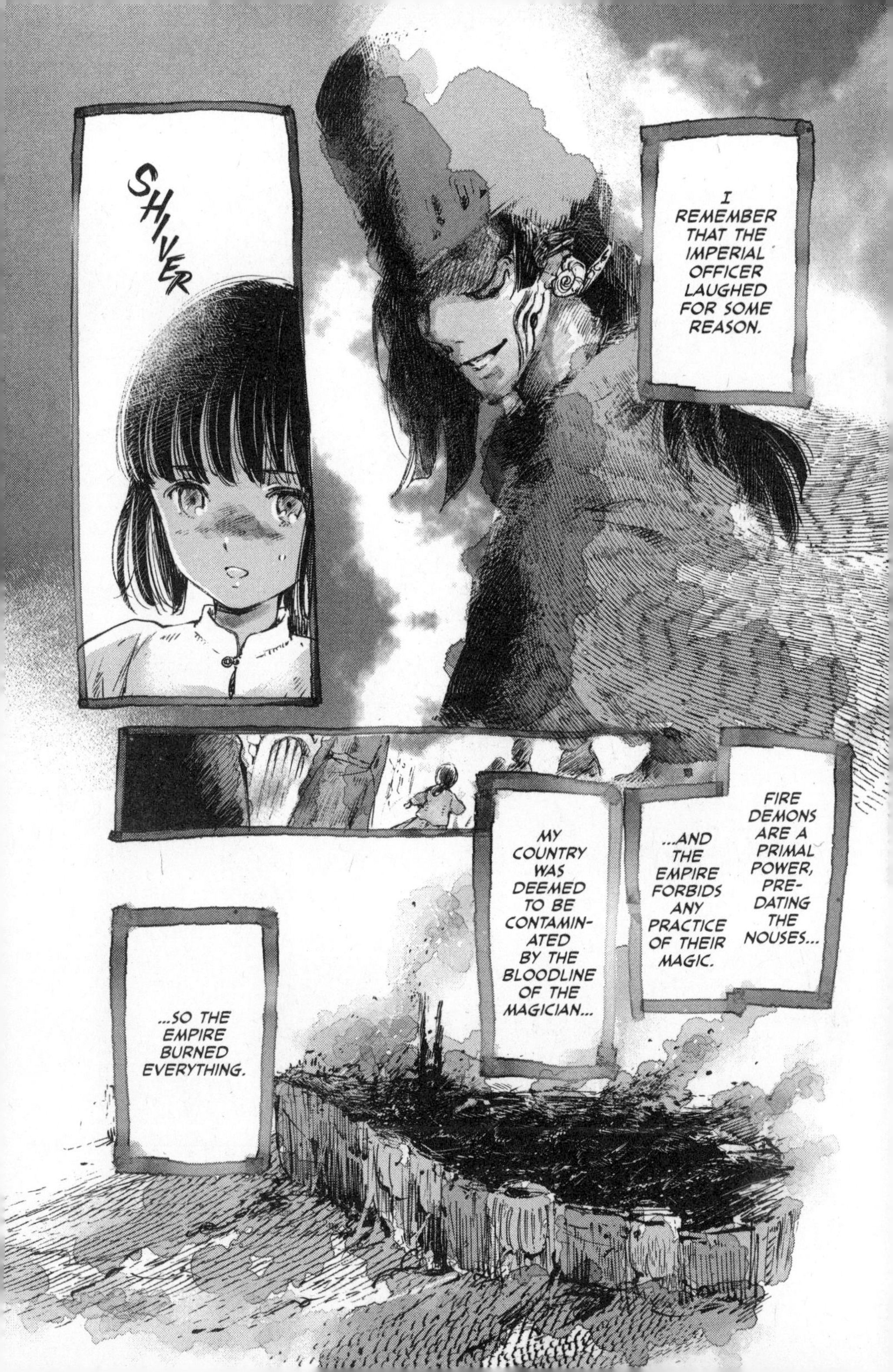
I REMEMBER THAT THE IMPERIAL OFFICER LAUGHED FOR SOME REASON.
SHIVER
FIRE DEMONS ARE A PRIMAL POWER, PRE-DATING THE NOUSES...
...AND THE EMPIRE FORBIDS ANY PRACTICE OF THEIR MAGIC.
MY COUNTRY WAS DEEMED TO BE CONTAMIN-ATED BY THE BLOODLINE OF THE MAGICIAN...
...SO THE EMPIRE BURNED EVERYTHING.

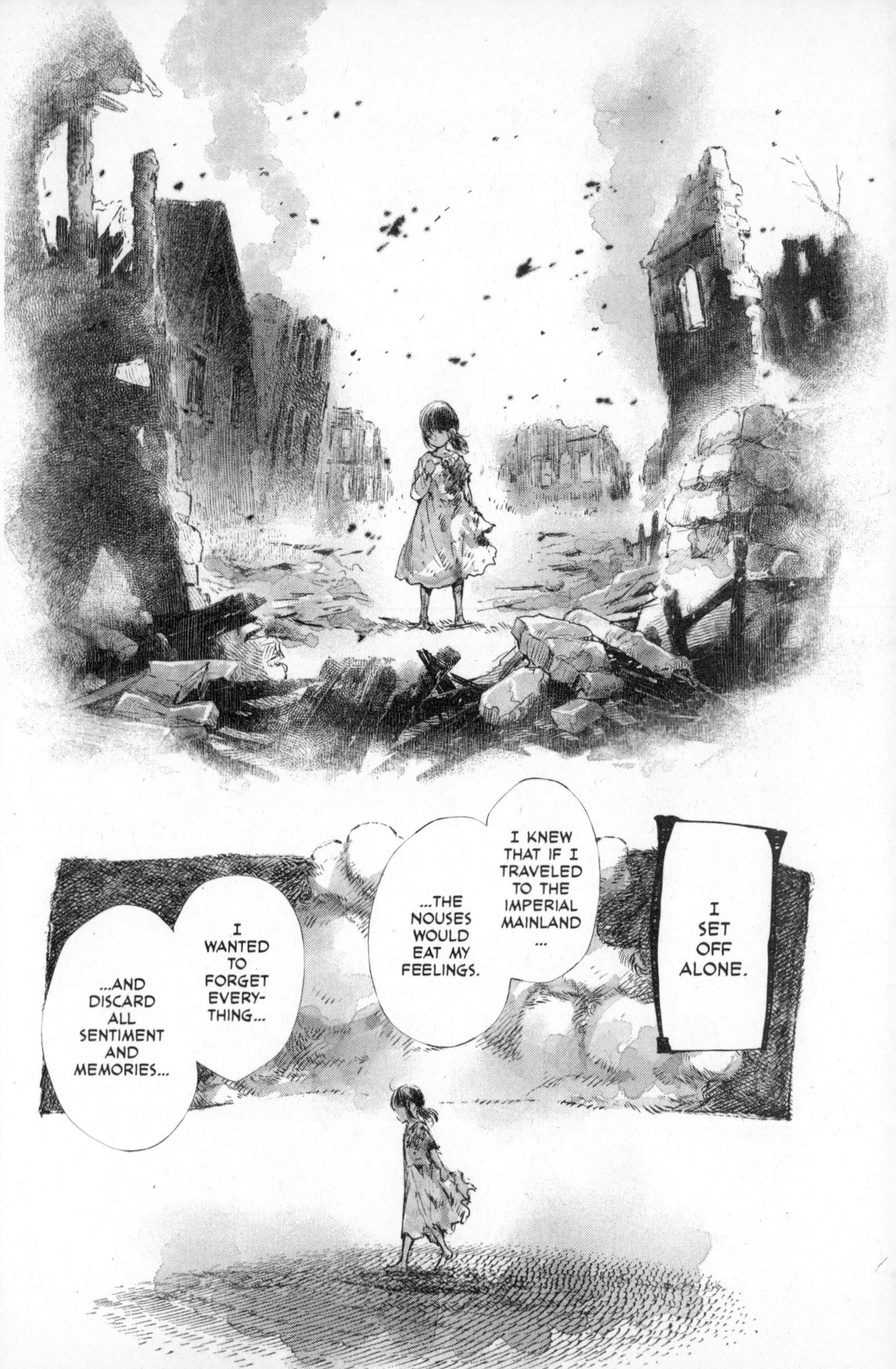
I SET OFF ALONE.
I KNEW THAT IF I TRAVELED TO THE IMPERIAL MAINLAND...
...THE NOUSES WOULD EAT MY FEELINGS.
I WANTED TO FORGET EVERY-THING...
...AND DISCARD ALL SENTIMENT AND MEMORIES...

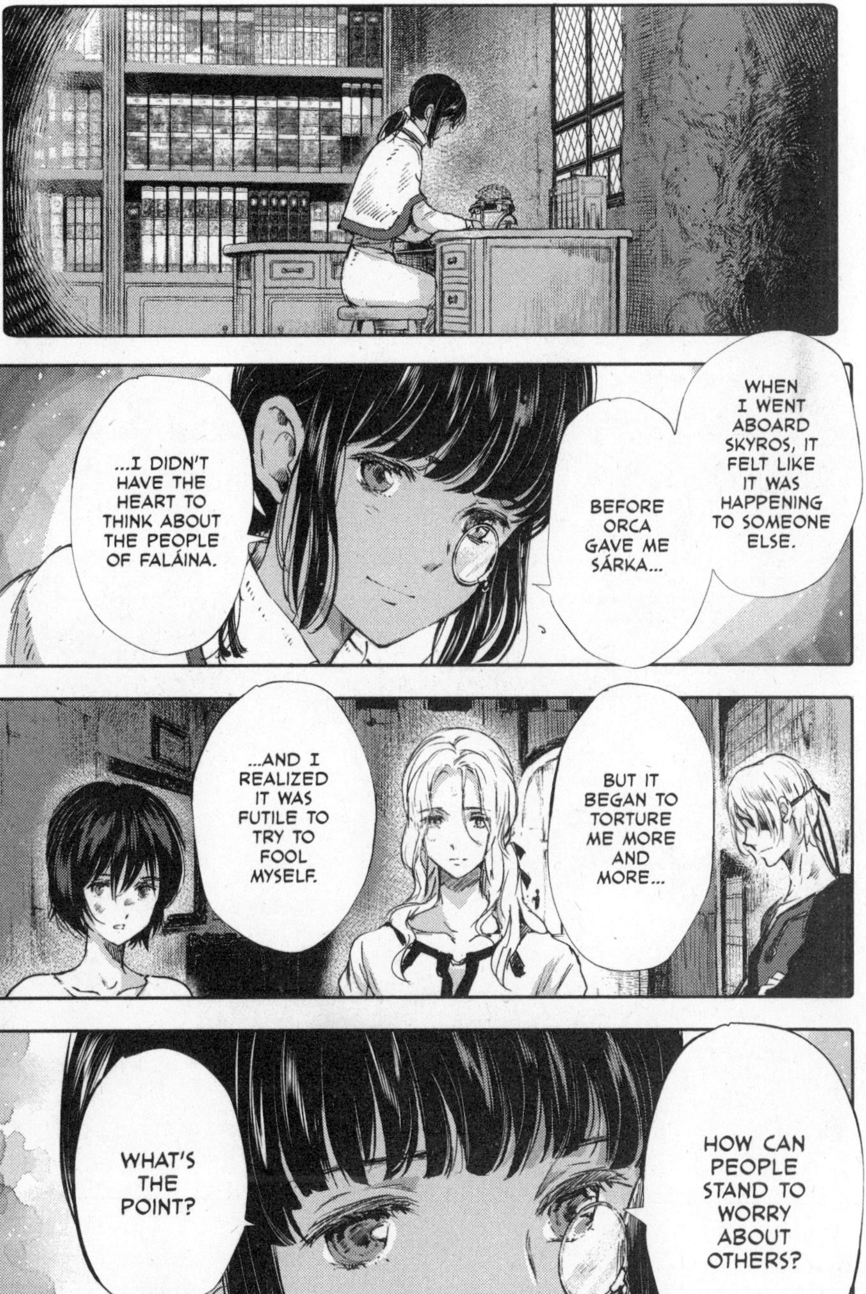
WHEN I WENT ABOARD SKYROS, IT FELT LIKE IT WAS HAPPENING TO SOMEONE ELSE.
BEFORE ORCA GAVE ME SÁRKA...
...I DIDN'T HAVE THE HEART TO THINK ABOUT THE PEOPLE OF FALÁINA.
BUT IT BEGAN TO TORTURE ME MORE AND MORE...
...AND I REALIZED IT WAS FUTILE TO TRY TO FOOL MYSELF.
HOW CAN PEOPLE STAND TO WORRY ABOUT OTHERS?
WHAT'S THE POINT?

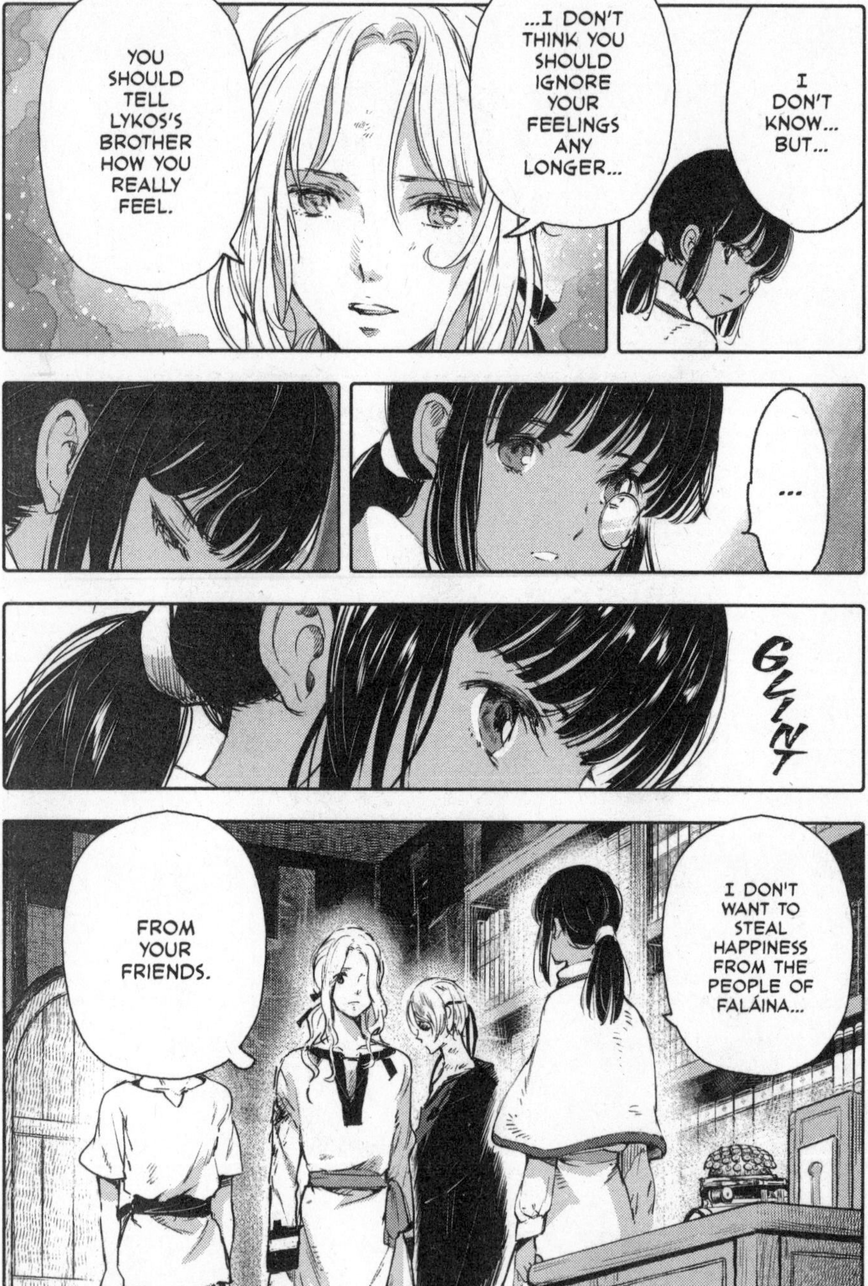
I DON'T KNOW... BUT...
...I DON'T THINK YOU SHOULD IGNORE YOUR FEELINGS ANY LONGER...
YOU SHOULD TELL LYKOS'S BROTHER HOW YOU REALLY FEEL.
...
GLINT
I DON'T WANT TO STEAL HAPPINESS FROM THE PEOPLE OF FALÁINA...
FROM YOUR FRIENDS.

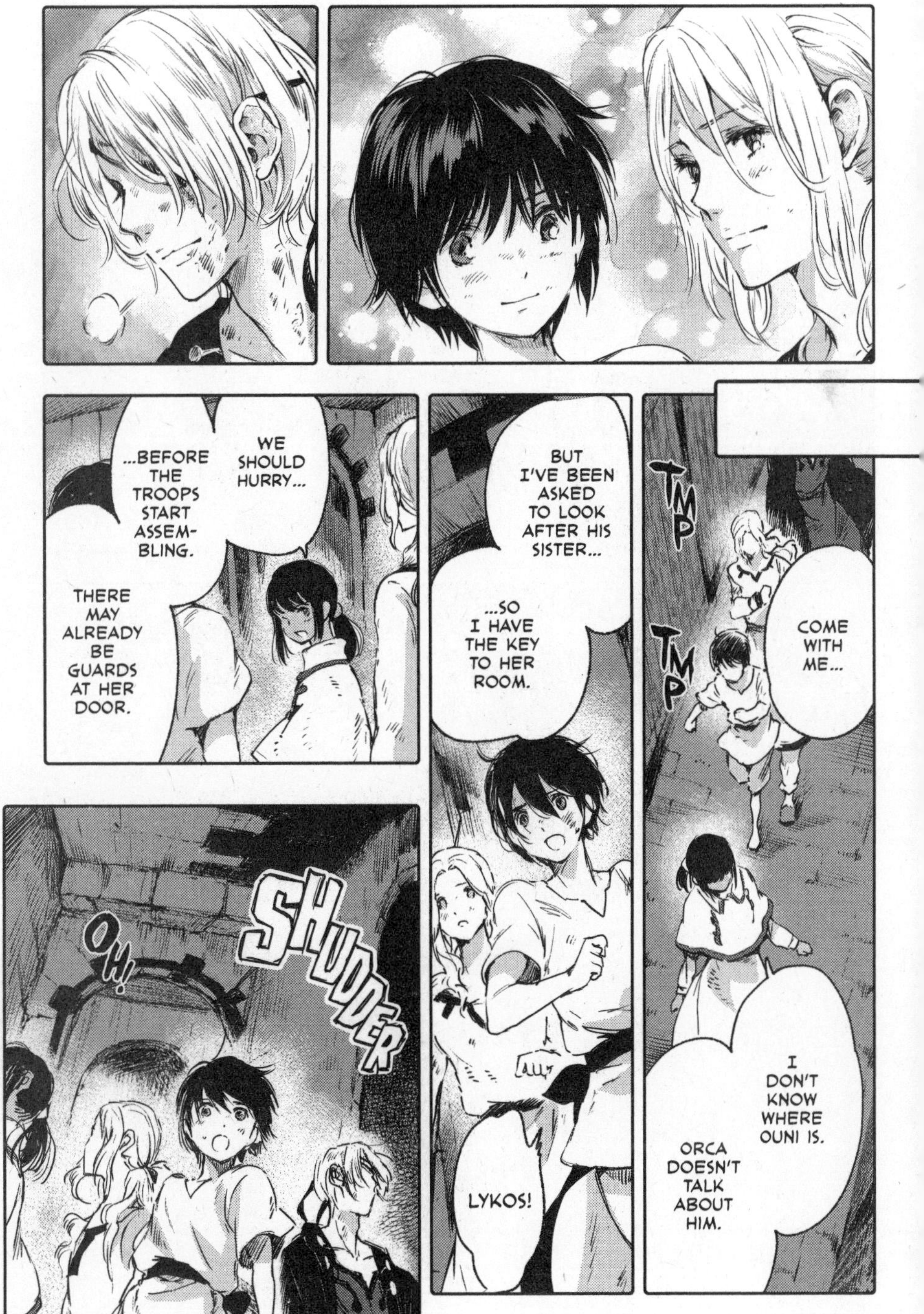
TMP
TMP
COME WITH ME...
I DON'T KNOW WHERE OUNI IS.
ORCA DOESN'T TALK ABOUT HIM.
BUT I'VE BEEN ASKED TO LOOK AFTER HIS SISTER...
...SO I HAVE THE KEY TO HER ROOM.
LYKOS!
WE SHOULD HURRY...
...BEFORE THE TROOPS START ASSEM-BLING.
THERE MAY ALREADY BE GUARDS AT HER DOOR.
SHUDDER
OH!

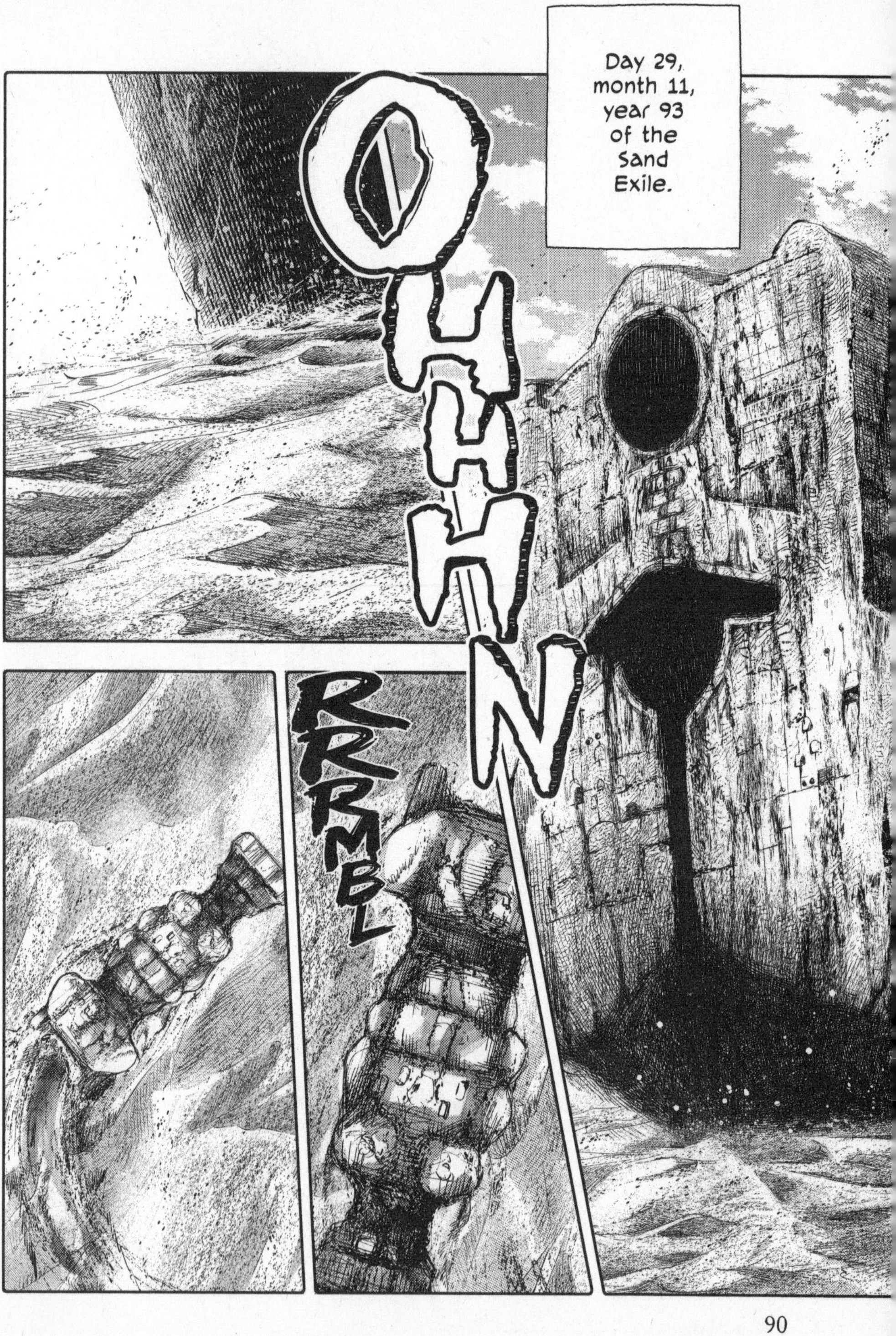
Day 29, month 11, year 93 of the Sand Exile.
OUHHHN
RRRMBL

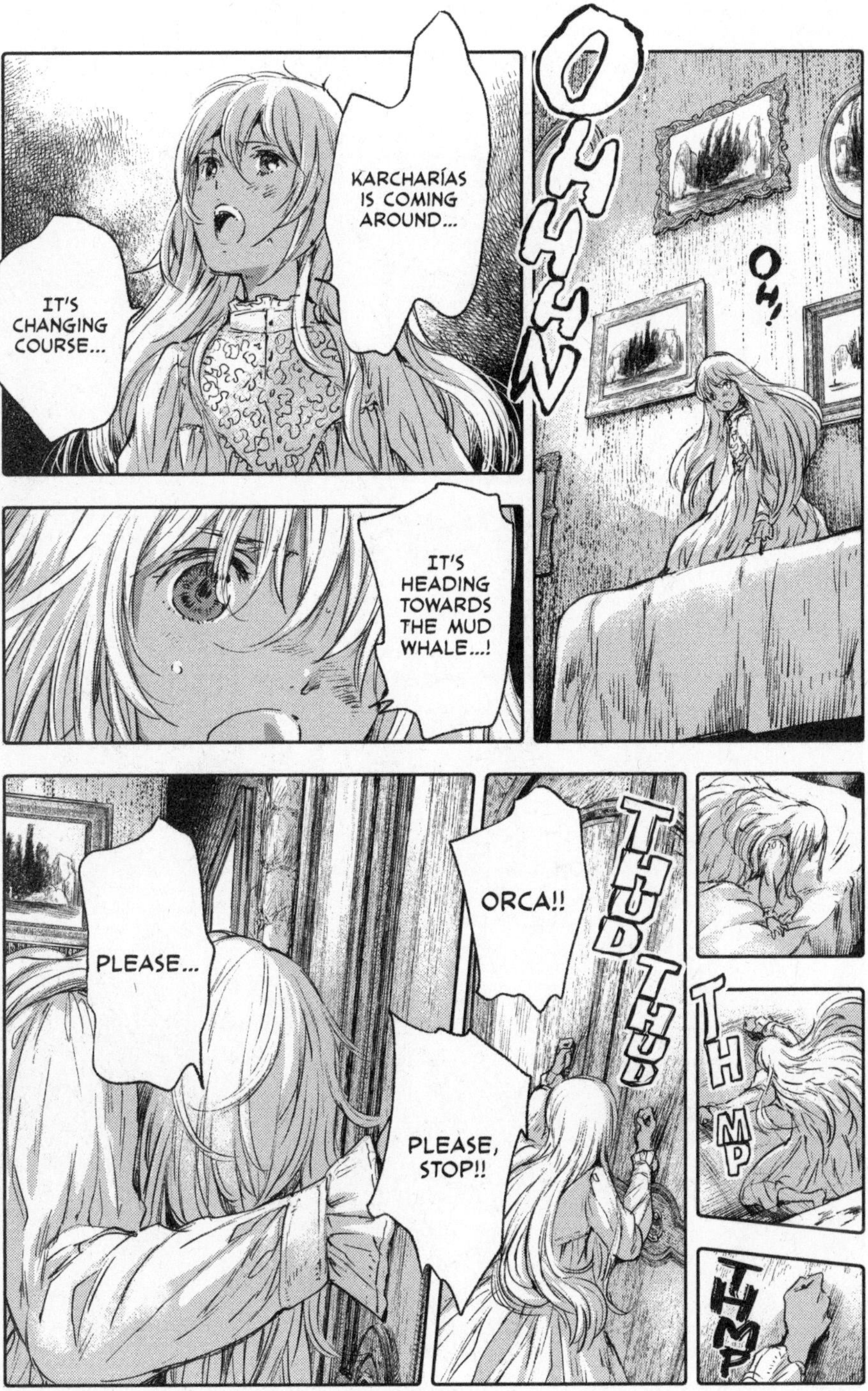
OHUHHN
OH!
KARCHARÍAS IS COMING AROUND...
IT'S CHANGING COURSE...
IT'S HEADING TOWARDS THE MUD WHALE...!
THUMP
THMP
ORCA!!
THUD THUD
PLEASE, STOP!!
PLEASE...

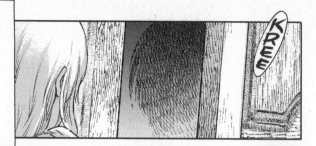

KREE

It had been several days since Lykos was taken.

CHA-KURO...

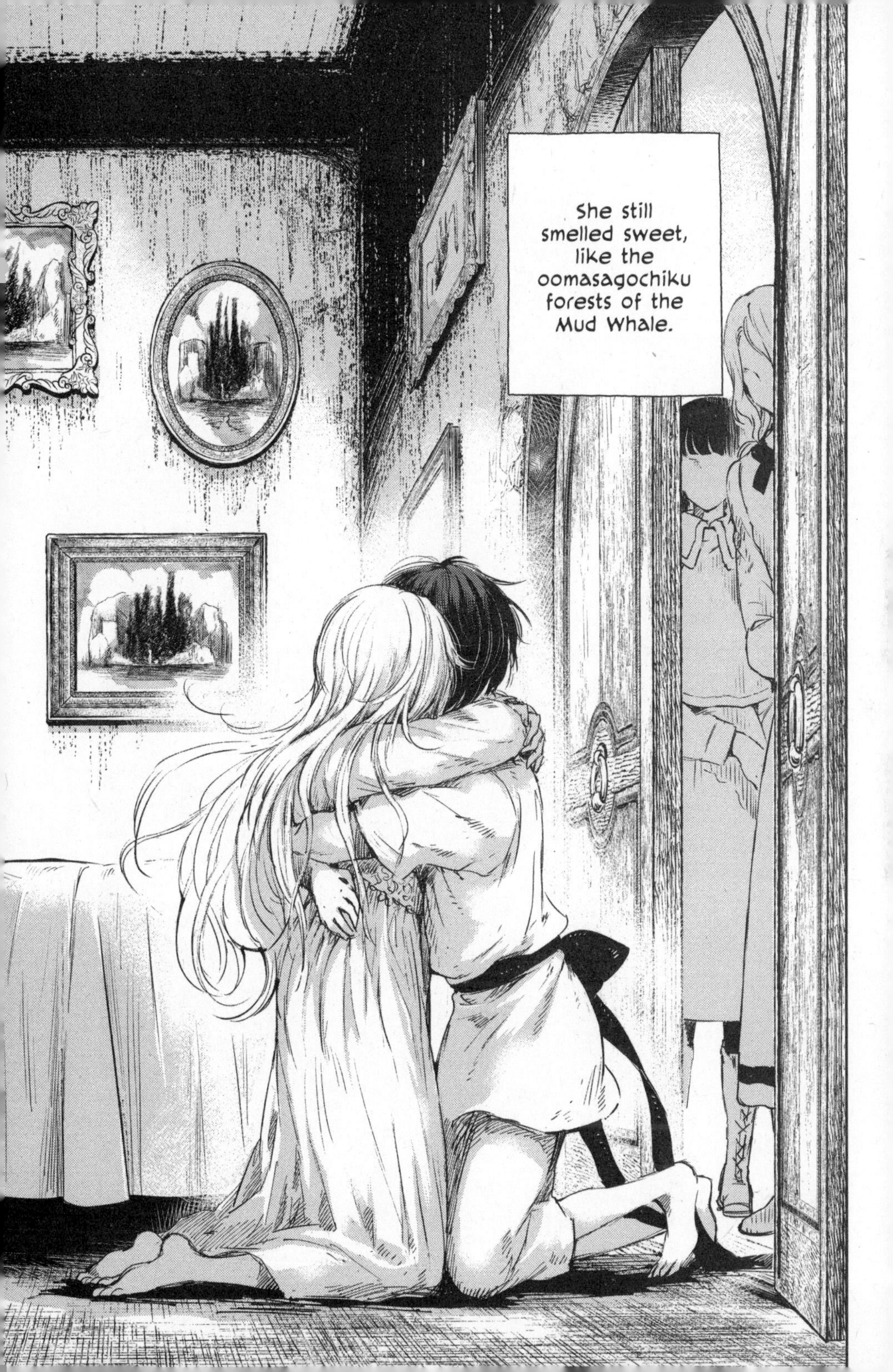
She still smelled sweet, like the oomasagochiku forests of the Mud Whale.

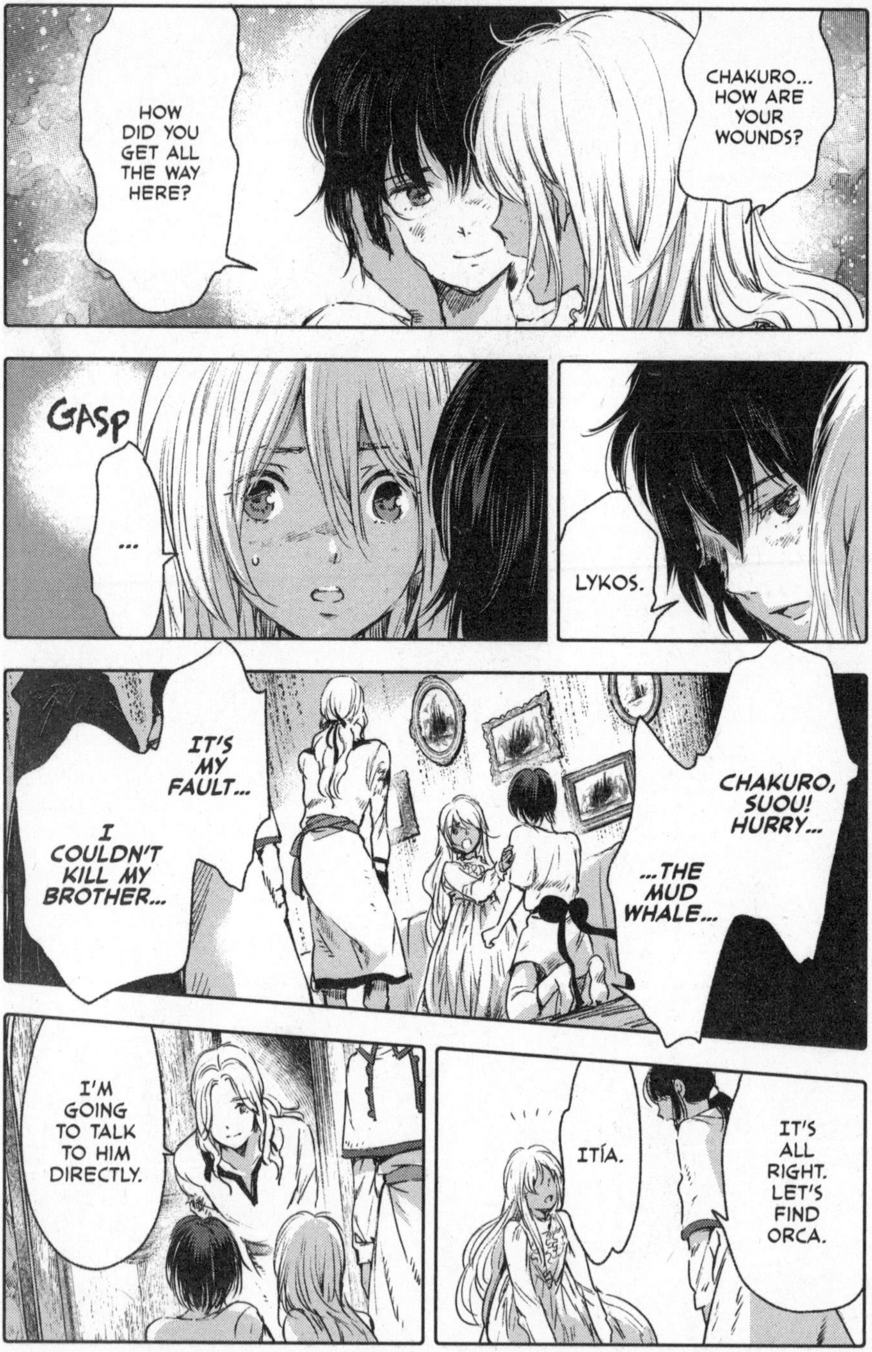
CHAKURO... HOW ARE YOUR WOUNDS?
HOW DID YOU GET ALL THE WAY HERE?
LYKOS.
GASP
...
CHAKURO, SUOU! HURRY...
...THE MUD WHALE...
IT'S MY FAULT...
I COULDN'T KILL MY BROTHER...
IT'S ALL RIGHT. LET'S FIND ORCA.
ITÍA.
I'M GOING TO TALK TO HIM DIRECTLY.

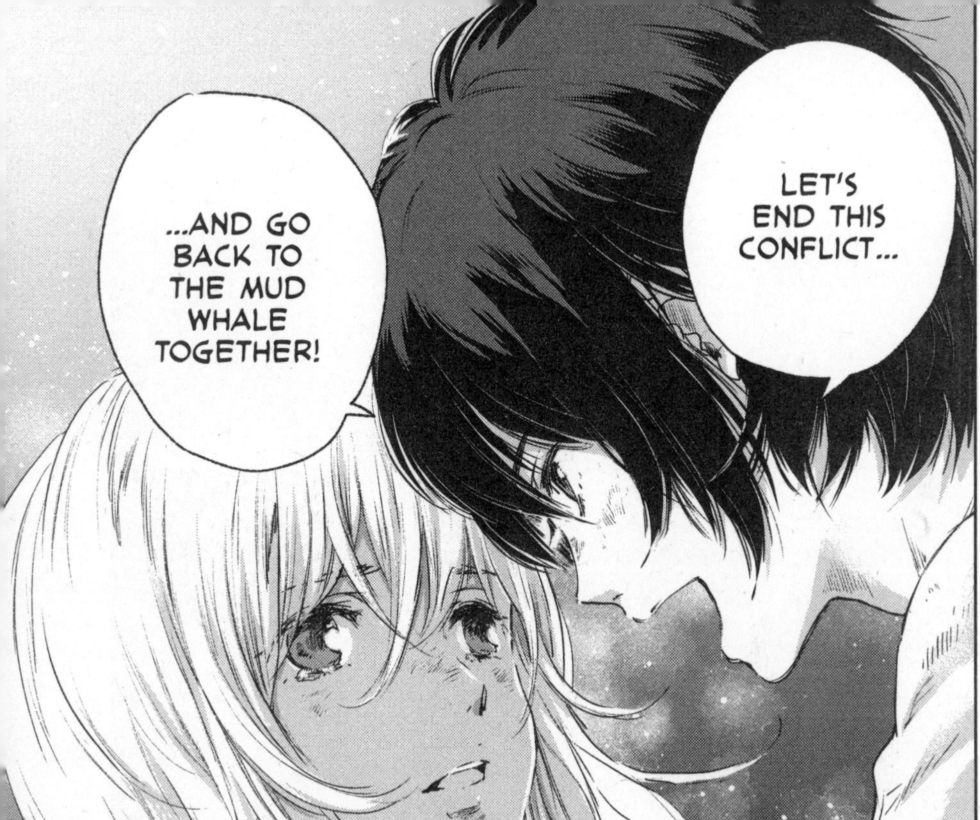
LET'S END THIS CONFLICT...
...AND GO BACK TO THE MUD WHALE TOGETHER!

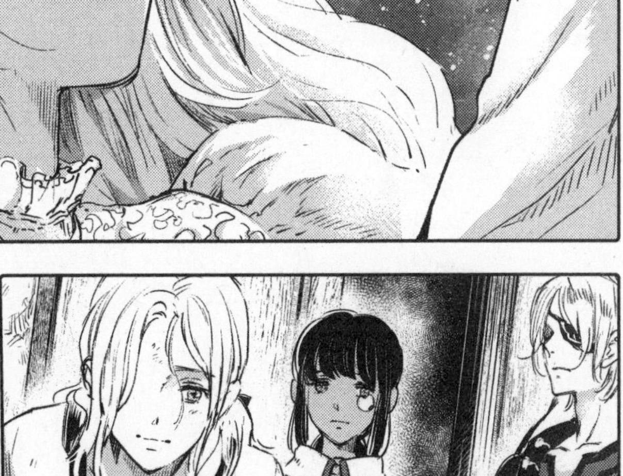

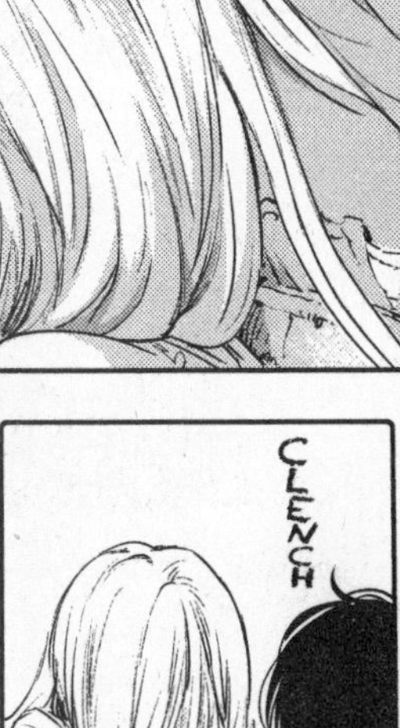
CLENCH

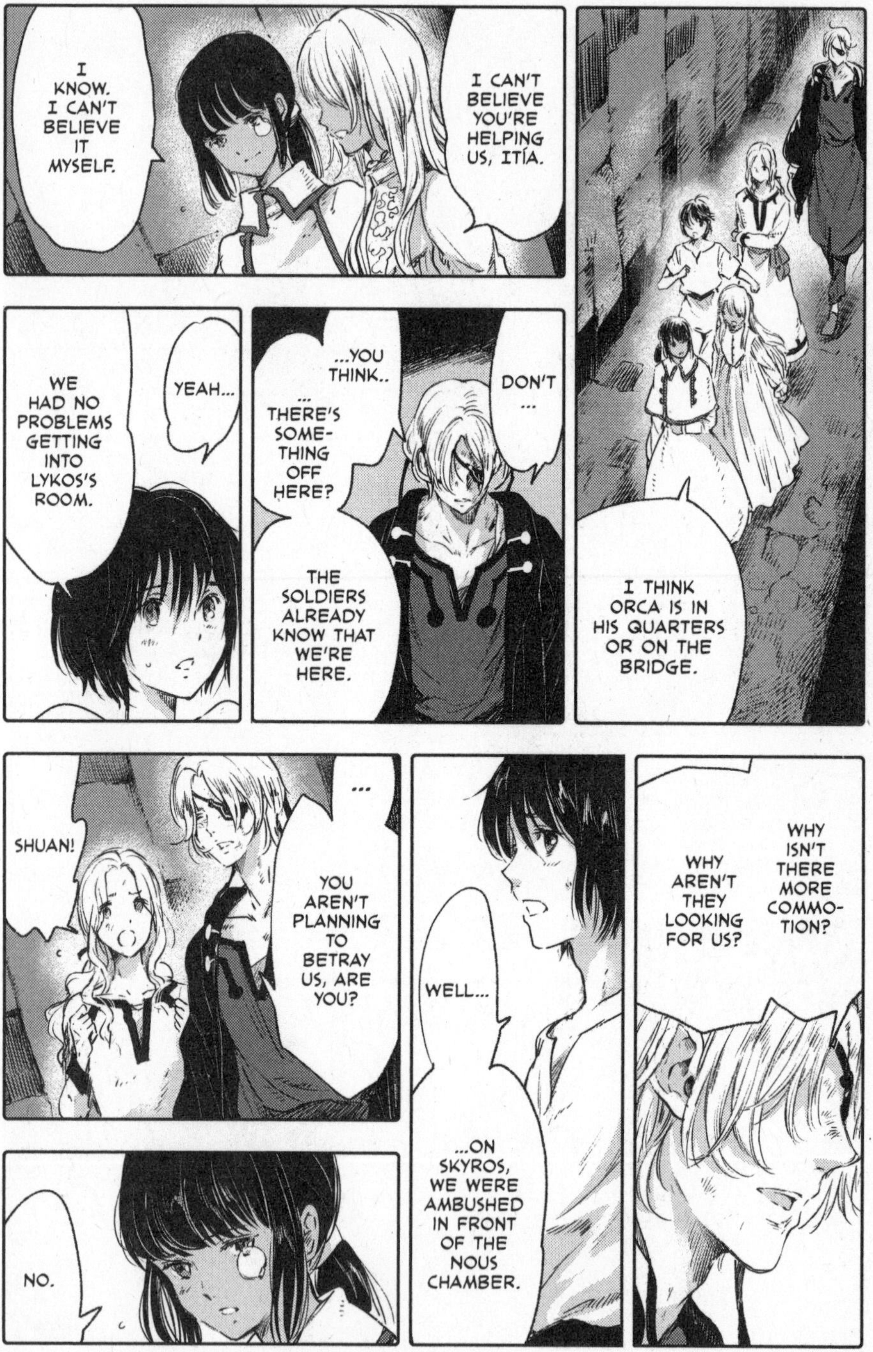
I THINK ORCA IS IN HIS QUARTERS OR ON THE BRIDGE.
I CAN'T BELIEVE YOU'RE HELPING US, ITÍA.
I KNOW. I CAN'T BELIEVE IT MYSELF.
DON'T ...
...YOU THINK.. ... THERE'S SOME-THING OFF HERE?
THE SOLDIERS ALREADY KNOW THAT WE'RE HERE.
YEAH...
WE HAD NO PROBLEMS GETTING INTO LYKOS'S ROOM.
WHY ISN'T THERE MORE COMMO-TION?
WHY AREN'T THEY LOOKING FOR US?
WELL...
...ON SKYROS, WE WERE AMBUSHED IN FRONT OF THE NOUS CHAMBER.
...
YOU AREN'T PLANNING TO BETRAY US, ARE YOU?
SHUAN!
NO.

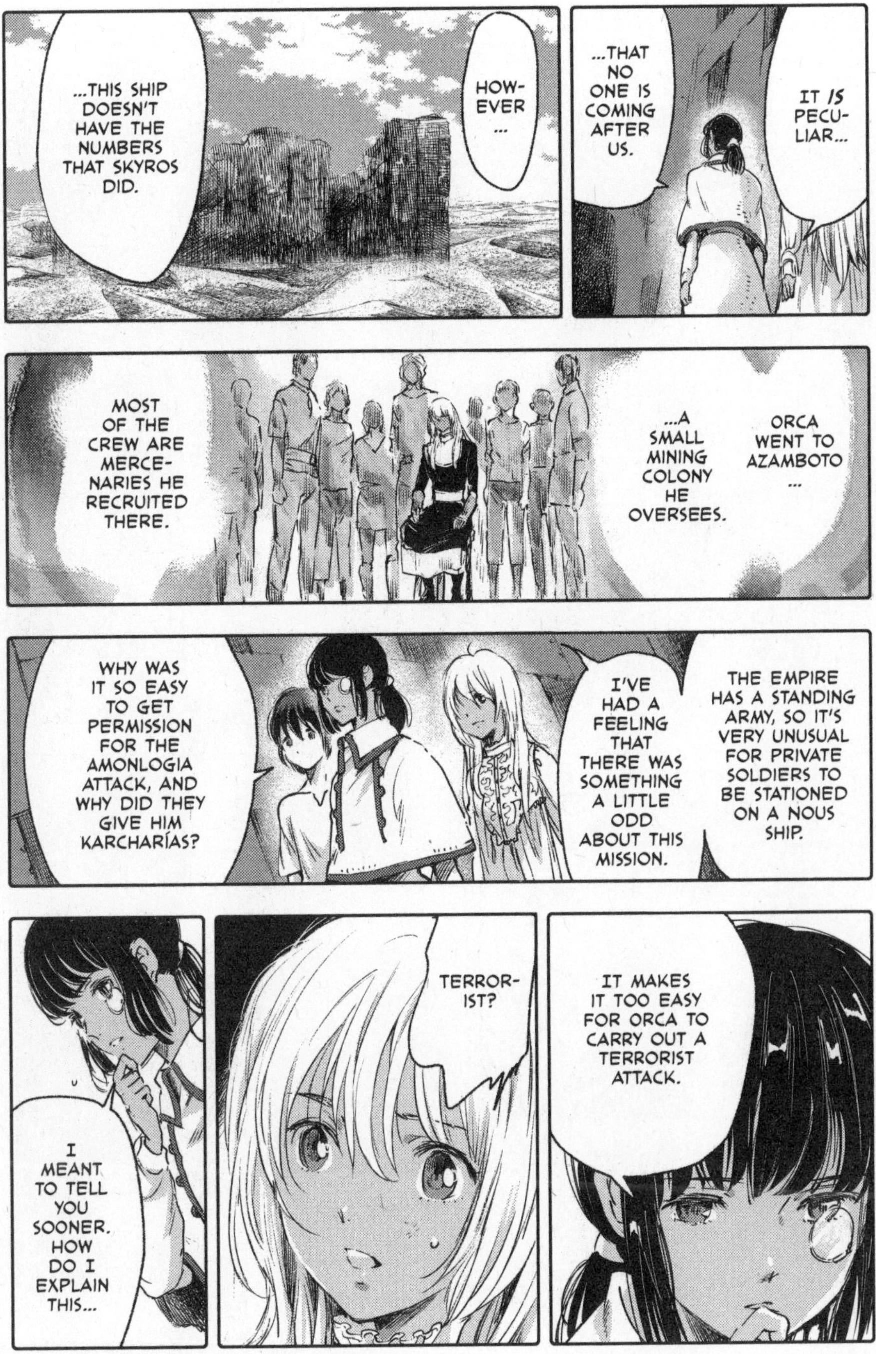
IT *IS* PECULIAR...
...THAT NO ONE IS COMING AFTER US.
HOWEVER...
...THIS SHIP DOESN'T HAVE THE NUMBERS THAT SKYROS DID.
ORCA WENT TO AZAMBOTO...
...A SMALL MINING COLONY HE OVERSEES.
MOST OF THE CREW ARE MERCENARIES HE RECRUITED THERE.
THE EMPIRE HAS A STANDING ARMY, SO IT'S VERY UNUSUAL FOR PRIVATE SOLDIERS TO BE STATIONED ON A NOUS SHIP.
I'VE HAD A FEELING THAT THERE WAS SOMETHING A LITTLE ODD ABOUT THIS MISSION.
WHY WAS IT SO EASY TO GET PERMISSION FOR THE AMONLOGIA ATTACK, AND WHY DID THEY GIVE HIM KARCHARÍAS?
IT MAKES IT TOO EASY FOR ORCA TO CARRY OUT A TERRORIST ATTACK.
TERRORIST?
I MEANT TO TELL YOU SOONER. HOW DO I EXPLAIN THIS...

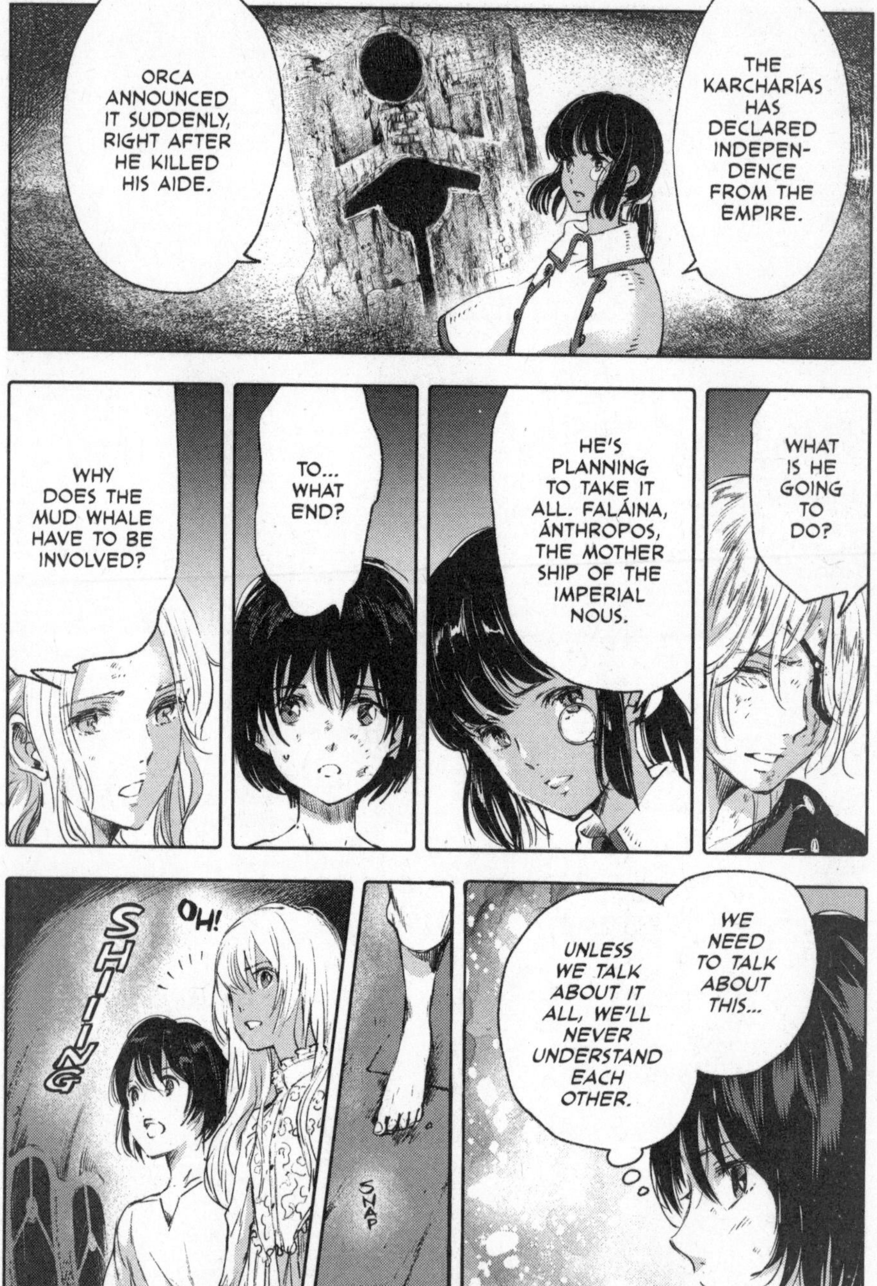
THE KARCHARÍAS HAS DECLARED INDEPEN-DENCE FROM THE EMPIRE.
ORCA ANNOUNCED IT SUDDENLY, RIGHT AFTER HE KILLED HIS AIDE.
WHAT IS HE GOING TO DO?
HE'S PLANNING TO TAKE IT ALL. FALÁINA, ÁNTHROPOS, THE MOTHER SHIP OF THE IMPERIAL NOUS.
TO... WHAT END?
WHY DOES THE MUD WHALE HAVE TO BE INVOLVED?
WE NEED TO TALK ABOUT THIS...
UNLESS WE TALK ABOUT IT ALL, WE'LL NEVER UNDERSTAND EACH OTHER.
SNAP
OH!
SHIIING

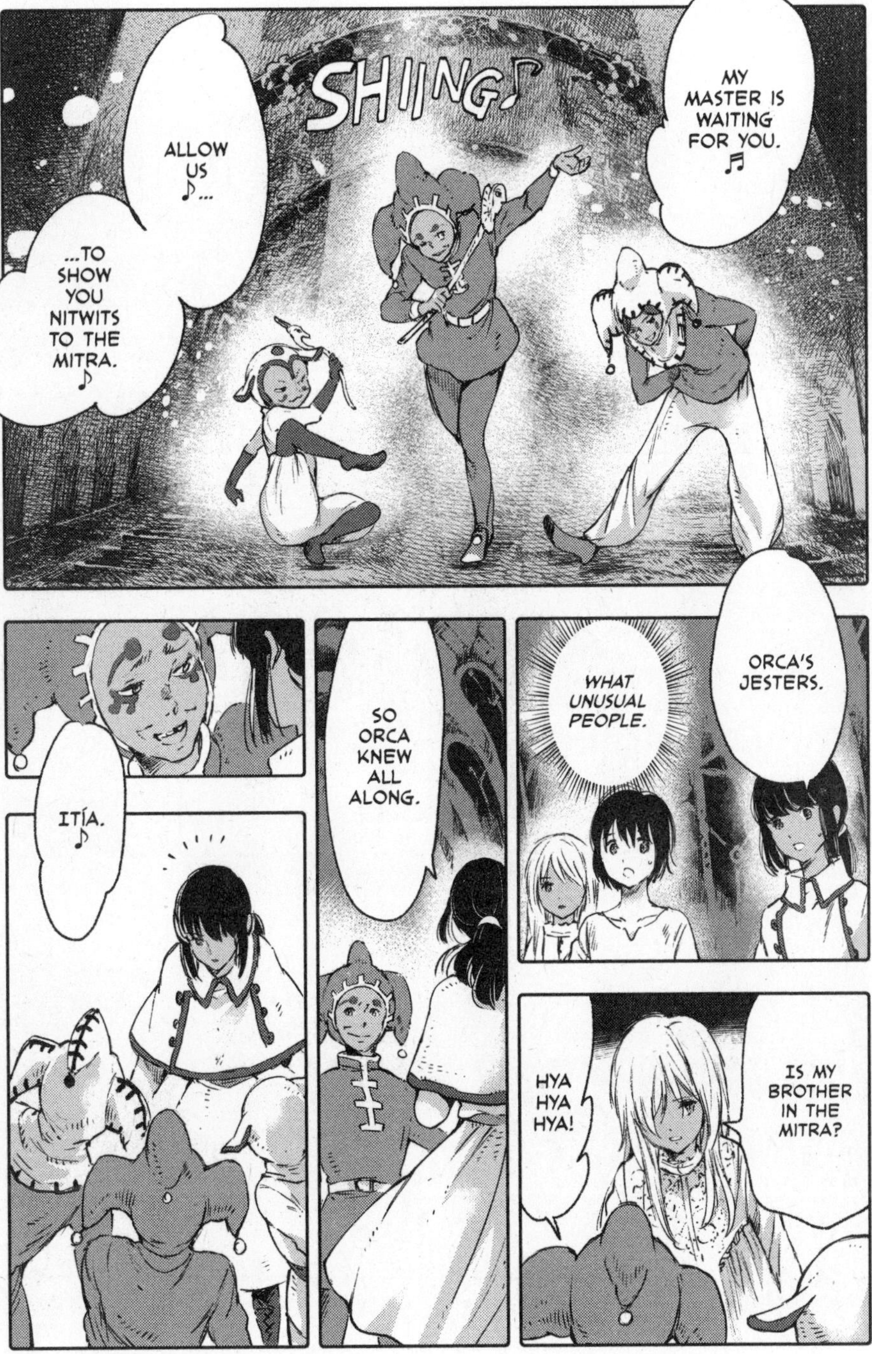
MY MASTER IS WAITING FOR YOU. ♬
SHIING♪
ALLOW US ♪...
...TO SHOW YOU NITWITS TO THE MITRA. ♪
ORCA'S JESTERS.
WHAT UNUSUAL PEOPLE.
IS MY BROTHER IN THE MITRA?
HYA HYA HYA!
SO ORCA KNEW ALL ALONG.
ITÍA. ♪

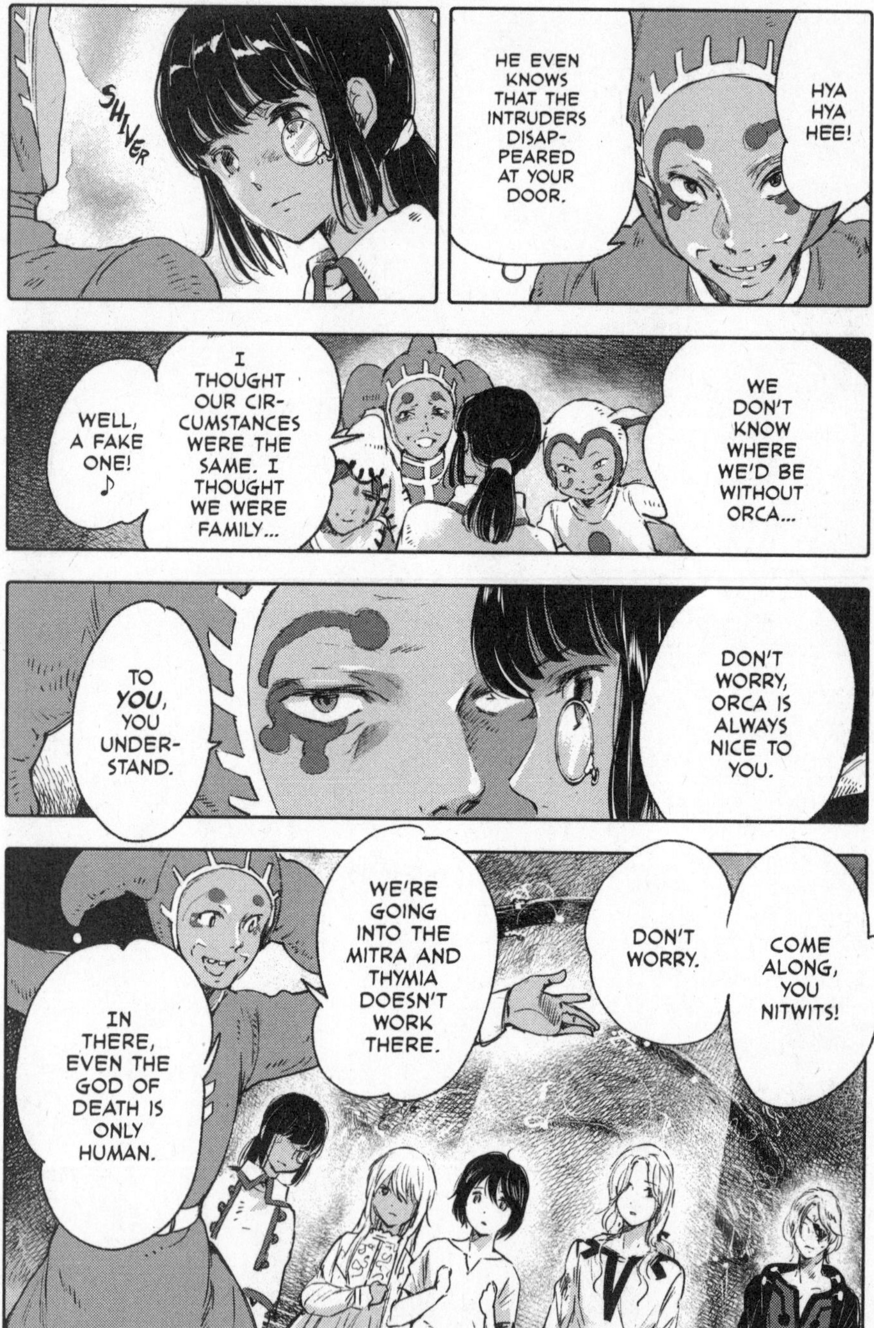
HYA HYA HEE!
HE EVEN KNOWS THAT THE INTRUDERS DISAP-PEARED AT YOUR DOOR.
SHIVER
WE DON'T KNOW WHERE WE'D BE WITHOUT ORCA...
I THOUGHT OUR CIR-CUMSTANCES WERE THE SAME. I THOUGHT WE WERE FAMILY...
WELL, A FAKE ONE! ♪
DON'T WORRY, ORCA IS ALWAYS NICE TO YOU.
TO *YOU*, YOU UNDER-STAND.
COME ALONG, YOU NITWITS!
DON'T WORRY.
WE'RE GOING INTO THE MITRA AND THYMIA DOESN'T WORK THERE.
IN THERE, EVEN THE GOD OF DEATH IS ONLY HUMAN.

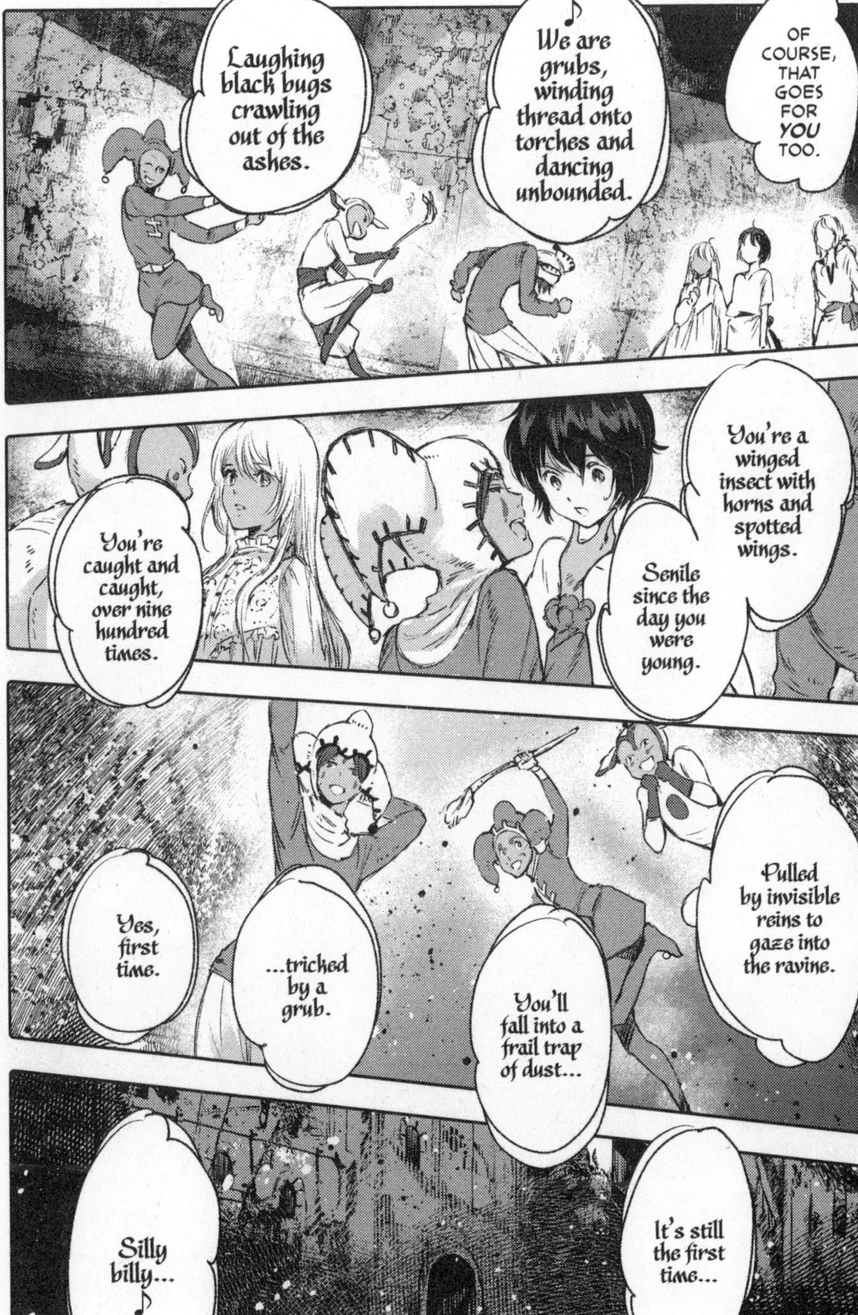
OF COURSE, THAT GOES FOR *YOU* TOO.
♪ We are grubs, winding thread onto torches and dancing unbounded.
Laughing black bugs crawling out of the ashes.
You're a winged insect with horns and spotted wings.
Senile since the day you were young.
You're caught and caught, over nine hundred times.
Pulled by invisible reins to gaze into the ravine.
You'll fall into a frail trap of dust...
...tricked by a grub.
Yes, first time.
It's still the first time...
Silly billy... ♪

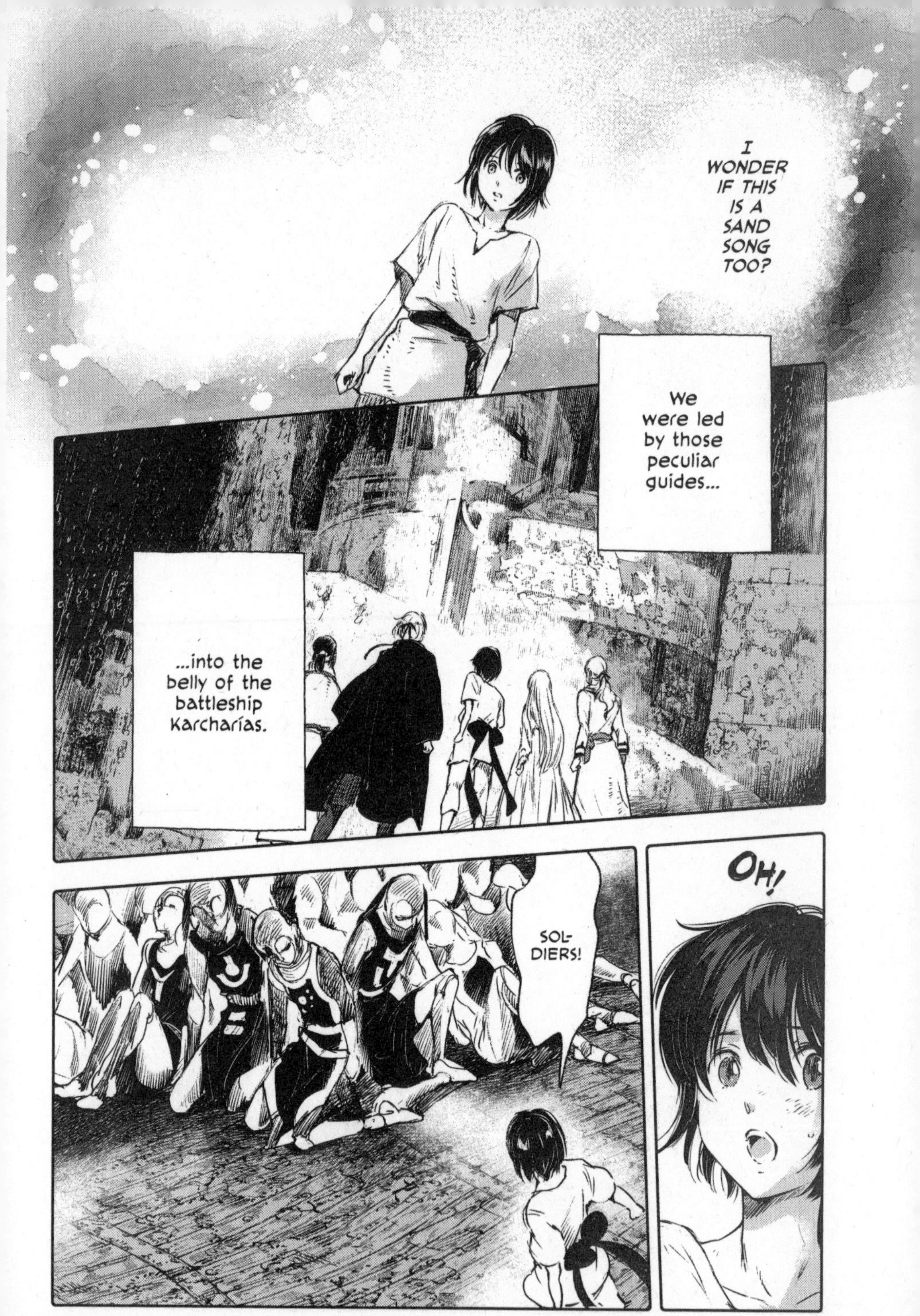
I WONDER IF THIS IS A SAND SONG TOO?
We were led by those peculiar guides...
...into the belly of the battleship Karcharias.
OH!
SOL-DIERS!

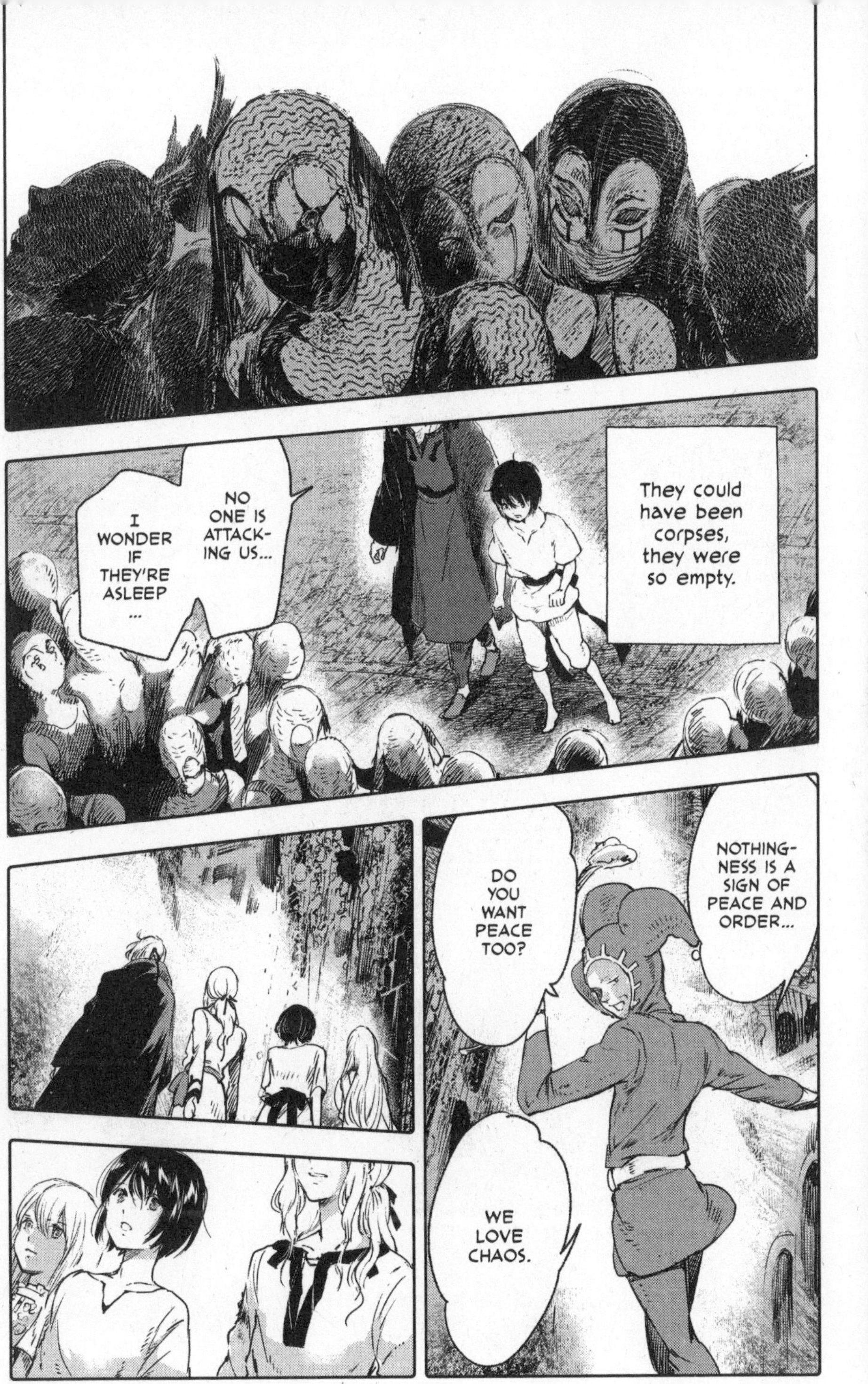
They could have been corpses, they were so empty.
NO ONE IS ATTACKING US...
I WONDER IF THEY'RE ASLEEP ...
NOTHINGNESS IS A SIGN OF PEACE AND ORDER...
DO YOU WANT PEACE TOO?
WE LOVE CHAOS.

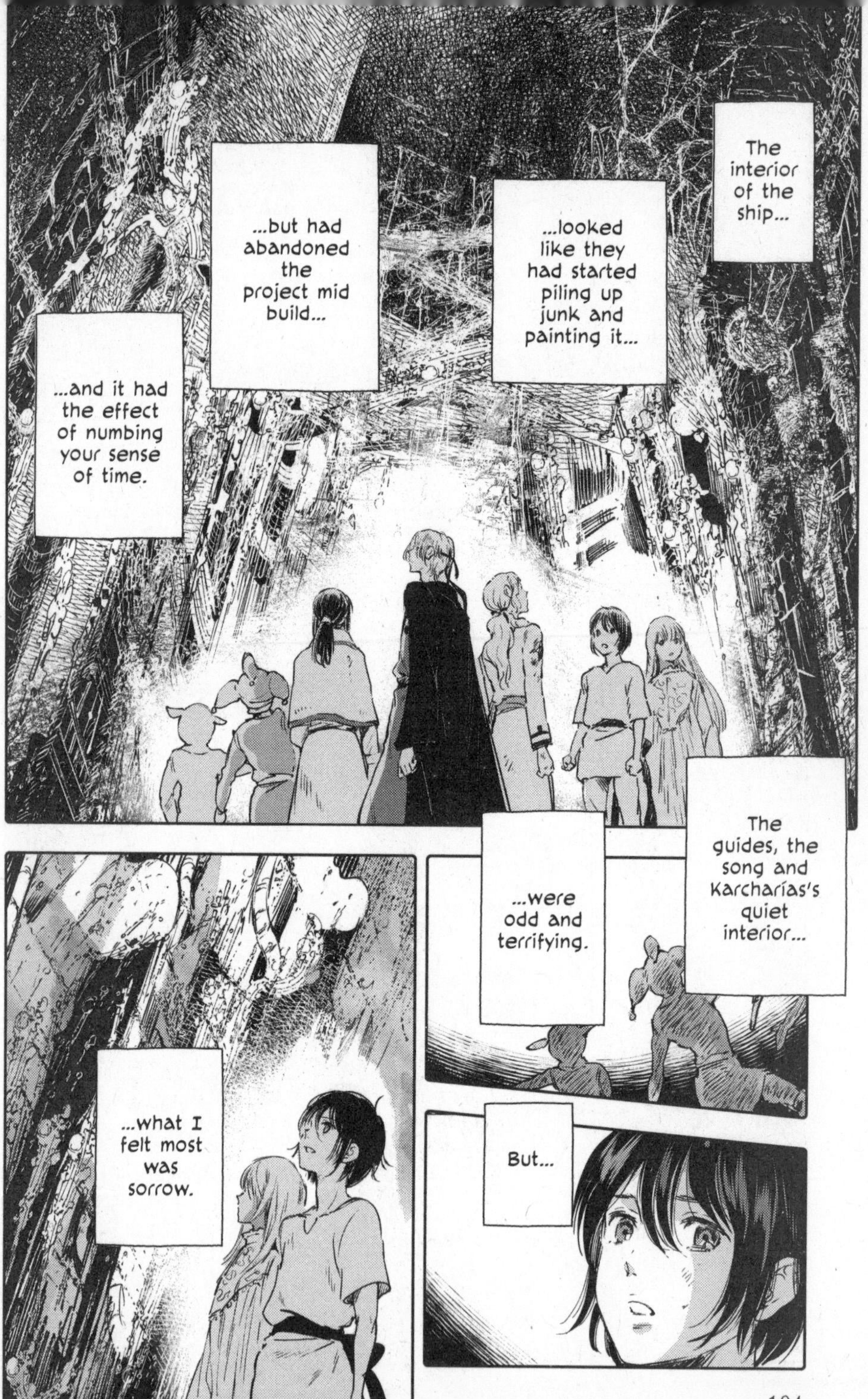
The interior of the ship...
...looked like they had started piling up junk and painting it...
...but had abandoned the project mid build...
...and it had the effect of numbing your sense of time.
The guides, the song and Karcharias's quiet interior...
...were odd and terrifying.
But...
...what I felt most was sorrow.

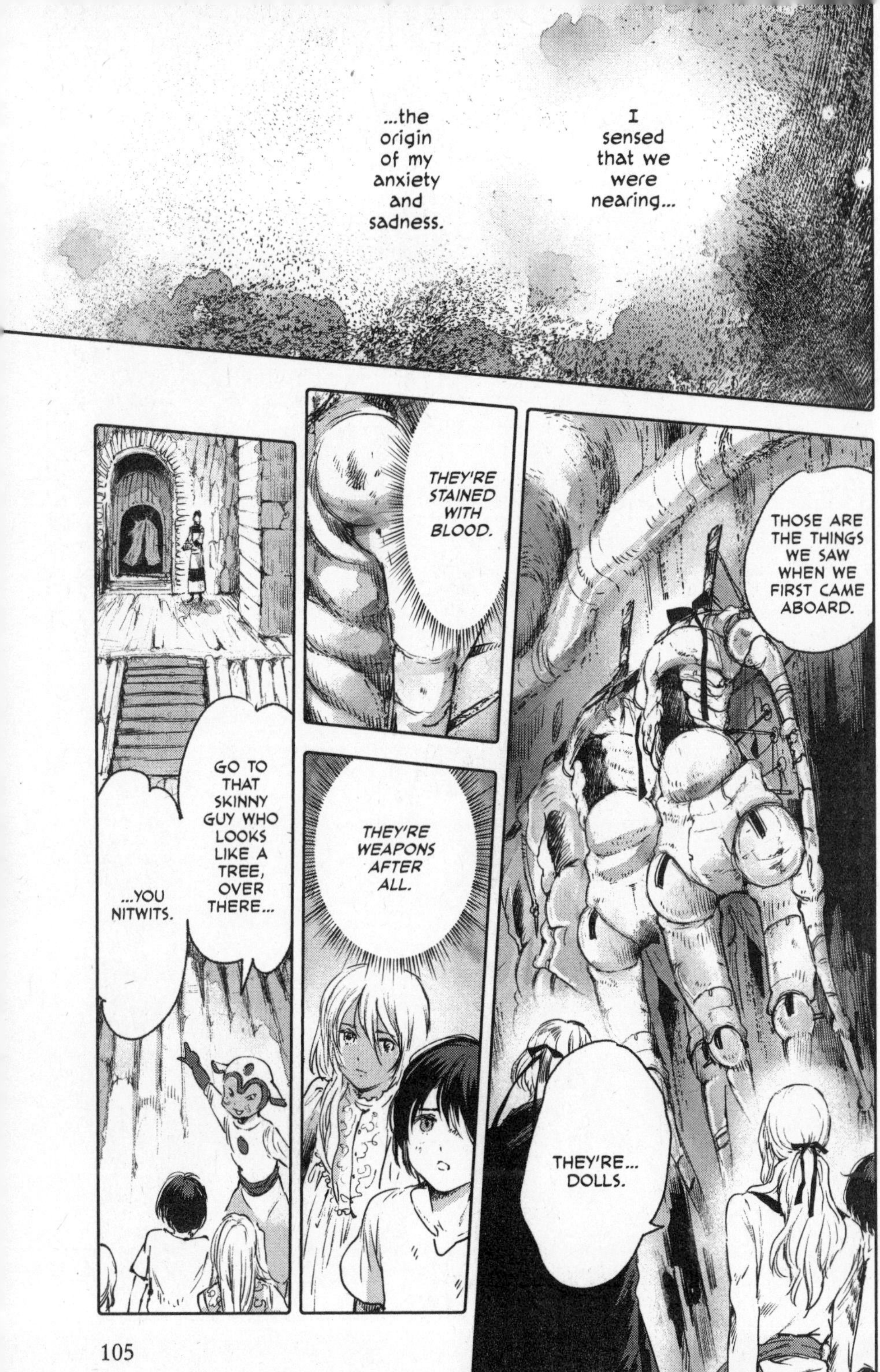
I sensed that we were nearing...
...the origin of my anxiety and sadness.
THOSE ARE THE THINGS WE SAW WHEN WE FIRST CAME ABOARD.
THEY'RE... DOLLS.
THEY'RE STAINED WITH BLOOD.
THEY'RE WEAPONS AFTER ALL.
GO TO THAT SKINNY GUY WHO LOOKS LIKE A TREE, OVER THERE...
...YOU NITWITS.

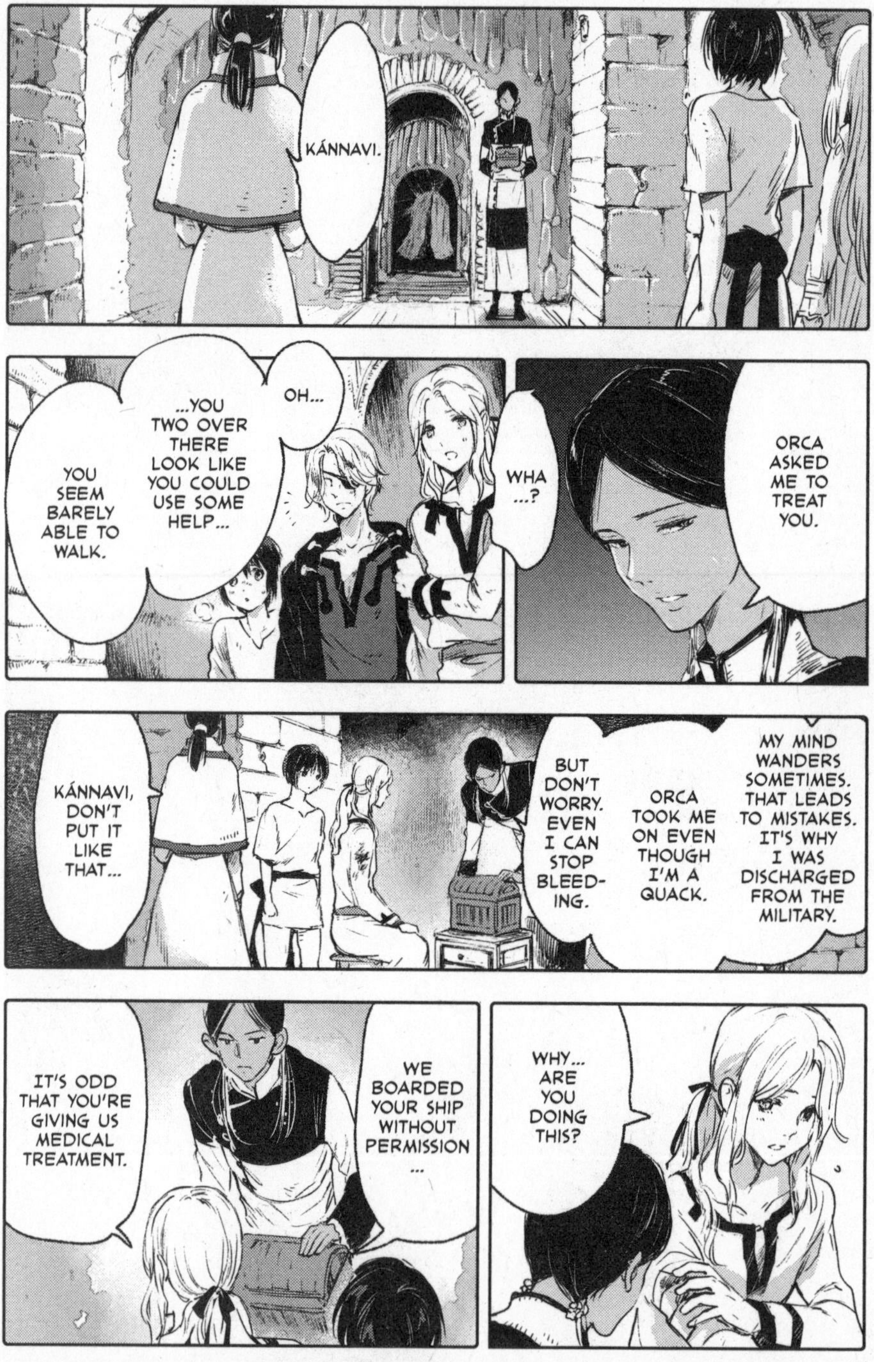
KÁNNAVI.
ORCA ASKED ME TO TREAT YOU.
WHA...?
OH...
...YOU TWO OVER THERE LOOK LIKE YOU COULD USE SOME HELP...
YOU SEEM BARELY ABLE TO WALK.
MY MIND WANDERS SOMETIMES. THAT LEADS TO MISTAKES. IT'S WHY I WAS DISCHARGED FROM THE MILITARY.
ORCA TOOK ME ON EVEN THOUGH I'M A QUACK.
BUT DON'T WORRY. EVEN I CAN STOP BLEED-ING.
KÁNNAVI, DON'T PUT IT LIKE THAT...
WHY... ARE YOU DOING THIS?
WE BOARDED YOUR SHIP WITHOUT PERMISSION...
IT'S ODD THAT YOU'RE GIVING US MEDICAL TREATMENT.

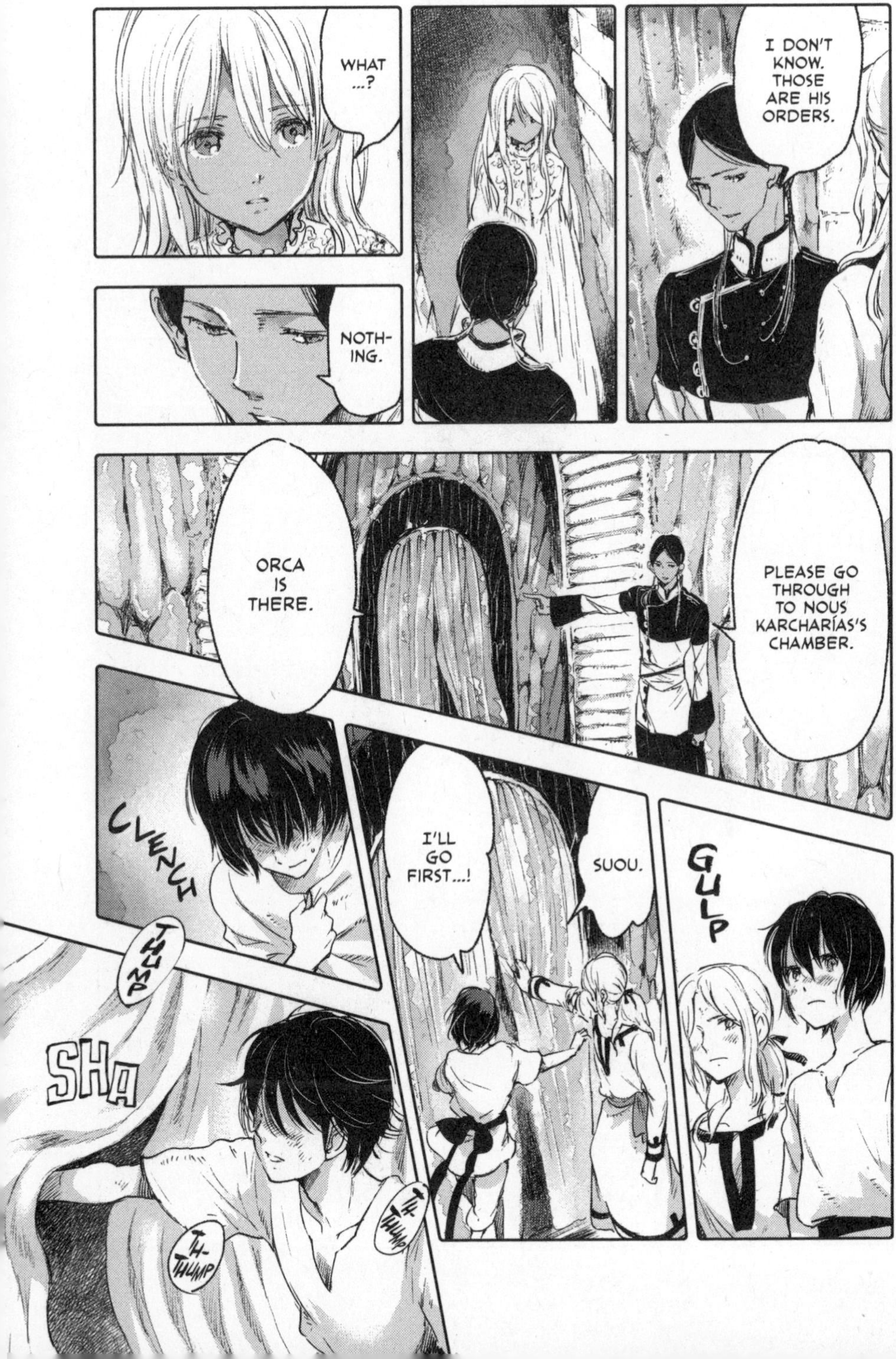
I DON'T KNOW. THOSE ARE HIS ORDERS.
WHAT ...?
NOTH-ING.
PLEASE GO THROUGH TO NOUS KARCHARÍAS'S CHAMBER.
ORCA IS THERE.
GULP
SUOU.
I'LL GO FIRST...!
CLENCH
THUMP
SHA
TH-THUMP
TH-THUMP

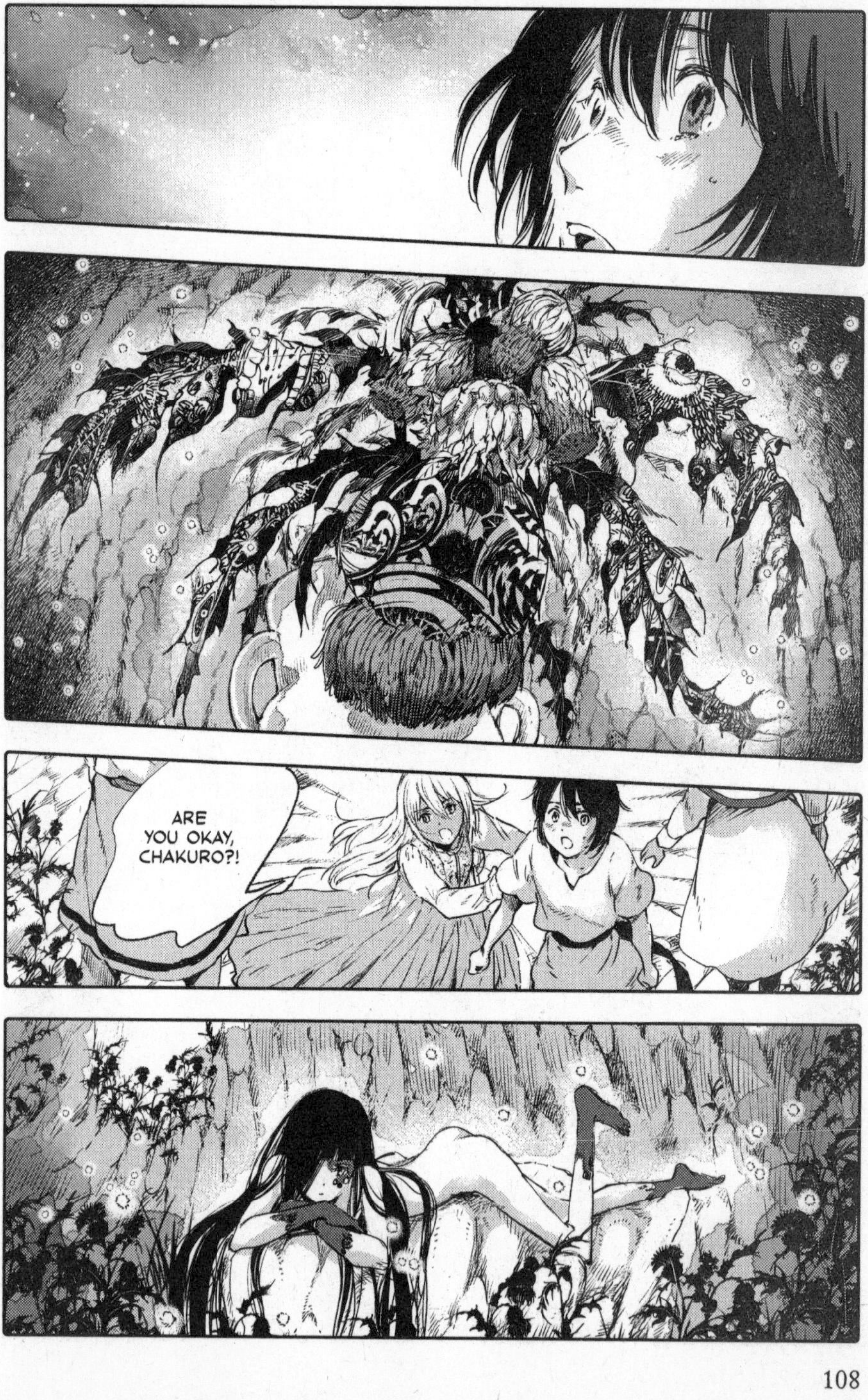
ARE YOU OKAY, CHAKURO?!

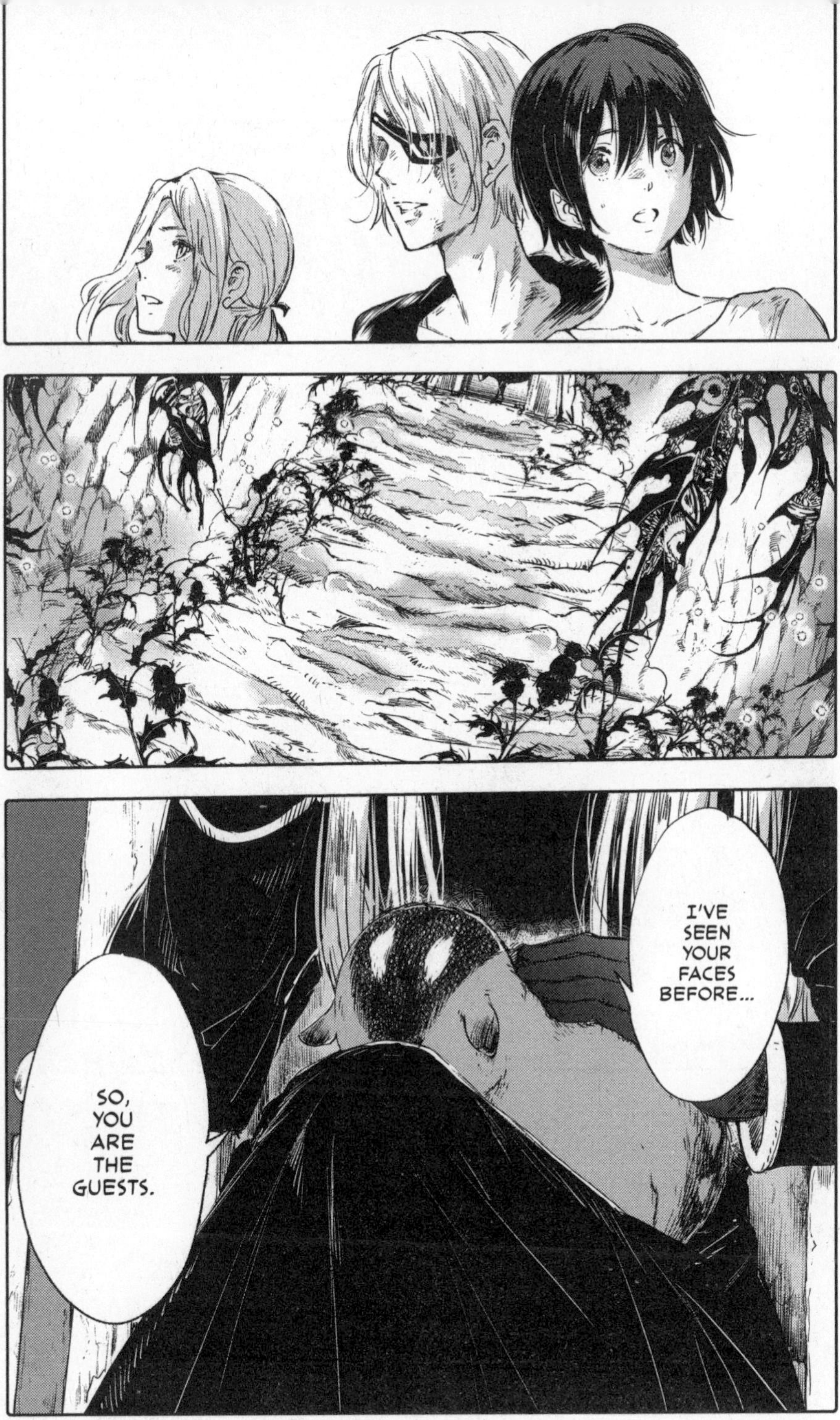
I'VE SEEN YOUR FACES BEFORE...
SO, YOU ARE THE GUESTS.

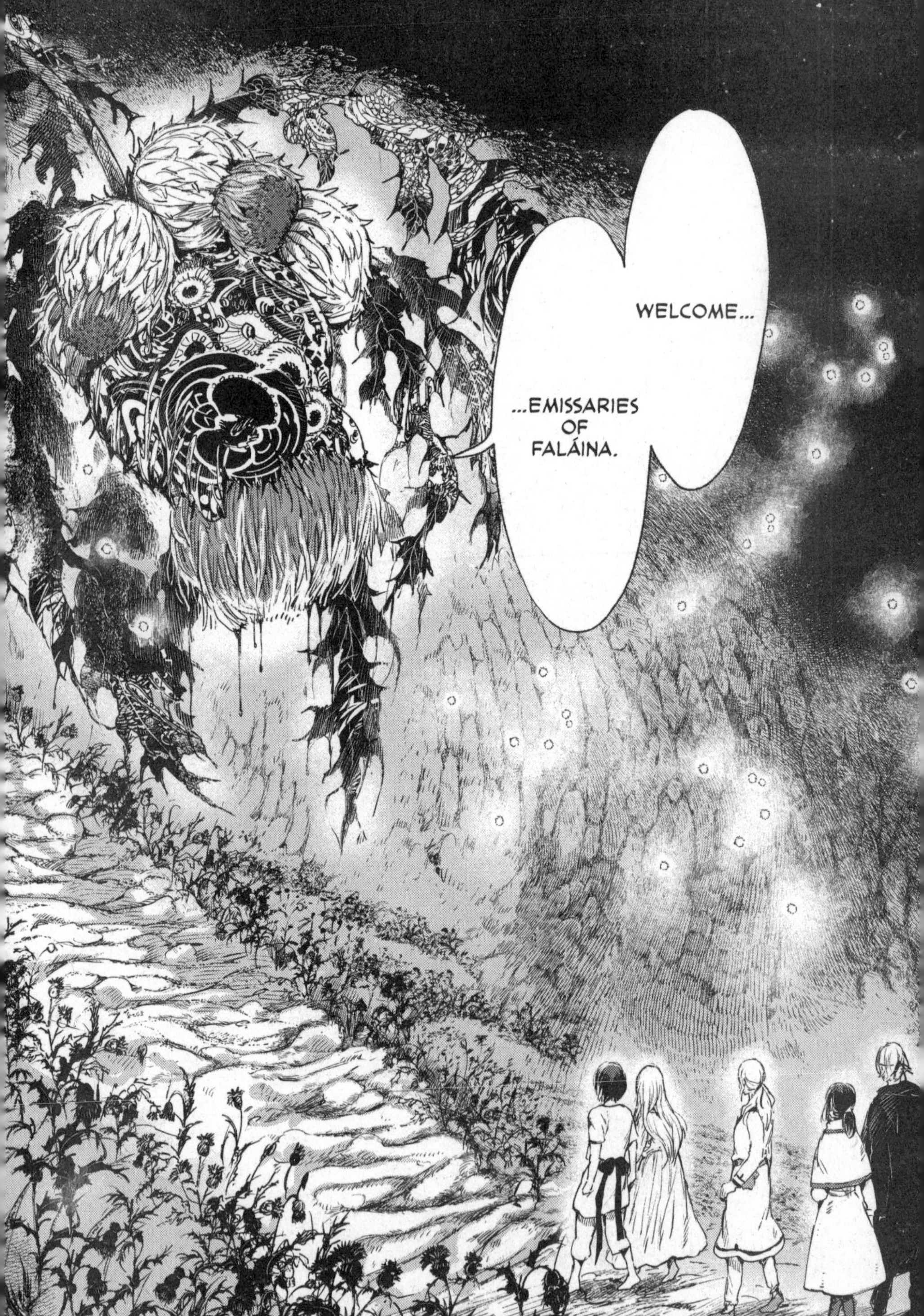
WELCOME...
...EMISSARIES OF FALÁINA.

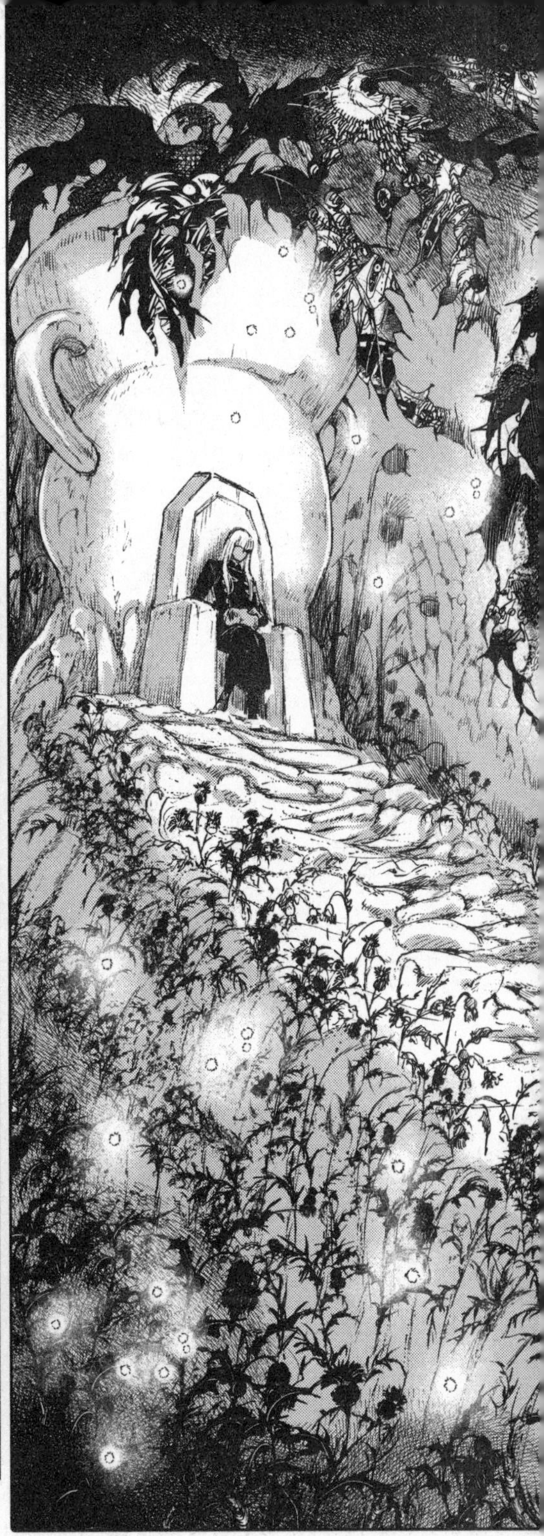

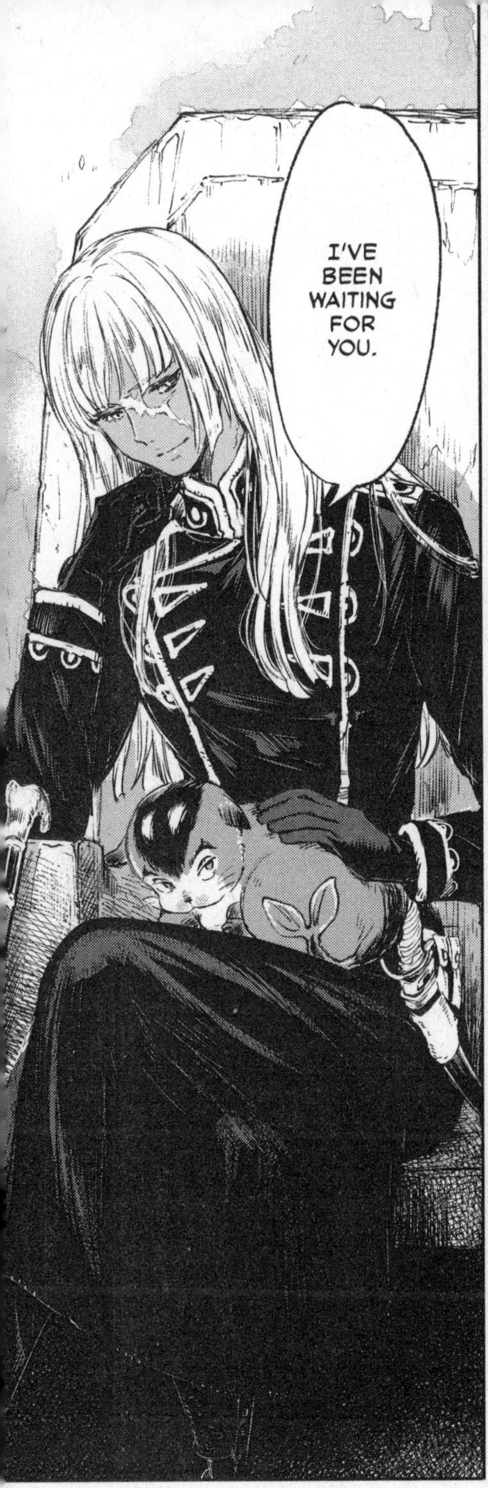
I'VE BEEN WAITING FOR YOU.

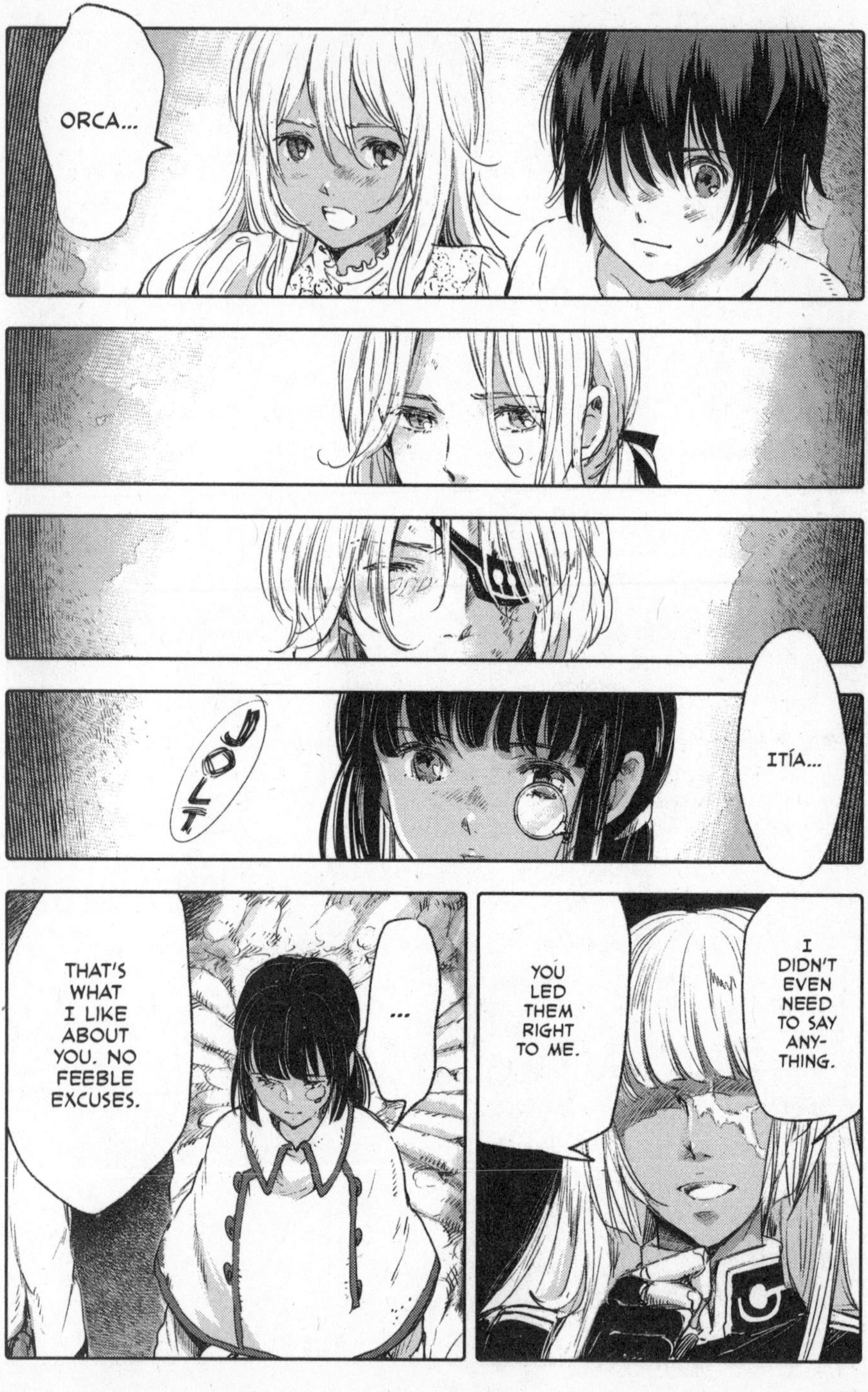
ORCA...
ITÍA...
JOLT
I DIDN'T EVEN NEED TO SAY ANY-THING.
YOU LED THEM RIGHT TO ME.
...
THAT'S WHAT I LIKE ABOUT YOU. NO FEEBLE EXCUSES.

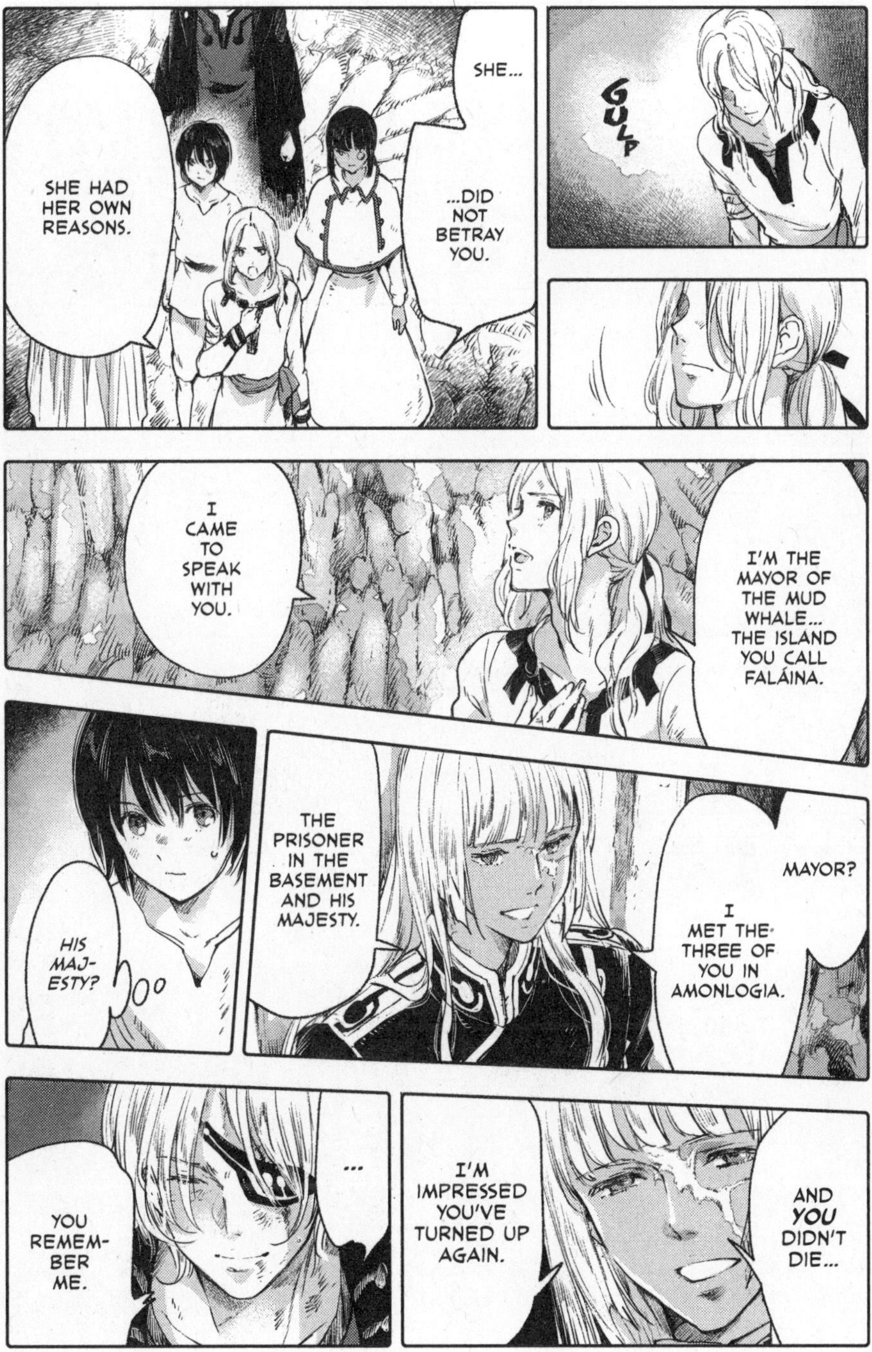
GULP
SHE...
...DID NOT BETRAY YOU.
SHE HAD HER OWN REASONS.
I'M THE MAYOR OF THE MUD WHALE... THE ISLAND YOU CALL FALÁINA.
I CAME TO SPEAK WITH YOU.
MAYOR?
I MET THE THREE OF YOU IN AMONLOGIA.
THE PRISONER IN THE BASEMENT AND HIS MAJESTY.
HIS MAJESTY?
AND *YOU* DIDN'T DIE...
I'M IMPRESSED YOU'VE TURNED UP AGAIN.
...
YOU REMEMBER ME.

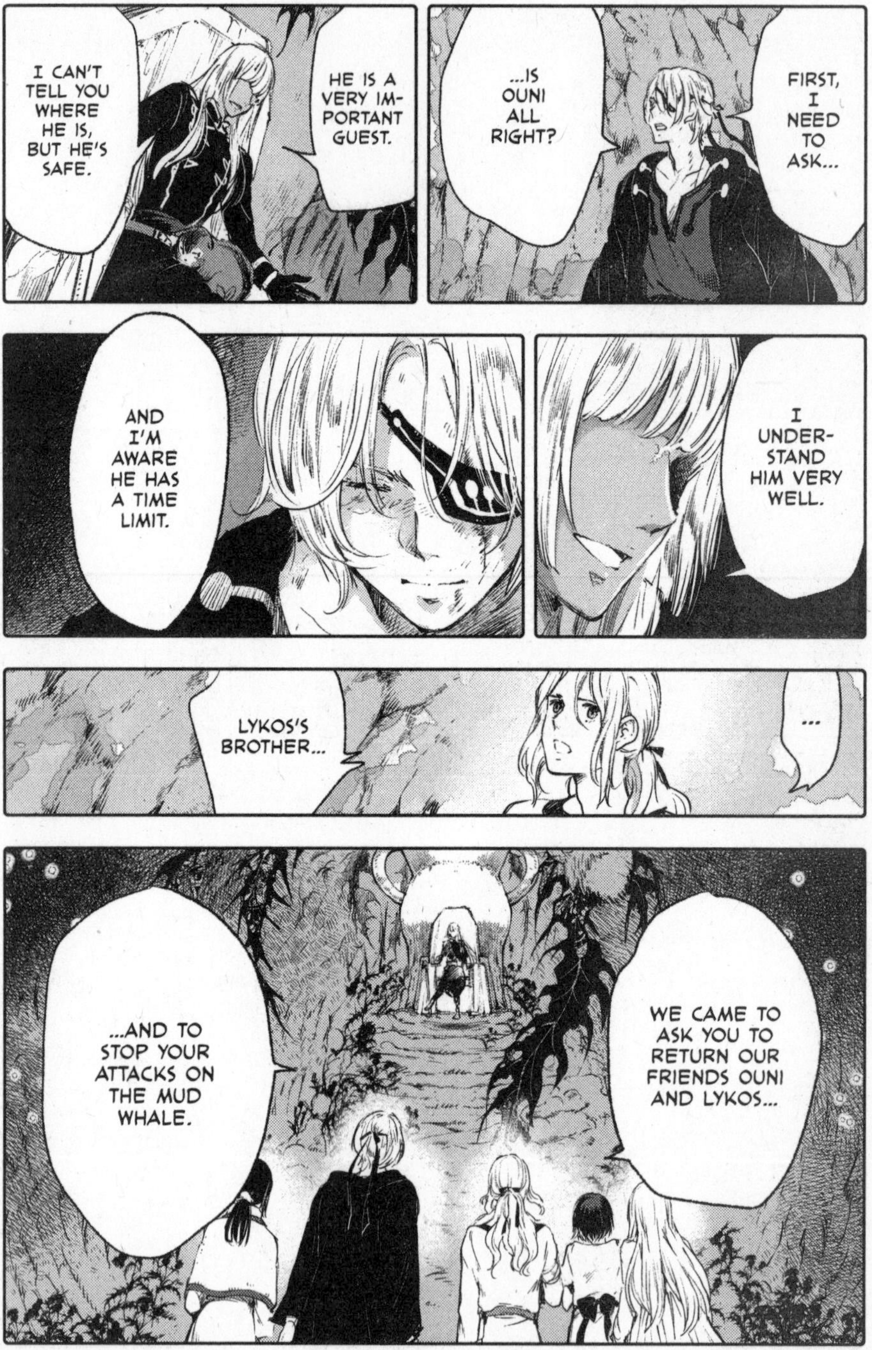

FIRST, I NEED TO ASK...
...IS OUNI ALL RIGHT?
HE IS A VERY IMPORTANT GUEST.
I CAN'T TELL YOU WHERE HE IS, BUT HE'S SAFE.
I UNDERSTAND HIM VERY WELL.
AND I'M AWARE HE HAS A TIME LIMIT.
...
LYKOS'S BROTHER...
WE CAME TO ASK YOU TO RETURN OUR FRIENDS OUNI AND LYKOS...
...AND TO STOP YOUR ATTACKS ON THE MUD WHALE.

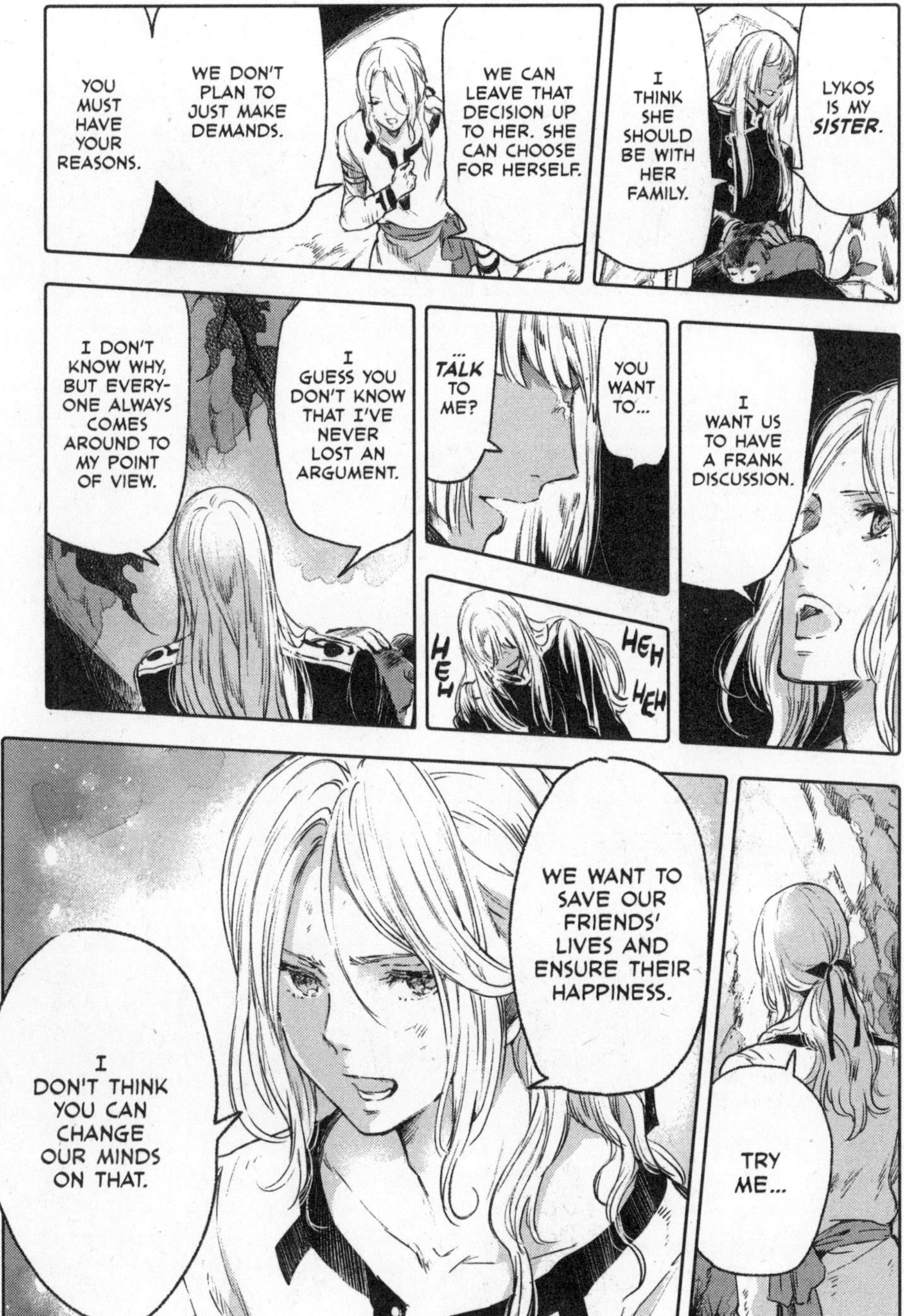
LYKOS IS MY *SISTER*.
I THINK SHE SHOULD BE WITH HER FAMILY.
WE CAN LEAVE THAT DECISION UP TO HER. SHE CAN CHOOSE FOR HERSELF.
WE DON'T PLAN TO JUST MAKE DEMANDS.
YOU MUST HAVE YOUR REASONS.
I WANT US TO HAVE A FRANK DISCUSSION.
YOU WANT TO...
...*TALK* TO ME?
HEH HEH
HEH HEH
I GUESS YOU DON'T KNOW THAT I'VE NEVER LOST AN ARGUMENT.
I DON'T KNOW WHY, BUT EVERY-ONE ALWAYS COMES AROUND TO MY POINT OF VIEW.
TRY ME...
WE WANT TO SAVE OUR FRIENDS' LIVES AND ENSURE THEIR HAPPINESS.
I DON'T THINK YOU CAN CHANGE OUR MINDS ON THAT.

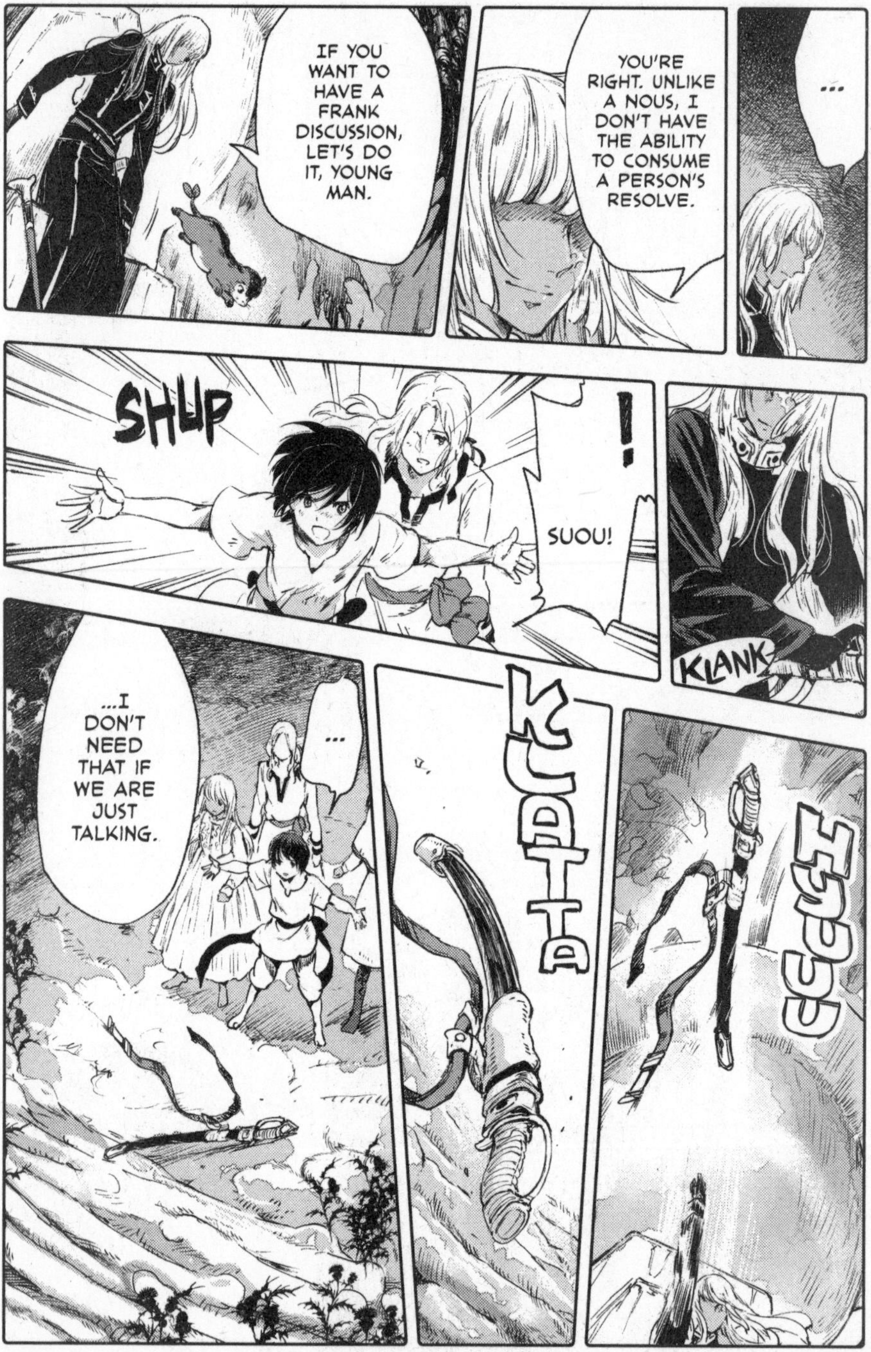
...
YOU'RE RIGHT. UNLIKE A NOUS, I DON'T HAVE THE ABILITY TO CONSUME A PERSON'S RESOLVE.
IF YOU WANT TO HAVE A FRANK DISCUSSION, LET'S DO IT, YOUNG MAN.
KLANK
!
SUOU!
SHUP
UUUGH
KLATTA
...
...I DON'T NEED THAT IF WE ARE JUST TALKING.

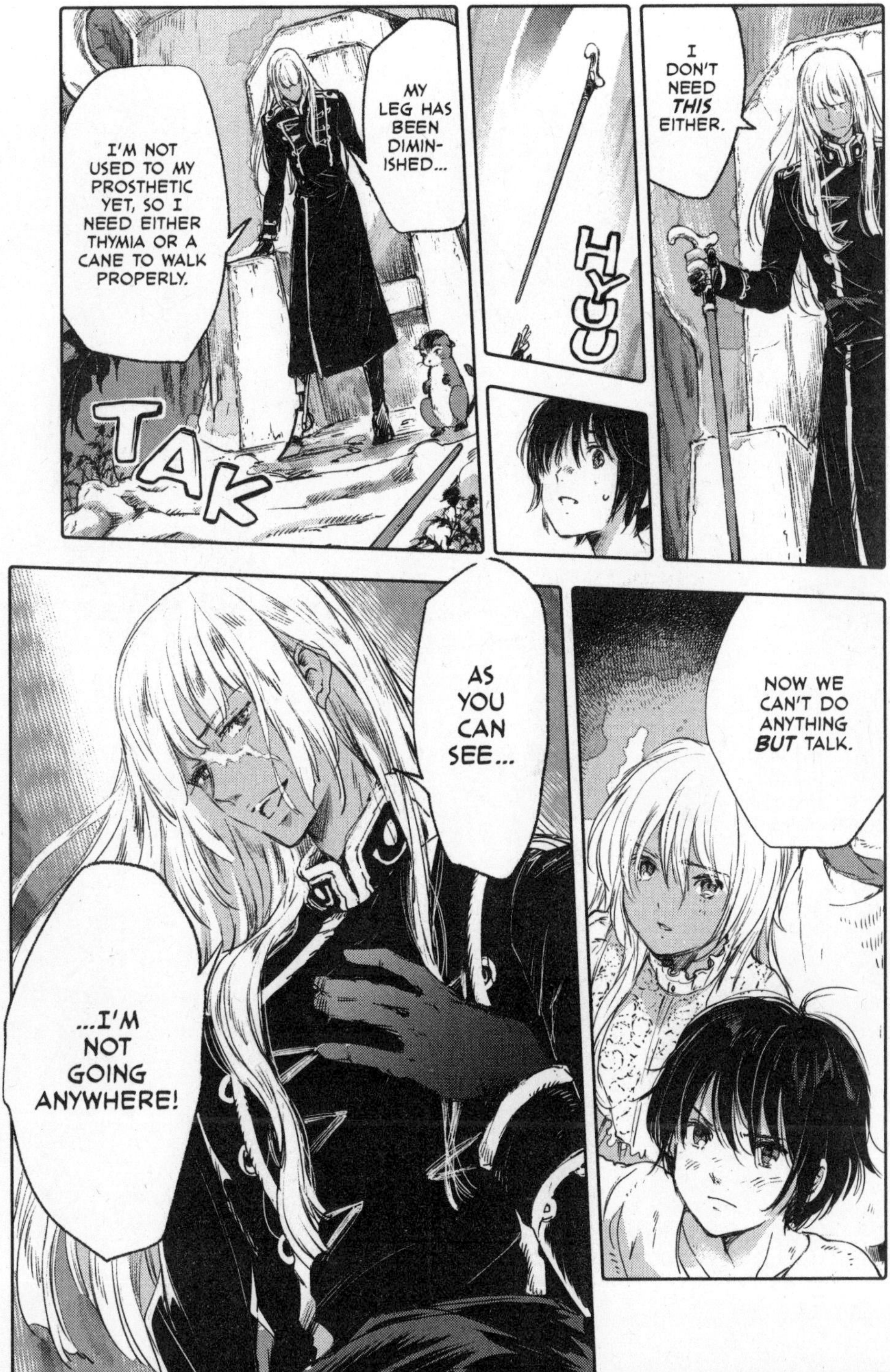
I DON'T NEED *THIS* EITHER.
HYUU
MY LEG HAS BEEN DIMIN-ISHED...
I'M NOT USED TO MY PROSTHETIC YET, SO I NEED EITHER THYMIA OR A CANE TO WALK PROPERLY.
TAK
NOW WE CAN'T DO ANYTHING *BUT* TALK.
AS YOU CAN SEE...
...I'M NOT GOING ANYWHERE!

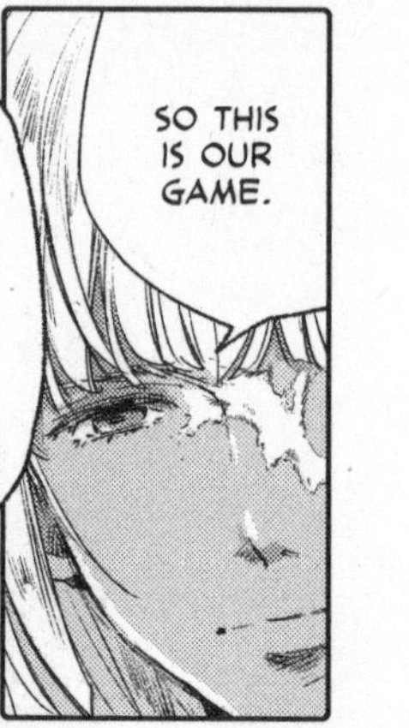
SO THIS IS OUR GAME.

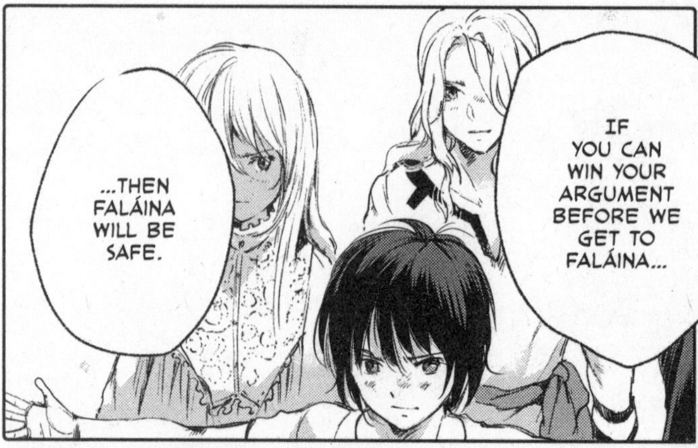
IF YOU CAN WIN YOUR ARGUMENT BEFORE WE GET TO FALÁINA...
...THEN FALÁINA WILL BE SAFE.

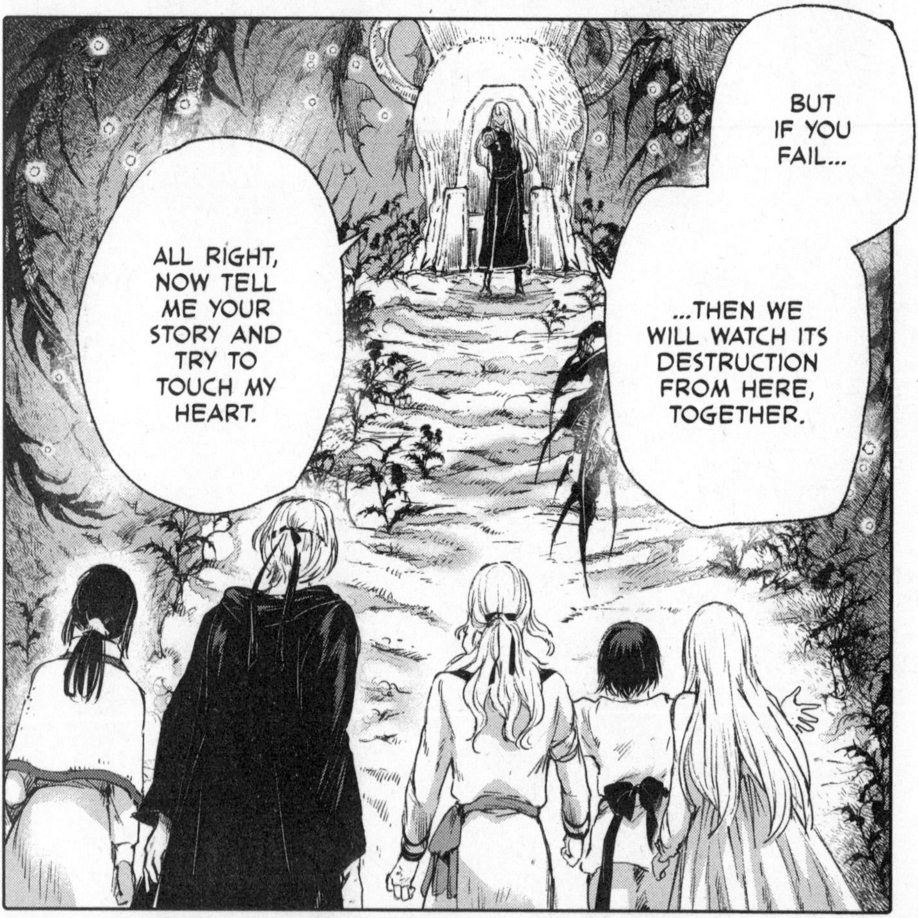
BUT IF YOU FAIL...
...THEN WE WILL WATCH ITS DESTRUCTION FROM HERE, TOGETHER.
ALL RIGHT, NOW TELL ME YOUR STORY AND TRY TO TOUCH MY HEART.

The Guide -The End-

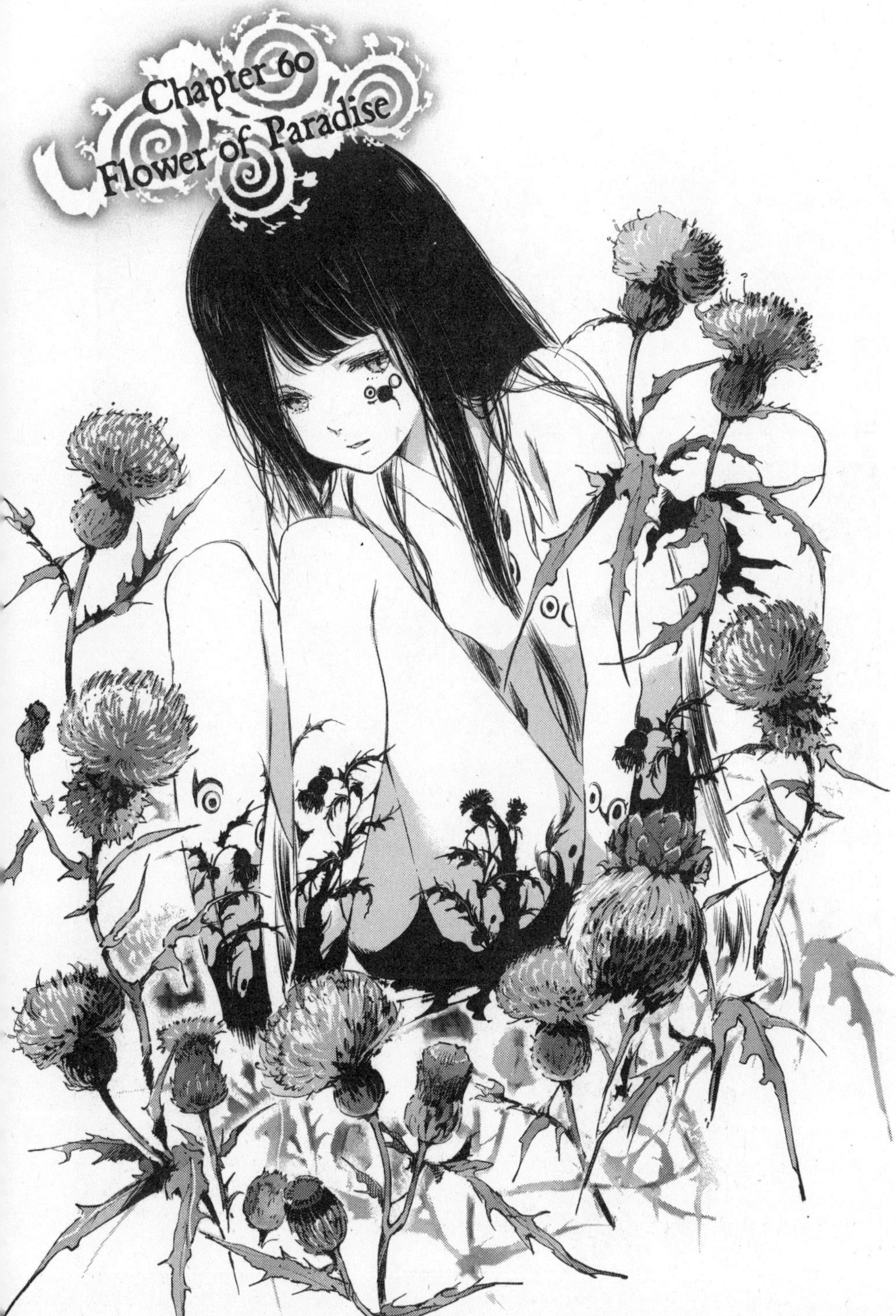
Chapter 60
Flower of Paradise

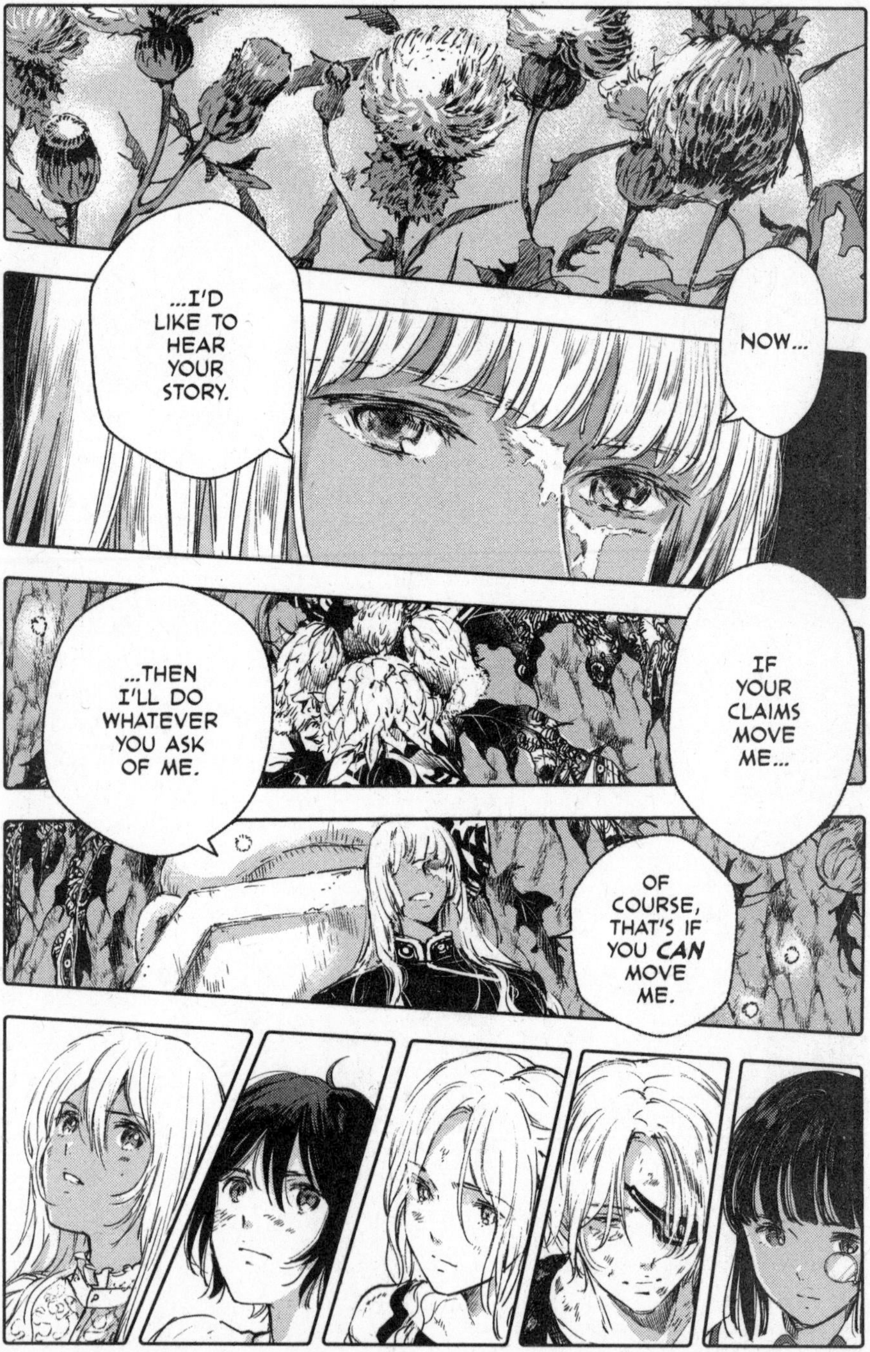
NOW...
...I'D LIKE TO HEAR YOUR STORY.
IF YOUR CLAIMS MOVE ME...
...THEN I'LL DO WHATEVER YOU ASK OF ME.
OF COURSE, THAT'S IF YOU *CAN* MOVE ME.

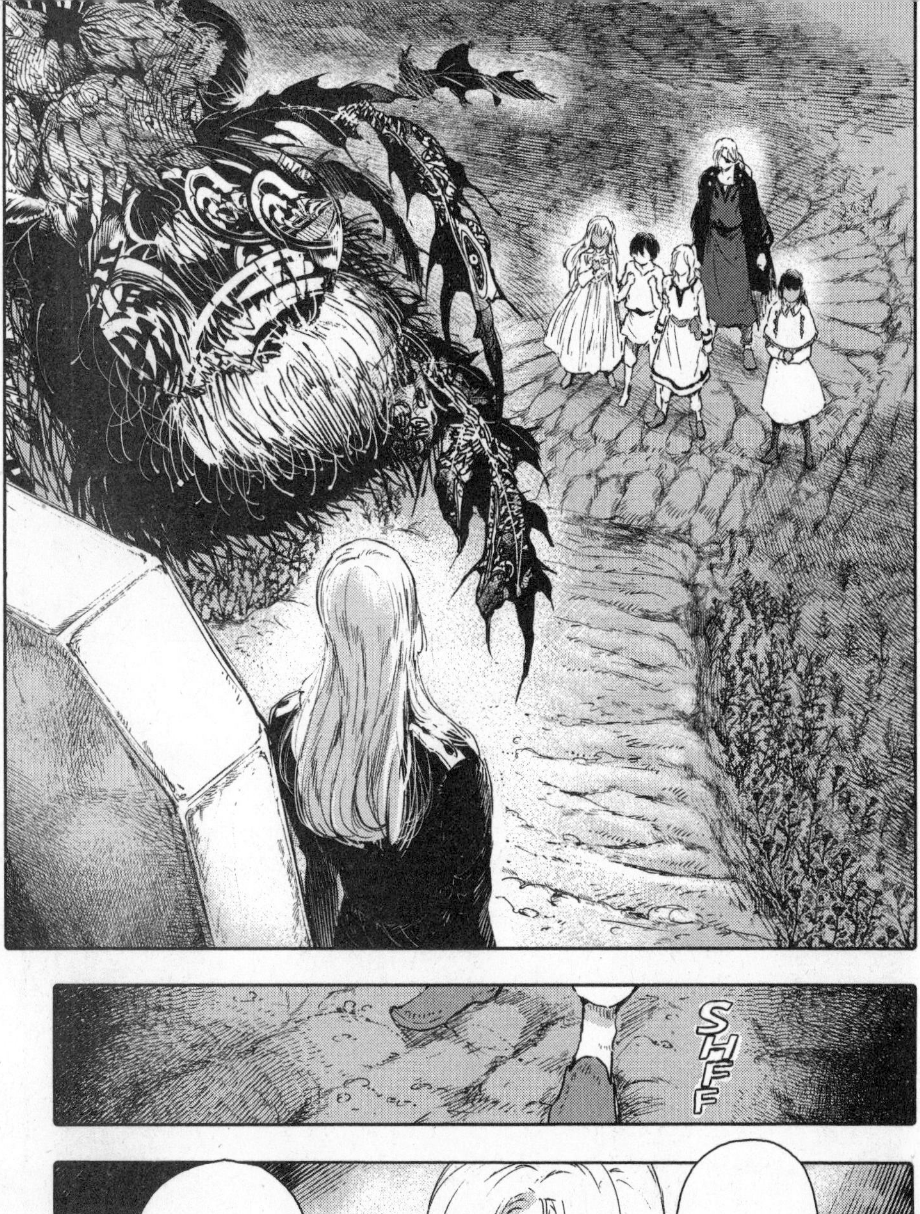
SHFF
UNFORTU-NATELY...
...WE DON'T HAVE A LOT TO SAY.

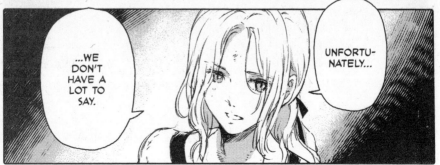

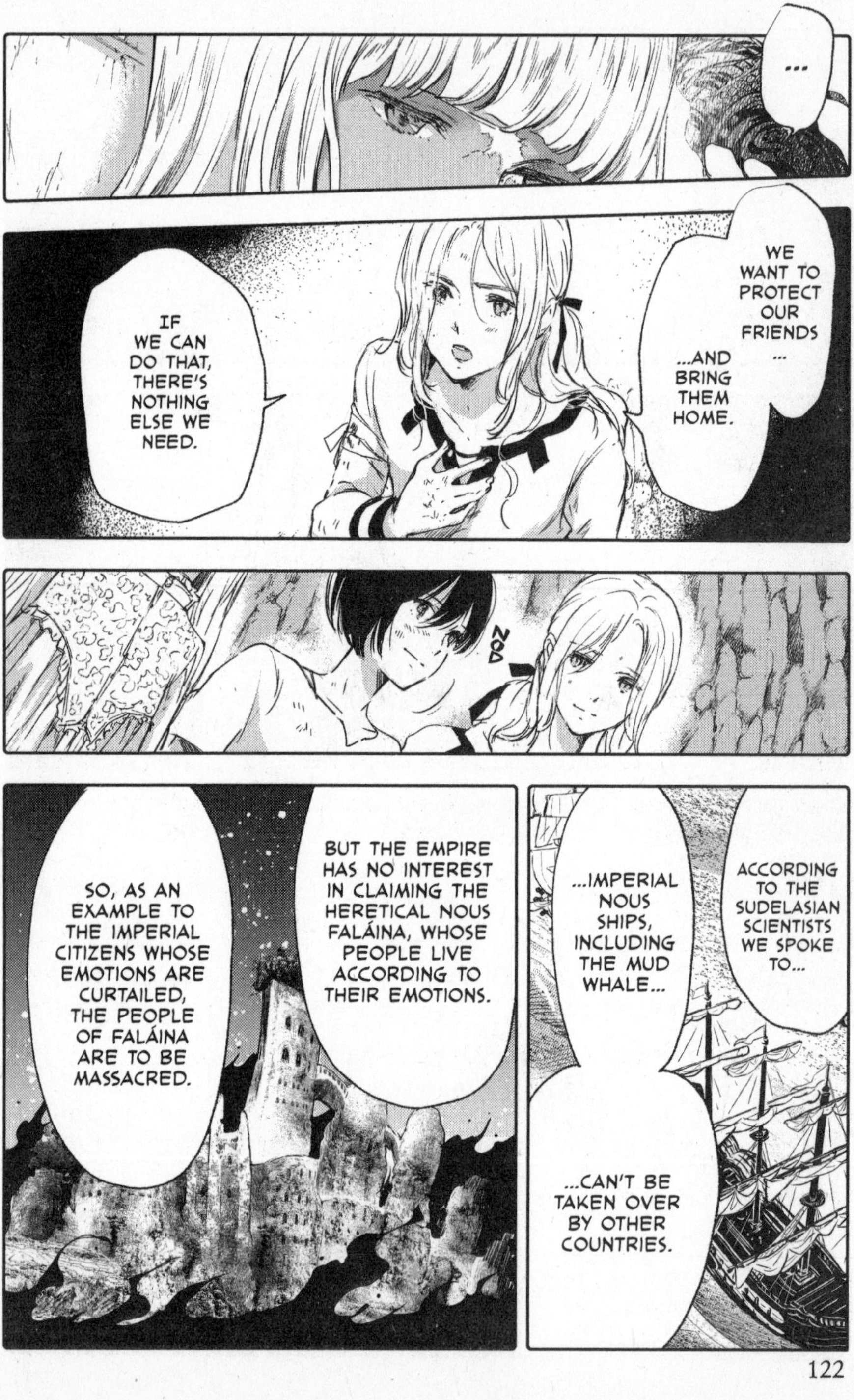
...
WE WANT TO PROTECT OUR FRIENDS...
...AND BRING THEM HOME.
IF WE CAN DO THAT, THERE'S NOTHING ELSE WE NEED.
NOD
ACCORDING TO THE SUDELASIAN SCIENTISTS WE SPOKE TO...
...IMPERIAL NOUS SHIPS, INCLUDING THE MUD WHALE...
...CAN'T BE TAKEN OVER BY OTHER COUNTRIES.
BUT THE EMPIRE HAS NO INTEREST IN CLAIMING THE HERETICAL NOUS FALÁINA, WHOSE PEOPLE LIVE ACCORDING TO THEIR EMOTIONS.
SO, AS AN EXAMPLE TO THE IMPERIAL CITIZENS WHOSE EMOTIONS ARE CURTAILED, THE PEOPLE OF FALÁINA ARE TO BE MASSACRED.

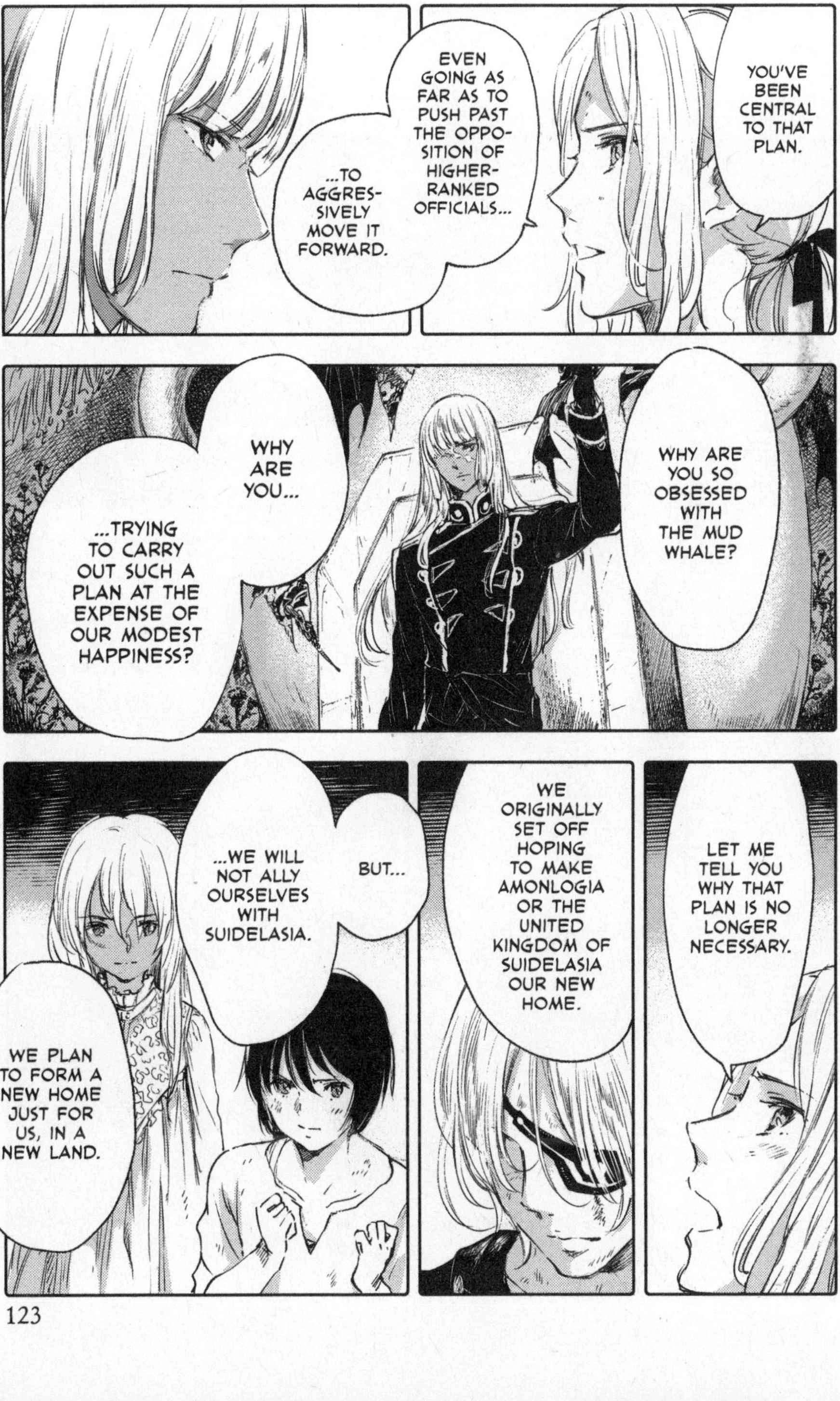
YOU'VE BEEN CENTRAL TO THAT PLAN.
EVEN GOING AS FAR AS TO PUSH PAST THE OPPOSITION OF HIGHER-RANKED OFFICIALS...
...TO AGGRESSIVELY MOVE IT FORWARD.
WHY ARE YOU SO OBSESSED WITH THE MUD WHALE?
WHY ARE YOU...
...TRYING TO CARRY OUT SUCH A PLAN AT THE EXPENSE OF OUR MODEST HAPPINESS?
LET ME TELL YOU WHY THAT PLAN IS NO LONGER NECESSARY.
WE ORIGINALLY SET OFF HOPING TO MAKE AMONLOGIA OR THE UNITED KINGDOM OF SUIDELASIA OUR NEW HOME.
BUT...
...WE WILL NOT ALLY OURSELVES WITH SUIDELASIA.
WE PLAN TO FORM A NEW HOME JUST FOR US, IN A NEW LAND.

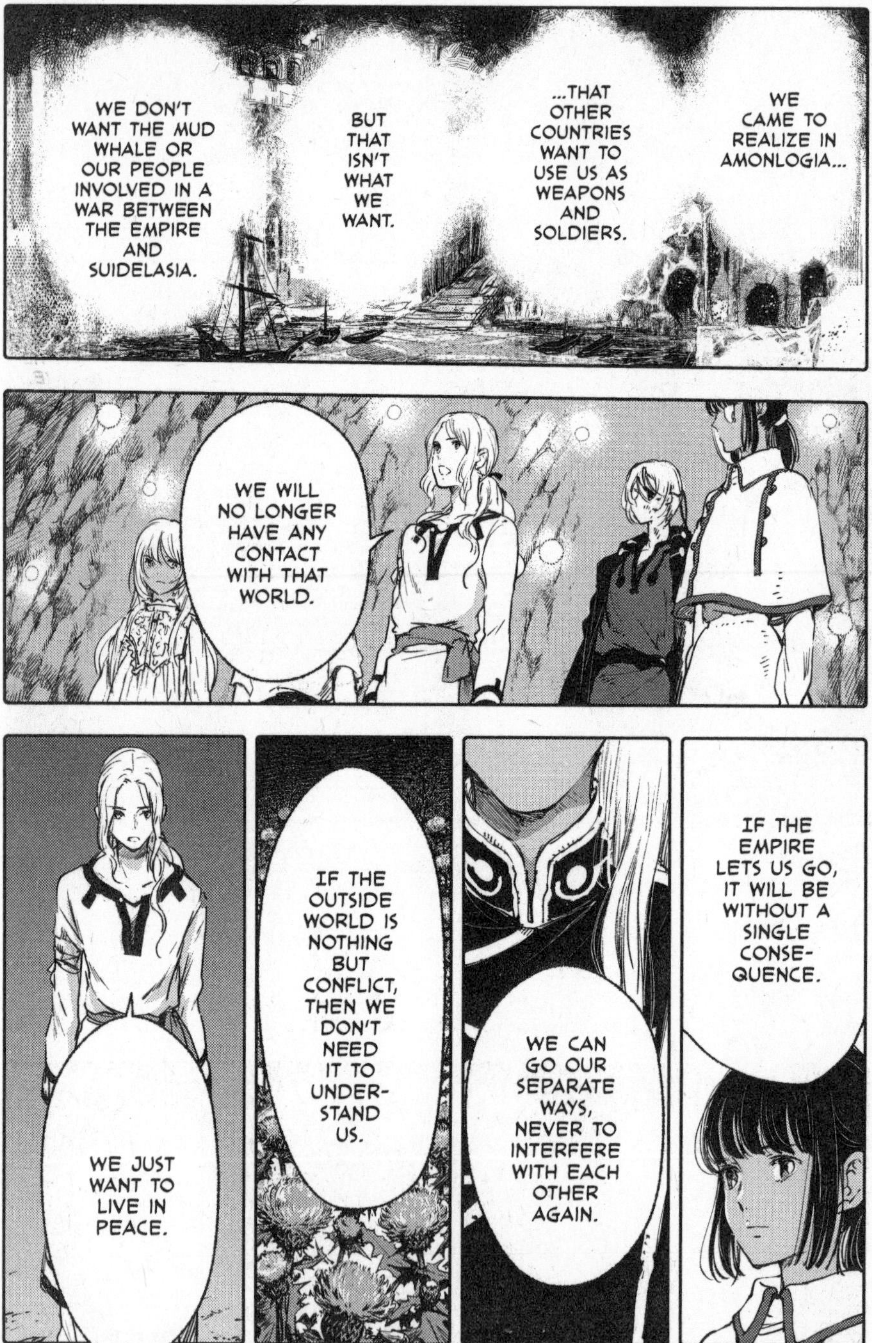
WE CAME TO REALIZE IN AMONLOGIA...
...THAT OTHER COUNTRIES WANT TO USE US AS WEAPONS AND SOLDIERS.
BUT THAT ISN'T WHAT WE WANT.
WE DON'T WANT THE MUD WHALE OR OUR PEOPLE INVOLVED IN A WAR BETWEEN THE EMPIRE AND SUIDELASIA.
WE WILL NO LONGER HAVE ANY CONTACT WITH THAT WORLD.
IF THE EMPIRE LETS US GO, IT WILL BE WITHOUT A SINGLE CONSE-QUENCE.
WE CAN GO OUR SEPARATE WAYS, NEVER TO INTERFERE WITH EACH OTHER AGAIN.
IF THE OUTSIDE WORLD IS NOTHING BUT CONFLICT, THEN WE DON'T NEED IT TO UNDER-STAND US.
WE JUST WANT TO LIVE IN PEACE.

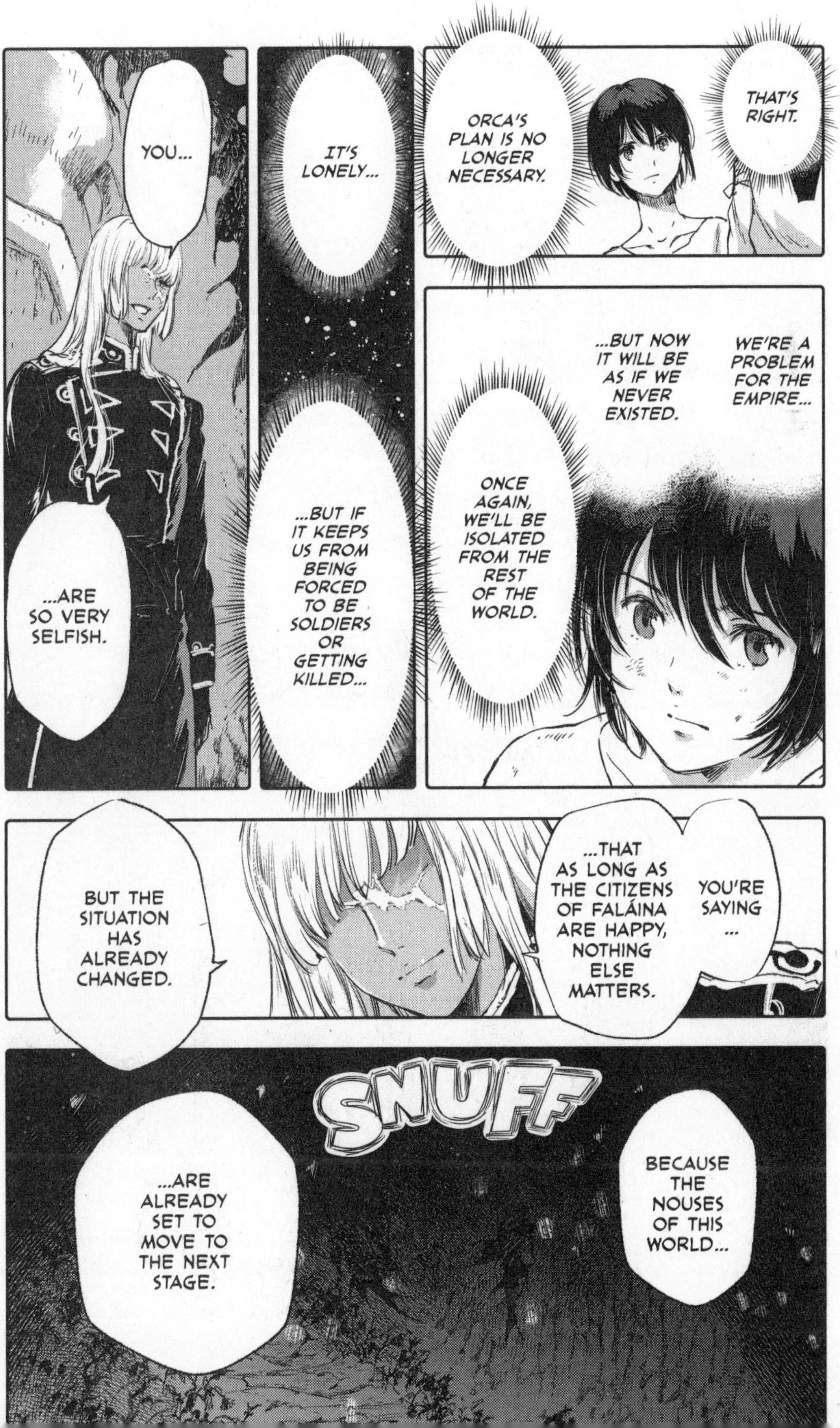
THAT'S RIGHT.
ORCA'S PLAN IS NO LONGER NECESSARY.
WE'RE A PROBLEM FOR THE EMPIRE...
...BUT NOW IT WILL BE AS IF WE NEVER EXISTED.
ONCE AGAIN, WE'LL BE ISOLATED FROM THE REST OF THE WORLD.
IT'S LONELY...
...BUT IF IT KEEPS US FROM BEING FORCED TO BE SOLDIERS OR GETTING KILLED...
YOU...
...ARE SO VERY SELFISH.
YOU'RE SAYING...
...THAT AS LONG AS THE CITIZENS OF FALÁINA ARE HAPPY, NOTHING ELSE MATTERS.
BUT THE SITUATION HAS ALREADY CHANGED.
SNUFF
BECAUSE THE NOUSES OF THIS WORLD...
...ARE ALREADY SET TO MOVE TO THE NEXT STAGE.

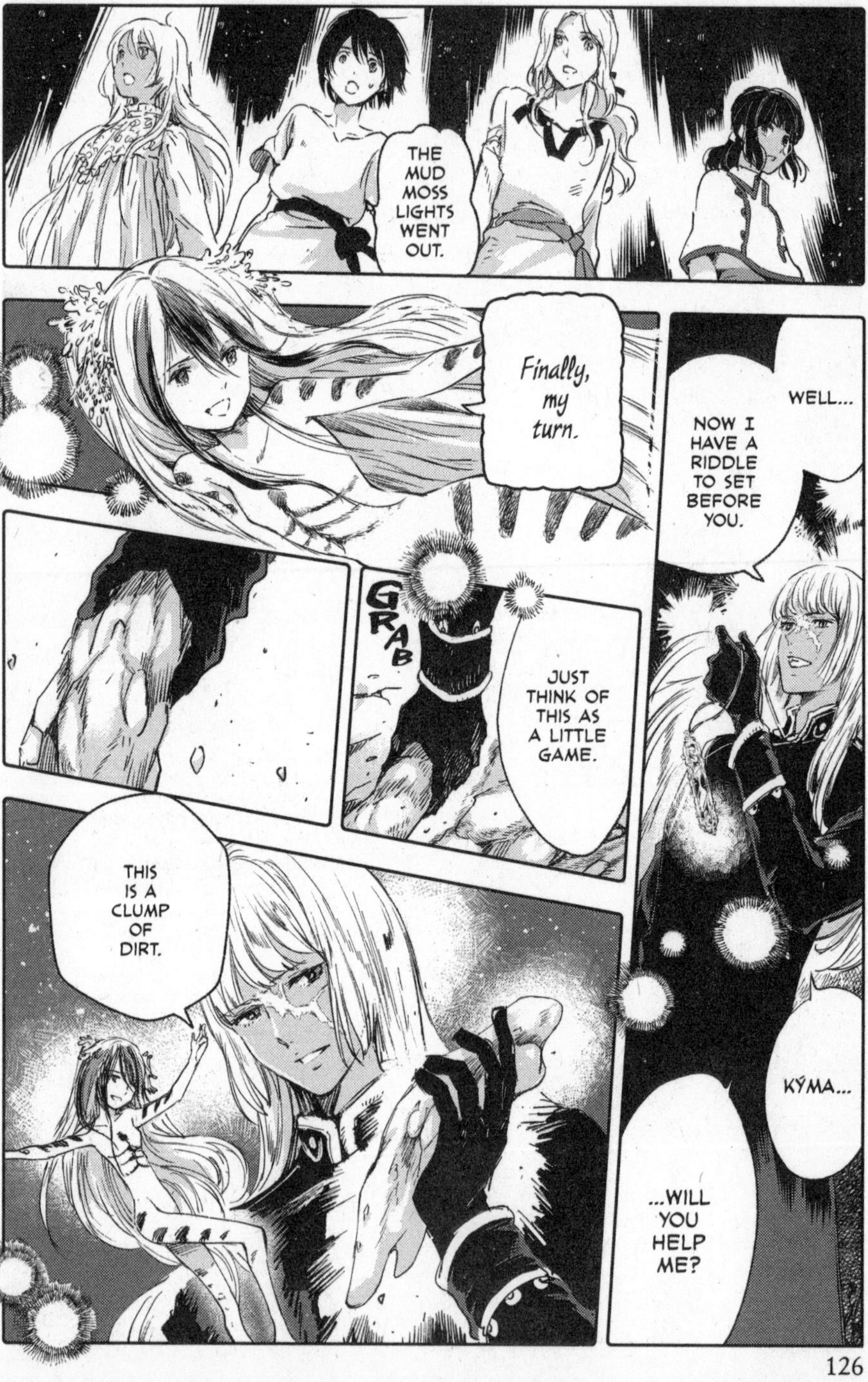
THE MUD MOSS LIGHTS WENT OUT.
WELL...
NOW I HAVE A RIDDLE TO SET BEFORE YOU.
KÝMA...
...WILL YOU HELP ME?
Finally, my turn.
GRAB
JUST THINK OF THIS AS A LITTLE GAME.
THIS IS A CLUMP OF DIRT.

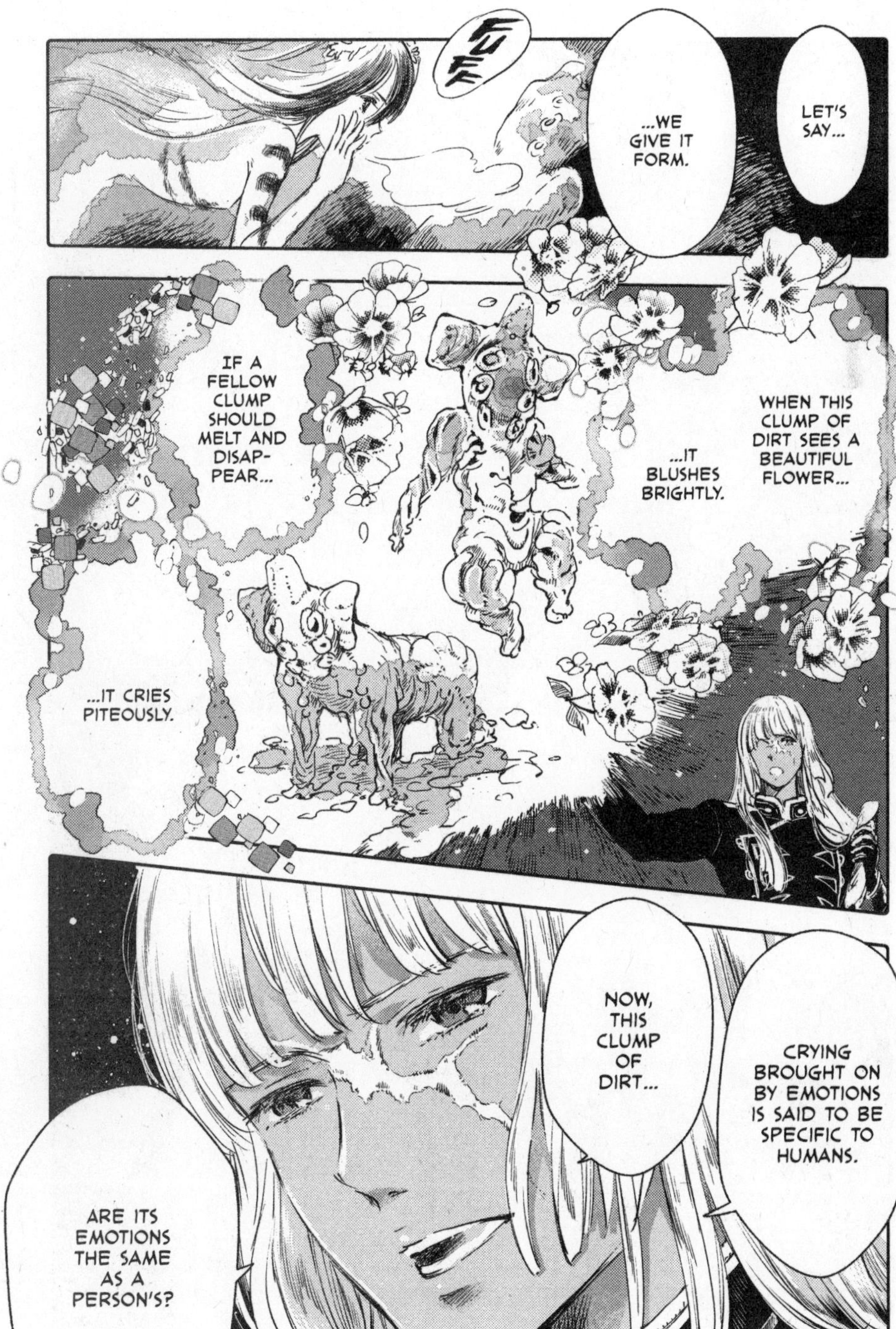
LET'S SAY...
...WE GIVE IT FORM.
FUFF
WHEN THIS CLUMP OF DIRT SEES A BEAUTIFUL FLOWER...
...IT BLUSHES BRIGHTLY.
IF A FELLOW CLUMP SHOULD MELT AND DISAPPEAR...
...IT CRIES PITEOUSLY.
CRYING BROUGHT ON BY EMOTIONS IS SAID TO BE SPECIFIC TO HUMANS.
NOW, THIS CLUMP OF DIRT...
ARE ITS EMOTIONS THE SAME AS A PERSON'S?

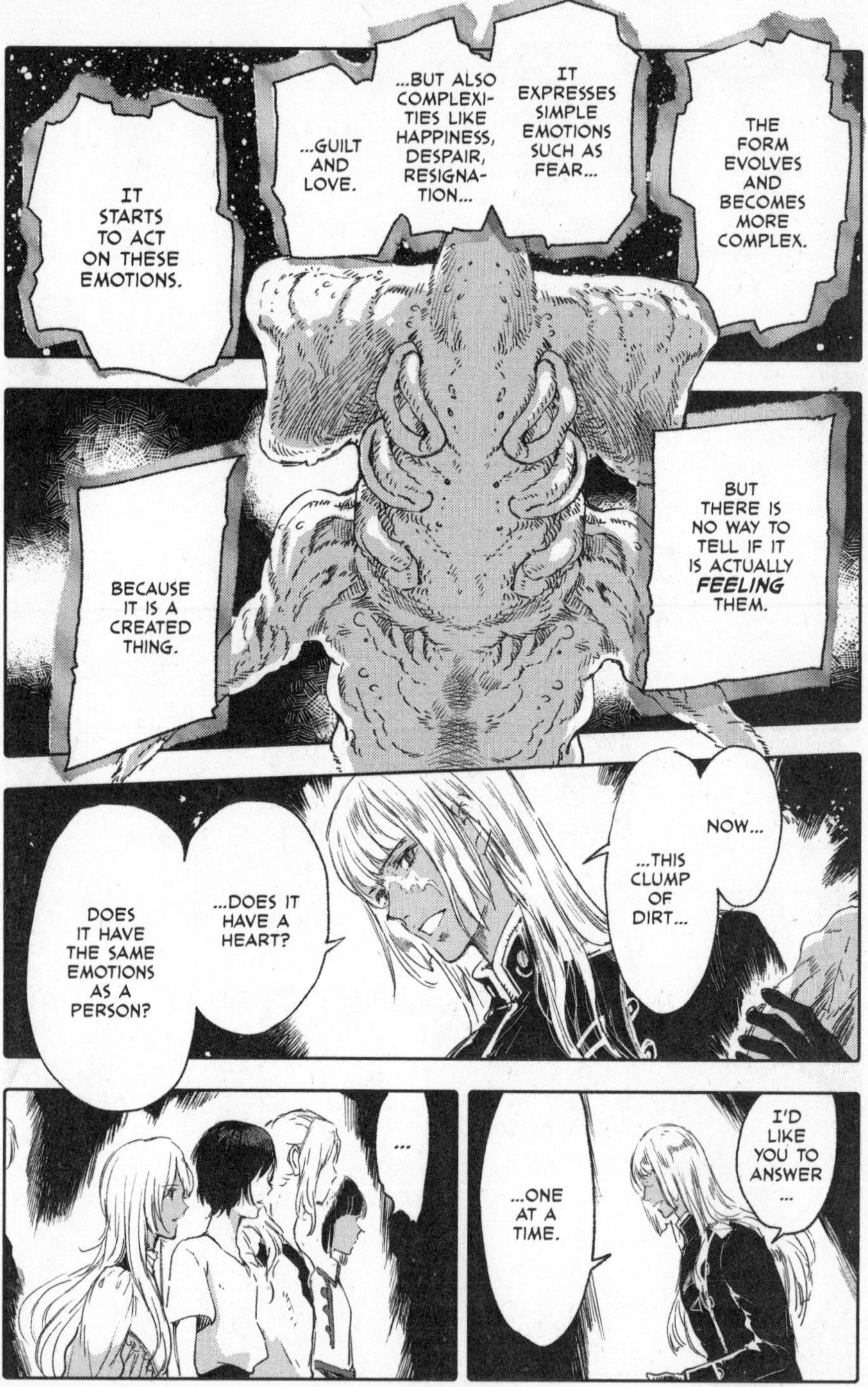
THE FORM EVOLVES AND BECOMES MORE COMPLEX.
IT EXPRESSES SIMPLE EMOTIONS SUCH AS FEAR...
...BUT ALSO COMPLEXITIES LIKE HAPPINESS, DESPAIR, RESIGNATION...
...GUILT AND LOVE.
IT STARTS TO ACT ON THESE EMOTIONS.
BUT THERE IS NO WAY TO TELL IF IT IS ACTUALLY *FEELING* THEM.
BECAUSE IT IS A CREATED THING.
NOW...
...THIS CLUMP OF DIRT...
...DOES IT HAVE A HEART?
DOES IT HAVE THE SAME EMOTIONS AS A PERSON?
I'D LIKE YOU TO ANSWER ...
...ONE AT A TIME.
...

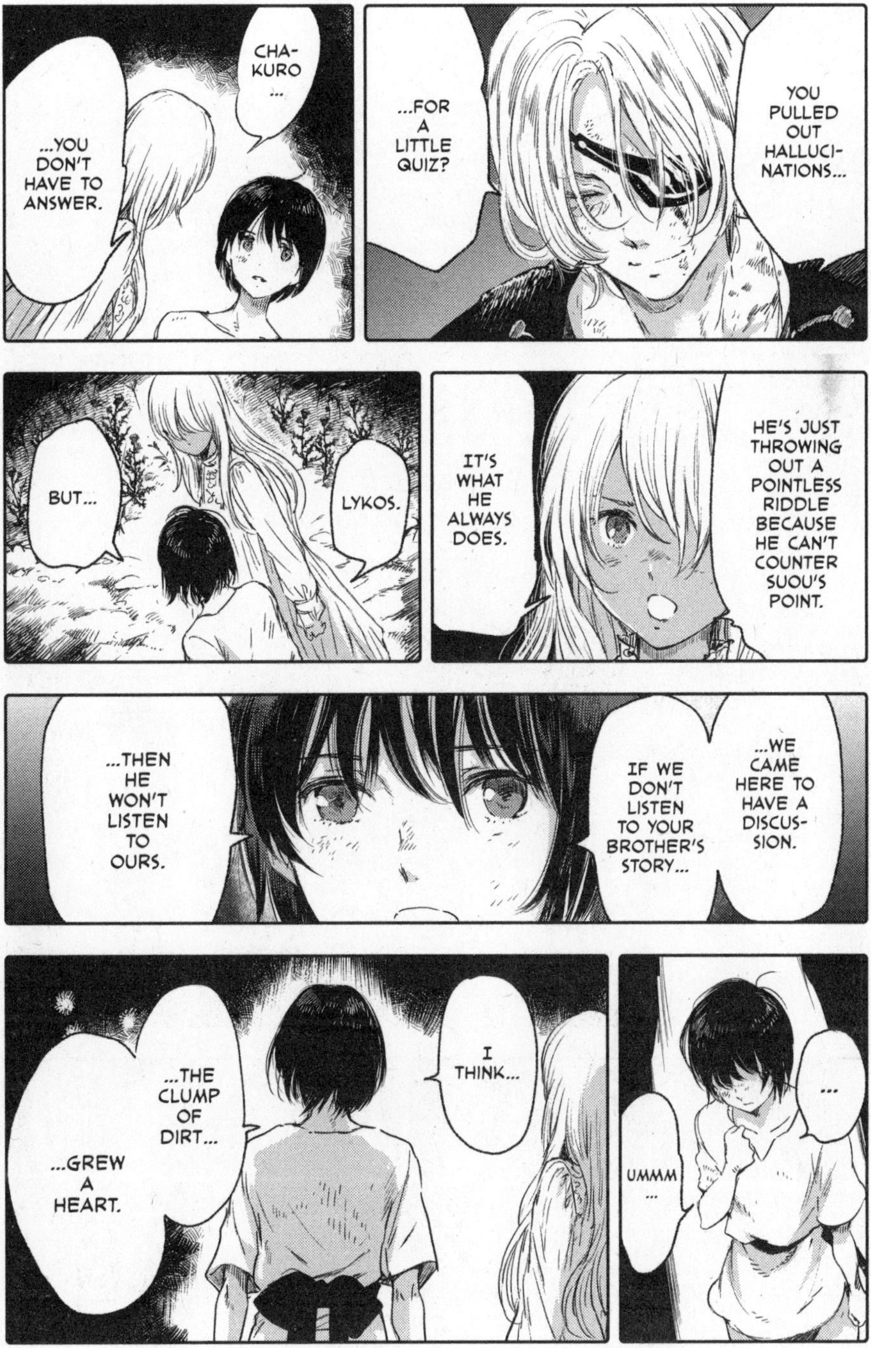
YOU PULLED OUT HALLUCINATIONS...
...FOR A LITTLE QUIZ?
CHAKURO...
...YOU DON'T HAVE TO ANSWER.
HE'S JUST THROWING OUT A POINTLESS RIDDLE BECAUSE HE CAN'T COUNTER SUOU'S POINT.
IT'S WHAT HE ALWAYS DOES.
LYKOS.
BUT...
...WE CAME HERE TO HAVE A DISCUSSION.
IF WE DON'T LISTEN TO YOUR BROTHER'S STORY...
...THEN HE WON'T LISTEN TO OURS.
...
UMMM...
I THINK...
...THE CLUMP OF DIRT...
...GREW A HEART.

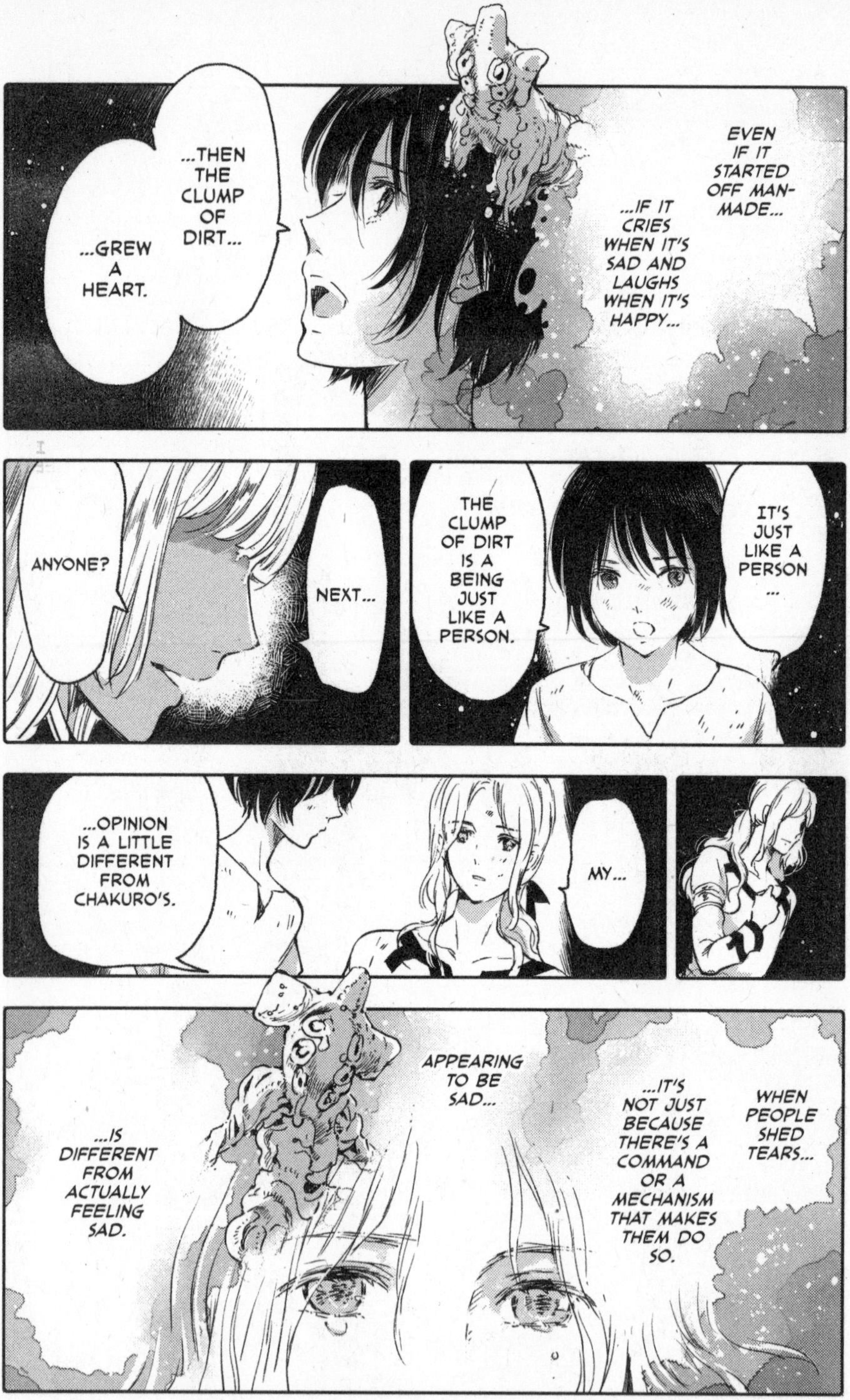
EVEN IF IT STARTED OFF MAN-MADE...
...IF IT CRIES WHEN IT'S SAD AND LAUGHS WHEN IT'S HAPPY...
...THEN THE CLUMP OF DIRT...
...GREW A HEART.
IT'S JUST LIKE A PERSON ...
THE CLUMP OF DIRT IS A BEING JUST LIKE A PERSON.
NEXT...
ANYONE?
MY...
...OPINION IS A LITTLE DIFFERENT FROM CHAKURO'S.
WHEN PEOPLE SHED TEARS...
...IT'S NOT JUST BECAUSE THERE'S A COMMAND OR A MECHANISM THAT MAKES THEM DO SO.
APPEARING TO BE SAD...
...IS DIFFERENT FROM ACTUALLY FEELING SAD.

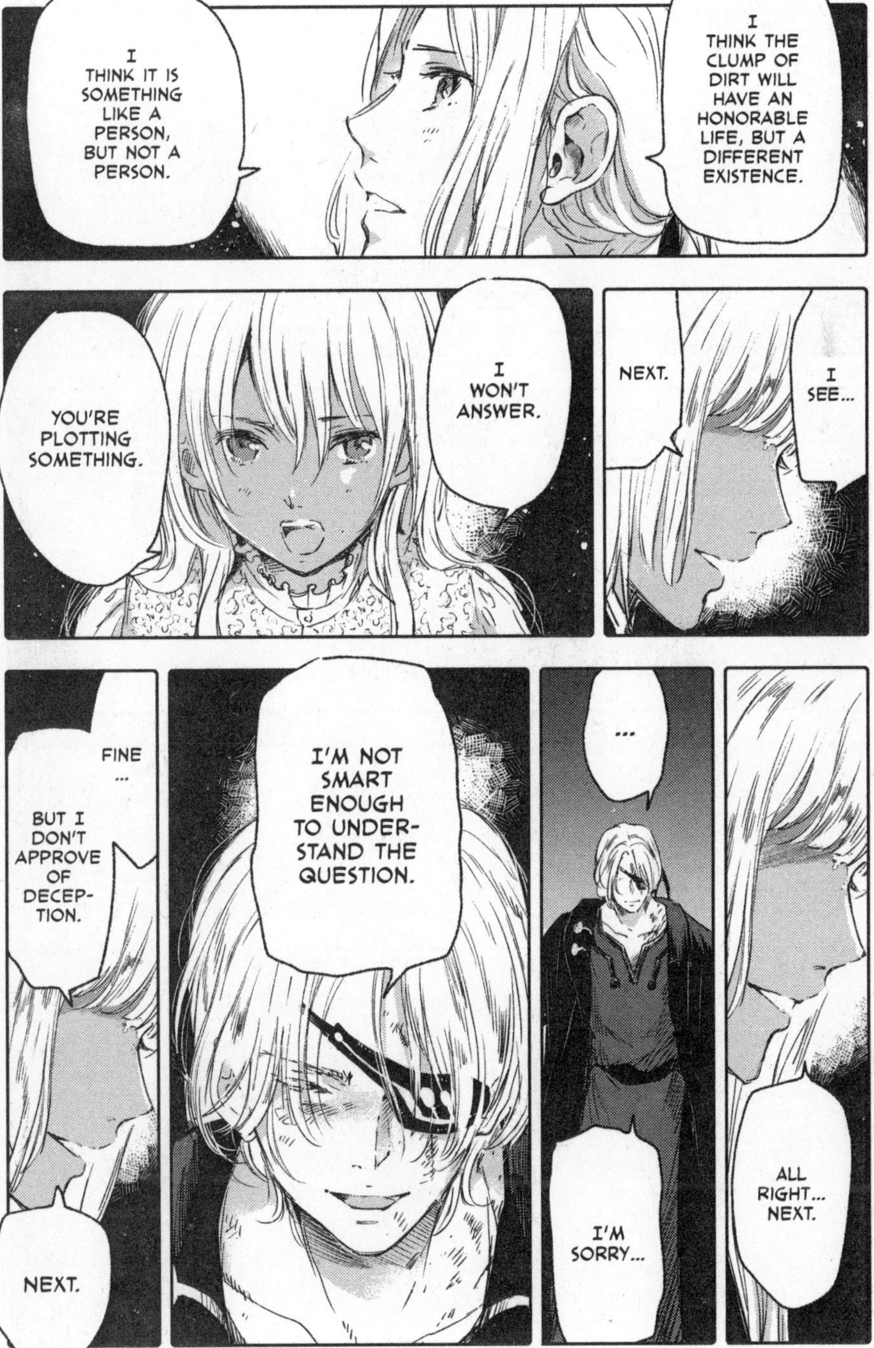
I THINK THE CLUMP OF DIRT WILL HAVE AN HONORABLE LIFE, BUT A DIFFERENT EXISTENCE.
I THINK IT IS SOMETHING LIKE A PERSON, BUT NOT A PERSON.
I SEE...
NEXT.
I WON'T ANSWER.
YOU'RE PLOTTING SOMETHING.
ALL RIGHT... NEXT.
...
I'M SORRY...
I'M NOT SMART ENOUGH TO UNDER-STAND THE QUESTION.
FINE ...
BUT I DON'T APPROVE OF DECEP-TION.
NEXT.

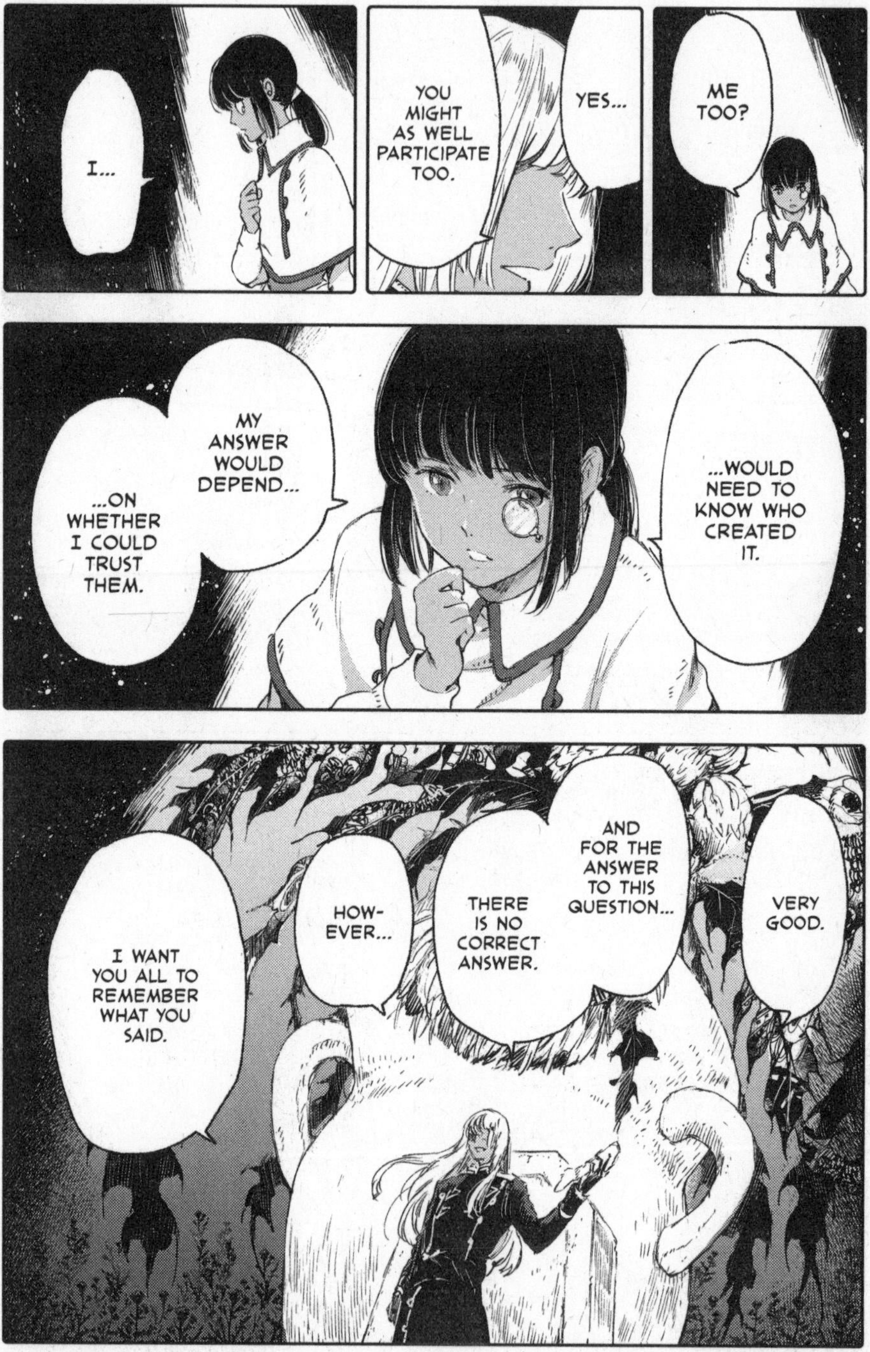
ME TOO?
YES...
YOU MIGHT AS WELL PARTICIPATE TOO.
I...
...WOULD NEED TO KNOW WHO CREATED IT.
MY ANSWER WOULD DEPEND...
...ON WHETHER I COULD TRUST THEM.
VERY GOOD.
AND FOR THE ANSWER TO THIS QUESTION...
THERE IS NO CORRECT ANSWER.
HOW-EVER...
I WANT YOU ALL TO REMEMBER WHAT YOU SAID.

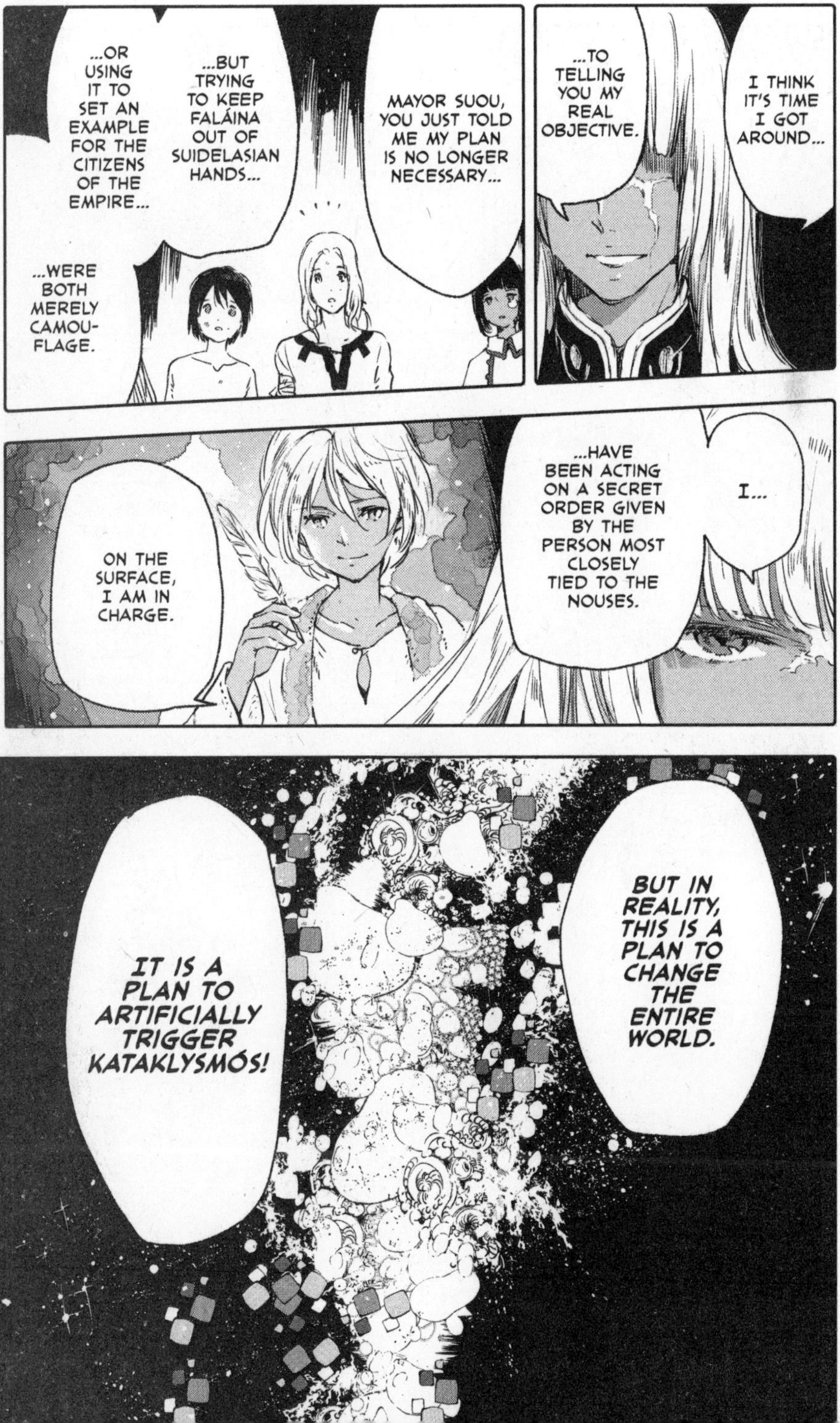
I THINK IT'S TIME I GOT AROUND...
...TO TELLING YOU MY REAL OBJECTIVE.
MAYOR SUOU, YOU JUST TOLD ME MY PLAN IS NO LONGER NECESSARY...
...BUT TRYING TO KEEP FALÁINA OUT OF SUIDELASIAN HANDS...
...OR USING IT TO SET AN EXAMPLE FOR THE CITIZENS OF THE EMPIRE...
...WERE BOTH MERELY CAMOU-FLAGE.
I...
...HAVE BEEN ACTING ON A SECRET ORDER GIVEN BY THE PERSON MOST CLOSELY TIED TO THE NOUSES.
ON THE SURFACE, I AM IN CHARGE.
BUT IN REALITY, THIS IS A PLAN TO CHANGE THE ENTIRE WORLD.
IT IS A PLAN TO ARTIFICIALLY TRIGGER KATAKLYSMÓS!

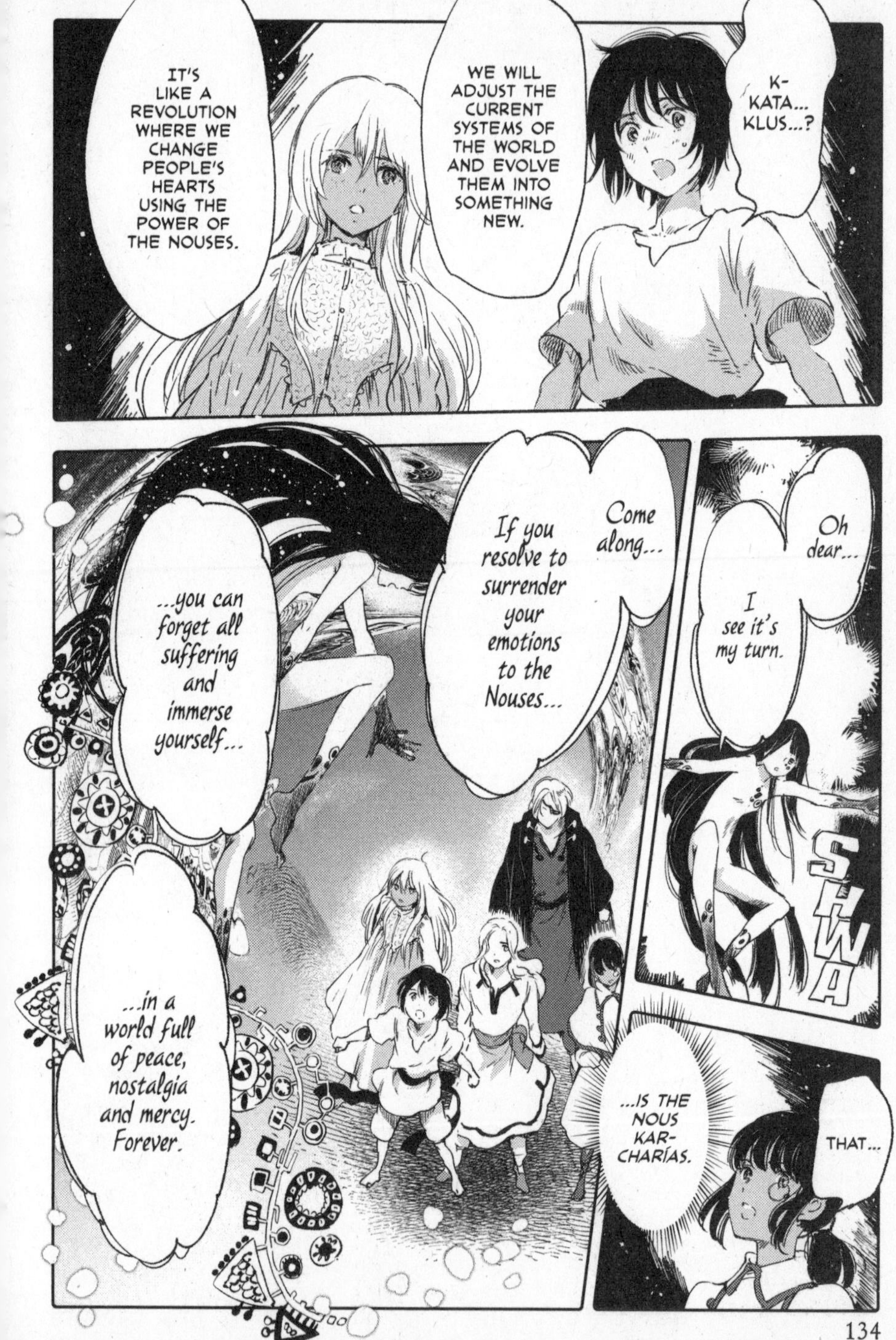

K-KATA... KLUS...?
WE WILL ADJUST THE CURRENT SYSTEMS OF THE WORLD AND EVOLVE THEM INTO SOMETHING NEW.
IT'S LIKE A REVOLUTION WHERE WE CHANGE PEOPLE'S HEARTS USING THE POWER OF THE NOUSES.
Oh dear...
I see it's my turn.
SHWA
THAT...
...IS THE NOUS KAR-CHARÍAS.
Come along...
If you resolve to surrender your emotions to the Nouses...
...you can forget all suffering and immerse yourself...
...in a world full of peace, nostalgia and mercy. Forever.

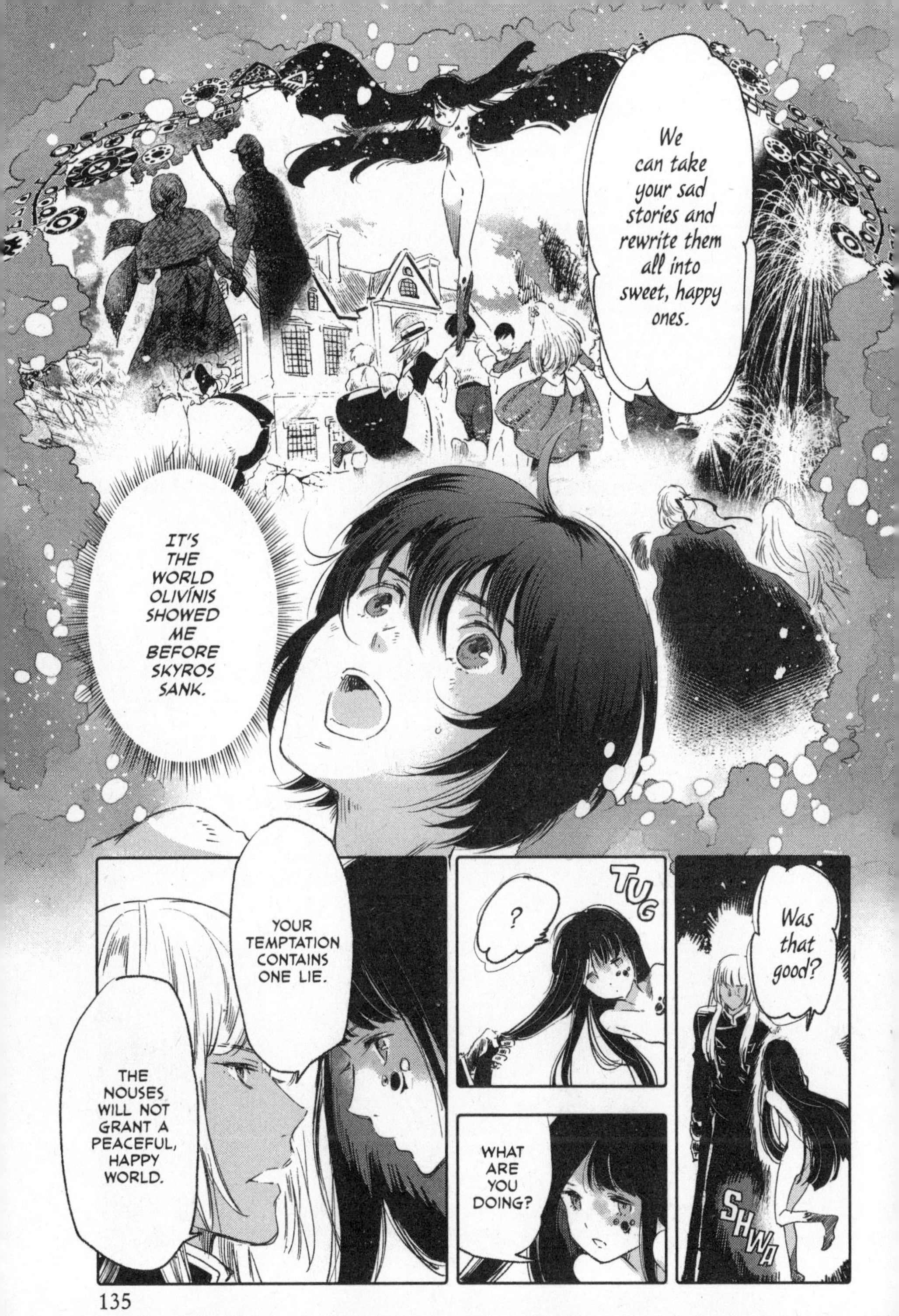
We can take your sad stories and rewrite them all into sweet, happy ones.
IT'S THE WORLD OLIVÍNIS SHOWED ME BEFORE SKYROS SANK.
Was that good?
SHWA
TUG
?
WHAT ARE YOU DOING?
YOUR TEMPTATION CONTAINS ONE LIE.
THE NOUSES WILL NOT GRANT A PEACEFUL, HAPPY WORLD.

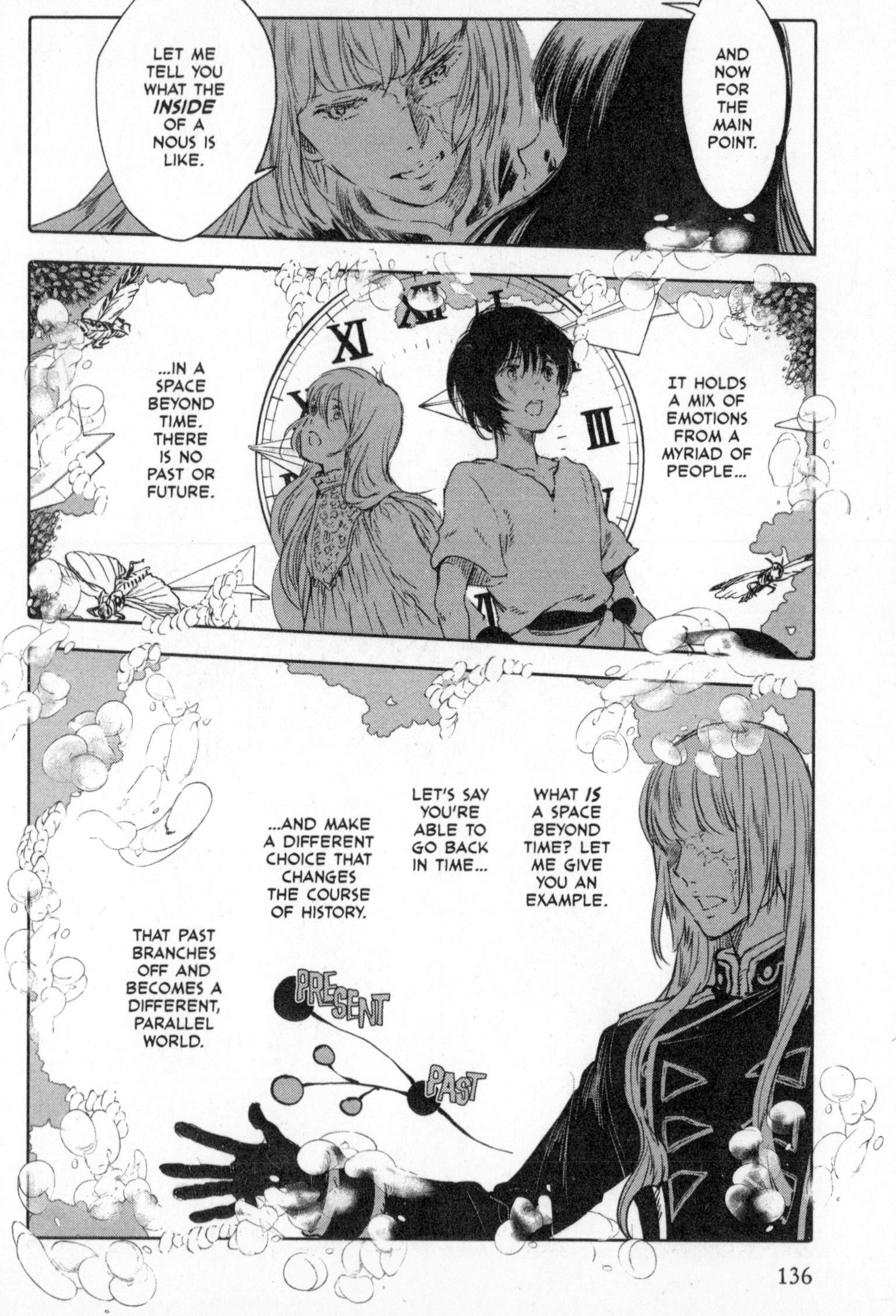
AND NOW FOR THE MAIN POINT.
LET ME TELL YOU WHAT THE *INSIDE* OF A NOUS IS LIKE.
IT HOLDS A MIX OF EMOTIONS FROM A MYRIAD OF PEOPLE...
...IN A SPACE BEYOND TIME. THERE IS NO PAST OR FUTURE.
WHAT *IS* A SPACE BEYOND TIME? LET ME GIVE YOU AN EXAMPLE.
LET'S SAY YOU'RE ABLE TO GO BACK IN TIME...
...AND MAKE A DIFFERENT CHOICE THAT CHANGES THE COURSE OF HISTORY.
THAT PAST BRANCHES OFF AND BECOMES A DIFFERENT, PARALLEL WORLD.
PRESENT
PAST

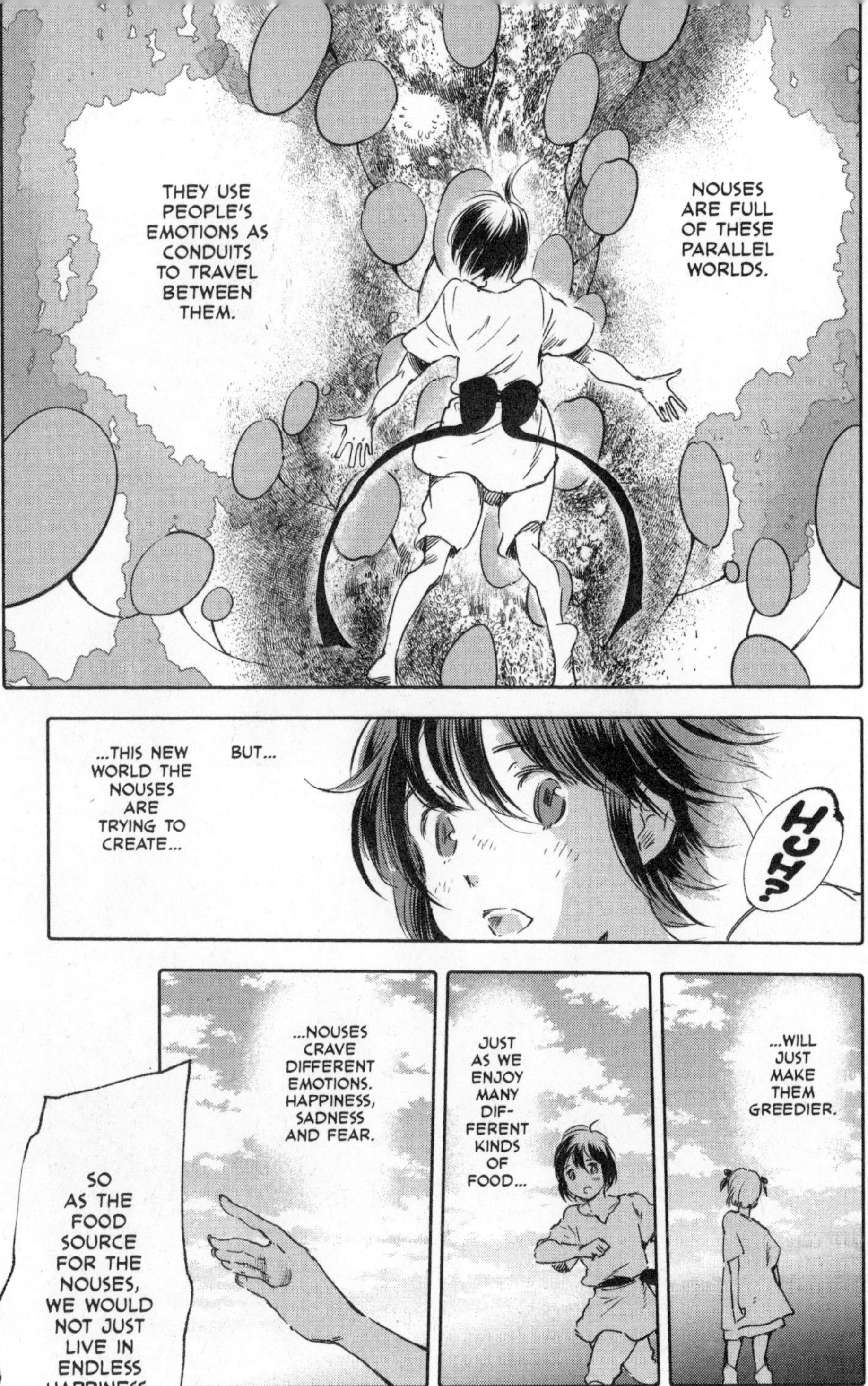
NOUSES ARE FULL OF THESE PARALLEL WORLDS.
THEY USE PEOPLE'S EMOTIONS AS CONDUITS TO TRAVEL BETWEEN THEM.
HUH?
BUT...
...THIS NEW WORLD THE NOUSES ARE TRYING TO CREATE...
...WILL JUST MAKE THEM GREEDIER.
JUST AS WE ENJOY MANY DIF-FERENT KINDS OF FOOD...
...NOUSES CRAVE DIFFERENT EMOTIONS. HAPPINESS, SADNESS AND FEAR.
SO AS THE FOOD SOURCE FOR THE NOUSES, WE WOULD NOT JUST LIVE IN ENDLESS HAPPINESS.

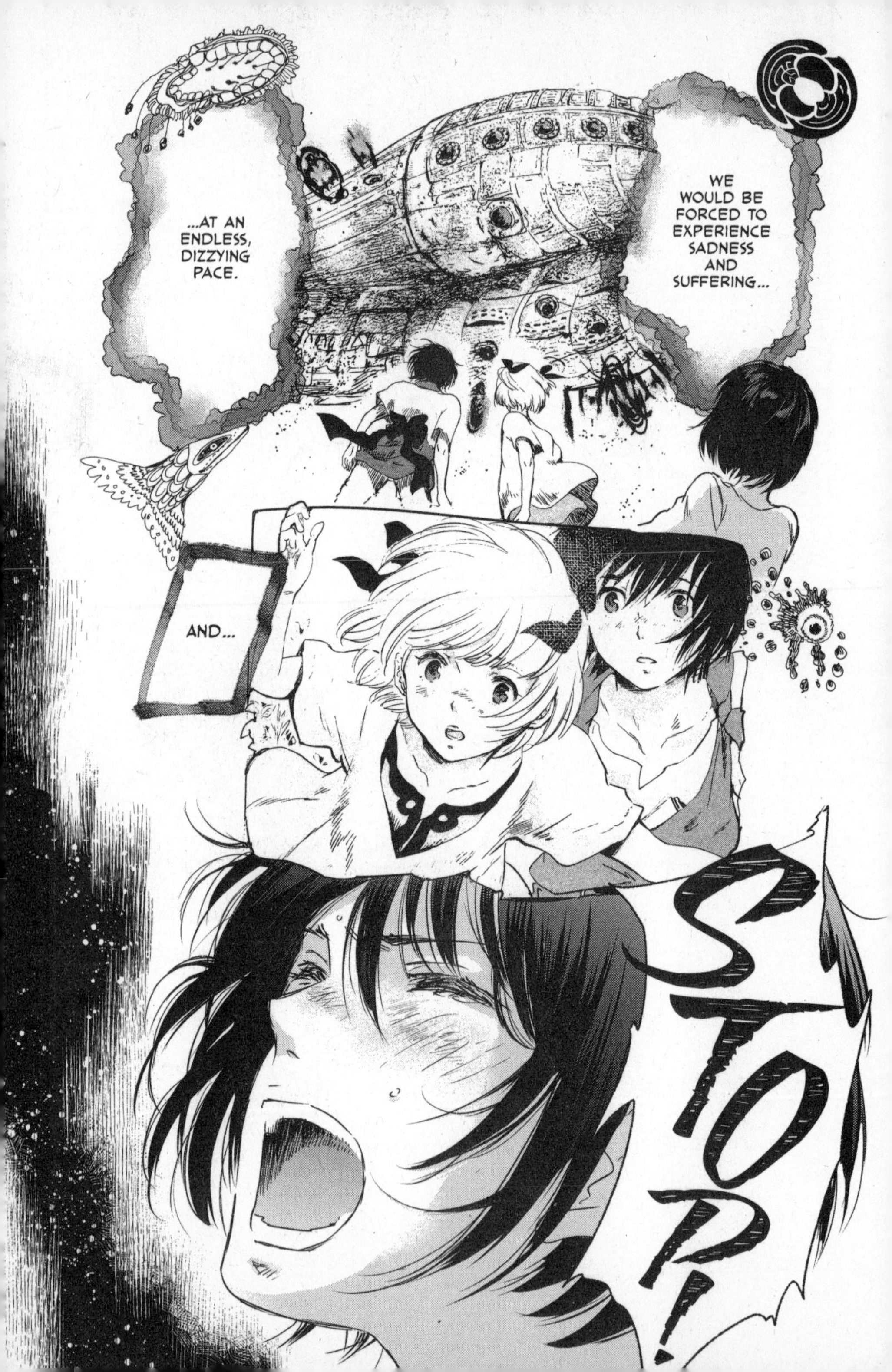
WE WOULD BE FORCED TO EXPERIENCE SADNESS AND SUFFERING...
...AT AN ENDLESS, DIZZYING PACE.
AND...
STOP?!

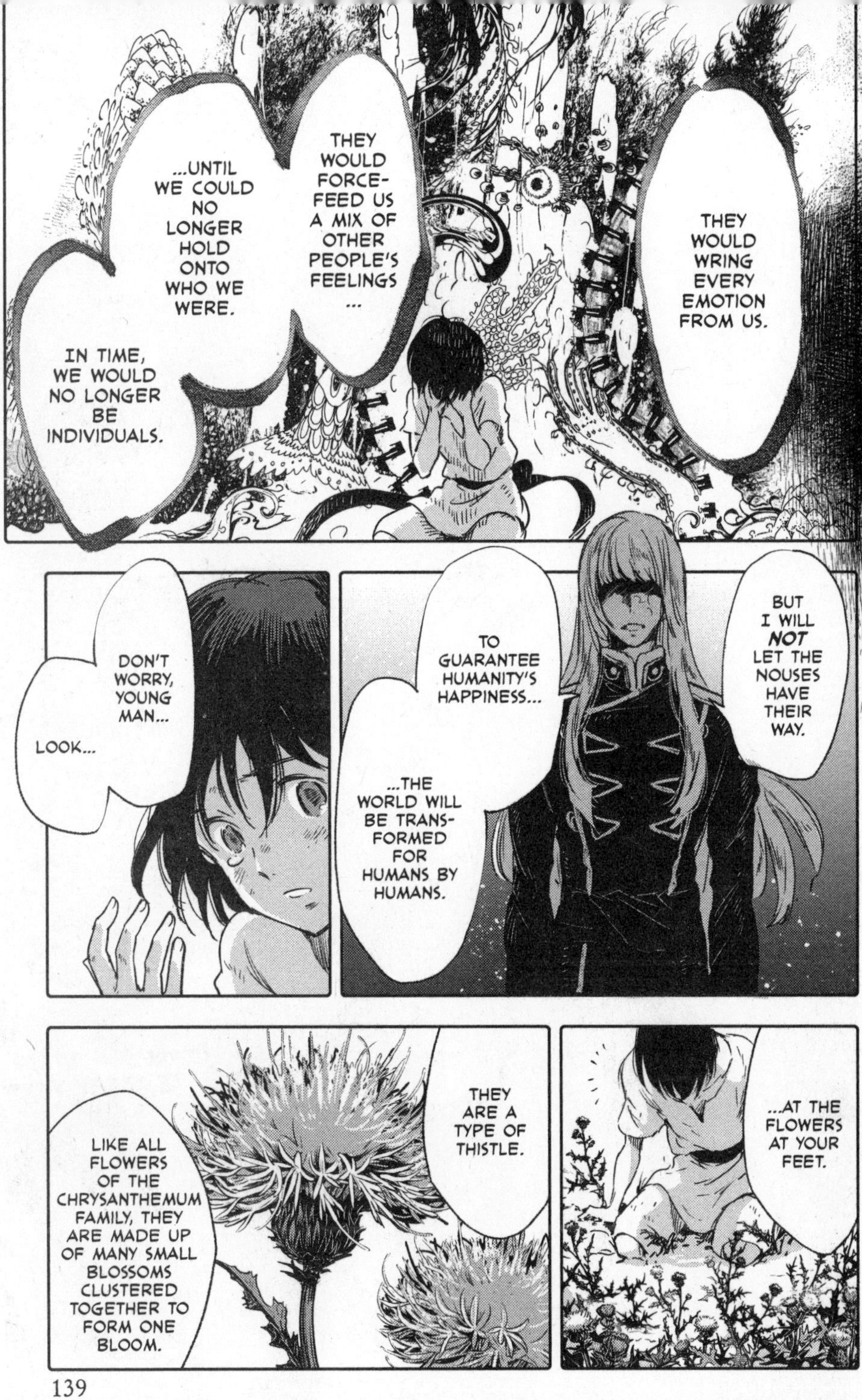
THEY WOULD WRING EVERY EMOTION FROM US.
THEY WOULD FORCE-FEED US A MIX OF OTHER PEOPLE'S FEELINGS...
...UNTIL WE COULD NO LONGER HOLD ONTO WHO WE WERE.
IN TIME, WE WOULD NO LONGER BE INDIVIDUALS.
BUT I WILL *NOT* LET THE NOUSES HAVE THEIR WAY.
TO GUARANTEE HUMANITY'S HAPPINESS...
...THE WORLD WILL BE TRANSFORMED FOR HUMANS BY HUMANS.
DON'T WORRY, YOUNG MAN...
LOOK...
...AT THE FLOWERS AT YOUR FEET.
THEY ARE A TYPE OF THISTLE.
LIKE ALL FLOWERS OF THE CHRYSANTHEMUM FAMILY, THEY ARE MADE UP OF MANY SMALL BLOSSOMS CLUSTERED TOGETHER TO FORM ONE BLOOM.

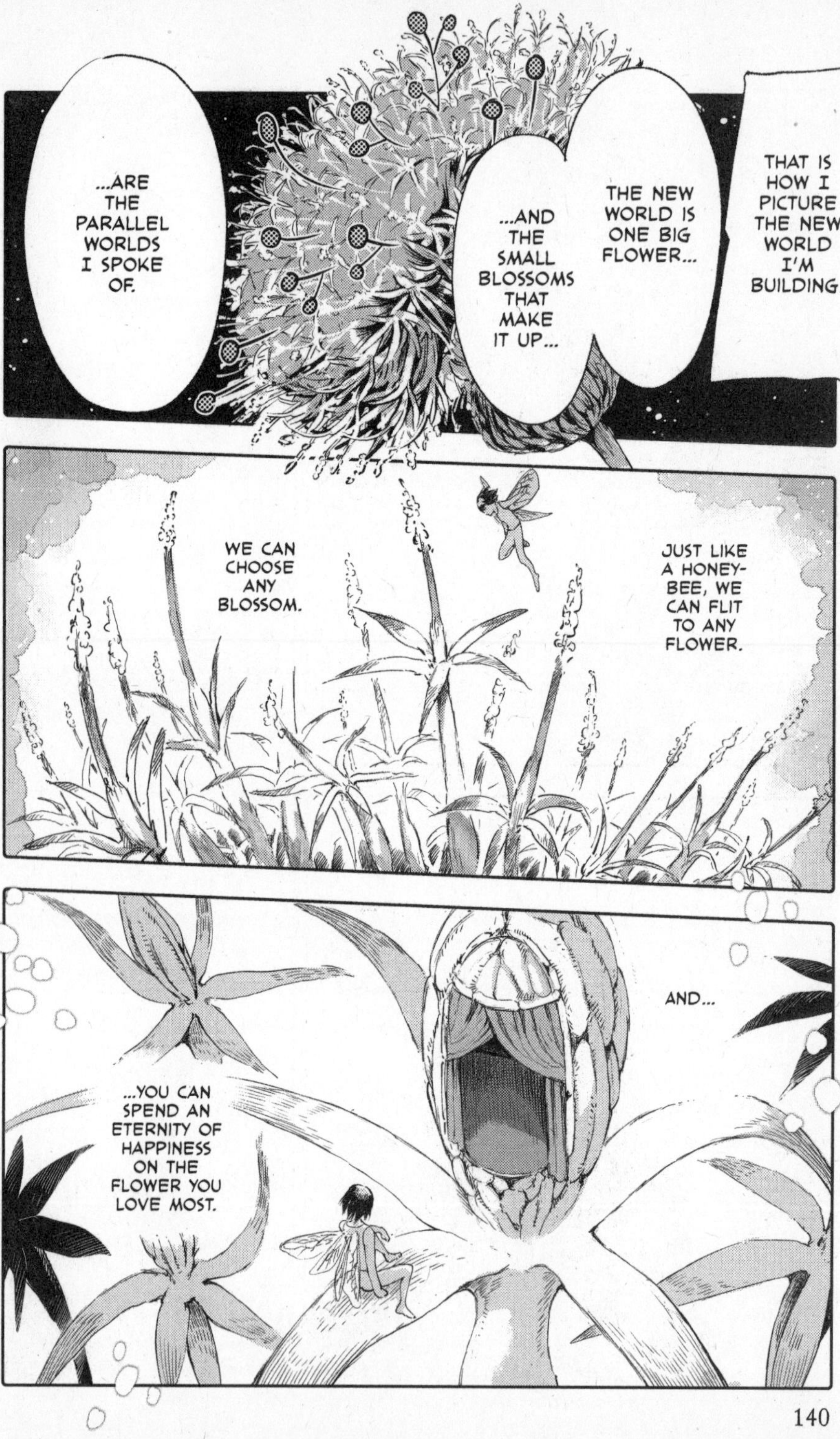
THAT IS HOW I PICTURE THE NEW WORLD I'M BUILDING.
THE NEW WORLD IS ONE BIG FLOWER...
...AND THE SMALL BLOSSOMS THAT MAKE IT UP...
...ARE THE PARALLEL WORLDS I SPOKE OF.
JUST LIKE A HONEY-BEE, WE CAN FLIT TO ANY FLOWER.
WE CAN CHOOSE ANY BLOSSOM.
AND...
...YOU CAN SPEND AN ETERNITY OF HAPPINESS ON THE FLOWER YOU LOVE MOST.

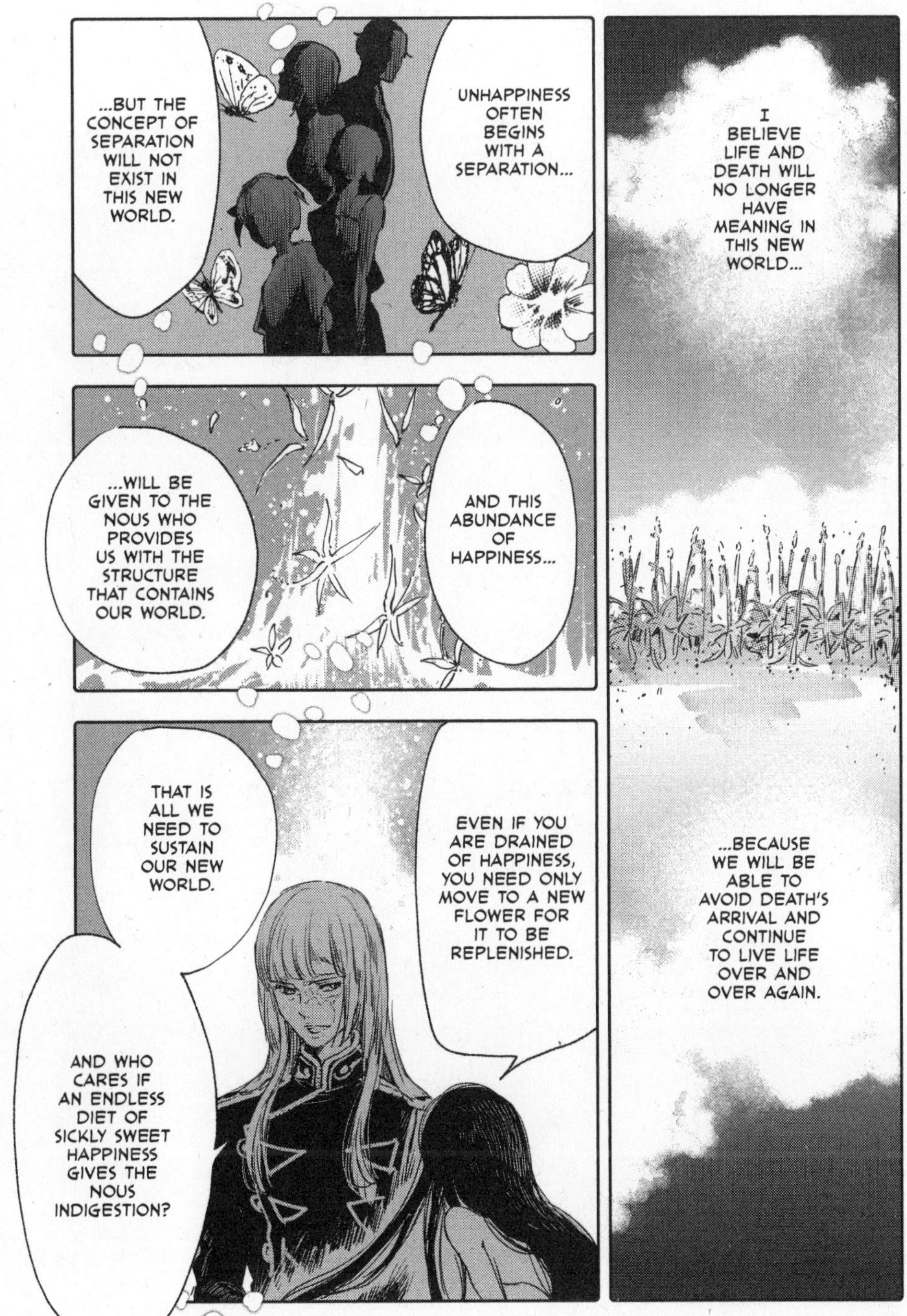
I BELIEVE LIFE AND DEATH WILL NO LONGER HAVE MEANING IN THIS NEW WORLD...
...BECAUSE WE WILL BE ABLE TO AVOID DEATH'S ARRIVAL AND CONTINUE TO LIVE LIFE OVER AND OVER AGAIN.
UNHAPPINESS OFTEN BEGINS WITH A SEPARATION...
...BUT THE CONCEPT OF SEPARATION WILL NOT EXIST IN THIS NEW WORLD.
AND THIS ABUNDANCE OF HAPPINESS...
...WILL BE GIVEN TO THE NOUS WHO PROVIDES US WITH THE STRUCTURE THAT CONTAINS OUR WORLD.
EVEN IF YOU ARE DRAINED OF HAPPINESS, YOU NEED ONLY MOVE TO A NEW FLOWER FOR IT TO BE REPLENISHED.
THAT IS ALL WE NEED TO SUSTAIN OUR NEW WORLD.
AND WHO CARES IF AN ENDLESS DIET OF SICKLY SWEET HAPPINESS GIVES THE NOUS INDIGESTION?

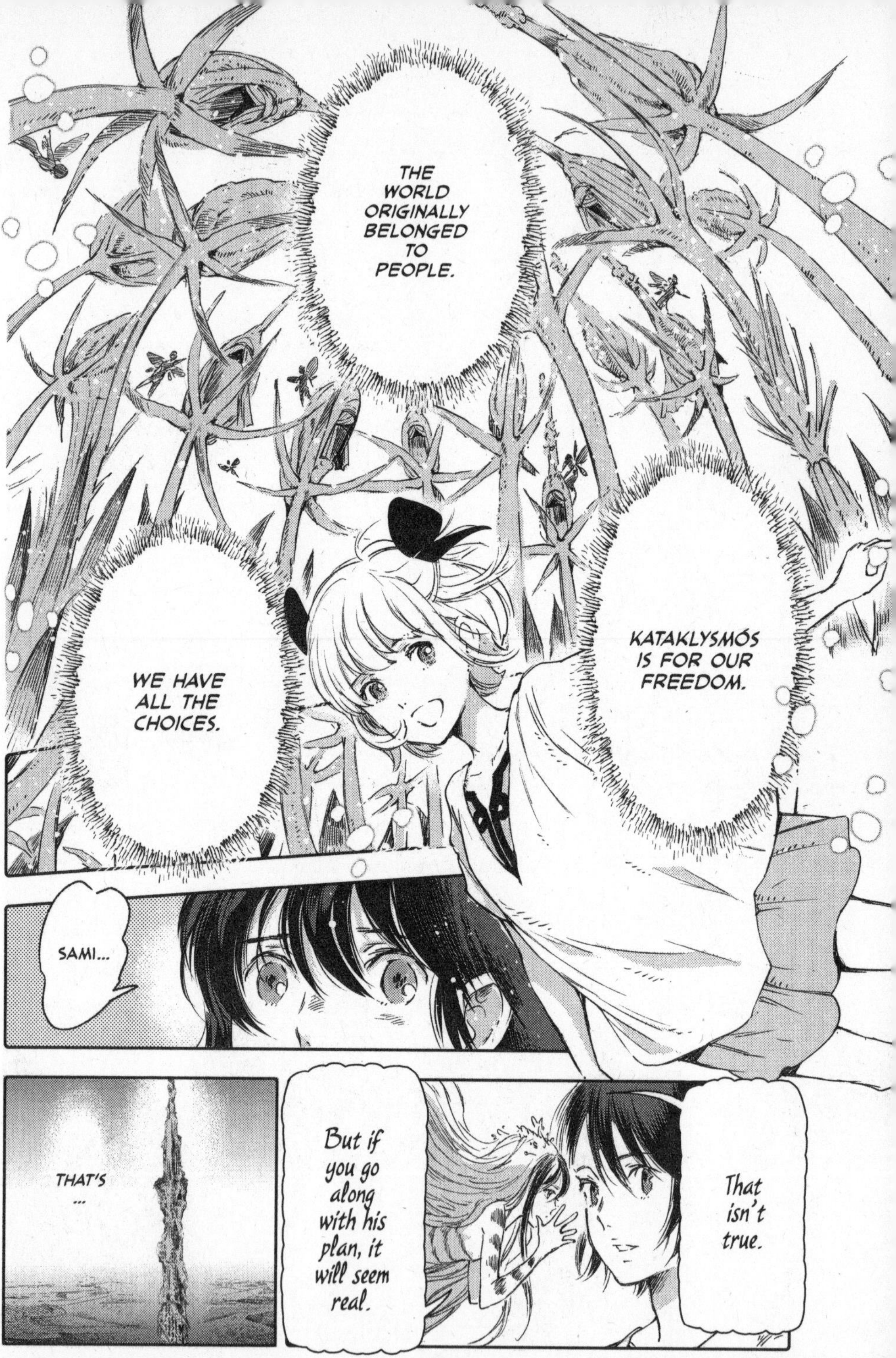
THE WORLD ORIGINALLY BELONGED TO PEOPLE.
KATAKLYSMÓS IS FOR OUR FREEDOM.
WE HAVE ALL THE CHOICES.
SAMI...
That isn't true.
But if you go along with his plan, it will seem real.
THAT'S ...

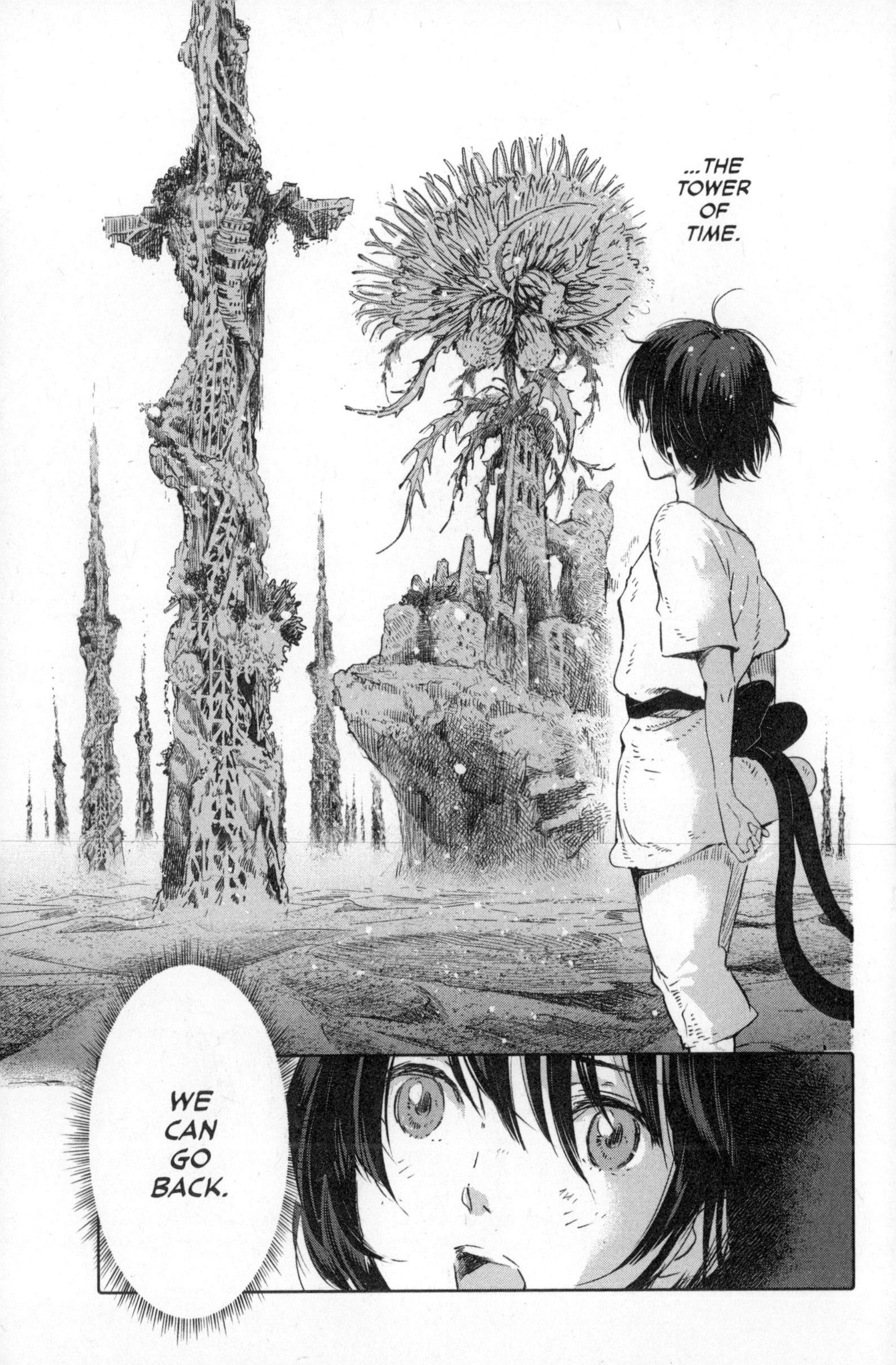
...THE TOWER OF TIME.
WE CAN GO BACK.

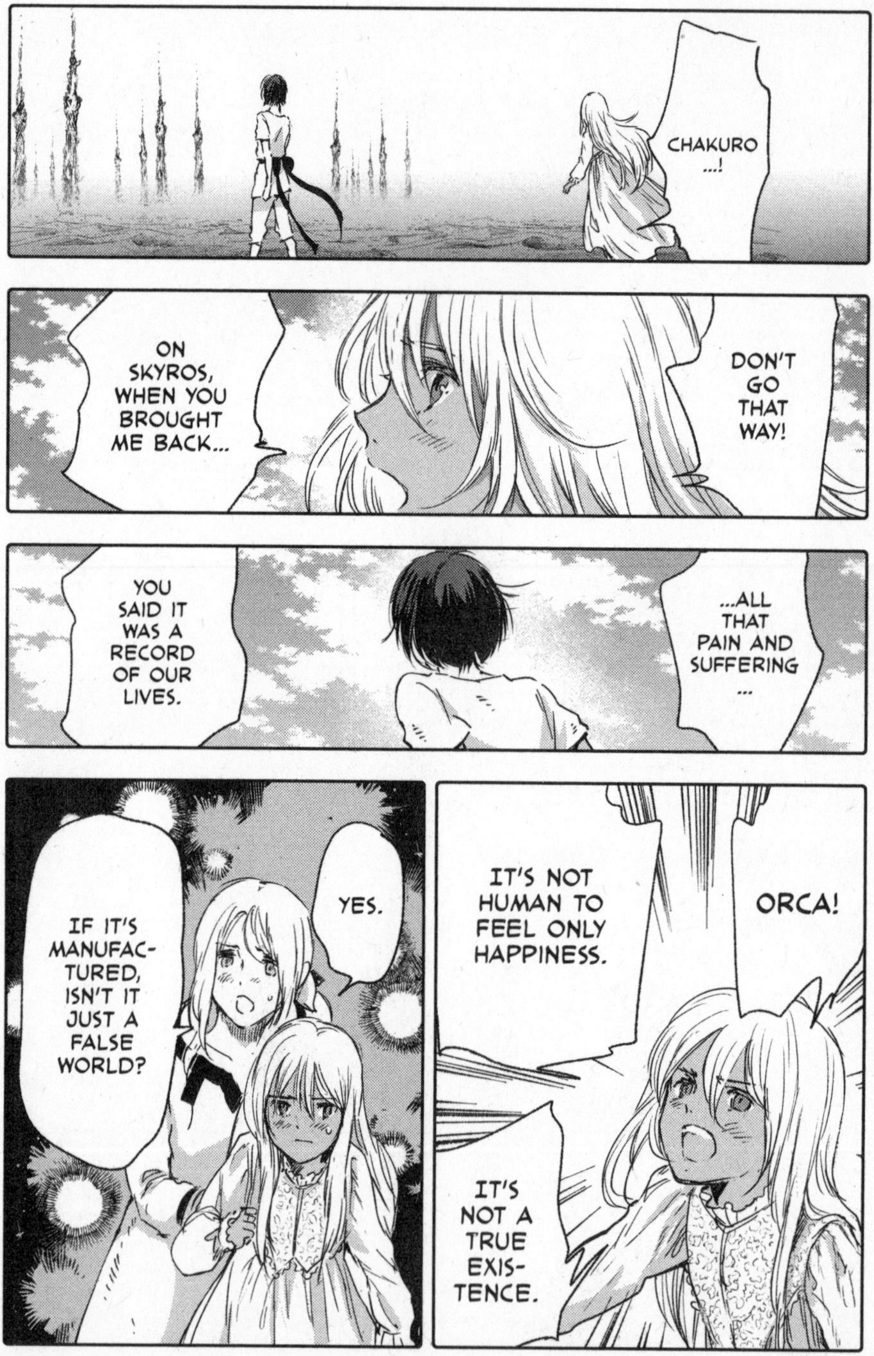
CHAKURO ...!
DON'T GO THAT WAY!
ON SKYROS, WHEN YOU BROUGHT ME BACK...
...ALL THAT PAIN AND SUFFERING ...
YOU SAID IT WAS A RECORD OF OUR LIVES.
ORCA!
IT'S NOT HUMAN TO FEEL ONLY HAPPINESS.
IT'S NOT A TRUE EXIS-TENCE.
YES.
IF IT'S MANUFAC-TURED, ISN'T IT JUST A FALSE WORLD?

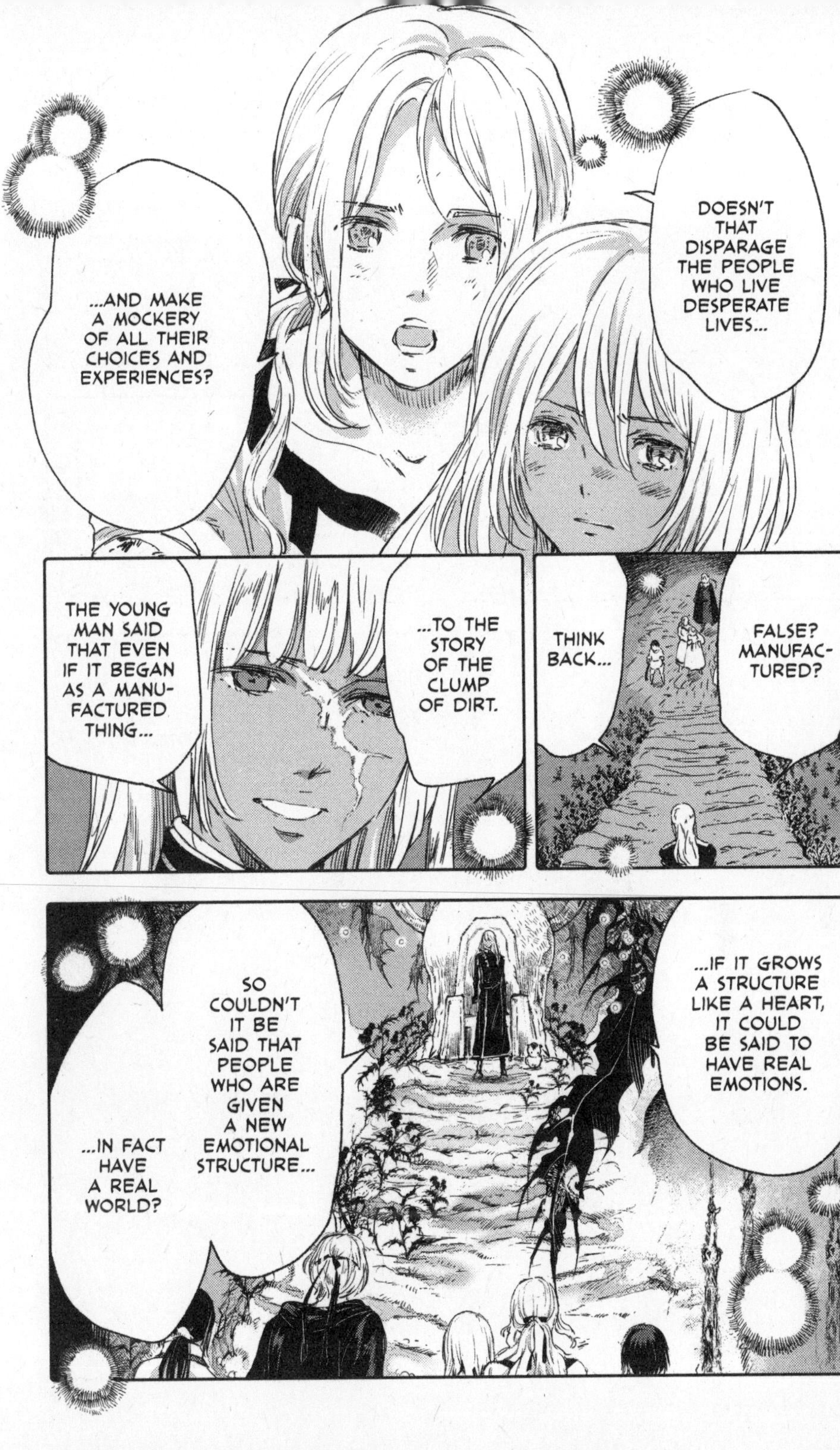
DOESN'T THAT DISPARAGE THE PEOPLE WHO LIVE DESPERATE LIVES...
...AND MAKE A MOCKERY OF ALL THEIR CHOICES AND EXPERIENCES?
FALSE? MANUFACTURED?
THINK BACK...
...TO THE STORY OF THE CLUMP OF DIRT.
THE YOUNG MAN SAID THAT EVEN IF IT BEGAN AS A MANUFACTURED THING...
...IF IT GROWS A STRUCTURE LIKE A HEART, IT COULD BE SAID TO HAVE REAL EMOTIONS.
SO COULDN'T IT BE SAID THAT PEOPLE WHO ARE GIVEN A NEW EMOTIONAL STRUCTURE...
...IN FACT HAVE A REAL WORLD?

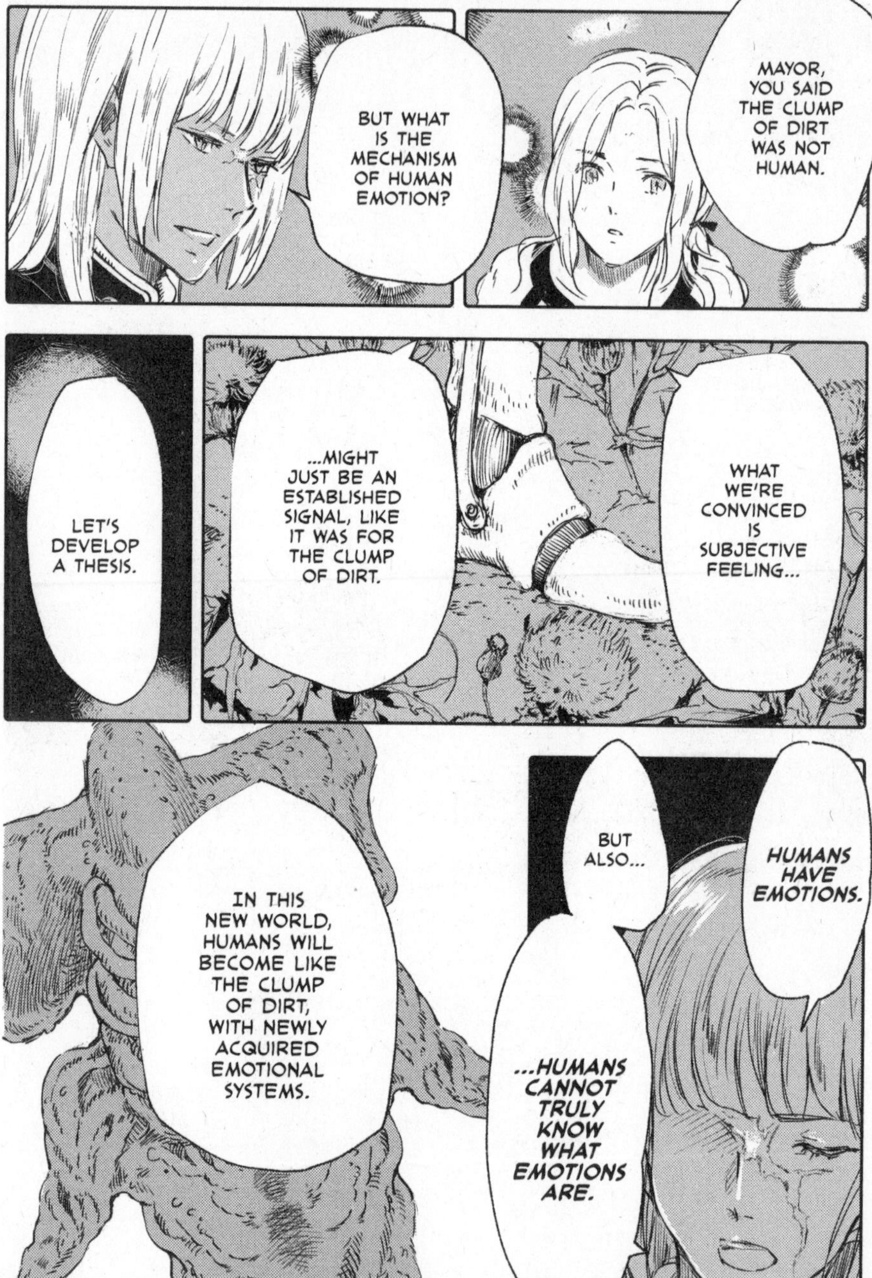
MAYOR, YOU SAID THE CLUMP OF DIRT WAS NOT HUMAN.
BUT WHAT IS THE MECHANISM OF HUMAN EMOTION?
WHAT WE'RE CONVINCED IS SUBJECTIVE FEELING...
...MIGHT JUST BE AN ESTABLISHED SIGNAL, LIKE IT WAS FOR THE CLUMP OF DIRT.
LET'S DEVELOP A THESIS.
HUMANS HAVE EMOTIONS.
BUT ALSO...
...HUMANS CANNOT TRULY KNOW WHAT EMOTIONS ARE.
IN THIS NEW WORLD, HUMANS WILL BECOME LIKE THE CLUMP OF DIRT, WITH NEWLY ACQUIRED EMOTIONAL SYSTEMS.

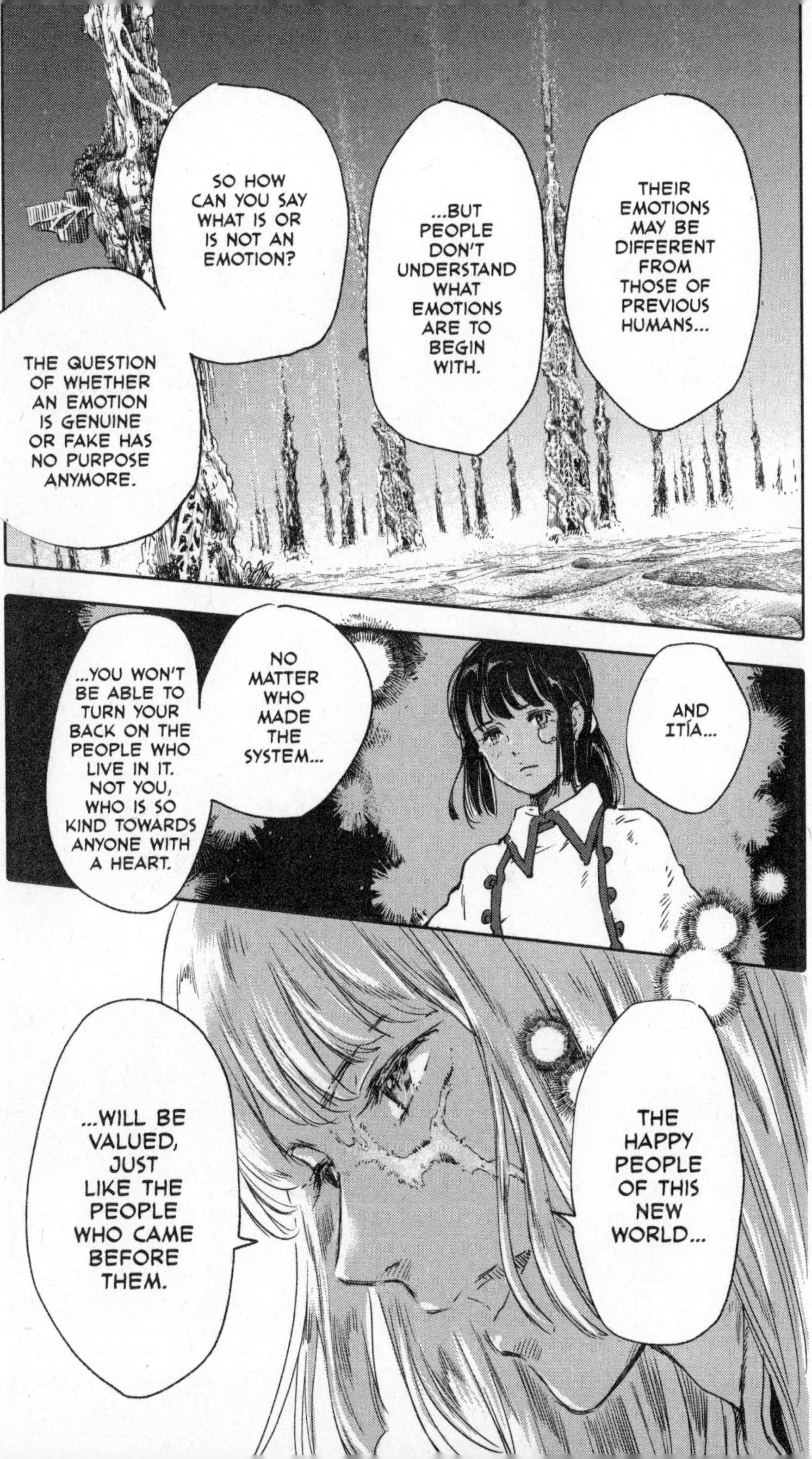
THEIR EMOTIONS MAY BE DIFFERENT FROM THOSE OF PREVIOUS HUMANS...
...BUT PEOPLE DON'T UNDERSTAND WHAT EMOTIONS ARE TO BEGIN WITH.
SO HOW CAN YOU SAY WHAT IS OR IS NOT AN EMOTION?
THE QUESTION OF WHETHER AN EMOTION IS GENUINE OR FAKE HAS NO PURPOSE ANYMORE.
AND ITÍA...
NO MATTER WHO MADE THE SYSTEM...
...YOU WON'T BE ABLE TO TURN YOUR BACK ON THE PEOPLE WHO LIVE IN IT. NOT YOU, WHO IS SO KIND TOWARDS ANYONE WITH A HEART.
THE HAPPY PEOPLE OF THIS NEW WORLD...
...WILL BE VALUED, JUST LIKE THE PEOPLE WHO CAME BEFORE THEM.

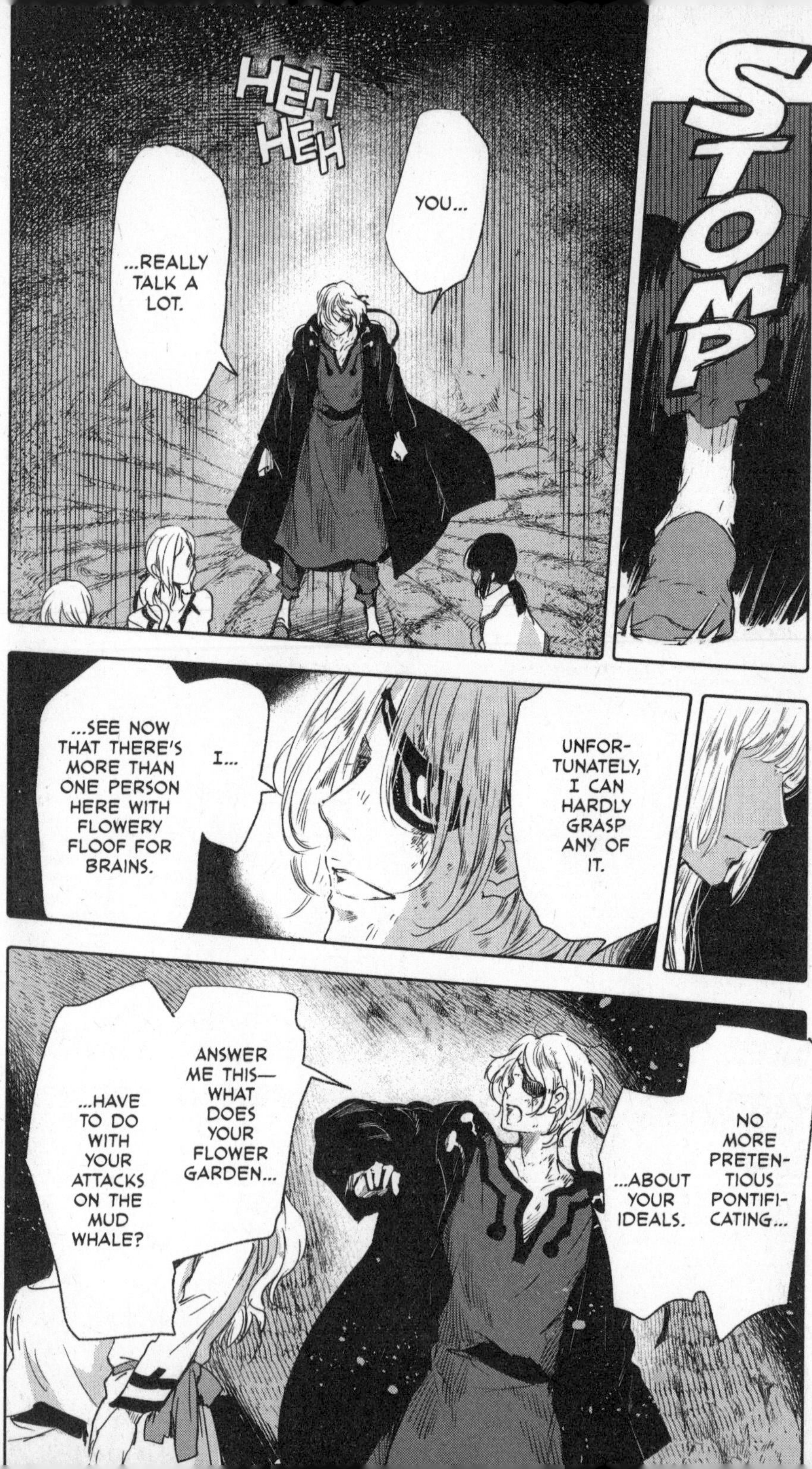
STOMP
HEH HEH
YOU...
...REALLY TALK A LOT.
UNFORTUNATELY, I CAN HARDLY GRASP ANY OF IT.
I...
...SEE NOW THAT THERE'S MORE THAN ONE PERSON HERE WITH FLOWERY FLOOF FOR BRAINS.
NO MORE PRETENTIOUS PONTIFICATING...
...ABOUT YOUR IDEALS.
ANSWER ME THIS—WHAT DOES YOUR FLOWER GARDEN...
...HAVE TO DO WITH YOUR ATTACKS ON THE MUD WHALE?

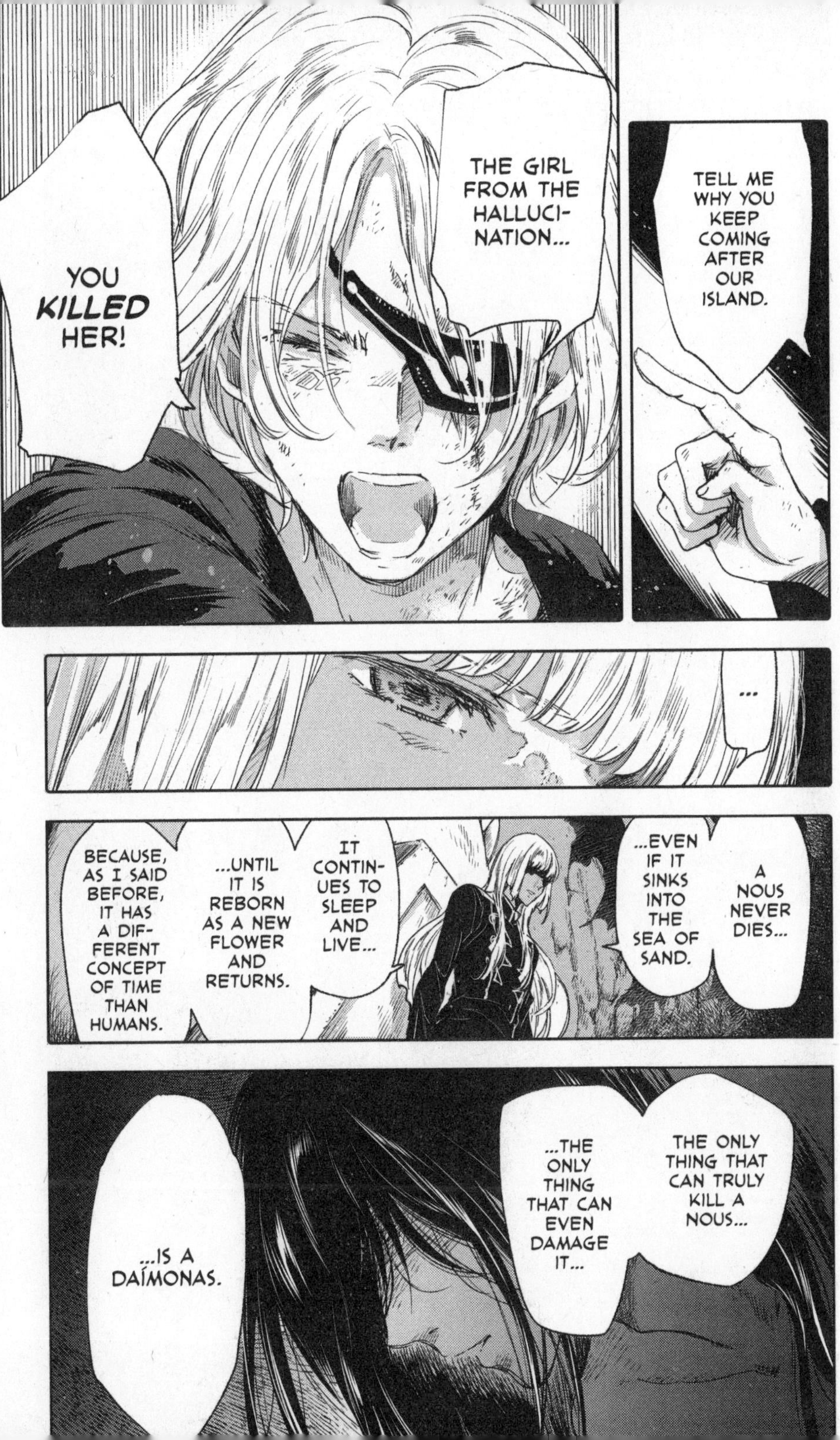
TELL ME WHY YOU KEEP COMING AFTER OUR ISLAND.
THE GIRL FROM THE HALLUCINATION...
YOU *KILLED* HER!
...
A NOUS NEVER DIES...
...EVEN IF IT SINKS INTO THE SEA OF SAND.
IT CONTINUES TO SLEEP AND LIVE...
...UNTIL IT IS REBORN AS A NEW FLOWER AND RETURNS.
BECAUSE, AS I SAID BEFORE, IT HAS A DIFFERENT CONCEPT OF TIME THAN HUMANS.
THE ONLY THING THAT CAN TRULY KILL A NOUS...
...THE ONLY THING THAT CAN EVEN DAMAGE IT...
...IS A DAÍMONAS.

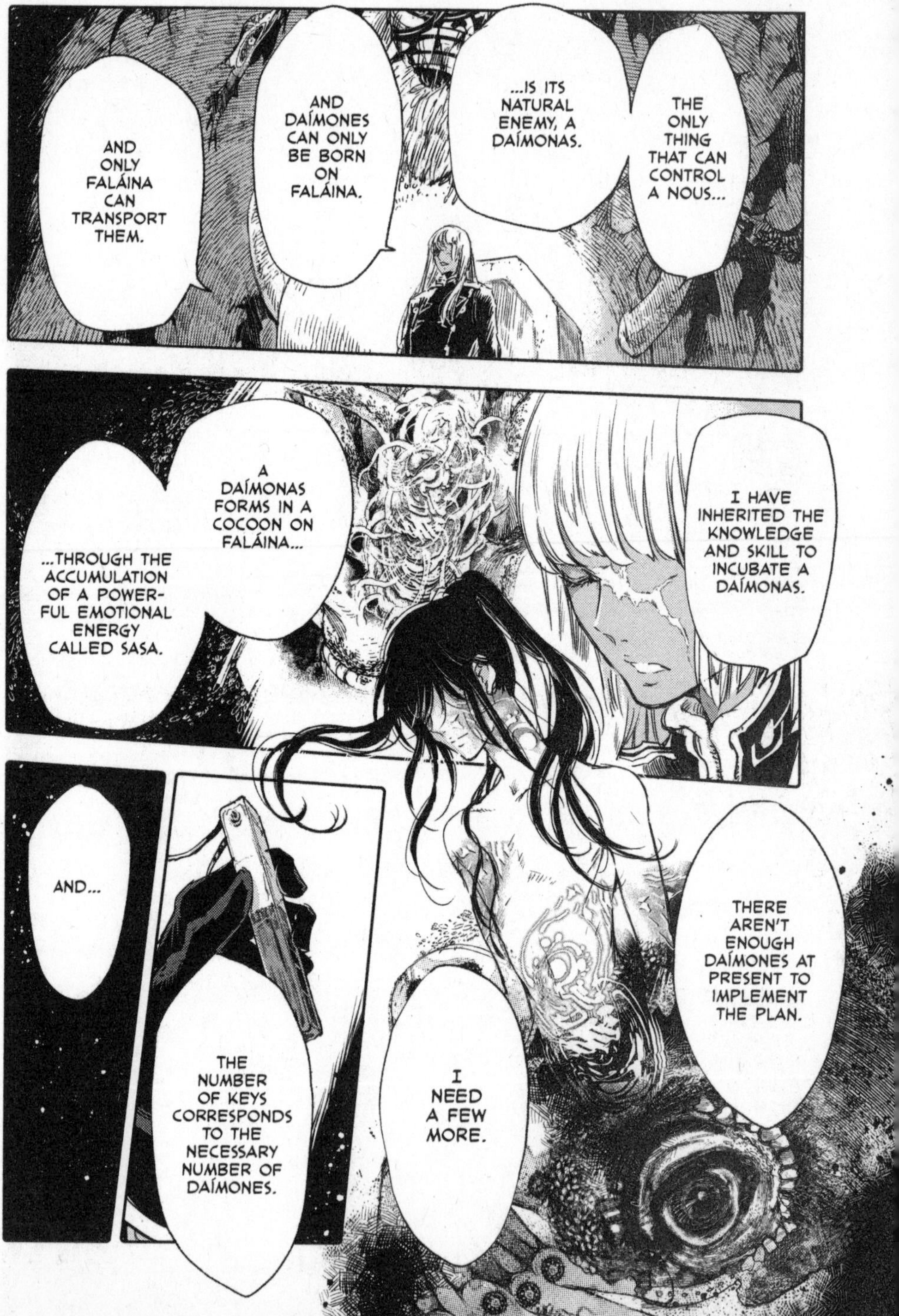
THE ONLY THING THAT CAN CONTROL A NOUS...
...IS ITS NATURAL ENEMY, A DAÍMONAS.
AND DAÍMONES CAN ONLY BE BORN ON FALÁINA.
AND ONLY FALÁINA CAN TRANSPORT THEM.
I HAVE INHERITED THE KNOWLEDGE AND SKILL TO INCUBATE A DAÍMONAS.
A DAÍMONAS FORMS IN A COCOON ON FALÁINA...
...THROUGH THE ACCUMULATION OF A POWER-FUL EMOTIONAL ENERGY CALLED SASA.
THERE AREN'T ENOUGH DAÍMONES AT PRESENT TO IMPLEMENT THE PLAN.
I NEED A FEW MORE.
THE NUMBER OF KEYS CORRESPONDS TO THE NECESSARY NUMBER OF DAÍMONES.
AND...

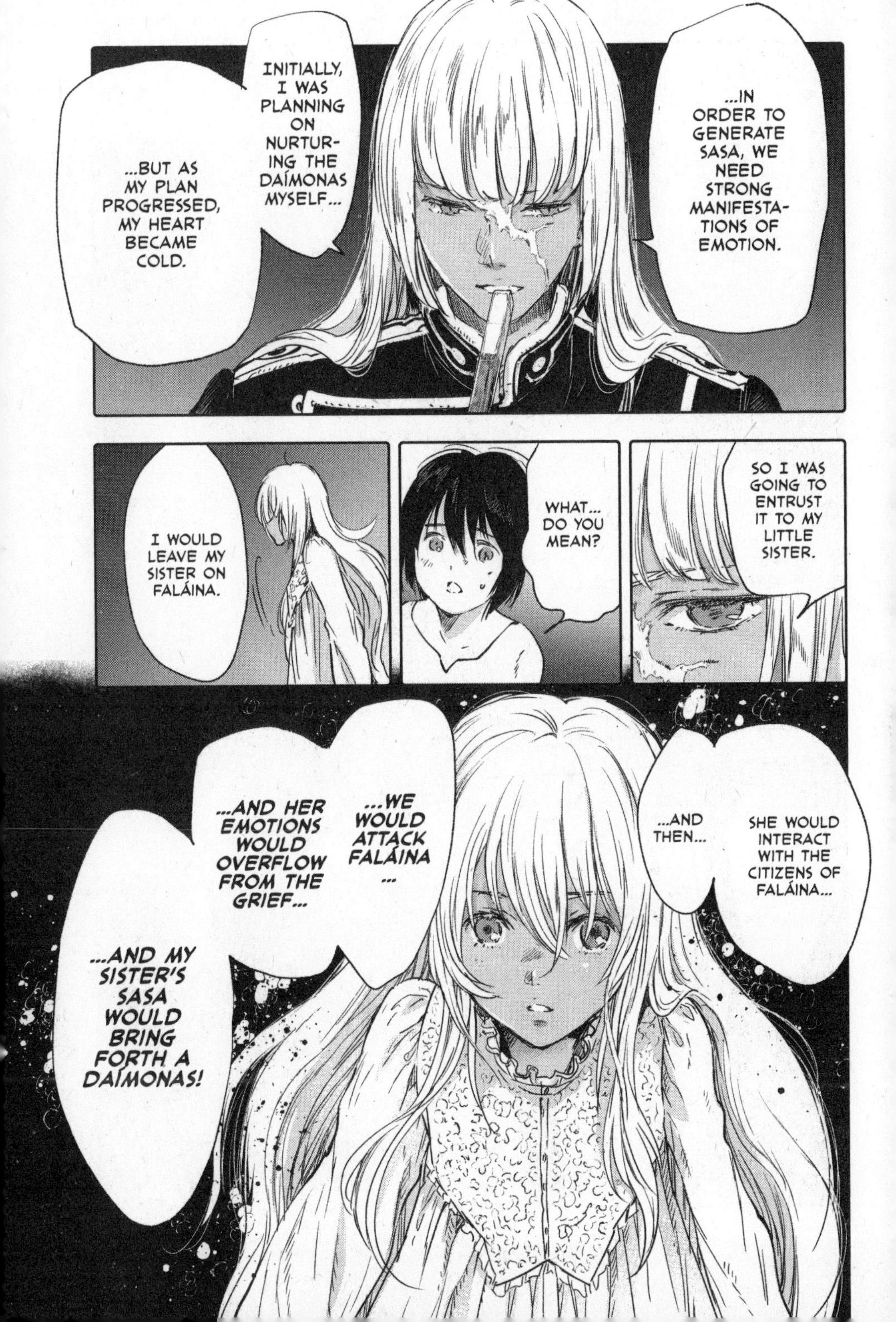
...IN ORDER TO GENERATE SASA, WE NEED STRONG MANIFESTATIONS OF EMOTION.
INITIALLY, I WAS PLANNING ON NURTURING THE DAÍMONAS MYSELF...
...BUT AS MY PLAN PROGRESSED, MY HEART BECAME COLD.
SO I WAS GOING TO ENTRUST IT TO MY LITTLE SISTER.
WHAT... DO YOU MEAN?
I WOULD LEAVE MY SISTER ON FALÁINA.
SHE WOULD INTERACT WITH THE CITIZENS OF FALÁINA...
...AND THEN...
...WE WOULD ATTACK FALÁINA...
...AND HER EMOTIONS WOULD OVERFLOW FROM THE GRIEF...
...AND MY SISTER'S SASA WOULD BRING FORTH A DAÍMONAS!

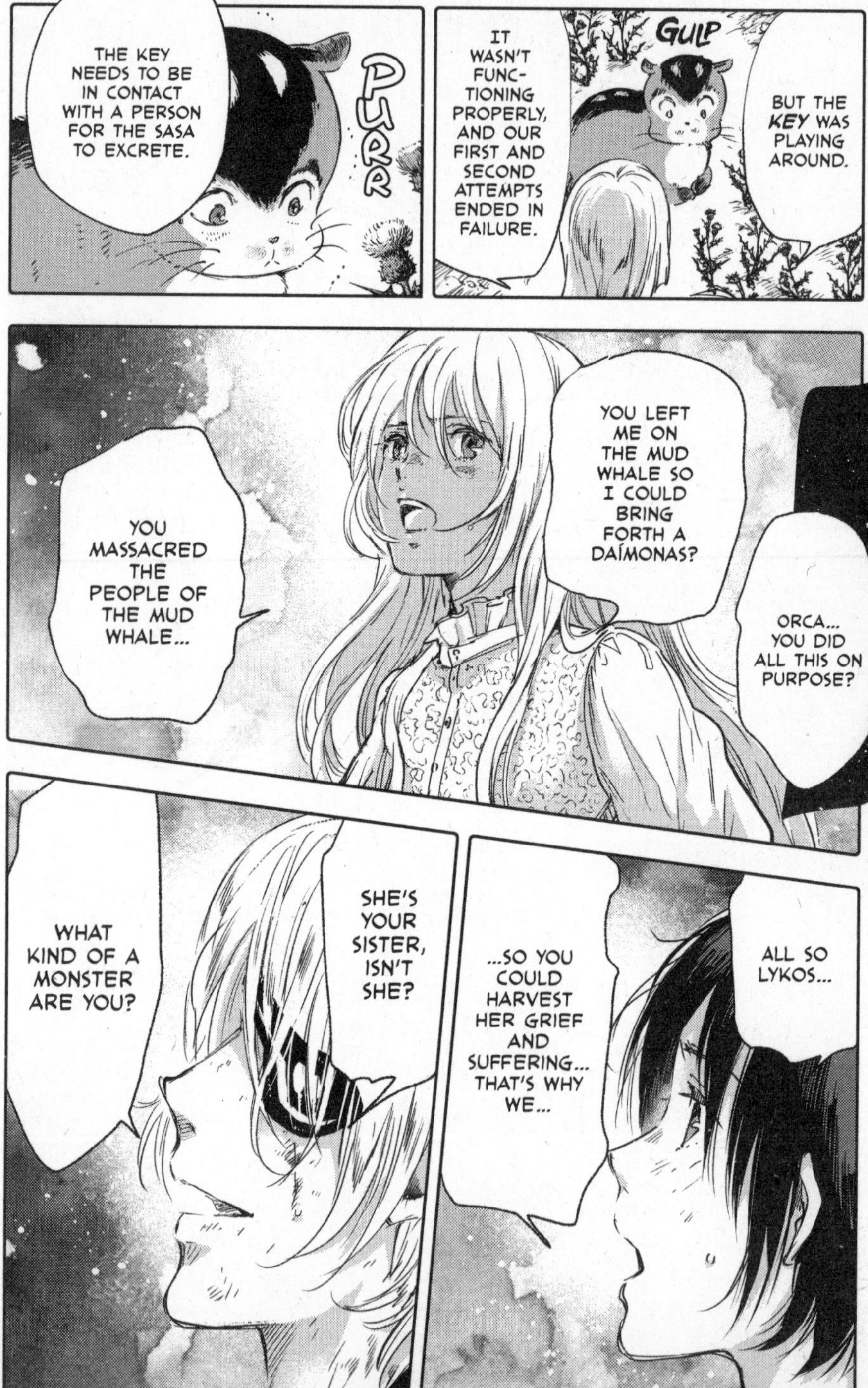

BUT THE KEY WAS PLAYING AROUND.
GULP
IT WASN'T FUNCTIONING PROPERLY, AND OUR FIRST AND SECOND ATTEMPTS ENDED IN FAILURE.
PURR
THE KEY NEEDS TO BE IN CONTACT WITH A PERSON FOR THE SASA TO EXCRETE.
ORCA... YOU DID ALL THIS ON PURPOSE?
YOU LEFT ME ON THE MUD WHALE SO I COULD BRING FORTH A DAÍMONAS?
YOU MASSACRED THE PEOPLE OF THE MUD WHALE...
ALL SO LYKOS...
...SO YOU COULD HARVEST HER GRIEF AND SUFFERING... THAT'S WHY WE...
SHE'S YOUR SISTER, ISN'T SHE?
WHAT KIND OF A MONSTER ARE YOU?

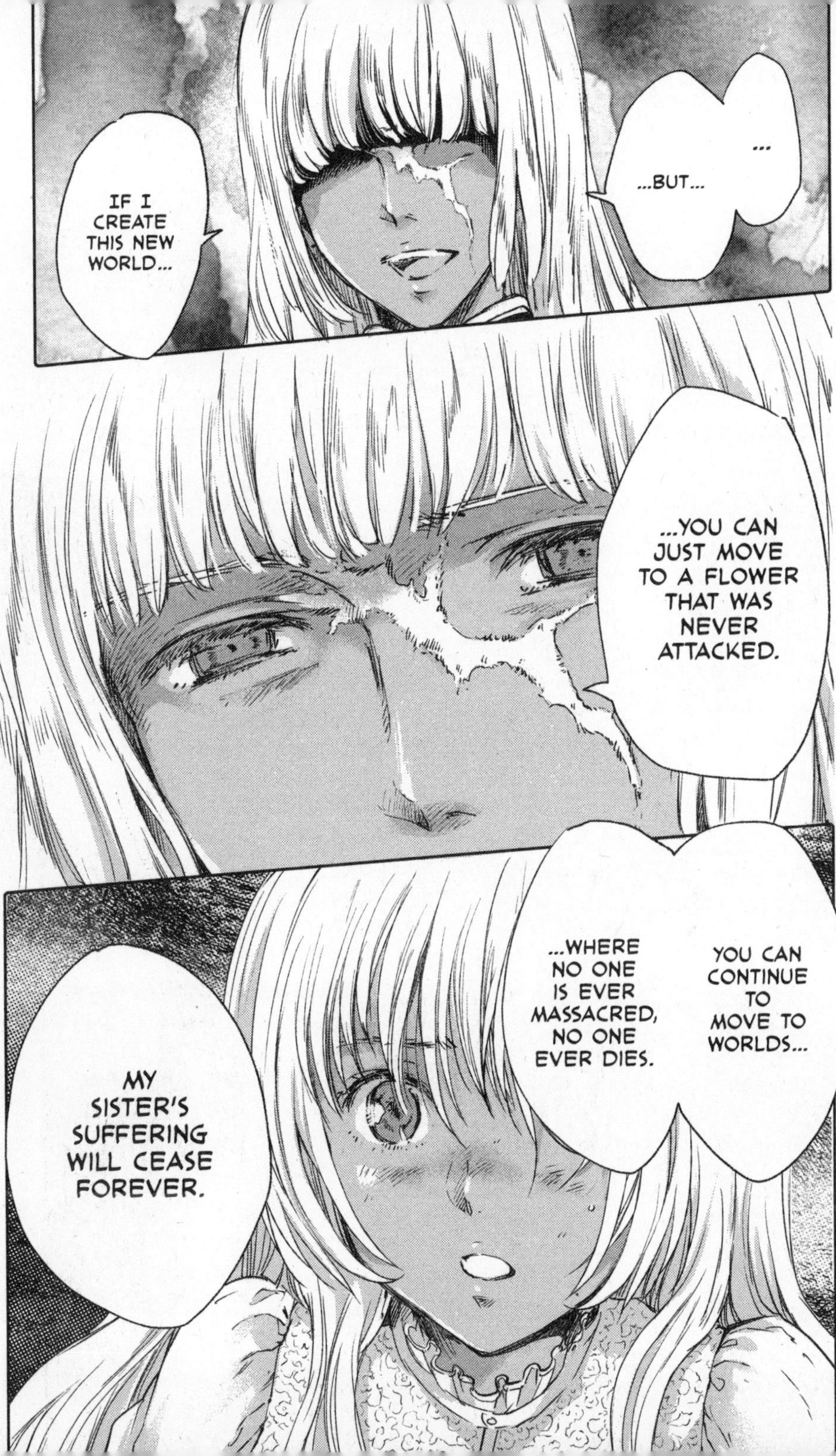
...
...BUT...
IF I CREATE THIS NEW WORLD...
...YOU CAN JUST MOVE TO A FLOWER THAT WAS NEVER ATTACKED.
YOU CAN CONTINUE TO MOVE TO WORLDS...
...WHERE NO ONE IS EVER MASSACRED, NO ONE EVER DIES.
MY SISTER'S SUFFERING WILL CEASE FOREVER.

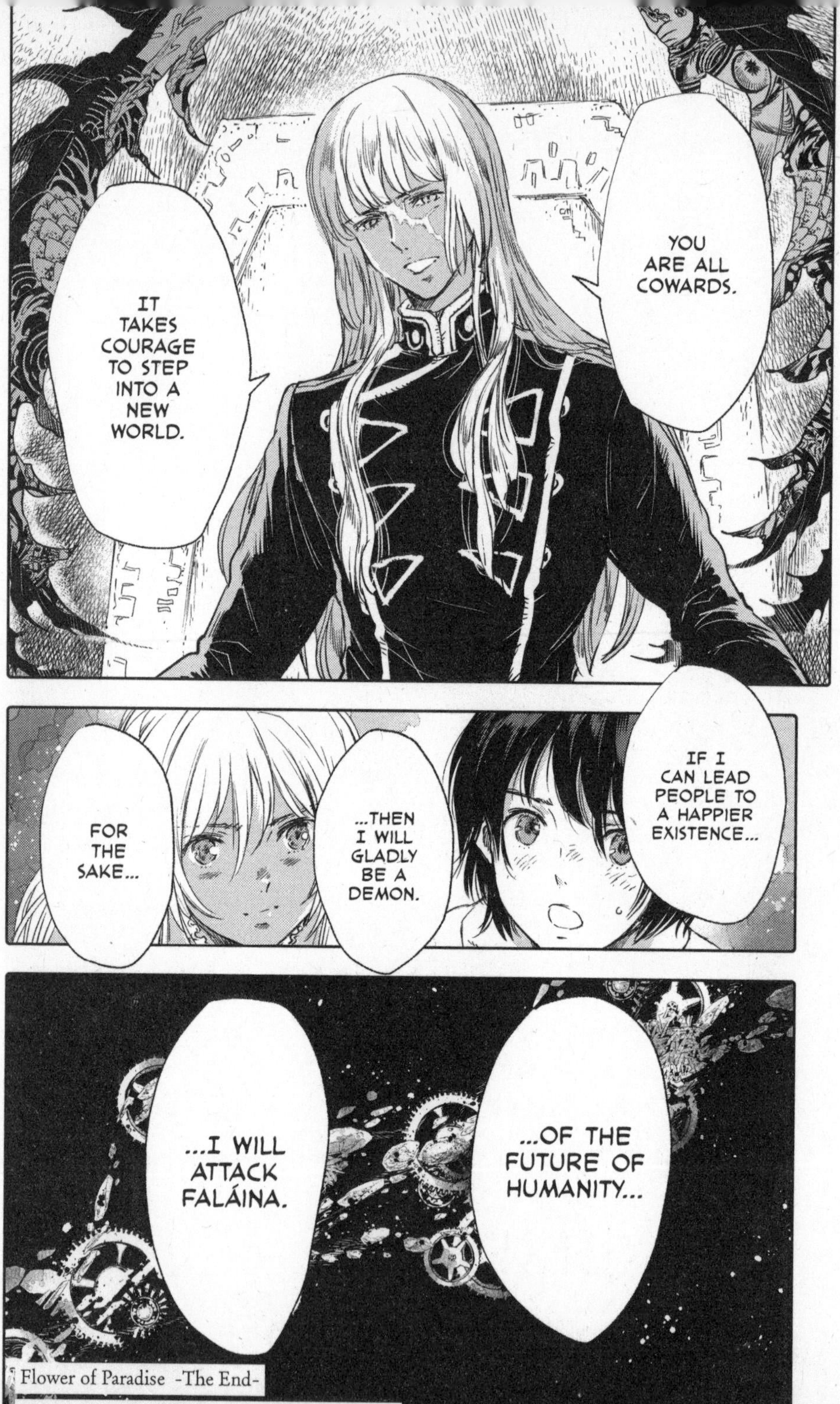
YOU ARE ALL COWARDS.
IT TAKES COURAGE TO STEP INTO A NEW WORLD.
IF I CAN LEAD PEOPLE TO A HAPPIER EXISTENCE...
...THEN I WILL GLADLY BE A DEMON.
FOR THE SAKE...
...OF THE FUTURE OF HUMANITY...
...I WILL ATTACK FALÁINA.

Flower of Paradise -The End-

Children of the Whales volume 14 -The End-

CHILDREN OF THE WHALES

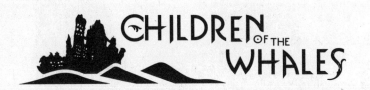

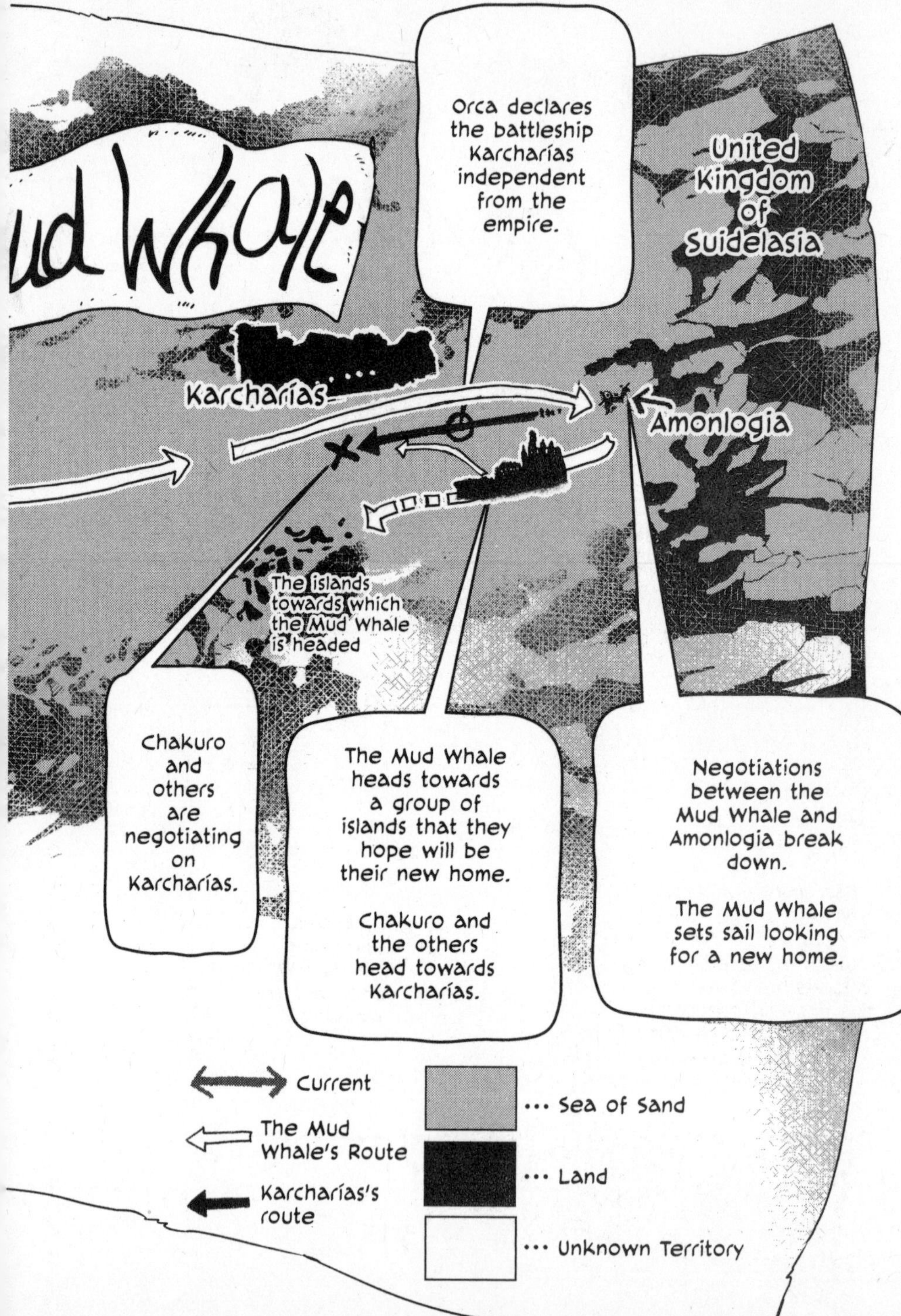
Mud Whale
Orca declares the battleship Karcharías independent from the empire.
United Kingdom of Suidelasia
Karcharías
Amonlogia
The islands towards which the Mud Whale is headed
Negotiations between the Mud Whale and Amonlogia break down.
The Mud Whale sets sail looking for a new home.
The Mud Whale heads towards a group of islands that they hope will be their new home.
Chakuro and the others head towards Karcharías.
Chakuro and others are negotiating on Karcharías.
Current
The Mud Whale's Route
Karcharías's route
··· Sea of Sand
··· Land
··· Unknown Territory

A lot has happened...!

The Voyage of the M

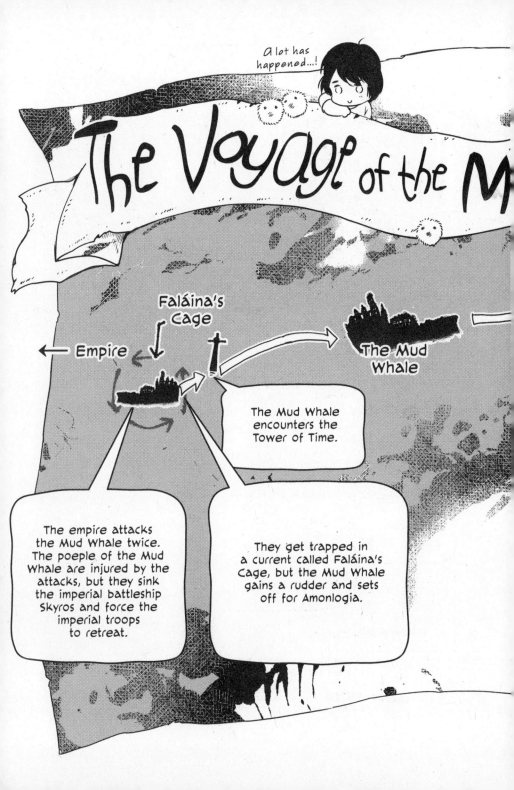

Faláina's Cage

← Empire

The Mud Whale

The Mud Whale encounters the Tower of Time.

The empire attacks the Mud Whale twice. The poeple of the Mud Whale are injured by the attacks, but they sink the imperial battleship Skyros and force the imperial troops to retreat.

They get trapped in a current called Faláina's Cage, but the Mud Whale gains a rudder and sets off for Amonlogia.

A Note on Names

Those who live on the Mud Whale are named after colors in a language unknown. Abi Umeda uses Japanese translations of the names, which we have maintained. Here is a list of the English equivalents for the curious.

Aijiro	pale blue
Benihi	scarlet
Buki	kerria flower (*yamabuki*)
Byakuroku	malachite mineral pigments, pale green tinged with white
Chakuro	blackish brown (*cha* = brown, *kuro* = black)
Furano	from "flannel," a soft-woven fabric traditionally made of wool
Ginshu	vermillion
Hakuji	porcelain white
Jiki	golden
Kicha	yellowish brown
Kikujin	koji mold, yellowish green
Kogare	burnt muskwood, dark reddish brown
Kuchiba	decayed-leaf brown
Masoh	cinnabar
Miru	seaweed green
Nashiji	a traditional Japanese crepe weave fabric
Neri	silk white
Nezu	mouse gray
Nibi	dark gray
Ouni	safflower red
Rasha	darkest blue, nearly black
Ro	lacquer black
Sami	light green (*asa* = light, *midori* = green)

Shikoku	purple-tinged black
Shikon	purple-tinged navy
Shinono	the color of dawn (*shinonome*)
Shuan	dark bloodred
Sienna	reddish brown
Sumi	ink black
Suou	raspberry red
Taisha	red ocher
Tobi	reddish brown like a kite's feather
Tokusa	scouring rush green
Tonoko	the color of powdered grindstone, a pale brown
Urumi	muddy gray

I really liked thistles when I was younger, and I used to wonder why they were that color. They appear in this volume.

—Abi Umeda

ABI UMEDA debuted as a manga creator with the one-shot "Yukokugendan" in *Weekly Shonen Champion*. *Children of the Whales* is her eighth manga work.

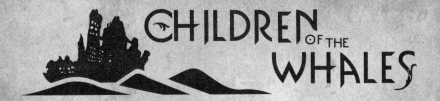

CHILDREN OF THE WHALES

VOLUME 14
VIZ Signature Edition

Story and Art by Abi Umeda

Translation / JN Productions
Touch-Up Art & Lettering / Annaliese Christman
Design / Julian (JR) Robinson
Editor / Pancha Diaz

KUJIRANOKORAHA SAJOUNIUTAU Volume 14

First published in Japan in 2019 by AKITA PUBLISHING CO., LTD., Tokyo
English translation rights arranged with AKITA PUBLISHING CO., LTD. through
Tuttle-Mori Agency, Inc., Tokyo

Printed in Canada

Published by VIZ Media, LLC
P.O. Box 77010
San Francisco, CA 94107

10 9 8 7 6 5 4 3 2 1
First printing, January 2020

VIZ MEDIA
viz.com

PARENTAL ADVISORY
CHILDREN OF THE WHALES is rated T+ for Older Teen and is recommended for ages 16 and up. Contains violence and death.

RATED T+ OLDER TEEN ratings.viz.com

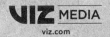

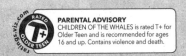

vizsignature.com

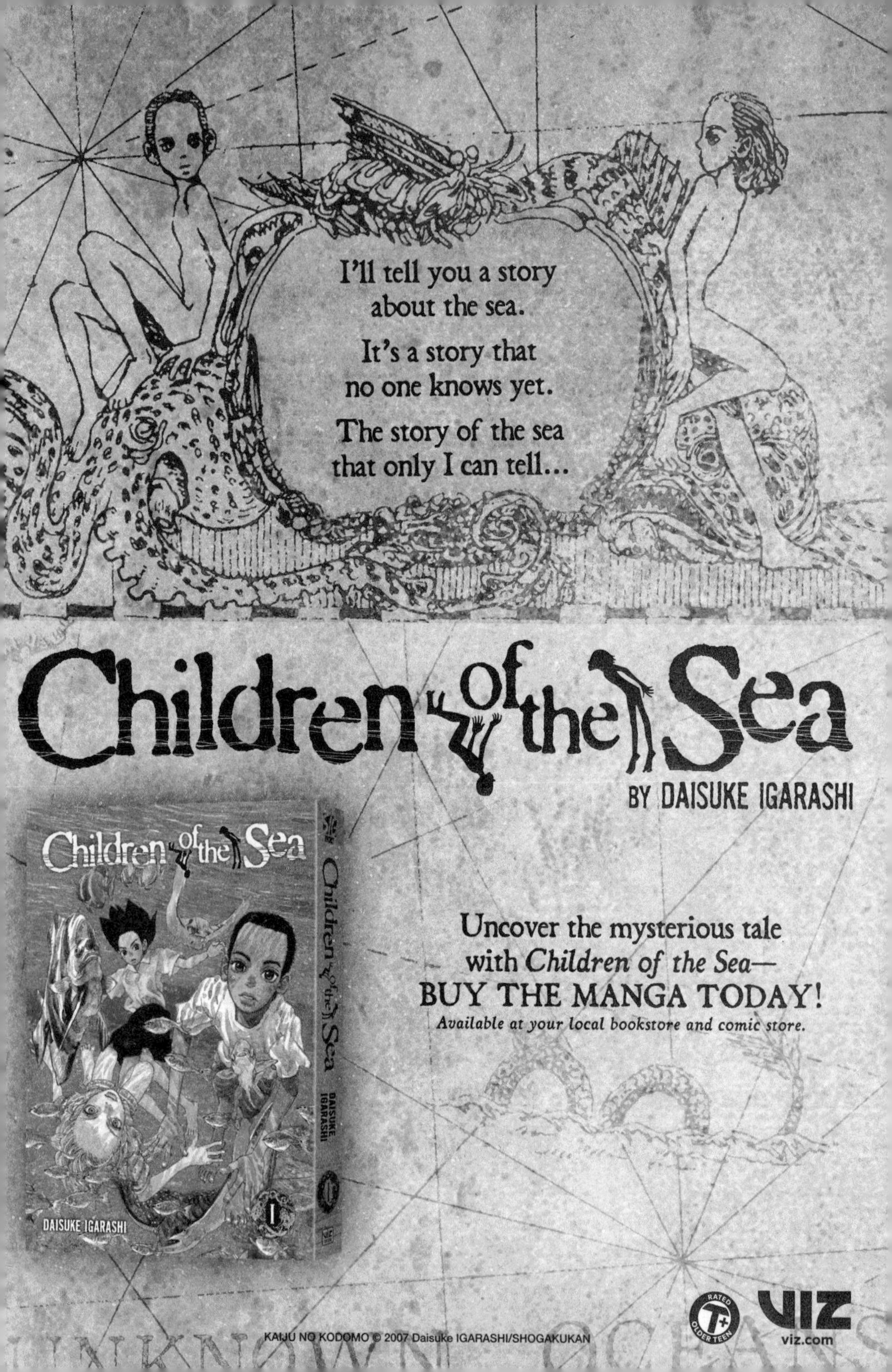
I'll tell you a story
about the sea.
It's a story that
no one knows yet.
The story of the sea
that only I can tell...
Children of the Sea
BY DAISUKE IGARASHI
Children of the Sea
DAISUKE IGARASHI
1
Uncover the mysterious tale
with Children of the Sea—
BUY THE MANGA TODAY!
Available at your local bookstore and comic store.
RATED T+ OLDER TEEN
VIZ
viz.com
KAIJU NO KODOMO © 2007 Daisuke IGARASHI/SHOGAKUKAN

A deluxe bind-up edition of Naoki Urasawa's award-winning epic of doomsday cults, giant robots and a group of friends trying to save the world from destruction!

20th Century Boys

THE PERFECT EDITION

NAOKI URASAWA

Humanity, having faced extinction at the end of the 20th century, would not have entered the new millennium if it weren't for them. In 1969, during their youth, they created a symbol. In 1997, as the coming disaster slowly starts to unfold, that symbol returns. This is the story of a group of boys who try to save the world.

RATED T+ OLDER TEEN

VIZ

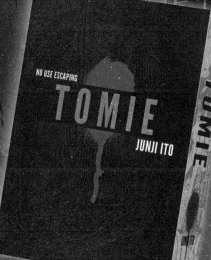

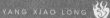

MOBILE SUIT GUNDAM THUNDERBOLT

In the Universal Century year 0079, the space colony known as Side 3 proclaims independence as the Principality of Zeon and declares war on the Earth Federation. One year later, they are locked in a fierce battle for the Thunderbolt Sector, an area of space scarred by the wreckage of destroyed colonies. Into this maelstrom of destruction go two veteran Mobile Suit pilots: the deadly Zeon sniper Daryl Lorenz, and Federation ace Io Fleming. It's the beginning of a rivalry that can end only when one of them is destroyed.

STORY AND ART
YASUO OHTAGAKI
ORIGINAL CONCEPT BY
HAJIME YATATE
AND **YOSHIYUKI TOMINO**

MOBILE SUIT GUNDAM
THUNDERBOLT

viz media
viz.com

RATED T+ FOR OLDER TEEN

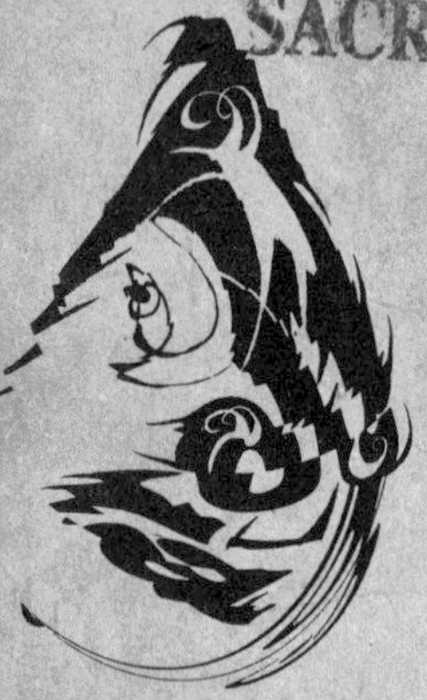

THIS IS THE LAST PAGE!

Children of the Whales has been printed in the original Japanese format to preserve the orientation of the original artwork.

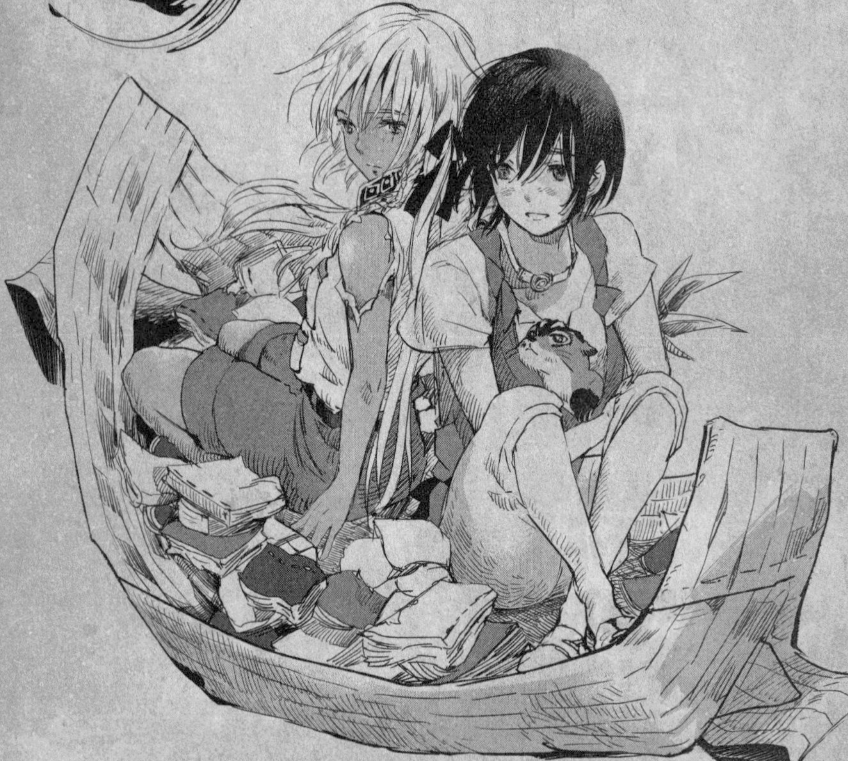